An International Look at Educating Young Adolescents

a volume in
The Handbook of Research in Middle Level Education

Series Editor:
Vincent A. Anfara, Jr.
The University of Tennessee

The Handbook of Research in Middle Level Education

Vincent A. Anfara, Jr., Series Editor

The Handbook of Research in Middle Level Education (2001)
edited by Vincent A. Anfara, Jr.

Middle School Curriculum, Instruction, and Assessment (2002)
edited by Vincent A. Anfara, Jr. and Sandra L. Stacki

*Leaders for a Movement: Professional Preparation and Development of
Middle Level Teachers and Administrators* (2003)
edited by P. Gayle Andrews and Vincent A. Anfara, Jr.

Reforming Middle Level Education: Considerations for Policymakers (2004)
edited by Sue C. Thompson

Making a Difference: Action Research in Middle Level Education (2005)
edited by Micki M. Caskey

The Young Adolescent and the Middle School (2007)
edited by Steven B. Mertens, Vincent A. Anfara, Jr.,
and Micki M. Caskey

An International Look at Educating Young Adolescents (2009)
edited by Steven B. Mertens, Vincent A. Anfara, Jr.,
and Kathleen Roney

An International Look at Educating Young Adolescents

Edited by

Steven B. Mertens
Illinois State University

Vincent A. Anfara, Jr.
The University of Tennessee

Kathleen Roney
University of North Carolina Wilmington

NMSA
National Middle School Association
Westerville, Ohio

MIDDLE LEVEL EDUCATION RESEARCH
SPECIAL INTEREST GROUP

INFORMATION AGE
PUBLISHING

Charlotte, North Carolina • www.infoagepub.com

Library of Congress Cataloging-in-Publication Data

An international look at educating young adolescents / edited by Steven B.
Mertens, Vincent A. Anfara, Jr.
    p. cm. — (Handbook of research in middle level education)
  Includes bibliographical references.
  ISBN 978-1-60752-041-2 (paperback) — ISBN 978-1-60752-042-9 (hardcover)
1. Middle school education—Cross-cultural studies. I. Mertens, Steven B.
II. Anfara, Vincent A.
  LB1623.I63 2009
  373.23'6—dc22

                                               2008054469

Printed in the United States of America.

MIDDLE LEVEL EDUCATION RESEARCH
SPECIAL INTEREST GROUP

The Handbook of Research in Middle Level Education is endorsed by the Middle Level Education Research Special Interest Group, an affiliate of the American Educational Research Association.

As stated in the organization's Constitution, the purpose of MLER is to improve, promote, and disseminate educational research reflecting early adolescence and middle-level education.

The Handbook of Research in Middle Level Education

EDITORIAL REVIEW BOARD

CONTENTS

FOREWORD

The World is Flat: A Brief History of the Twenty-First Century is an international best selling book by Thomas L. Friedman (2005). The title is a metaphor for viewing the world as a level playing field where all nations have an equal opportunity to compete. Following the premise of the book, globalization has leveled the playing fields between industrial and emerging-market countries. The title of this book, though, also alludes to the historic shift of perception once people realized that the world was not flat, but round. We believe that a similar shift in perceptions is required if we are going to face the challenge of effectively educating young adolescents in the United States and around the world. We can no longer afford to wait to increase cross-national and cross-cultural understandings of the educational processes that are involved in structuring schools and the teaching and learning environments for students 10-15 years old.

We need to engage in global educational discourses where we can learn from others and find out if there are any generalized statements about the schooling of young adolescents that are valid across the world. We need to benefit from the collective knowledge that can be generated from across the globe as we face challenges associated with educating young adolescents. In many other fields, scholars, policymakers, professionals and even members of the public are demonstrating an increased interest in learning about other countries—in "making the strange familiar" (von Hardenberg, 1800, as cited in Wood, 2007). In education, though, we don't seem to know much about each other. Pajares and Urdan (2003), in

An International Look at Educating Young Adolescents
pp. ix–xi
Copyright © 2009 by Information Age Publishing
All rights of reproduction in any form reserved.

responding to this gap in our knowledge as it related to the education of adolescents, noted, "The vast majority of Americans are poorly acquainted with the customs, habits, and education of adolescents outside their own country" (p. xi). With this seventh volume of the *Handbook of Research in Middle Level Education*, we make the same claim as it relates to the schooling of young adolescents and call for a broadening of our perspectives in this regard. We have much to learn from each other.

The intent of this volume, *An International Look at Educating Young Adolescents*, is to broaden our understanding of middle level schooling by critically examining the education of young adolescents (ages 10-15, typically Grades 6-8) through an international lens. In addition to looking at how schooling and students are organized for teaching and learning, the chapters in this volume focus on the successes and failures that are evident in a wide variety of nations, present the indictments and praises that have been offered by supporters and critics alike, and review the research that has been generated about educating young adolescents in an effort to cross national boundaries. This volume of the handbook series explores what international perspectives teach us about the effective education of young adolescents.

Contributing authors were asked to set the stage for their readers by providing information about their country and its significant cultural norms and issues, including issues like the role of women, compulsory education, infant mortality, illiteracy, population migration, religious issues, location/ geography, individualist/competitive versus collectivist/ cooperation beliefs, economic well-being, and other social issues deemed to be critical to understanding the education system.

Following this introductory narrative, we asked the authors to address the following items: (1) the history of educating young adolescents in your country, including descriptions of curricula, instructional practices, assessment systems, schools structures, organization, and teaching practices; (2) the academic performance and social and emotional development of young adolescents; (3) current issues related to the schooling of young adolescents in your country, including concerns about the current educational system, and benefits of the current educational system; (4) reform initiatives (e.g., national, curricular, pedagogical) that currently exist that are being encouraged for the education of young adolescents; (5) the middle level education research that has been conducted in your country and what is the nature of this research (e.g., national in scope; quantitative, qualitative, and/or mixed methodologies used; what topics have been studied; what student outcomes have been measured); and lastly, (6) possible future directions in the education of young adolescents in your county.

The 14 chapters contained in this volume span five continents and include submissions on Turkey, Lebanon, the United Arab Emirates, India, China, South Korea, New Zealand, Australia, Rwanda, South Africa, Russia, Germany, Ireland, and Brazil. We are hopeful that these chapters provide readers with a comprehensive understanding and international perspective of the current issues, concerns, and practices of educating today's young adolescents.

The *Handbook of Research in Middle Level Education* was established in 2001 by Vincent A. Anfara, Jr., series editor, to address emerging research on issues related to middle level education. Prior volumes in the series have addressed topics specific to middle schools and young adolescents predominantly from a U.S. perspective, including curriculum, instruction, and assessment (volume 2), teacher and principal preparation and training (volume 3), policy implications of middle level reform (volume 4), action research in middle schools (volume 5), and young adolescent development and middle schools (volume 7). To a degree, this volume is an extension—an international extension—of the last volume.

REFERENCES

Friedman, T. L. (2005). *The world if flat: A brief history of the twenty-first century.* New York: Farrar, Straus and Giroux.

Pajares, F., & Urdan, T. (2003). *International perspectives on adolescence.* Greenwich, CT: Information Age.

Wood, D. W. (Ed. & Trans.). (2007). *Novalis: Notes for a romantic encyclopaedia* [*Das Allgemeine Brouillon*]. New York: State University of New York Press.

INTRODUCTION

Comparative and International Education and Middle Level Education Research: A World of Possibilities

David C. Virtue

INTRODUCTION

In a keynote address at a meeting of middle level professors in 2008, National Middle School Association (NMSA) Executive Director Betty Edwards (2008a) called attention to the poor performance of U.S. students in the Program for International Student Assessment (PISA), an international assessment of student performance in mathematics, reading, and science literacy conducted under the auspices of the Organization for Economic Cooperation and Development (OECD). In recent PISA assessments, 15-year-olds in the United States who took the tests scored at or below the OECD average in all three areas tested. These results, Edwards argued, support the call for greater attention to middle level education in the United States (Edwards, 2008a).

An International Look at Educating Young Adolescents
pp. xiii–xxix
Copyright © 2009 by Information Age Publishing

The rhetoric was familiar. International comparisons have long been used to call attention to weaknesses in the U.S. education system (e.g. National Commission on Excellence in Education, 1983) and to the challenges facing middle level education, in particular (Juvonen, Le, Kaganoff, Augustine, & Constant, 2004). However, while some of the rhetoric may have been familiar, Edwards' (2008a) address took a unique turn as she began to discuss at length ways in which globalization is impacting the middle level reform movement and then call for increased internationalization of NMSA and, more broadly speaking, the middle school movement. Her message echoed a growing realization within the middle school movement that middle level educators need to be aware of and responsive to global conditions, particularly in the post-9/11 world (Erb, 2001).

According to Tom Erb, editor of *Middle School Journal*, NMSA has been "leading the fight to improve the education of young adolescents in North America and throughout the world" (2005, p. x). Active NMSA affiliates thrive throughout Canada and in Australia and New Zealand, yet the organization has no affiliates in Asia, Africa, or Latin America. There is a European League of Middle Schools, but it consists largely of international schools in which English is the language of instruction.

International perspectives in *Middle School Journal* have been largely limited to Australia, New Zealand, and Canada. De Jong and Chadbourne (2007) described a teacher preparation program at an Australian university which sought to model middle school principles and practices in instruction. Whitehead (2005) drew attention to issues and practices in curriculum integration by looking comparatively at the United States and Australia. Nolan and Brown (2002) reported on trends and issues in the development of middle level education in New Zealand, with a particular emphasis on structural organization and grade spans and integration of middle level philosophy in nonmiddle school settings, while Neville-Tisdale (2004) provided a more general overview of young adolescent education there. Kist (2004) and Peterson and Belizaire (2006) have contributed Canadian perspectives on literacy education, emphasizing new literacies and literature circles, respectively. In the 1990s, Ziegler and Mulhall (1994) provided an international perspective on advisory programs in Toronto, Canada, and Waggoner and McEwin (1993) reported results of a survey of 140 international schools and Department of Defense schools in Europe. Indeed, nearly all of the mainstream middle level scholarly work that has been published in NMSA-sponsored journals and other outlets focuses on young adolescent education in the English speaking world, yet most of the world's young adolescent learners are not native English speakers.

The middle school movement will be strengthened and enriched through cross-national and cross-cultural scholarship and dialogue about young adolescent education. This will only occur if middle level education researchers find ways to internationalize the work they do and if they work collaboratively and constructively with researchers in comparative and international education whose scholarship is relevant to the middle level. After briefly introducing the field of comparative and international education, this chapter provides a rationale for conducting comparative and international research in middle level education and outlines a tentative, working agenda for this proposed effort.

THE FIELD OF COMPARATIVE AND INTERNATIONAL EDUCATION (CIE)

Educators have looked abroad for ideas to improve systems of education and schooling since the very beginning of formal schooling many centuries ago (Wilson, 2003), yet comparative and international education has only been recognized as a distinct academic field since the 1950s. Comparative and international education is "a very amorphous field of pure and applied studies" characterized by its theoretical and methodological eclecticism (Halls, 1990, p. 11). Researchers in the field employ theoretical frames and methodologies drawn from all of the social sciences, including history, economics, sociology, anthropology. From these varied perspectives, researchers study virtually all aspects of education at all levels of analysis; from microlevel ethnographies of individual classrooms to macro-level analyses of national school systems.

While some consider comparative and international education to be "twin fields" (e.g., Wilson, 2003, p. 18), most view it as a single, unified field that encompasses international, comparative, and cross-national educational research. Citing Bray (1999), Hahn (2006) defined these three types of research in the following way.

> Such research may be referred to as international (in which phenomena are studied in more than one country or simply outside the researcher's or reader's home country), cross-national (in which the same questions are asked of samples in different countries), or comparative (in which authors deliberately draw conclusions about how phenomena are similar and different across different settings, regions, or national contexts). (p. 139)

Halls (1990) identified four basic goals of comparative and international education research:

1. to provide an educational morphology, that is, a global description and classification of the various forms of education;

2. to determine the relations and interactions between different aspects or factors in education, and between education and society;

3. to distinguish the fundamental conditions of educational change and persistence and relate these to more ultimate philosophical laws; and

4. to "stimulate a better life for society and the individual" by assisting in the development of educational institutions and practices (pp. 9, 22; see also Noah, 1986).

Infrastructure

Today, the field of CIE has a well-established infrastructure that includes graduate degree programs, national and international professional associations, and scholarly journals. In the United States, some of the leading graduate programs in CIE are housed at Columbia University, Stanford University, and the University of Pittsburgh, while leading centers abroad include the Comparative Education Research Centre at the University of Hong Kong, the Centre for Comparative and International Education at Oxford University, and the Comparative, International and Development Education Centre at the Ontario Institute for Studies in Education (OISE) located in Toronto. While some CIE research is conducted by pure academics, a great deal of work is done by "academic practitioners" (Wilson, 2003, p. 18) who conduct research to solve problems or address issues for national ministries of education, nongovernmental organizations (NGOs), or entities like the United Nations Educational Scientific Organization (UNESCO), the Organization for Economic Cooperation and Development (OECD), and the World Bank.

The World Council of Comparative Education Societies Web site lists 35 member associations throughout the world (World Council of Comparative Education Societies, 2008). Among the largest of these is the Comparative and International Education Society (CIES), an international organization based in the United States which was founded in 1956 to promote cross-disciplinary, international study of education. Through its conferences, publications, and other activities the Society helps its members:

1. promote understanding of the many roles that education plays in the shaping and perpetuation of cultures, the development of nations, and in influencing the lives of individuals;

2. improve opportunities for the citizens of the world by fostering an understanding of how education policies and programs enhance social and economic development; and

3. increase cross-cultural and cross-national understanding through educational processes and by the study and critique of educational theories, policies and practices that affect individual and social well being (CIES, 2008).

Traditions, Trends, and Issues

Altbach and Kelly (1986) identified five traditions in the field of comparative education. The oldest tradition in the field is the exchange of "travelers' tales" describing educational practices abroad (Wilson, 2003, p. 26). As Spaulding (1989) noted, "for over two millennia … comparative studies in education were essentially reports of scholars, government officials, and others who described educational institutions, systems, and programs they saw while they were traveling" (p. 1).

A second tradition, called "lending and borrowing," emerged as educators sought to transfer educational practices from one country to another. This tradition encompasses both the *borrowing* of practices (e.g., United States educators borrowing lesson study and problem-based mathematics from Japan), as well as the *lending* of practices (e.g., Britain and France lending curriculum, materials, and expertise to colonies in Africa and the Americas). Lending has often been neither neutral nor meliorative in its intent. For example, during the Cold War period the focus of much comparative scholarship in the United States shifted toward the developing world and areas of strategic interest around the globe, as education became a tool to promote economic development and capitalist ideology in the Third World (Steiner-Khamsi, 2006).

A tradition of historical and cultural studies of education emerged during the modern period of comparative education research, beginning in the mid-twentieth century. Scholars working within this tradition have sought to understand how language, culture, and historical forces shape educational process and outcomes. An excellent example of scholarship in this tradition is John Ogbu's cultural-ecological framework for understanding the relationship between minority group status and school performance (see e.g., Ogbu, 1982, 1983; Ogbu & Simons, 1998).

A fourth tradition identified by Altbach and Kelly (1986) is the tradition of conducting comparative and international research to improve international understanding and to promote world peace and development—what Wilson (2003) calls the "melioristic function" of comparative education (p. 26). This tradition continues today as comparativists work with organizations like UNESCO, the World Bank, and USAID to improve education globally.

The attempt toward building a science of comparative education is the fifth tradition described by Altbach and Kelly (1986). This tradition was initiated in the 1960s by noted scholars in the field, including George Bereday, Harold Noah, Max Eckstein and Brian Holmes (e.g., Bereday, 1964; Eckstein & Noah, 1969; Holmes, 1965; Noah & Eckstein, 1969). These researchers used statistical methods from the social sciences to develop theory and to inform educational policy decisions with quantifiable data. In addition, they began laying a foundation for a "comparative methodology" in the study of education, though the field today remains methodologically eclectic.

The five traditions mentioned above continue to influence and inform scholarship in the field of comparative education, yet the field possesses tremendous vitality as scholars continually develop new approaches and foci for their research. For example, Kubow and Fossum (2003) observed a recent shift in comparative and international education research from studies of education systems and components of those systems toward examination of education-related issues, such as access and equality of educational opportunity across diverse populations (Rotberg, 2004; Simon & Banks, 2003), teacher accountability and systems of rewards/sanctions (Black & William, 2005), and school choice (Black & William; Glenn, 1989).

In recent decades, comparative and international education research has experienced a theoretical shift from the neoclassical economic and structural-functionalist social theories that dominated the field from roughly the 1950s through the 1970s to critical perspectives that include post-structuralist, postcolonial, and feminist theoretical frameworks (see e.g., Bloch, Kennedy, Lightfoot, & Weyenberg, 2006). Critical perspectives value political democracy and urge for the struggle for social justice against oppression. While Klees (2008) recognized distinctions among the numerous critical research perspectives in the field, he argued that they are fundamentally the same in the way they answer two basic questions: "How do we understand our social world?, and What can we do about it?" (p. 309). In relation to this sameness, Klees wrote:

> They see the world as composed of systems and structures that maintain, reproduce, and legitimate existing inequalities. From these perspectives, inequalities are not system failures but the logical consequence of successful system functioning. (p. 309)

The shift in theoretical perspectives noted above has been accompanied by a methodological shift in the field. Researchers in comparative and international education have increasingly engaged in ethnographic work at the local level (e.g., Anderson-Levitt, 1984, 2004; Levinson, 1999) as well as mixed-methods approaches to research (Klees, 2008).

COMPARATIVE AND INTERNATIONAL RESEARCH IN THE MIDDLE

Perhaps because it is such a critical stage in human development, many comparative and international education researchers have conducted work in middle or junior high schools, or they have chosen to focus on young adolescent learners. Researchers have examined diverse phenomena and settings—from formal and informal education for young adolescent girls in Ghana (Robertson, 1984), to ethnic relations among Indonesian and Chinese junior high students (Bjork, 2002), to concepts of adolescence evident in junior high schools in Mexico (Levinson, 1999), to curriculum implementation in Israeli junior high schools (Benavot & Resh, 2001). These are just a few of the dozens of studies published by comparative and international education researchers that focus on issues, school settings, student populations, and educational phenomena of interest to middle level education researchers.

In fields like mathematics education, science education, and literacy education, interest in comparative and international education research seems to peak after large-scale international assessments of young adolescent student achievement. For example, numerous studies follow the International Association for the Evaluation of Educational Achievement (IEA) assessments, such as the Trends in Mathematics and Science Studies (TIMSS) (Anderson, 1987; Ban & Cummings, 1999; Beaton et al., 1996a, 1996b; Brown, 1996; Bursten, 1992; Hiebert et al., 2003) or the International Civic and Citizenship Education Study (ICCS) (Hahn & Torney-Purta, 1999; Torney-Purta, 2000). Not surprisingly, researchers are most attentive to the education systems in high achieving countries, as was the case after the 1999 TIMSS results were released. Researchers highlighted mathematics instruction in high-achieving East Asian countries such as Japan (Martinez & Martinez, 2003), Taiwan (Reys, 1998), and Singapore (Ferrucci, Yeap, & Carter, 2003; Menon, 2000). In addition, math educators in the United States have also looked to English, Greek, and Portuguese middle level schools to improve critical thinking, problem solving skills, and motivation in mathematics (Georgakis, 1999; Johnson, 2001; Swan, 1996).

A RATIONALE FOR COMPARATIVE AND INTERNATIONAL RESEARCH IN MIDDLE LEVEL EDUCATION

Why should middle level scholars do comparative and international research? What does the field stand to gain from such work? A rationale for comparative and international scholarship in the field of middle level education can be built on three sets of imperatives.

The first is an epistemological imperative concerned with the way middle level educators construct knowledge about effective education for young adolescents. How do we know what we know about middle level education? What perspectives and voices are included in research in the field, and which ones are silenced or omitted? As argued earlier, the knowledge base in middle level education is built on a foundation of research conducted in the United States and elsewhere in the English-speaking world. The field of middle level education research needs to embrace diverse perspectives and alternative ways of knowing if it is to transcend Anglophonic parochialism and achieve relevance abroad. From studies of indigenous and non-Western societies we can learn much about distinctions between formal and informal (or nonformal) education, the role of family and community in the education and development of young adolescents, perspectives on civic and vocational education (and the role of the individual in society), language learning and teaching, and values, morality, and spirituality (e.g., Reagan, 2000, pp. 205-209).

Comparative and international research in middle level education can serve as a catalyst for critical self-reflection within the field. As Beane (2005) argued,

> What is needed is a reexamination of the middle school concept to see where it has the strength to sustain itself, where it must face up to persistent contradictions, and how it might be pushed to a stronger, more complete, and more compelling vision of its possibilities. (p. xiv)

Comparative and international research can open the field to new possibilities in middle level education. It can offer a broader perspective of philosophies, problems, and practices that exist in diverse social, cultural, and political contexts around the globe. Comparative and international research can confirm or challenge long-held assumptions about young adolescents and the best ways to meet their educational needs, and it can engender the kind of critical reflection that may move the field forward in new directions.

The second set of imperatives is ontological in nature, deriving from the universal realities of adolescence and cultural responses to it through institutions like schooling. In addition, it is important to consider how these realities are continually shaped and internationalized by the ubiquitous phenomenon of globalization that is impacting all facets of human activity throughout the world.

John Harrison, former president of the National Forum to Accelerate Middle Grades Reform, recently spoke to a group of middle level educators in Charleston, South Carolina about a trip to visit schools in China. In a school serving young adolescents in a remote part of China, Harrison noticed fingerprints above the door frames in the school. "How did the fingerprints get there?" he asked the audience of teacher educators. Harrison answered his own question, telling the group what it already knew: "The kids are jumping up and slapping the wall above the door frame, just like American kids. Why? *Because they can.* Kids are kids, whether you are somewhere in China or in Charleston, South Carolina" (personal communication, May 22, 2008).

Indeed, cross-cultural studies of child development show tremendous developmental similarities among young adolescents from country to country (e.g., Brown & Larson, 2002; Gibbons & Stiles, 2004; Konner, 1991; Pajares & Urdan, 2003; Schlegel & Barry, 1991). At the onset of puberty, young adolescents face "the most stunningly *biological* phase of childhood" (Konner, p. 17). At this stage, young people throughout the world begin the "serious business" of life "as they struggle to cope with the social pressure to conform and often to excel" (Schlegel & Barry, p. 43). While there is tremendous variation in the rituals and rites of passage that cultural groups have created to usher children into adolescence, it is important to note that they all do *something* to mark this critical stage of development. As Brown and Larson have observed,

> Whether it is short or long, whether it is unnamed or named, or understood through a variety of terms in different situations, nearly all societies have a period of transition when young people continue a process, begun in childhood, of equipping themselves to be full adult members of society. (p. 6)

In nearly every society, schooling is a central part of this transition. In some places, the onset of adolescence coincides with an intensification of schooling, while in other places it marks the end of a child's formal education. In most countries the quantity and quality of a child's education during young adolescence depends on age, gender, nationality, and a host of other determinants that may be out of his or her control. Middle level education researchers can play a vital role in building the knowledge base about young adolescent education worldwide and highlighting the often subtle relationships that exist between and among the student, societal characteristics, educational opportunities, and educational outcomes.

As argued earlier, middle level education research has proliferated within particular culturally and linguistically bound systems in the English-speaking world; however, these systems, like all cultural systems, have permeable boundaries and are continually changing from within and without. Schools in the United States, United Kingdom, and Canada are serving increasingly diverse student populations as segments of society become increasingly multicultural and internationalized. As education systems are impacted by internal internationalization, the also feel the effects of globalization. Globalization is not just a phenomenon associated with the economy and world markets; rather, it impacts all aspects of society including education. Globalization is a powerful force that influences patterns of schooling worldwide as it brings about internal and external pressure for reform (Popkewitz, 2006). As a result of internationalization and globalization, it is becoming increasingly problematic to study educational systems anywhere in the world as closed, bounded systems. The field of middle level education research must become sensitive to the realities of internationalization and globalization, or its explanations of middle level reform will be incomplete.

The third basis for comparative and international middle level education research derives from a central normative imperative of the field: to improve education for all young adolescent learners. While the field has concentrated its efforts in North America and, to some extent, Australia, New Zealand, and the United Kingdom, NMSA Executive Director Betty Edwards suggested that the middle level reform movement should strive to "positively influence the education of young adolescents wherever they live, wherever they go to school, to ensure that they can be whoever they want to be" (Edwards, 2008b, p. 5). Together with the world community, middle level educators share a humanitarian commitment to certain educational values and ideals that are encoded in documents such as the United Nations Declaration of the Rights of the Child. The declaration outlines its position on education in Principle 7, which states:

- The child is entitled to receive education, which shall be free and compulsory, at least in the elementary stages. He shall be given an education which will promote his general culture and enable him, on a basis of equal opportunity, to develop his abilities, his individual judgment, and his sense of moral and social responsibility, and to become a useful member of society.

- The best interests of the child shall be the guiding principle of those responsible for his education and guidance; that responsibility lies in the first place with his parents.

- The child shall have full opportunity for play and recreation, which should be directed to the same purposes as education; society and the public authorities shall endeavour to promote the enjoyment of this right (Office of the United Nations High Commissioner for Human Rights, 1959, Principle 7, para. 1).

These principles, including child-centered education and a commitment to social justice, are consistent with principles in *This We Believe* and other statements of middle level education philosophy (National Middle School Association, 2003). Middle level education researchers are in a position to enact these principles as they strive to improve conditions for young adolescent learners worldwide.

AN AGENDA FOR COMPARATIVE AND INTERNATIONAL RESEARCH IN MIDDLE LEVEL EDUCATION

How might middle level scholars proceed to develop a program of comparative and international research in middle level education? All research begins with a question or a set of questions, and some questions middle level scholars might consider include the following.

- What kinds of curricula, instructional practices, assessment systems, and school organizational structures exist for young adolescent learners (a) in places outside the USA, (b) in non-English speaking and/or non-Western countries, or (c) in cross-cultural contexts in the United States or elsewhere?
- How is the concept of "young" or "early" adolescence constructed in societies within which such a concept exists? How is young adolescence defined by educational policies and practices in different cultural contexts around the world?
- What can international, comparative, or cross-cultural research teach us about effective education for young adolescent learners?
- How are educators prepared to teach and counsel young adolescent learners in countries throughout the world? What policies govern their preparation and licensure?

The questions suggested above represent a "starting point;" the possibilities for comparative and international research in middle level education are virtually unlimited. Current middle level education researchers should begin by reflecting upon their own scholarship and identifying international or cross-cultural dimensions within it, or they might consider aspects of their research that would be further illuminated through cross-national comparison.

Networking and collaboration will be key components of an effort to initiate comparative and international work in middle level education. NMSA and its higher education counterpart, National Professors of Middle Level Education (NaPOMLE), could more aggressively seek to internationalize their memberships and engage in international outreach, as some organizations have successfully done. For example, National Coun-

cil for the Social Studies (NCSS) has a group called the International
Assembly of Social Educators, or IA. The membership of the IA comes
from all parts of the globe and includes school teachers, higher education
faculty, and other members interested in social studies education worldwide. The International Reading Association, an organization based in
the United States, has an international membership and an extensive program of international outreach. In the field of mathematics education,
members of organizations from around the globe convene every four
years for an International Congress on Mathematics Education. NMSA
could initiate a similar special interest group consisting of educators and
policy makers who are interested in the education of young adolescent
learners. In addition, NMSA could consider disseminating materials in
languages other than English to broaden its impact.

Middle level education researchers could join with researchers in comparative and international education or related fields whose focus is
young adolescent learners or the schools that serve them. The Middle
Level Education Research SIG could network with other AERA SIGs to
identify scholars throughout the organization who may work with young
adolescents in the United States or abroad but who might not immediately identify themselves as "middle level" researchers. Possible collabora-
tions might involve members of the International Studies SIG, the
Postcolonial Studies and Education SIG, Research Focus on Education in
the Caribbean and Africa SIG, or the Research in Global Child Advocacy
SIG. A comparative and international approach to middle level research
may initiate exciting new synergies among researchers, uniting communities of scholars around the world who share an interest in understanding
and improving education for young adolescent learners.

CONCLUSION

Recent initiatives by National Middle School Association signal a trend
toward internationalization in the field of middle level education
(Edwards, 2008b). Until now, international perspectives in the field of
middle level education have been limited to places in the English-speaking world, notably Canada, Australia, New Zealand, and the United Kingdom. This is problematic, as most of the world's young adolescent
students and their teachers live outside the English-speaking world. For
decades, researchers in fields like comparative and international education have studied educational issues, practices, and policies relevant to
middle level education in settings around the globe. This work has
occurred largely outside the academic sphere of scholars who identify
themselves as middle level education researchers. The forces of globaliza-

tion, the universality of young adolescence and schooling, and the ethical imperatives of educational research demand that middle level education researchers broaden the geographic scope of their activities. The present volume of *The Handbook of Research in Middle Level Education, An International Look at Educating Young Adolescents*, is an important first step in that direction. Engaging in comparative and international research will open up a world of possibilities for the field of middle level education. Most importantly, this effort will contribute significantly to the improvement of education for young adolescent learners worldwide.

REFERENCES

Altbach, P. G., & Kelly, G. P. (Eds.). (1986). *New approaches to comparative education*. Chicago: University of Chicago Press.

Anderson, L. W. (1987). The classroom environment study: Teaching for learning. *Comparative Education Review, 31*(1), 69–87.

Anderson-Levitt, K. M. (1984). On taking everything into account. *Anthropology and Education Quarterly, 15*(4), 316-319.

Anderson-Levitt, K. M. (2004). Reading lessons in Guinea, France, and the United States: Local meanings or global culture? *Comparative Education Review, 48*(3), 229-252.

Arnove, R. F., Altbach, P. G., & Kelly, G. P. (Eds.). (1992). *Emergent issues in education: Comparative perspectives*. Albany: State University of New York Press.

Ban, T., & Cummings, W. K. (1999). Moral orientations of school children in the United States and Japan. *Comparative Education Review, 43*(1), 64-85.

Beane, J. A. (2005). Foreword. In E. R. Brown & K. J. Saltman (Eds.), *The critical middle school reader* (pp. xi-xv). New York: Routledge.

Beaton, A. E., Mullis, I. V. S., Martin, M. O., Gonzalez, E. J., Kelly, D. L., & Smith, T. A. (1996a). *Mathematics achievement in the middle school years: IEA's Third International Mathematics and Science Study*. Chestnut Hill, MA: Boston College.

Beaton, A. E., Mullis, I. V. S., Martin, M. O., Gonzalez, E. J., Kelly, D. L., & Smith, T. A. (1996b). *Science achievement in the middle school years: IEA's Third International Mathematics and Science Study*. Chestnut Hill, MA: Boston College.

Benavot, A., & Resh, N. (2001). The social construction of the local school curriculum: Patterns of diversity and uniformity in Israeli junior high schools. *Comparative Education Review, 45*(4), 504-536

Bereday, G. Z. F. (1964). *Comparative method in education*. New York: Holt, Rinehart, & Winston.

Bjork, C. (2002). Reconstructing rituals: Expressions of autonomy and resistance in a Sino-Indonesian school. *Anthropology & Education Quarterly, 33*(4), 465-491.

Black, P., & William, D. (2005). Lessons from around the world: How policies, politics, and cultures constrain and afford assessment practices. *The Curriculum Journal, 16*(2), 249-261.

Bloch M., Kennedy, D., Lightfoot, T., & Weyenberg, D. (Eds.). (2006). *The child in the world: The world in the child: Education and the configuration of a universal, modern, and globalized childhood.* New York: Palgrave Macmillan.

Bray, M. (1999). Methodology and focus in comparative education. In M. Bray & R. Koo (Eds.), *Education and society in Hong Kong and Macau: Comparative perspectives on continuity and change* (pp. 209-223). Hong Kong: Comparative Education Research Centre, University of Hong Kong.

Brown, B. B., & Larson, R. W. (2002). *The kaleidoscope of adolescence: Experiences of the world's youth at the beginning of the 21st century.* In B. B. Brown, R. W. Larson, & T. S. Saraswathi (Eds.), *The world's youth: Adolescence in eight regions of the world* (pp. 1-20). New York: Cambridge University Press.

Brown, M. L. (1996). FIMS and SIMS: The first two IEA international mathematics surveys. *Assessment in Education: Principles, Policy, and Practice, 3*(2), 193-212.

Bursten, L. (Ed.). (1992). *The IEA study of mathematics III: Student growth and classroom* process. Oxford: Pergamon.

Comparative and International Education Society. (2008). *About us.* Retrieved July 7, 2008, from http://www.cies.us/aboutus.htm

De Jong, T., & Chadbourne, R. (2007). A challenge for middle grades teacher education programs to practice what they preach: An Australian experience. *Middle School Journal, 38*(3), 10-18.

Eckstein, M., & Noah, H. (1969). *Scientific investigations in comparative education.* New York: Macmillan.

Edwards, B. (2008a, March). Keynote address, Southeast Regional Middle Teacher Education Symposium, Charleston, SC.

Edwards, B. (2008b). Executive director's note. NMSA to consider name change. *Middle Ground, 12*(1), 5.

Erb, T. (2001). 9/11/01: Not just another date to memorize. *Middle School Journal, 33*(2), 4.

Erb, T. O. (2005). (Ed.). *This we believe in action: Implementing successful middle level schools.* Westerville, OH: National Middle School Association.

Ferrucci, B. J., Yeap, B., & Carter, J. A. (2003). A modeling approach for enhancing problem solving in the middle grades. *Mathematics Teaching in the Middle School, 8*(9), 470-475.

Georgakis, P. (1999). Oh good, it's Tuesday! *Mathematics Teaching in the Middle School, 5*(4), 224-226.

Gibbons, J. L., & Stiles, D. A. (2004). *The thoughts of youth: An international perspective on adolescents' ideal persons.* Greenwich, CT: Information Age.

Glenn, C. L. (1989). *Choice of schools in six nations: France, Netherlands, Belgium, Britain, Canada, West Germany.* Washington, DC: U.S. Dept. of Education, Office of Educational Research and Improvement, Programs for the Improvement of Practice.

Hahn, C. L. (2006). Comparative and international social studies research. In K. C. Barton (Ed.), *Research methods in social studies education: Contemporary issues and perspectives* (pp. 139-158). Greenwich, CT: Information Age.

Hahn, C. L., & Torney-Purta, J. (1999). The IEA Civic Education Project: National and international perspectives. *Social Education, 63*, 425-431.

Halls, W. D. (Ed.). (1990). *Comparative education: Contemporary issues and trends*. London: J. Kingsley/UNESCO.

Hiebert, J., Gallimore, R., Garnier, H., Bogard Givvin, K., Hollingsworth, H., Jacobs, J., et al. (2003). *Teaching mathematics in seven countries: Results from the TIMSS 1999 video study*. Washington, DC: National Center for Education Statistics.

Holmes, B. (1965). *Problems in education: A comparative approach*. London: Routledge & Kegan Paul.

Johnson, I. D. (2001). Standards-based teaching: Alive and well in Portugal. *Mathematics Teaching in the Middle School, 6*(9), 538-542.

Juvonen, J., Le, V. N., Kaganoff, T., Augustine, C., & Constant L. (2004). *Focus on the wonder years: Challenges facing the American middle school*. Arlington, VA: RAND Corporation.

Kist, W. (2003). Student achievement in new literacies for the 21st century. *Middle School Journal, 35*(1), 6-13.

Klees, S. J. (2008). Reflections on theory, method, and practice in comparative and international education. *Comparative Education Review, 52*(3), 301-324.

Konner, M. (1991). *Childhood: A multicultural view*. Boston: Little, Brown, & Co.

Kubow, P. K., & Fossum, P. R. (2003). *Comparative education: Exploring issues in international context*. Upper Saddle River, NJ: Merrill/Prentice Hall.

Levinson, B. A. (1999). "Una etapa siempre dificil": Concepts of adolescence and secondary education in Mexico. *Comparative Education Review, 43*(2), 129-161.

Martinez, J. G. R., & Martinez, N. C. (2003). Raising middle school math standards without raising anxiety. *Middle School Journal, 34*(4), 27-35.

Menon, R. 2000. On my mind: Should the United States emulate Singapore's education system to achieve Singapore's success in the TIMSS? *Mathematics Teaching in the Middle School, 5*(6), 345-347.

National Commission on Excellence in Education. (1983). *A nation at risk: The imperative for educational reform*. Washington, DC: U.S. Department of Education.

National Middle School Association. (2003). *This we believe: Successful schools for young adolescents*. Westerville, OH: Author.

Neville-Tisdall, M. (2002). Pedagogy and politics in New Zealand's middle schools. *Middle School Journal, 33*(4), 45-51.

Noah, H. J. (1986). The use and abuse of comparative education. In P. G. Altbach & G. P. Kelly (Eds.), *New approaches to comparative education* (pp. 153-165). Chicago: University of Chicago Press.

Noah, H. J., & Eckstein, M. A. (1969). *Toward a science of comparative education*. New York: Macmillan.

Nolan, C. J. P., & Brown, M. A. (2002). The fight for middle school education in New Zealand. *Middle School Journal, 33*(4), 34-44.

Office of the United Nations High Commissioner for Human Rights. (1959). *Declaration of the Rights of the Child*. Retrieved August 7, 2008, from http://www.unhchr.ch/html/menu3/b/25.htm

Ogbu, J. U. (1982). Cultural discontinuities and schooling. *Anthropology and Education Quarterly, 13*(4), 290-307.

Ogbu, J. U. (1983). Minority status and schooling in plural societies. *Comparative Education Review, 27*(2), 168-190.

Ogbu, J. U., & Simons, H. D. (1998). Voluntary and involuntary minorities: A cultural ecological theory of school performance with some implications for education. *Anthropology & Education Quarterly, 29*(2), 155-188.

Pajares, F., & Urdan, T. (2003). *Adolescence and education: International perspectives on adolescence.* Greenwich, CT: Information Age.

Peterson, S., & Belizaire, M. (2006). Another look at roles in literature circles. *Middle School Journal, 37*(4), 37-43.

Popkewitz, T. (2006). Foreword: Hopes of inclusion/recognition and production of difference. In M. N. Bloch, D. Kennedy, T. Lightfoot, & D. Weyenberg (Eds.), *The child in the world, the world in the child: Education and the configuration of a universal, modern, and globalized childhood* (pp. ix-xiv). New York: Palgrave.

Reagan, T. G. (2000). *Non-Western educational traditions: Alternative approaches to educational thought and practice.* Mahwah, NJ: Erlbaum.

Reys, R. E. (1998). Computation versus number sense. *Mathematics Teaching in the Middle School, 4*(2), 110-112.

Robertson, C. C. (1984). Formal or nonformal education? Entrepreneurial women in Ghana. *Comparative Education Review, 28*(4), 639-658.

Rotberg, I. (2004). Concluding thoughts: On change, tradition, and choices. In I. Rotberg (Ed.), *Balancing change* (pp. 385-413). Lanham, MD: Scarecrow Education.

Schlegel, A., & Barry, H. (1991). *Adolescence: An anthropological inquiry.* New York: The Free Press.

Shimizu, K. (1992). Shido: Education and selection in a Japanese middle school. *Comparative Education 28*(2), 109-129.

Simon, R. J., & Banks, L. (2003). *Global perspectives on social issues: Education.* Lanham, MD: Lexington Books.

Spaulding, S. (1989). Comparing educational phenomena: Promises, prospects, and problems. In A. C. Purves (Ed.), *International comparisons and educational reform* (pp. 1-16). Alexandria, VA: Association for Supervision and Curriculum Development

Steiner-Khamsi, G. (2006). The development turn in comparative education. *European Education, 38*(3), 19-47.

Swan, M. (1996). Assessing mathematical processes: The English experience. *Mathematics Teaching in the Middle School, 1*(9), 706-711.

Torney-Purta, J. (2000). Comparative perspectives on political socialization and civic education. *Comparative Education Review, 44*(1), 88-95.

Waggoner, V. C., & McEwin, C. K. (1993). Middle level practices in European international and Department of Defense schools. *Middle School Journal, 24*(5), 29-36.

Whitehead, K. (2005). Integrated curriculum in the context of challenges to middle schooling: An Australian perspective. *Middle School Journal, 36*(4), 41-50.

Wilson, D. N. (2003). The future of comparative and international education in a globalized world. *International Review of Education, 49*(1-2), 15-33.

World Council of Comparative Education Societies. (2008). *Member societies.* Retrieved August 7, 2008, from http://www.wcces.net/members/index.html

Ziegler, S., & Mulhall, L. (1994). Establishing and evaluating a successful advisory program in a middle school. *Middle School Journal, 25*(4), 42-46.

CHAPTER 1

YOUNG ADOLESCENT EDUCATION IN TURKEY

**Serkan Özel, Z. Ebrar Yetkiner,
Robert M. Capraro, and Ali Riza Küpçü**

After the foundation of the Republic of Turkey in 1923, the establishment of widespread compulsory education in 1924 started Turkey's steady path to rigorous and standardized educational practices. Middle-school education has benefited from various reform movements specifically the provision for 8-year compulsory education. As part of the increase in the compulsory-education years to include young adolescents, the investment in school infrastructure and educational materials, the government's active role in assigning underutilized teaching professionals to schools, and the development and incentives provided to families to enroll students who had formerly not been able to take advantage of schooling resulted in a dramatic increase in the compulsory-education enrollment rates. In response to the international and national achievement reports, Turkey established young adolescent education curriculum and assessment reform that started in 2004 and is to be completed in 2009. One consequence of the curriculum and assessment reform has been to codify changes in the leaning theory from behaviorism to constructivism taking into account the stress of high-stakes testing on students.

An International Look at Educating Young Adolescents
pp. 1–23

CONTEXTUAL NARRATIVE

Location and Geography

With 3% of its overall area lying in Europe and 97% in Asia, Turkey forms a bridge between two old world continents. Because of its unique geographic location, Turkey has been home to various societies and cultures and is often called "the cradle of civilizations." Turkey's diverse neighbors, Greece and Bulgaria to the northwest, Armenia and Georgia in the northeast, Iran and Azerbaijan to the east, Iraq on the southeast, and Syria on the south, give it increasing strategic importance. Turkey's 2007 population was 70,586,256 (Turkish Statistical Institute [TSI], n.d.), and there is a decrease in the population growth rate with a 1.83% growth during 1990-2000 period compared to the expected growth rate of 1.21% between 2004 and 2020. Turkey has an area of 814, 578 square kilometers including its lakes and is divided into seven geographical regions: Marmara, Black Sea, Eastern Anatolia, Southeastern Anatolia, Mediterranean, Aegean, and Central Anatolia. Each of these regions has their own geographic and climate characteristics as well as cultural and historical features.

Turkey has significant regional differences in education, both between western and eastern regions and rural and urban areas, partly due to differences in economic development. Rural areas in eastern and southeastern regions have a large number of remote and secluded villages lacking easy access to education. A considerable number of schools in these areas have insufficient facilities (e.g., substandard schools lack much of the essential elements of formalized schools such as heating infrastructure and windows) and insufficient academic necessities such as libraries and instructional materials.

Cultural Norms and Religion

Cultural identity, secularism, and religion are intertwined, each struggling for its identity within the Turkish populace. Turkey is a secular country whose population is 99% Muslim. The largest sect is Sunni followed by Alevis, estimated to be between 15 and 20 million people. The other major religions are Christianity and Judaism. Minority rights are protected by law and people of different religions are equally free to practice their beliefs. Culturally, Turkey is largely monoethnic with the main alternate ethnic group being the Kurdish. Along with a strong cultural identity, the people are more collectively minded than Western countries but less than far eastern countries. The culture tends to foster patriarchal family units. As an integral part of the cultural system, Turks are a high context and indirect society. That is, understanding the context is essential to understanding the message, and this is often conveyed through indirect conversation.

Religious Education in Turkey

The Ministry of National Education's (MoNE, Turkish acronym, MEB) mandated curriculum starts religious education at fourth grade. However, non-Muslim minorities can be exempted from religious courses by request. Within the recent reform movement, the Religious Culture and Moral Knowledge course curriculum has been redesigned. Even though the religion course is based on Islamic values, it has shifted to a more pluralistic perspective and reaches beyond one specific belief. The new religious education curriculum aims to educate students with accurate knowledge about religion and moral values and to nurture ethical sensitivity (Kaymakcan, 2006).

Role of Women

The Turkish constitution ensures that women and men are equal before the law. However, there are considerable gender differences between women and men in their education levels and participation in the workforce. The Turkish workforce consists of only 26% of the total female population as compared to 73% of the male population (KA-DER, 2003). While the law affords equal rights to women, they are underrepresented in the local, regional, and national government, therefore, they have less participation in the decision-making processes. The underrepresentation of women in the labor market and the government is partially due to complex cultural and social reasons such as traditional women's roles at home and a gender double standard against women in the labor market.

Economic Well-Being

Turkish economy has experienced remarkable growth in recent years. In 2001, Turkish people experienced a severe economic crisis, a 7.5% decrease in gross domestic product (GDP), but the recovery was very fast, a 7.9% increase in 2002 (Organization for Economic Cooperation Development [OECD], 2008). Also the GDP per capita increased 34.7%

from 2001 to 2006. The country is working progressively toward the goal of increasing its GDP per capita, which is still among the lowest, $8,766, with Luxembourg being the highest, $78,138, of the OECD countries. There is a significant difference in economic development between eastern and western regions. The contribution of the eastern cities to the GDP is as low as 0.1% compared to western cities that can be as high as 21.3% (TSI, n.d.).

Per child expenditures for education is one factor in academic performance. Turkey annually spends $869 per student on primary education. This level of funding is in the bottom quartile of OECD countries, where the average is $5,450 (OECD, 2007).

Infant Mortality

According to Turkish Population and Health Research results (Hancioglu & Alyanak, 2004), during the 1998-2003 period, infant mortality rate was 29 per 1000 live births. Fifty-nine percent of the infant deaths occur in the neonatal period, and on average 37 out of 1000 children die before the age of five. Both infant and under-five mortality rates are higher in the northern and eastern regions of Turkey because of complex social and economic issues, such as low economical development, lack of access to suitable health care, and low parental education levels. However, when comparing 1993-1998 and 1998-2003 periods, both infant and under-5 mortality rates decreased 29% and 34%, respectively (Hancioglu & Alyanak).

Illiteracy

There has been meaningful improvement in literacy rates since the early 1990s as a result of literacy programs and campaigns developed by national and local government agencies, independent organizations, and international associations such as the United Nations Children's Fund (UNICEF). However, illiteracy rates still remain high. In 2006, the adult illiteracy rate was 11.9% (4% of men and 19.6% of women) as compared to 21.6% (10.2% of men and 32.6% of women) in 1990 (TSI, n.d.). Illiteracy rates differ by region in addition to gender. In some eastern cities the illiteracy rates for men and women can be as high as 26% and 39%, respectively, and in some western cities as low as 8% and 12%, respectively. Not surprisingly, high illiteracy mainly affects people from the lower socioeconomic status and the elderly as compared to middle or high socioeconomic stratuses and the younger population (Nohl & Sayilan, 2004).

The overall educational level in Turkey is low. In general, there is differential access to education by region in addition to gender, which is more apparent in the eastern regions. On average, in western regions males have 8.70 and females have 8.27 years of formal education, whereas, in the southeastern region it is 6.71 and 4.49 for males and females, respectively. One explanation is differential participation in compulsory education.

Compulsory Education

In 1997, compulsory schooling was extended for elementary education—from 5 years (ages 6-10) to 8 years (ages 6-14), and to include middle school education—and named as primary education. Thus, all public and private primary schools have grades one through eight, and they follow the national curriculum developed by MoNE. Since the 2003-2004 academic year, MoNE has been providing primary public school students with textbooks and practice workbooks. Public school teachers have also been supplied with the accompanying teacher's version of the books, free of charge. Students and teachers in private schools must purchase their textbooks, which need to be chosen from among the ones sanctioned by MoNE.

Overall, the compulsory education completion rate was 66% (i.e., 72.3% and 59.1% for males and females, respectively) (TSI, n.d.). The participation rate in compulsory education in western cities ranges between 72% and 75%, whereas, in eastern cites it ranges between 41% and 58% (TSI, n.d.). Currently there is a high rate of school-age children, 10.21% (7.63% of males and 11.6% of females), who do not participate in compulsory education.

HISTORY AND ORGANIZATION OF
SCHOOLING FOR YOUNG ADOLESCENTS

Historical Background

The Ministry of National Education is the modern equivalent of the Ministry of Public Instruction, established in 1857 during the period of the Ottoman Empire. Substantive reforms in education followed the foundation of the Republic of Turkey. The contemporary Turkish education system was established in 1924 with secular schools replacing religious ones. Compulsory education was established as 5 years of elementary schooling, although the educational infrastructure was not yet established to provide universal education for many years. With the ratification of the 1924 Unity of Education Law, all schools became coeducational (Wolf-Gazo, 1996) and came under the supervision of the MoNE. Before this law, there were different educational systems for different purposes rather than a uniform national education system. For example, *medreses* were religion-based, *rusdiye* (elementary school), *idadiye* (lower secondary school), and *sultaniye* (secondary school) provided education based on practices learned from Europe, and some schools, specifically for minorities, offered instruction in the students' native languages. However, after the Independence War (1919-1923), it was important to foster a new generation with national sovereignty and to strengthen nationalism. Therefore, the Unity of Education Law precludes even the largest ethnic group from an education in their native language.

To democratize the educational system and foster educational secularism, Mustafa Kemal Ataturk, founder of the Republic of Turkey, invited John Dewey to share his ideas about reforms for the educational system in 1924. Dewey prepared two reports, which mainly concentrated on teacher education but also included recommendations on topics such as instructional strategies and the role of the ministry of education. Dewey's reports and his progressive ideas about education influenced Turkish education in some aspects. The most readily accepted idea was the development of teacher education schools, which in turn improved the social and financial status of teachers. However, some ideas, such as his pluralistic perspective of providing foreign schools with more independence were not implemented due to the social and political situation of the era. Dewey's long-term influence on Turkish education and teachers was through his work translated into Turkish. In those formative years of the Turkish educational system, educators from Germany, Switzerland, and the United States were also invited to provide their insights (Buyukduvenci, 1995).

In 1926 with the Law on Education Organization, MoNE was charged with providing contemporary national education for Turkish citizens by opening primary, secondary, and vocational schools and developing courses. Further, this law established the Language Commission to protect the integrity of the Turkish language. Establishing a uniform teacher preparation program was of paramount importance. Today the ministry is responsible for staffing public schools with teachers and administrators. Furthermore, curriculum development and the establishment of educational regulations and programs are under MoNE's responsibility; consequently, there are no local school boards.

In order to increase the educational quality, science boards and National Education Summits (NES) were established where the issues of training and basic educational principles were discussed. Science boards were responsible for overseeing the structure of schooling while the summits were responsible for the content of schooling. For example, in 1923, the first science boards' meeting established that compulsory education would increase to 6 years, and primary school students would be banned from enrollment in foreign schools. One year later, the same group reduced compulsory education back to 5 years. However, optional high school education had increased to 6 years, 3 years preliminary and 3 years specialization, and there has ben an increase in teacher education from 3 to 5 years. Science boards served in this capacity until they were replaced by the Board of Education and Discipline (BoED) in 1926. The National Education Summits still remain the same as they were, the first was in 1939 and the seventeenth in 2006. Each summit addresses specific educational issues although the focus has been on improving the curriculum, selecting content, and course developments (MoNE, 2002).

Curriculum, Instruction, and Assessment Practices

The classroom environment. In middle schools, a teacher who is certified in a subject area instructs the class. Students are assigned to classrooms and the teachers circulate to classrooms as different subjects are taught. This is in direct contrast to schools where teachers remain stationary in one classroom and students move from classroom to classroom. When teachers are not teaching, they have a shared lounge where students can find them. The average teacher working time in primary education is 4.8 hours per day, which is below the OECD average of 6.2. However, the workload can vary widely based on region, number of students per grade, and number of students in the school. When compared to the OECD countries, Turkish middle school teachers have one of the lowest annual statutory salaries (OECD, 2007).

The school environment. The MoNE is responsible for public school buildings. The primary school age population is very large with an insufficient number of school buildings and teachers to accommodate the need. As a consequence, half-day school sessions are adopted by a large number of public schools, with morning and afternoon sessions. The national average for students per classroom is 36. In some rural and urban areas the number of students reaches 50 or 60 per class (MoNE, n.d.-a). Currently, most of the primary schools lack science laboratories or the necessary lab equipment, which hinders the transition from traditional teaching practices to application-oriented instruction. Very few schools have gyms, thus physical education commonly occurs either in the garden or in the classrooms.

Weekly schedule and courses. Students in primary schools are required to attend 30 class hours per 5-day week. In Grades 1 through 7, required courses comprise 28 of the 30 hours, with 2 hours for elective courses. Required courses include Turkish, mathematics, social studies, science and technology, English as a second language, visual arts, music, and physical education. In addition to the required courses, religious studies start at fourth grade, traffic safety is included in fourth and fifth grades, and technology and design start at sixth grade. Students, starting in fourth grade, select two elective art courses from the following options: drama, folk dancing, band, art, photography, or foreign language (only English). Kinesiology-based physical education electives include wrestling, soccer, basketball, volleyball, or ping-pong. Finally, enrichment courses include information technologies and chess, but from sixth grade forward they may also choose folklore, horticulture, or media literacy. While new options are added at certain grade levels, students select only two from the available courses for the year.

In eighth grade, 29 hours are spent on required courses with a 1-hour elective. In eighth grade the same required courses exist with history of the Republic of Turkey and Kemalism, first-aid, citizenship, and human rights replacing traffic safety and social studies. Nevertheless, only one elective course per week is offered in eighth grade and those elective courses add to the previous options: speech, creative writing, information technologies, tourism, agriculture, foreign language other than English, or local handicraft (MoNE, n.d.-b).

Instructional practices. In middle school classrooms, traditional teaching instructional practices were prominent until 2004 curriculum reform movement. For example, direct teaching and lecturing were the main teaching methods virtually in all middle schools. Students' involvement in the lessons was mainly through narrow teacher questioning, which mainly evaluated student understanding or preparation. Students were given a lot of homework that involved mostly drill and practice rather than tasks that improve problem solving and critical thinking skills.

Although the reform brought a constructivist curriculum and professional development opportunities for teachers to implement modern instructional practices, teachers' transition from their old practices to the newly encouraged methods has proved not to be easy. For example, in order to improve instructional practices, middle school classrooms were enhanced with educational technologies such as computers and smartboards, and teachers were provided professional development to integrate these technologies. However, given the lack of necessary infrastructure to integrate technology and teachers' inadequate experience with these tools, effective and consistent technology integration has yet to be achieved.

Measurement and assessment. Educational measurement and student assessment are major issues for the Turkish educational system. Until very recently, instructional models were based on a behaviorist approach, which is still prominently reflected in both K-12 instructional settings and assessment systems (Kucuk & Cepni, 2004). The behaviorist approach focuses on observable and measurable behavior, and student learning/ achievement is assessed dichotomously as to be correct or incorrect. Therefore, the aim of the instruction for the behaviorist paradigm is mainly to increase students' correct answers. This promotes assessment models that require responses that can be categorized as either right or wrong. Consequently, the most common assessment methods used by teachers are multiple choice tests or well-structured problems that have a clearly right or wrong solution. Generally, assessment is a teacher's domain. Although the insufficiency of these assessment models in evaluating student learning and skills precipitate a need for alternate and more complex authentic assessment tools such as essays, presentations, or portfolios (Birgin & Baki, 2007), research on the effects of authentic assessment and its requisite pedagogical techniques is not prevalent in Turkey.

Organization and Structure

The MoNE has established two main structures of education: formal and nonformal (see Figure 1.1). Formal education consists of four levels: early childhood education, primary school (elementary and middle), high school, and postsecondary school. Nonformal education is not limited by age nor is designed for those who never participated in compulsory education. Likewise it is not limited to or designed for those who exited the system before completing the compulsory education or those who need additional training. The nonformal education system provides alternate training focused on developing reading, writing, or job skills with the goal of enhancing participants' standard of living. The national public education system provides formal and nonformal education for free and there are comparable private schools. The MoNE is responsible for the legislation and supervision of both public and private formal and nonformal education, except for postsecondary schools. For the local administrative management of public primary schools, MoNE assigns provincial directors of education that work under the provincial governor.

Preschool education is voluntary for children ages 3 to 5 and is free in public schools. The participation rate in preschool education remains

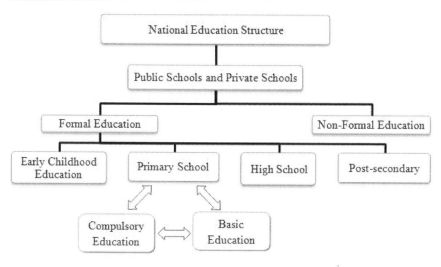

Figure 1.1.   National education structure.

very low—about 13% in 2003, although the number of children attending preschools has almost doubled since the early 1990s. There was an important increase in the number of preschools, particularly public preschools since 1997, resulting from MoNE's emphasis on programs for children's cognitive and physical development.

Primary education is characterized as both basic and compulsory (Gultekin, 1998) and is defined as the fundamental education that helps to develop physical, cognitive, and moral values for all students. Primary education refers to a level in the education system which comes after preschool education and before secondary school. Basic education is at the heart of the educational system and refers to the education that everyone must, by law, is permitted to be a productive citizen. However, basic education is insufficient without an expectation about how long it should take to learn this information, therefore, compulsory education sets the term for the basic education to be accomplished. The main goal of compulsory education is to prepare students for higher education or the job market, thus receiving the basic education is necessary for individual professional and social development, and guidance for career choices and vocational education (Gultekin).

Secondary school education comprises at least 4 years of schooling in general or vocational high schools. Secondary schools follow the national curriculum and in the 2006-2007 academic year MoNE started providing public secondary school students with free textbooks. All postsecondary schools are affiliated with the Higher Education Council rather than MoNE.

OUTCOMES OF THE SCHOOLING OF YOUNG ADOLESCENTS

Academic Performance Outcomes

Turkey has participated in various administrations of major international comparative studies: Trends in Mathematics and Science Study-R (TIMMS-R, 1999), TIMSS (2007), the Progress in International Reading Literacy Study [PIRLS] (2001) (International Association for the Evaluation of Educational Achievement, n.d.), and Programme for International Student Assessment (PISA, 2003, 2006) (OECD, n.d). Turkey's results on these tests are important in that they provide information about the international benchmarks that Turkish students have or have not achieved as well as a comparison of Turkish students' achievement across other participating countries. Further, MoNE's primary school curriculum reform movement utilized Turkish students' results on these international studies to understand students' weaknesses and strengths as compared to the international benchmarks and prompted the examination of curricula and assessment policies used in other countries.

PIRLS is an assessment of fourth graders' reading comprehension. Turkey ranked 28th out of 35 countries on reading achievement with a mean score of 449, which was below the international average of 500. Moreover, Turkish students' achievement was below their European Union (EU) counterparts and other EU candidates. Only 58% of Turkish students met the lower quartile benchmark, which is associated with the capability of interpreting explicitly stated information. Seven percent of students reached the upper quartile, which corresponds to more advanced reading comprehension skills such as making inferences and providing interpretations through connections to their own experiences.

On both the 2003 and 2006 administrations of PISA, which assesses the ability of 15-year-olds to use their knowledge and skills for future life challenges in the information age, Turkey ranked among the lowest achievers within the participating countries as well as EU and OECD countries. The majority of Turkish students' achievements did not go beyond the lowest international benchmarks, whereas, in general the majority of the students from OECD countries achieved at least the middle level benchmarks. One important finding on PISA was the substantive performance differences among schools.

The impact of education funding is difficult to disentangle from other school variables, especially in light of international comparisons with a broad spectrum of school funding strategies that make direct country comparisons ambiguous at best. Therefore, when international comparisons are made, economic conditions should be considered. For example, regarding available school resources and technology, the majority of Turkish students (i.e., 65% in 2003) who took PISA were from schools that had very few resources, whereas in high achieving countries, this proportion was very small (e.g., 0% in New Zealand in 2003) (OECD, 2004).

In addition, both the 2003 and 2006 PISA took place before the implementation of the curriculum reform. The areas identified as weaknesses on PISA were addressed in the curriculum improvement plans. For example, careful comparison between the previous curriculum and the PISA results showed that problem solving was not adequately addressed and this area was addressed by the new curriculum. This comparison revealed other weaknesses in the curriculum such as probability, change, and relationships between mathematics and reading comprehension. These content areas have benefited from renewed interest and emphasis in the new curriculum.

Other Important Outcomes

The MoNE has launched a new primary and secondary school guidance and counseling program. Within this program major social and emotional outcomes were identified and to achieve these outcomes sample activities have been developed to be implemented by school counselors. These outcomes have been spread across the academic year as weekly benchmarks. Yearly reports are developed about students' achievements of these benchmarks, as well as difficulties within the implementation of these benchmarks. These reports are then used to improve the program.

As part of the reform movement in middle school education, specifically 8-year compulsory education, guidance in primary schools has been emphasized. Educating young adolescents is not only limited to intellectual development but also social, emotional, and physical developments. Guidance had been mostly prominent on academic success and career choice in secondary schools, whereas now it starts at the fourth grade. In the Turkish education system the prerequisite to attend formal job training is the completion of middle school. During primary school parent, teacher, and student seminars are held to introduce various secondary schools and the job opportunities after graduation from these schools.

Research Supporting Academic Performance and Other Outcomes

The most respected research on the academic outcomes is the afore-mentioned international studies, whose results have had a lot of impact on Turkish policy decisions. Educational research is also conducted to improve social and emotional, as well as academic, outcomes of primary school students. Various research in the area of social and emotional development include strategies to deal with classroom misbehaviors (Sadik, 2008), conflict resolution (Bilgin, 2008), and different aspects of bullying (Kartal & Bilgin, 2008). In addition, research can be found on the career choices of middle school students such as the difficulties they encounter as they decide their careers (Kesici, Hamarta, & Arslan, 2008).

CURRENT ISSUES RELATED TO THE SCHOOLING OF YOUNG ADOLESCENTS

Concerns About the Current Education System

Conflicting worlds: High-stakes assessment does not equal assessment reform. One important barrier to assessment reform has been the status quo for high-stakes national selection examinations. Despite the movement toward more authentic classroom assessment, the major national selection exams given at middle and high school levels reinforce traditional assess-ment approaches, thus impeding transition to authentic classroom assess-ment. The major high stakes testing at the end of the primary school level was the Secondary School Student Selection and Placement Examination (SSE, Turkish acronym OKS) through 2007. The MoNE, at the end of eighth grade, administered this centralized test yearly across the country. The SSE was an optional test but highly competitive for those wishing to move into the most desirable secondary schools. Primary education grad-uates who wanted to attend a well-resourced and high-quality secondary school had to take the test and attain the score required by the school(s) of their choice. The schools that are considered prestigious public and pri-vate high schools required the SSE and established their own admission criteria. These schools include general and vocational Anatolian high schools, science high schools, and many private schools. However, stu-dents who did not earn a sufficient score to attend these schools could still enroll in general and public vocational schools as well as private schools that did not require the SSE.

Private tutoring: An integral component of the education system. Private tutoring occurs in mainly three forms (a) individual tutoring, (b) at private tutoring centers in small groups, and (c) as supplementary classes at schools (Tansel & Bircan, 2008). Using external resources to prepare for the SSE and the university entrance examinations at the secondary level creates a substantial economic burden for parents. The expenditure on high-stakes tests preparation was approximately $650 million in 2002, which constituted 11.7% of the total private expenditure on education (Chawla, 2005). The estimated average cost of attending private tutoring center was $550.

The reliance on private tutoring created a great inequity for students—privileged the upper and the middle SES over the lower SES students. Given the high cost of tutoring centers, Tansel and Bircan (2006) found that household income was the major indicator of expenditures on private tutoring together with parents' education levels, particularly the education level of the mother. A corollary is the increased inequity in access to better secondary schools, which are believed to offer high quality education that in turn increase students' potential success on university entrance examinations.

In response to the issues related to high-stakes testing, as of 2008 the MoNE initiated a program to phase in testing reform for advancing from primary to secondary school. The new system does not rely on one single test, namely SSE, instead students are administered the optional Academic Proficiency Examinations (APeX) at the end of sixth, seventh, and eighth grades. One of the important differences of the new test is it includes a foreign language section in addition to previously tested subjects. Students earn individual scores but they are not ranked as they were on SSE. The APeX, which is directly linked to the curriculum objectives established during the curriculum reform movement, is used for placement into the schools previously requiring the SSE, however, it has no impact on students' passing or failing at any grade level. Furthermore, the composite scores for admission consideration into select secondary schools include students' performance on the APeX for three years, the students' grade point average (GPA) (weighted 25%), and their discipline scores (weighted 5%). The new system requires monitoring not only academic achievement but also social development continuously. Because students' school performances as reflected in their GPAs and discipline scores affect their access to the high school of their choice, the MoNE expects a substantial decrease in the demand for private tutoring centers, thereby improving equity in access to secondary school education. However, some educators are worried that the new system will result in attending private tutoring centers at an even earlier age than before to get ready for the first APeX at sixth grade (Sahin, 2007).

Access to a university education is extremely competitive because of high expectations established by notably selective universities and an insufficient number of post-secondary institutions. Only 10% of the students who take the Student Selection Examination for Universities (SSEU) are accepted into a 2- or 4-year post-secondary program, which includes distance education. Admission is determined by performance on the SSEU. The university entrance examination is required for college admittance and is given at the end of each academic year by the Student Selection and Placement Center. College-bound students must attain at least the minimal score required by the university and departments of their choices.

The SSEU has a paramount effect on the education system as well as students' and their families' lives. Some major reasons for the great demand for a university education is the differential income for university graduates (Tansel, 2005), the increased likelihood of finding full employment, and the prestigious social status. Sixty percent of senior high school students ($N = 1,078$) and 66% of high school graduates ($N = 1,073$) stated that there is nothing more important than the SSEU in their lives (Tansel & Bircan, 2008). This shows the profound impact the test has on students. There have been numerous studies on various aspects of university entrance examination anxiety such as how it differs across genders or due to perception of achievement among students (e.g., Sahin, Gunay, & Bati, 2006).

Benefits of the Current Education System

One of the major benefits of the current education system to the improvement in literacy rates and overall education level is the 8-year compulsory education. Through the funding made available for educational reforms to get every Turkish student complete 8-year compulsory education, there has been a substantive improvement in both the young adolescents completing the middle school and the facilities and staff.

REFORM INITIATIVES AND NATIONAL POLICIES

As a result of poor performance on international comparisons and a lack of progress toward meeting education system goals, the MoNE started educational reform in 2004. The reform included curriculum improvements that moved from subject-centered to learner-centered and changing from behaviorism to constructivism (Bulut, 2007; Sahin, 2007). The objectives of curriculum reform were to reduce the amount of content and number of concepts, arrange the units thematically, develop nine core competencies across the curriculum, move from a teacher-centered didactic model to a student-centered constructivist model, incorporate technologies into instruction, monitor student achievement through formative assessments, move away from traditional assessment of recall and toward authentic assessment, and enhance citizenship education.

This major school reform was supported by a $300 million infusion of credit by the World Bank. As a result, emphasis was placed on technology integration and the acquisition of computers, and instructional software, games, and televisions. Additionally, large monetary infusion has provided for professional development to support proper implementation of the new curriculum, student-centered and active learning, and to de-emphasize memorization. The MoNE also commissioned new instruction and active teaching handbooks aligned with the reform.

In addition, in-service teachers were provided workshops to improve pedagogical skills and to help them transition to more student centered and conceptually-based teaching strategies. The MoNE has adopted a new strategy where schools apply for grants to implement promising instructional practices. This competitive strategy provides targeted funds to schools that undertake the most rigorous attempts at educational reform.

Another area where reform has been taking place is foreign language education. The Ministry of National Education implemented a new foreign language program. Within this program, initially foreign language instruction begins in fourth grade and continues through middle school with a second foreign language added to the curriculum in eighth grade.

A New Paradigm

The primary school curriculum reform movement, begun in 2004, was grounded in the constructivist paradigm. Within the new paradigm, MoNE encourages teachers' use of alternative assessment models such as project-based assessment, rubrics for scoring complex problems, and group- and self-assessment in addition to the traditional assessment tools and methods. However, an obstacle to the implementation of these new assessment techniques is insufficient pedagogical knowledge for successful implementation (Isman, 2005). In a survey conducted by Education Sciences Association, teachers stated their major difficulties implementing the new instructional programs were integrating assessment models such as authentic and performance assessments. Teachers also indicated that the lack of professional development to implement the new measurement and assessment programs was a substantial barrier to effective classroom integration. The teachers requested access to measurement and evaluation specialists at their schools as they attempted to incorporate the new strategies into their every day practice. Based on these findings, MoNE is considering adopting a model that places measurement and evaluation departments in public and private schools to support teachers in the implementation of reform assessment methods.

Testing Reform

Several serious flaws in the SSE led to testing reform. First, the SSE represented only a limited range of the intended curriculum and thus was insufficient to measure the whole corpus of what students were expected to learn. Only Turkish, Mathematics, Science and Technology, and Social Sciences were tested and the rest of the curriculum was excluded. Because SSE was the gatekeeper for a better high school education, students favored these four disciplines and marginalized instruction in foreign language, music, art, and physical education. Given the narrowness of the test, it also was not aligned to the reform curriculum standards within the subject areas tested. Second, because of the high-stakes nature of the test, the content of the instruction in schools became limited to what the test covered. The style of instruction followed the SSE's scope, and classroom assessment was conducted in the style of the tests' items. The SSE consisted of multiple-choice items, limited in their ability to evaluate the full scope of student learning. The test did not include open-ended or essay items which could evaluate a broader range of learning. Consequently, the assessments used in everyday instruction were multiple-choice and short answer open-ended questions. These assessment models encouraged procedural knowledge and rote memorization of facts rather than promoting higher-order thinking skills or critical thinking and problem solving.

Another disadvantage of SSE was its status as the sole test that determined who benefited from the best secondary education options. Students who had the means used private tutoring centers and other resources to prepare for the test. This placed undue stress on students and a costly financial burden on parents. Unfortunately, a consequence of the SSE was overreliance on private tutoring centers.

Military, Noncommissioned Preparatory, and Police Academy High Schools

Another high-stakes testing is required if middle-school students prefer to enter the military's high schools and Noncommissioned (NCO) Preparatory schools, which are supervised by Turkish Armed Forces. Admission to these schools is voluntarily but not open enrollment and is based on student performance on a two-phase examination taken at the end of eighth grade. Military high schools and NCO Preparatory School graduates do not hold military status, but they are eligible to attend military post-secondary schools. The Police Academy Entrance Examination, conducted by the Director's Office of Ankara Police Academy, is also given at the end of eighth grade. The Police Academy graduates become police officers and are assigned to positions by the government.

RESEARCH

Current Research Topics

Young adolescent education research in Turkey has benefited from renewed interest since the new millennia. In recent years there has been improvement in the quantity and scope of the research conducted regarding middle school education (Ozgentas, 1975; Ulutas & Ubuz, 2008) as reflected in the emergence of new research journals some of which are international, such as *Elementary Education Online, Journal of Theory and Practice in Education,* and *Eurasia Journal of Mathematics, Science and Technology Education.* The majority of education research occurs in mathematics, science, and instructional technology, whereas research in social studies, fine arts, physical education, and guidance is lacking. The research mainly focuses on cognitive and affective domains, curriculum and textbook analyses, instructional strategies and material development, student outcomes, and teacher education.

There is current emphasis on the effectiveness of the reform curriculum, international comparisons of student achievement, educational administration, technology integration, measurement and assessment, learning environment, and rural versus urban education. Little research in middle school education is found on the emotional development and career choices of students. Traditionally, there has been a lack of interest in issues related to length of the school day, block scheduling, transitions between primary school and secondary schools, or the use of uniforms. In regards to research on teachers, the emphasis is on preservice teachers, whereas inservice teacher research is not as prevalent but is a new priority for MoNE.

Methodologies

The nascent state of educational research can be characterized as predominantly local. Most researchers use convenience sampling. Random sampling is beginning to emerge as a method in the research reviewed for this chapter (e.g., Gencel, 2008; Kirikkaya & Gullu, 2008; Sagir, Aslan, & Cansaran, 2008). An apparent trend in research is its rareness in eastern, southeastern, and northern parts of Turkey as compared to its prevalence in western and central regions. National studies are mainly on the results of national high-stakes tests and the international studies such as PIRLS and PISA. Middle school education research in general is quantitative in nature followed by qualitative research and rare use of mixed methods.

Important Research Findings

The Turkish educational system has benefited substantially from the international studies in terms of understanding both the international standing of Turkish students' achievement levels and the curricula and pedagogical strategies used in high-achieving countries. These international studies were conducted in the fields of science, mathematics, and reading. Regarding the students' reading environment, the PIRLS results showed that, on average, students in participating countries had at least 25 books, whereas only 19% of Turkish students had 25 books or more. Turkey was also one of the two countries with the highest number of students who did not attend pre-K schooling and with the largest class sizes. The reported instructional strategies in PIRLS showed Turkish reading instruction was mainly based on textbook passages and rarely included children's literature books, magazines, or newspapers. Given the low achievement and the importance of reading skills for both in- and out-of-school success, it is essential that Turkey take steps to improve reading comprehension. The results of these studies have informed the current reform movement in primary school education. An important finding of current research is the significant differences among Turkish schools in their achievement levels.

Reading skills and mathematical and scientific literacy are assessed in PISA. The PISA results showed that in reading, mathematics, and science, Turkish students are below the OECD country averages. However, Turkey's GDP is below almost all of the OECD countries. The positive relationship between achievement in PISA and GDP explains Turkey's low scores. The results of these studies have been used in program development and as resources in educational research (MoNE, n.d.-c).

FUTURE DIRECTIONS

While many of the educational initiatives are still in their infancy, they seem to be aligned with the current international research base. Turkey's strong reliance on international testing will continue as it pursues admittance into the EU. Most of the current educational reforms are based on students' standings on international studies such as TIMSS and PISA.

The recent infusion of EU monies into education bodes well to address issues between eastern and western regions of Turkey. The infusion of money has not only helped educational reform but also facilitated the building of schools in remote areas and paying for teachers to work in them. Turkey, like most other countries, does not have a teacher surplus. Therefore, MoNE continues to have difficulty fully staffing many schools in rural and remote areas. A policy exists that requires new teachers to teach in remote locations for a period of 3 years, but few remain beyond their required length of service. This is similar to innovations in the United States where new teachers are placed in difficult inner-city locations, but leave as soon as they can secure another position.

CONCLUDING DISCUSSION

While there are many positives about Turkey's initiatives for the improvement of education for young adolescents, there are some important obstacles. The lack of multiculturalism in education makes it difficult for some ethnic minorities to gain access to education in their native language. For this reason they lag behind their native Turkish speaking counterparts academically and they find it difficult to compete on national tests. Furthermore, Turkey continues to struggle with adopting multicultural strategies to incorporate ethnic minorities into the educational system. Because of location and poverty, tutoring agencies do not move into remote areas and therefore, students cannot take advantage of the services their counterparts use readily. This cycle perpetuates the inequities among students from different SES. Further, the lack of coherent and consistent professional development for in-service teachers remains a barrier to full implementation of educational initiatives.

Both the advantages and barriers will provide legislators and citizens with issues to grapple with as they attempt to deal with equity and multiculturalism to improve the education level of overall population. The current reform in middle school education will open ways to raise competent young adolescents to perform in the information age.

REFERENCES

Bilgin, A. (2008). The impact of conflict resolution training on elementary school children. *Elementary Education Online, 7,* 541-556.

Birgin, O., & Baki, A. (2007). The use of portfolio to assess student's performance. *Journal of Turkish Science Education, 4*(2), 75-90.

Bulut, M. (2007). Curriculum reform in Turkey: A case of primary school mathematics curriculum. *Eurasia Journal of Mathematics, Science, and Technology, 3*, 203-212.

Buyukduvenci, S. (1995). John Dewey's impact on Turkish education. *Studies in Philosophy and Education, 13*, 393-400.

Chawla, M. (2005). *National education accounts in Turkey. Turkey ESS: Commissioned paper.* Washington, DC: The World Bank.

Gencel, I. E. (2008). The effect of instruction based on Kolb's experiential learning theory on attitude, achievement and retention in social studies. *Elementary Education Online, 7*, 401-420.

Gultekin, M. (1998). *Turkiye ve Avrupa Birligine uye bazi ulkelerde zorunlu egitim* [Compulsory education in Turkey and some EU countries]. Retrieved July 1, 2008, from http://www.aof.anadolu.edu.tr/kitap/IOLTP/1266/unite05.pdf

Hancioglu, A., & Alyanak, I. Y. (2004). Bebek ve cocuk olumlulugu [Infant and child mortality]. In *Hacettepe Universitesi Nufus Etutleri Enstitusu, Turkiye nufus ve saglik arastirmasi 2003* (pp. 109-118). Ankara, Turkey: Hacettepe Universitesi Nufus Etutleri Enstitusu.

International Association for the Evaluation of Educational Achievement. (n.d.). *TIMSS & PIRLS International Study Center.* Retrieved August 31, 2008, from http://timss.bc.edu/

Isman, A. (2005). *Türk egitim sisteminde olçme ve degerlendirme* [Measurement and assessment in Turkish education]. Ankara, Turkey: Pegem A.

KA-DER. (2003). *Kadin sorunlarina cozum arayisi kurultayi: Kadin ve ekonomi calisma grubu.* Retrieved August 31, 2008, from ka-der.org.tr/raporlar/kadin_ekonomi .doc

Kartal, H., & Bilgin, A. (2008). Bullying in the elementary schools: From the aspects of the students, the teachers and the parents. *Elementary Education Online, 7*, 485-495.

Kaymakcan, R. (2006). Religious education culture in modern Turkey. In M. Souza, G. Durka, K. Engebretson, R. Jackson, & A. McGrady (Eds.), *International handbook of the religious, moral, and spirititual dimensions in education* (pp. 449-460). Dordrecht, The Netherlands: Springer.

Kesici, S., Hamarta, E., & Arslan, C. (2008). Prediction of elementary school students' career decision making difficulties by their parental attitudes and guidance needs. *Elementary Education Online, 7*, 361-367.

Kirikkaya, E. B., & Gullu, D. (2008). Fifth grade students' misconceptions about heat-temperature and evaporation-boiling. *Elementary Education Online, 7*, 15-27.

Kucuk, M., & Cepni, M. (2004). Measurement and assessment for science education in the Turkish educational context: Problems and reflections. *Asia-Pacific Forum on Science Learning and Teaching, 5*(3), Article 1.

Ministry of National Education. (2002). *Education since the republic.* Retrieved July 1, 2008, from http://www.meb.gov.tr/Stats/apk2001ing/Section_3/ 1TransformationMotivated.htm

Ministry of National Education. (n.d.-a). *Istatistik subesi* [Statistics department]. Retrieved September 3, 2008, from http://iogm.meb.gov.tr/pages.php?page =sube&id=12

Ministry of National Education. (n.d.-b). *Yeni uygulmaya konulan ilkogretim kurumlari derslerine ait ogretim programlari ve haftalik ders saatleri cizelgesine iliskin hususlar* [Issues related to the currently adopted primary education curriculum and weekly course schedule]. Retrieved June 17, 2008, from http:// eokul.meb.gov.tr/Dokumanlar/2007_ogrt_yili_ilkogretim_kurumlari_ derslerine_iliskin_hususlar.pdf

Ministry of National Education. (n.d.-c). *PISA: Uluslar arasi ogrenci basarilarini degerlendirme programi* [PISA: Programme for International Student Assessment]. Retrieved September 5, 2008, from http://earged.meb.gov.tr/pisa/dil/ tr/sunum.html

Nohl, A. M., & Sayilan, F. (2004). *Teaching adult literacy in Turkey.* Retrieved July 1, 2008, from http://www.meb.gov.tr/duyurular/duyurular/proj/ tedpbilgilendirme.pdf

Organization for Economic Cooperation Development. (2004). *Learning for tomorrow's world: First results from PISA 2003.* Retrieved August 31, 2008, from http: //www.oecd.org/document/55/0,3343,en_32252351_32236173 _33917303_1_1_1_1,00.html

Organization for Economic Cooperation Development. (2007). OECD insights human capital: How what you know shapes your life. *Education and Skills, 1,* 1-150.

Organization for Economic Cooperation Development. (2008). *OECD factbook 2008: Economic, environmental, and social statistics.* Retrieved August 1, 2008, from http://puck.sourceoecd.org/vl=1649599/cl=16/nw=1/rpsv/factbook/

Organization for Economic Cooperation Development. (n.d.). *OECD Programme for International Student Assessment (PISA).* Retrieved August 31, 2008, from http://www.pisa.oecd.org/pages/0,2987,en_32252351_32235731_1_1_1_1_ 1,00.html

Ozgentas, I. (1975). *Educational research in Turkey, 1973-1974.* Ankara, Turkey: Ministry of National Education. (ERIC Document Reproduction Service No. ED118517)

Sadik, F. (2008). The investigation of strategies to cope with students' misbehaviors according to teachers and students' perspectives. *Elementary Education Online, 7,* 232-251.

Sagir, S. U., Aslan, O., & Cansaran, A. (2008). The examination of elementary school students' environmental knowledge and environmental attitudes with respect to the different variables. *Elementary Education Online, 7,* 496-511.

Sahin, I. (2007). Assessment of new Turkish curriculum for grade 1 to 5. *Elementary Education Online, 6,* 284-304.

Sahin, H., Gunay, T., & Bati, H. (2006). University entrance exam anxiety of senior high school students in the Province of Izmir, District of Bornova. *STED, 15*(6), 107-113.

Tansel, A. (2005). Public-private employment choice, wage differentials, and gender in Turkey. *Economic Development and Cultural Change, 53*(2), 453-477.

Tansel, A. & Bircan, F. (2006). Demand for education in Turkey: A tobit analysis of private tutoring expenditures. *Economics of Education Review, 25*, 303-313.

Tansel, A., & Bircan, F. (2008). *Private supplementary tutoring in Turkey: Recent evidence on its various aspects.* Retrieved July 1, 2008, from http://ftp.iza.org/dp3471.pdf

Turkish Statistical Institute. (n.d.). *Statistics.* Retrieved July 8, 2008, from http://www.tuik.gov.tr/

Ulutas, F., & Ubuz, B. (2008). Research and trends in mathematics education: 2000 to 2006. *Elementary Education Online, 7*, 614-626.

Wolf-Gazo, E. (1996). John Dewey in Turkey: An educational mission. *Journal of American Studies of Turkey, 3*, 15-42.

CHAPTER 2

EDUCATING YOUNG ADOLESCENTS IN LEBANON

Huda Ayyash-Abdo, Rima Bahous, and Mona Nabhani

This chapter focuses on the contemporary state of educating young adolescents in Lebanon after 1997, when the new structure and organization of all school curricula was introduced. Previews of the major factors that influence further development of education are presented along with the chief impediments including political violence, instability, migration, a dearth of research, and inequity. In spite of these factors, there are many signs of hope residing in the recent political settlement signed by all parties. There is a wide spread belief among most Lebanese that education is the way to promote positive change among youth. It is also believed to be a vehicle for young adolescents to succeed and learn to live together in peace. Lebanon does not lack the human capital to develop its middle-school education, but it is in need of making education a priority. While private schools have always played an important role in educating young adolescents in Lebanon, it is now time for public schools to catch up to the educational outcomes of the private schools.

An International Look at Educating Young Adolescents
pp. 25–46
Copyright © 2009 by Information Age Publishing
All rights of reproduction in any form reserved.

CONTEXTUAL NARRATIVE

Lebanon is a small country located on the eastern shore of the Mediterranean Sea. It is an Arab country that shares a common language, history, and culture with other Arab states. Nevertheless, the Lebanese culture is marked by strong Western influences, mainly French and American—Lebanon was under French colonial mandate from 1918 to 1943. Arabic is the official language, but French and English are widely spoken, especially in the cities. Lebanon's population is about 4 million, consisting mainly of Muslims and Christians. It is the only Middle Eastern country that does not have an official state religion and it remains the most heterogeneous of all Arab countries. There are 19 officially recognized religious sects, and the political system is based on a confessional distribution of power, which means that all government positions and political appointments are based on religious affiliation. For example, the president of the republic is always a Maronite (Christian), the speaker of the house a Shiite (Muslim), and the prime minister a Sunni (Muslim) (Kobeissy, 1999).

Most of the population—87%—lives in urban centers (World Bank, 2004). Lebanon has the highest literacy rates (Bashur, 2004; United Nations Children's Fund, 2005) highest percentage of females in the work force, as well as the finest universities, and publishing houses in the Arab world (Haidar, 2002). The 15-year Lebanese civil war, that took place between 1975 and 1990, left strong physical, mental, psychological, and social effects on the people. In addition, the recent political violence and instability between 2005 and 2008 has diverted attention of decision makers from reform and development to pressing security issues in the country. There are no reliable statistics, but it is estimated that about 60% of Lebanese families earn under $800 per month (World Bank).

According to United Nations Children's Fund (2005) figures, 50% of the population is between the ages of 0-25 years, with 17.5% falling in the age group of 10-19 years. According to the United Nations Development Programme (UNDP) (2008), the net enrollment rate in primary education is 92% with no gender differences for 2004. Moreover, according to UNDP (2008), the net enrollment in primary education reached 98.3% in 2000, up from 97.6% in 1996. The percentage of students completing primary education increased from 91.1% in 1997, to 95.3% in 2000; and recent studies indicate that the literacy rate for those aged 15-24 reached 97.5% in 2000.

Compulsory free education covers Grades 1 to 8 for all Lebanese children. Accordingly, in the newly revised curriculum, the 6 to 15 age group corresponds to basic education and includes elementary (6- to 11-year-olds) and intermediate (or middle) school levels (12- to 15-year olds) (Kobeissy, 1999).

Lebanon has witnessed significant improvement in reproductive health outcomes and indicators are clearly demonstrated in the results and findings of the Pan Arab Survey for Family Health (PAPFAM) conducted in 2004. The infant mortality rate has dropped from 28/1000 in 1996 to 26/1000 in 2000 to 19/1000 in 2004 (UNDP, 2008).

Migration

Emigration is not a new or limited phenomenon in Lebanon—indeed, the Lebanese emigrated (and continue to do so) all over the world, from the United States of America to West Africa. The emigration involved is quite substantial—indeed, estimates vary between 3 to 14 million émigrés (including descendents) have left Lebanon (Labaki, 1998). The Lebanese government did little to restrain emigration, and thus the Lebanese were permitted to leave Lebanon in a laissez-faire fashion. Indeed, there are inter-linked political, economic, and social reasons for the substantial emigration of the Lebanese.

On the political level, Lebanon is a place of local, regional, and international political unrest, and several times, outright war. Owing to the effects of such instability and violence, the Lebanese economy as a whole is suffering. The reason for this is that war leads to inflation, stagnation, higher taxation, a lack of direct foreign investment, unemployment, and higher poverty rates.

All of these factors culminate in a desire to leave Lebanon in search of more peaceful places that would provide opportunities for economic prosperity. Indeed, most of the Lebanese who emigrate and find work in other places send remittances back to their relatives. It is safe to deduce that emigration is an integral part of Lebanon's economy and the survival of the Lebanese themselves.

On a social level, prolonged political unrest leads to a long-term deterioration of infrastructure, a lack of social progress, and lack of significant sustainable social and economic development. As such, the Lebanese move to places where there is sustainability and improvement in all of these areas.

The results of such mass emigration are several. Many of the Lebanese emigrants adopt the citizenship of the country in which they reside, and often give up their original Lebanese citizenship. Given that second and third generation émigrés are raised outside Lebanon, many of them speak little Arabic and do not plan on returning to Lebanon. Indeed, about one third of these emigrants return to Lebanon, although many expatriates invest in the country (Brand, 2007).

Migration to Lebanon includes but is not limited to Palestinians (some of whom have become citizens), Armenians (most of whom have become citizens), Syrians, Iraqis, and semiskilled laborers. The number of Palestinians refugees registered with the United Nations Relief and Works Agency for Palestine Refugees in the Near East (UNRWA) in Lebanon is currently 409,714, or an estimated 10% of the population of Lebanon (Oh & Roberts, 2006). The UN Refugee High Commission for Refugees (UNHCR) puts the number of Iraqi refugees in Lebanon at 50,000 people, of whom only 8,476 are registered.

At present, Lebanon can be classified as a state in limbo. Indeed, there are Lebanese and expatriates all over the world; thus, an adoption and integration of many cultures are present within the state.

Individualism-Collectivism/Cooperation Beliefs

In a study conducted by Ayyash-Abdo (2001) to assess the social orientation of youth pertaining to individualism and collectivism (I-C), it was found that about 70% were relatively collectivists and 30% were relatively individualists. As is known, the I-C terms are not mutually exclusive constructs. Of the collectivist group, 75% were females, 62% were Muslims, and 48% preferred the use of the Arabic language over French or English.

The study corroborated the finding by Kashima and Kashima (1998) that languages allowing subject pronouns (I, he, she, and they) to be dropped show a lower level of individualism. In the Arabic language, subject pronouns are dropped and subsumed in the action verb, while in English and French the use of subject pronouns is obligatory. For example, in Arabic one says or writes *"thehabto ila el-madrassa"* (literally, "went to school") instead of "I went to school."

The general cultural orientation in Lebanon is collectivistic, although young adolescent orientation is increasingly individualistic in goal achievement (Faour, 1998). Religious courts, representing the 19 existing religious sects, apply their laws in matters of personal status, such as marriage, divorce, inheritance, and adoption.

In terms of religious practice, more Muslim young adolescents practice their religion than Christian or Druze adolescents (Ayyash-Abdo, 2001; Faour, 1998; Read, 2003). Membership in religious organizations was higher during and after the civil war, especially among the poor and young who saw religious identity and, at times, fanaticism as an escape from despair and lack of economic opportunity.

Lebanese society has often been described as neopatriarchal (Barakat, 1977; Faour, 1998; Sharabi, 1988). Like other societies in the region, male births are preferred, which is indicative of the ascribed cultural value of males over females and perpetuates gender inequality. For example, girls' menarche is associated with increased restrictions of mobility and more participation in household chores. Puberty for boys, however, expands male mobility outside the home and community (Mensch, Ibrahim, Lee, & El-Gibaily, 2003). Interestingly, no gender difference is found between males and females in access to basic education in Lebanon—98.1% for boys and 98.4% for girls in 2000 (UNDP, 2002).

Related to the individualist and collectivists' orientation and cooperation beliefs is a Lebanese saying that goes as follows: "My brother and I collaborate against my cousin, my cousin and I collaborate against the foreigner." Concurrently, with this collectivist's orientation is an equal assertion of individuality as evidenced by this old proverb "Al-Qraeb Aqareb"—"blood relatives can sting like scorpions."

Role of Women

Women in Lebanon have taken an active role in education and in the economy. Females represent close to 30% of the labor force and 50% of all university enrollment in Lebanon (Khalaf, 2002). Almost 25% of employed females work in the professional sector—in medicine, law, academia, arts, business, media, and in different fields of government. That said, they are still underrepresented in senior positions. The weakest representation of females is in politics, where only 5% of the 128 recently elected members of parliament are females. In fact, it was not until November 2004 that the Lebanese cabinet, for the first time in Lebanon's history, included two women ministers. Although progress is being made in developing a more gender equitable society in Lebanon, it is far from being an accomplished goal. Presently, young adolescents, unlike their forebears, have excellent role models of competitive working women in every field.

Notwithstanding the persistence of traditional attitudes regarding the role of women, Lebanese women have equal civil rights. Personal status laws, however, are under the control of religious courts, where a frequent imbalance of male/female equality still exists. The mosaic that is Lebanon represents two dichotomous female trends: one, an Islamist image symbolized by women wearing the headscarf or the *Hijab* and the *Abayia* (usually a long black robe), and the other symbolized by women dressed in jeans or mini skirts and backless tops. Together, they share the same sidewalk. Main street Lebanon, though, is alive with a significant number of females who are right in the middle.

Child Labor

National legislation sets the minimum age of employment at 14 years of age, but an expected amendment of the law is likely to increase the age from 14 to 15. The legal minimum wage has been raised recently (An-Nahar Staff, 2008) from 300,000 Lebanese Liras to 500,000 Lebanese Liras (from the equivalent of $200 to $330 U.S. dollars, respectively) and a rate that is not commensurate with the cost of living—is only applicable to workers above the age of 18. Child labor is a serious problem and represents an average of about 10% among 10-14 year olds, and over 15% among the 15-18 year olds (Central Administration for Statistics, 2004; Partners for Development, Civil Group, Khalidi, Nahhas, & Nuwayhid, 2004). Ninety percent of all child laborers are not covered by any health insurance. Poverty, large family size, and low level of educational attainment of heads of families are major factors in children who dropout and those who repeat their grade levels (El-Hassan, 1998).

HISTORY AND ORGANIZATION OF SCHOOLING FOR YOUNG ADOLESCENTS

Historical Background

Under the French mandate in 1920, the Lebanese government established a public education system close to that of the French. French became the primary second language in all public and private schools. It also became Lebanon's official language, for education and even daily conversation, in addition to Arabic. Many Anglo-Saxon schools shifted to a French program (Abu Rjeily, 1999). However, schools that were closely affiliated to religious groups did not make this shift. A system of official public examinations similar to the French was established. The Lebanese curriculum, which is a duplicate of that of the French, became official in 1920 (Atiyeh, 1970). Jarrar, Mikati, and Massialas (1988) noted that in 1920 the ruling of the Lebanese government established elementary and middle schools in major towns following the French system, using French as the first and official language but including Arabic and accrediting the French Baccalaureate for Lebanese students.

In 1968, official exams at the end of the primary level were cancelled (Kobeissy, 1999). Since independence in 1943, middle school education had often been considered complementary to elementary schooling and called higher elementary education with the purpose of preparing students for vocational schools or for finding a job. In 1946, decree number 6999 (Kobeissy, 1999) was issued and resulted in an independent curriculum culminating in official exams to obtain "the higher elementary degree." Another inclination was to consider intermediate schooling part of secondary education that aims at preparing elite citizens as declared by the 1946 curricula issued by decree number 7001. Thus, to satisfy both inclinations intermediate schooling was increased from 3 to 4 years, and in 1970 unified curricula were approved for intermediate education culminating in official exams and degree named "Brevet," replacing the higher elementary degree.

Lebanon has always had three types of schools: public schools, operated by the Lebanese government; subsidized private schools, religiously affiliated and run by Lebanese; and private schools, not subsidized and sometimes, but not always, religiously affiliated and owned by non-Lebanese. Private school education has always played a major role in Lebanon and during the war grew to fill the gap left by the weakened public education system. After the war, however, because of worsening economic conditions, the number of public school students increased. It is currently estimated that 50.5% of all elementary and intermediate level students are in private schools, 12% are in private subsidized schools, and 35% are in public schools (Kobeissy, 1999). The increase in the number of students in public schools has been particularly observed at the middle school level. The curriculum focus is on mathematics, science, history, civics, geography, Arabic and French/English or both languages. Art, music, computer science, and physical education are also offered, but are not considered core courses (Center for Educational Research and Development [CERD], 1995). In fact, the general objectives of the new curriculum state the importance of forming a citizen who "consolidates peace within the self and others through relationships, and through national and social relationships" (CERD, 1994, p. 12).

Education is highly centralized in Lebanon. All schools, both public and private, are required to follow the curriculum set by the Ministry of Education, although private schools are free to add other subject matter. Article 10 of the Constitution of Lebanon reflects these concerns as they impact the character of Lebanon as a democratic society: "Education is free in so far as it is not contrary to public order and good morals and does not affect the dignity of the several faiths" (Chapman, 1964, p. 8). Most Lebanese (those who can afford the tuition fees) prefer to send their children to private schools because they believe that education and discipline are better in those schools. Disparities in the quality of educational standards exist according to the socioeconomic and sociocultural level, however, especially in impoverished areas, where the public schools may be poorly staffed and the facilities and equipment are inadequate.

Curriculum, Instruction, and Assessment Practices

Most private schools practice an enrollment selection policy that may limit the availability of education and bias educational outcomes. Since the end of the war in 1990, the reconstruction, rehabilitation, and renovation of schools in the country have been proceeding at a rapid pace. Schooling that includes both young adolescent and adolescent age groups is divided into two levels: the 3-year intermediate cycle (age 12 to 14), and a 3-year secondary cycle (age 15 to 18) divided into tracks (scientific, literary, and technical/vocational). In general, the education sector has witnessed some progress: primary education (Grades 1 to 8) is almost universal, with the net enrollment ratio at 91.2%; the net enrollment in secondary education reached 70% in 1999; and, in the same year, the adult literacy rate reached 88% (United Nations Educational, Scientific & Cultural Organization [UNESCO], 2002). Despite the general improvement in all areas of education, some weaknesses remain. For example, high dropout at the intermediate level is observed, at 20% (Central Administration for Statistics, 2004).

After the Brevet degree, Lebanese students have the option of either choosing the vocational track or continuing secondary education. The vocational track remains unattractive to most students who prefer to pursue secondary school education hoping to gain access to one of the universities in Lebanon or abroad. For example, in 1993-1994 almost one million students were enrolled in public and private intermediate schools compared to 2,510 students enrolled in public and private vocational/technical education at the secondary level and 13,305 students enrolled in fast track vocational schools. It is worth mentioning that vocational education is available (CERD, 1995) for those students who attend elementary school and wish to shift to vocational at the intermediate level. Students who choose this track are usually the ones who fail in the academic field.

In 1975, civil war broke out, and the development of educational programs ceased. Many educational buildings and schools were destroyed; schools were closed for months at a time. Whenever possible, huge numbers of students were gathered in the same classrooms in two different shifts: some students would attend in the early mornings and others early afternoons. The government had to take this measure as many schools were completely destroyed and the remaining ones could not accommodate all the registered students.

CERD statistics for 1981-1982 show that 340 out of 1000 students dropped out of elementary schools, and 247 out of intermediate, and 223 out of secondary levels. With the Ta'if Accord that was signed in 1989 by the various Lebanese political factions and ended the civil war, several recommendations were set to improve the Lebanese education system.

By 1995, the curriculum reform movement known as the new organizational structure, or "Haykalyah," in Arabic had emerged. The educational reform was initiated by CERD but was the outcome of collaborative efforts of many leaders in the fields of public and private education and education experts from Lebanon and international organizations mainly, UNESCO (CERD, 1995). The educational reform plan was accompanied by several preliminary studies. For example, one study involved a survey regarding the behavior of children ages 3-15 years old as affected by the Lebanese civil war, which took place between the years of 1975-1991. In term of education, public education was to be reformed to "enhance national belonging, social integration, and respect for spiritual and cultural diversity" (CERD, p. 60). Improvement included unified textbooks mainly in history and civics.

The new system of education was approved in 1995 by the Lebanese Cabinet of Ministers and the curricula were elaborated on in 1997. Implementing CERD's education reform plan of 1994 began in the academic year 1998-1999 (Kobeissy, 1999). The educational reform provides general framework and organization for the various education tracks, for the relationship between academic and vocational technical education, for the relationship of pre-university with higher education, and for relationship between education, market and the needs and aspirations of the Lebanese society.

Organization and Structure

Public schooling according to the new organizational structure includes, as before, 12 years for 6- to18-year-old students, but elementary education requires 6 instead of 5 years. Middle and secondary education require an additional 3 years each. The "Haykalya" also reorganized intermediate school years to include three grade levels (7, 8, and 9) instead of the previous four years of middle school education (Grades 6, 7, 8, and 9). Thus, the curriculum would consist of four cycles of three grade levels each. In years to come, compulsory basic education should include both the elementary and intermediate phases of schooling. A new branch was added to the Baccalaureate II curriculum: social and economic sciences to develop new skills as found in developed countries' curriculum. Vocational education also requires three years and includes industry, agriculture, and public service such as tourism, management and trade. The new education system states that students should stay in regular school until the age of 15 before being allowed to move to vocational track.

OUTCOMES OF THE SCHOOLING OF YOUNG ADOLESCENTS

Academic Performance

In general, the emphasis of the Lebanese curriculum is on academics and the young adolescent is expected to conform to those standards almost to the exclusion of other dimensions of development. Table 2.1 reflects the percentage of students who passed the official Brevet exams that mainly measure achievement on academic subjects.

While knowledge and facts are important, teaching young adolescents survival skills that include social and emotional competence for modern day life are equally consequential to their overall development. Adolescents are faced with challenges of adjusting to a postwar Lebanon and an unstable political situation that is marked with ongoing and unpredictable changes (Ayyash-Abdo, 2007). Teachers and administrators need to be cognizant of the significance of engaging students in the inevitable redefinition of the educational process. Young adolescents are more likely to be happier and better students if they are able to connect aspects of academic subject matter with their everyday interactions. Moreover, the new organizational structure allows automatic promotion from elementary to intermediate level and stipulates national exams for all Lebanese students at the end of the intermediate and secondary levels. This means that private schools have to cover the basic components of this new curriculum, but it is not clear how the government will maintain supervision over private schools (Inati, 1999).

Table 2.1.   Percentages of Success in the Brevet Official Exams

Academic Year	Percentage of Success in the "Brevet"
2001-2002	64.71%
2002-2003	62.10%
2003-2004	68.49%
2004-2005	77.84%
2005-2006	67.49%
2006-2007	66.95%
2007-2008	67.07%

Source: CERD (2008)

Other Important Outcomes

There is a plethora of research in psychology that focuses on self-perception, identity development, and achievement in young adolescents. Bandura (1997) explained the relationship between self-perception and achievement if school achievement is viewed as a source of self-worth. Moreover, learning to regulate behaviors, emotions, and impulse control is a life long process that children and young adolescents need to develop and practice in order to become more successful adults. Adolescents who have a combination of academic skills and self-control are better learners.

Education cannot be separated from the cultural context. Curriculum content that portrays girls in limited traditional roles needs to be re-evaluated. Teachers need to examine instructional practices that may be more responsive to boys than girls. In addition, adolescents should develop critical thinking skills that challenge the status quo. Adolescents are not only recipients and participants in culture but are also agents of change (Ayyash-Abdo, 2003). Teachers can create real life contexts and encourage students to question social norms.

Those who teach and work with young adolescents must be aware of the multidimensionality of the young adolescent self. The needs of young adolescents differ greatly with respect to identity and, hence, may require varying counseling services that are not usually available except in elite schools. Teachers especially must be encouraged to see variation in identity formation and status as a developmental phase that may enhance well-being.

One of the specific implications for education of the Lebanese young adolescent is a basic cognizance that religion is an important source of variation in identity formation. Even though the impact of religion on social and emotional development is potentially politically sensitive, the impact of religion on identity must be dealt with in the education of young adolescents.

In any multicultural society, young adolescents can easily be stereotyped or categorized on the basis of dress, language, value system or religion. In Lebanon, for example, young adolescents' religion may be identified based on the name alone; such tendencies to categorize or stereotype individuals obviously can be detrimental to developing attitudes that are more accepting.

Research Supporting Academic Performance and Other Outcomes

Emotional and psychosocial education needs to be added to the curriculum in middle schools in Lebanon. It is noteworthy to mention that school counselors and school psychologists are not fully part of the educational process in the country (Ayyash-Abdo, Alamuddine, & Mukallid, in press).

The Lebanese place a high premium on affluence and appearances. With the help of socially responsive teachers, young adolescents should be accorded the right to question the social and educational inequities.

Providing quality educational opportunities to all is at the core of education for social justice and regarding students as partners in the process as opposed to passive recipients. In fact, research on the impact of social justice elements in Lebanese schools on student achievement shows differences in the quality of education, teachers and resources between private and public school, higher achievement outcomes, positive school culture, social cohesion and self-esteem in students of effective private schools (Bahous & Nabhani, 2008).

CURRENT ISSUES RELATED TO THE SCHOOLING OF YOUNG ADOLESCENTS

Concerns and Benefits of the Current Educational System

In the new educational reform, it was decided that each intermediate grade level should consist of a minimum of 34 class hours divided as follows: Arabic language (6 periods/week), first foreign language (i.e., English or French) (6 periods/ week), second foreign language (English or French) (2), civics, history, geography (1 period each), sciences (6), math (5), technology and computer (2 each), arts and activities (2), and sports (2) (Ministry of Education, 1995). This middle school curriculum (see Table 2.2) promotes more rounded individual because the focus is not only on academics.

The Ministry of Education has set the school curriculum that follows a spiral (hierarchical) approach. A topic is introduced in one cycle, is developed more fully in other classes, and then is further developed at higher educational levels.

After 1971, the government chose to use textbooks produced locally by the CERD as the main books for all public schools. In fact, a committee of subject specialists, mainly lecturers from various universities in the country, wrote these textbooks. Since 1995, CERD has tried to involve as many professionals as possible in this textbook writing process to avoid complaints and pressure from influential people. Unfortunately, textbook writing was done over a short period of time. In addition, there was not enough piloting of the textbooks and some of the "specialists" were not experienced in curriculum material developers. This lack of expertise in

Table 2.2. Weekly Distribution of School Subjects at the Intermediate Level

Class	Arabic Language	Foreign Language	2nd Foreign Language	Civics	Geography	History	Science	Math	Technology/ Computer	General Arts/ Activities	Sport	Total
7	6	6	2	1	1	1	6	5	2	2	2	34
8	6	6	2	1	1	1	6	5	2	2	2	34
9	6	6	2	1	1	1	6	5	2	2	2	34
%	50%						32%		18%			100%

Source: CERD (1995, p. 51).

writing school textbooks, especially books for the early, primary, and middle levels has led to new textbooks being quite theoretical and lacking elements that would attract and motivate children to read and enjoy learning.

Private schools can at present choose any textbook as long as the course book follows the government curriculum. The only two exceptions are the civics and history books. All schools, whether public or private, have to use the civics and history textbooks produced by CERD (Ministry of Education, 1995). Although civics books are at this time being used in Lebanese schools, there is still a problem with history textbooks as experts so far have not been able to decide what to include in the textbooks (El-Amine, 1994; Kobeissy, 1999). With reform and the 1995 modifications, the government decided that not only civics book should be used in all schools but also the history one (Ministry of Education), given that the history of Lebanon has been written many times and from different perspectives.

REFORM INITIATIVES AND NATIONAL POLICIES

The new organizational structure took students' needs for knowledge, values, and attitudes as well as activities and life skills into consideration (CERD, 1995). Thus, new positions were created for academic advising, extra-curricular activities, and career guidance counselors for middle schools. Additional academic courses were incorporated into the curriculum that included technology, computer literacy, and a second foreign language. The number of science sessions increased from five to six sessions per week and two sessions of weekly activities were added (CERD). The "Haykalya" proposed curriculum changes for seventh grade to prepare students for a smoother transition to the subsequent grade levels. Furthermore, it required the implementation of new assessment systems (CERD).

Accordingly, the goals for Middle School Education emphasized the acquisition of knowledge and skills in order to:

1. Ensure that Lebanese students develop into cultured citizens;
2. Identify and reinforce individual abilities;
3. Educate students with knowledge and skills and train them in values of citizenship;
4. Increase/ supplement students social environmental, cultural, and health education and provide opportunities to discuss contemporary issues to develop objective reasoning;

5. Strengthen basic linguistic communication skills leading to creative expression and literary taste;

6. Develop computer literacy and the use of technology as education medium and source of information;

7. Acquaint students with manual activities and with various careers to develop positive attitudes towards work and to provide training and readiness in preparation for future careers; and

8. Enhance students' self-esteem as independent and socialized individuals capable of balancing freedom and responsibilities (CERD, 1995).

The new curricular organization ensures alignment among the goals, content, teaching methods and assessment. Consequently, this facilitates translating these to education outcomes including skills and attitudes. The "Haykalya" facilitates the application of recent education strategies, so students have a more active role in the learning process in discussing, analyzing, and evaluating information and in using technology.

With the new framework for education, the Lebanese national curriculum was revised (CERD, 1995). Though one of the main issues was to stress the teaching and use of the national language, Arabic, nothing was done about this concern until 2000. The number of language class hours is the same for Arabic as for foreign languages, (i.e., English or French), throughout the primary, middle, and secondary sectors (Inati, 1999). English and French are no longer in competition and Arabic is labeled as the "native language" (Ministry of Education, 1995).

The old programs were reshuffled, and new subjects were added. Some changes were overdue, given the previous Lebanese curriculum (based on the 1945 French system) had not changed while the French curriculum itself had been reviewed several times. Thus, in the revised Lebanese national curriculum, some subjects received more emphasis (e.g. technology, computers) while others were left untouched.

In the area of foreign language teaching, a committee produced the curricula with three choices: English/French as a second language, English/French as a third language, and English/French as a vocational subject (Shaaban, 1997). A theme-based curriculum was developed; the emphasis was on English for Academic Purposes (EAP) as much as on the promotion of cultural understanding, cooperative learning, and the development of language proficiency (Shaaban & Ghaith, 1997). The key emphasis in all the three choices is on communication, not only as the second language but also as the language of instruction in all content areas. These changes have not been fully implemented in schools. For example, the government decided to include technology in the new curriculum, but many teachers are still not trained, and some schools cannot cover the expenses involved.

As stated earlier, application of technology and its implication was a subject added to the middle level grades. For example, students study the history of science and technology development and the role that research plays in developing tools that affect society and the culture at large. Students become acquainted with the practical uses of technology and its maintenance in agriculture, industry, and other areas. Students engage in technical workshops using instruments to transfer their designs to actual products. The subject of computer literacy introduces students to the parts and functions of computers such as memory, CD-ROM, networking, and programming. Students learn the basic terms and concepts that enable them to use computers in further education and as a means for supporting office and administrative functions.

Another addition to the intermediate/middle curriculum is that of Arts and activities that include music, singing, acting, drawing, photography, sculptor, folk dance, home economics, and others. These subjects aim to familiarize students with various careers and especially promote environmental fieldwork, data collection, and analysis. Schools select activities that suit their local needs and that are supported by school clubs (CERD, 1995).

RESEARCH

Current Research Topics

There are issues outside the classroom that need further study, given the fragmented and unstable state of affairs in Lebanon. The issue of preventing youth from violence and radicalism is one that needs to be addressed in most countries, particularly in this part of the world. There are few programs geared toward youth ages 14 and above that teach diplomacy, communication, and conflict resolution skills to Lebanese youth. This trend has been growing since the end of the civil war in 1990.

One such program is that of Global Classrooms Model United Nations (GC-MUN). As implied by its name, this program is worldwide. The program targets students who are in middle and high schools all over the world, regardless of their religion, socioeconomic status, race, country, and region.

In Lebanon, the GC-MUN is initiated, executed, and administered (largely) by undergraduate students at the Lebanese American University. Quite successfully, students at the Lebanese American University teach students the diplomacy and communication skills that they have been taught via training sessions within the GC-MUN program. As such, both university and school age students are taught diplomacy and communication. This fosters understanding—and leads away from violent extremism.

However, in Lebanon, this particular program is still in its infancy stage—it is only three years old. Furthermore, while the number of Lebanese schools involved in Global Classrooms Model United Nations (GC-MUN) is increasing, the schools involved are so far all private or subsidized schools. To date, no public schools are involved in this program.

That said, the efforts towards diplomacy, communication, and conflict resolution should not be underestimated. This is a new (but growing) program in Lebanon and one can only hope that it will reach more and more students as the program solidifies.

Another program that will begin this fall is "Teach for Lebanon." Unlike GC-MUN, this program is intended for public and private schools in impoverished areas. Students in Grades 7 and 8 in middle school and 10 and 11 in high school will be taught life skills including academic-linguistic proficiency, computer literacy, and conflict resolution strategies.

There are three major universities that are designing the curriculum for this program (the Lebanese American University, the American University of Beirut, and Saint Joseph University). Universities supporting this program select and train student teachers. The criteria for the selection of student teachers include: top-ranking students who demonstrate leadership ability and community service spirit, a bachelor's degree, and a six week in-service training program. As incentives, these student-teachers are offered scholarships and stipends and are given priority in the job market.

Methodologies

The educational system in Lebanon required change in content and organization. This change was only partially met and implemented by the "Haykalya" of 1995, a structured method towards educational reform as stated earlier. In 2000, the Ministry of Education issued an educational strategy for Lebanon for the next 15 years, i.e., until 2015. This strategy remains a guideline for examining important issues, such as: education administration, quality education, access to education, expenditure, and catering to demands of the job market.

In 2003, the World Bank called for another subsidized education development project but this project did not materialize. Consequently, this attempt in strategic planning for education is based on a renewed belief in the need for such a strategy as a framework for reform efforts and for restructuring educational institutions in line with general reform efforts.

This attempt builds on local needs and a Lebanon-centered approach. As is apparent, the most successful and effective educational strategies are those based on understanding the context and culture of students. In addition, conducting continuous needs assessment and revising plans accordingly is correlated with enhanced educational outcomes.

Important Research Findings

The 2006 educational research report of the Ministry of Education (MOE, 2006) focused on the following, two main issues:

Diagnosing the status quo by highlighting the critical education issues and matters in order to create awareness of their situation and the need for immediate remedies. This diagnosis will highlight specific problems that the suggested reform policies will address depending on their nature and priorities and the policies will then be discussed accordingly.

Creating a realistic and practical vision that gives priority to the critical matters and cases that the diagnosis highlighted so that the suggested short term policies will produce effective long term changes.

Achieving the subsequent goals depends on understanding the schools' internal capacities, responsiveness, and the level of external support provided for them.

The 2006 report states that like the 2000 reform plan, priority was given to reforming education administration and concurrently dealing with human resources capabilities and with cost effective use of available resources. Success of this reform plan requires a new educational administration that can move to the next phase of formulating new education strategies liberated from the pressures of the past and obstacles of the present and can anticipate future needs (Ministry of Education, 2006, p. vi).

FUTURE DIRECTIONS

In Lebanon, there are several initiatives to improve education at the middle school level in private schools. In one school, differentiated instruction is applied in writing and reading. It began as one teacher's experiment in an elementary class and became a policy for both elementary and middle schools. The teacher assesses students' writing at the beginning of term then identifies three groups according to criteria that are provided by rubrics. The teacher then prepares lessons, projects, and conferences with students in accordance with these data. At the end of the school year, all students should demonstrate achievement based on the differentiated objectives. In another school, block scheduling is implemented in the elementary and intermediate grade levels. Teachers teach a block of 80-90 minutes, instead of the traditional 40-45 minute class period and thus provide ample time for students to apply whatever concepts they have learned during the session. This also facilitates integrating the various subjects by working with other teachers who teach different subjects. In another private school, middle school teachers of civics are working with university professors on a pilot project to integrate technology. Teachers will continue their lesson plans by using computers and help students link to relevant Web sites that enrich the subject matter. For example, Computer Technology on the Web (WebCT) classes are used where teachers share their lesson plans and blogs and teach middle school civics by involving the students in similar experiences. Students will also integrate technology in their daily work and in required projects instead of relying on traditional methods of responding to the content.

Moreover, several private schools in Lebanon have recently begun an international baccalaureate (IB) degree and thus had to readjust middle school education to be less traditional and rote learning oriented and be more inductive and hands on in order to lead to the IB program. It begins with the primary year's program where students learn research skills then in middle years' program, students construct their own learning and discover how they learn, and teachers become guides and facilitators.

CONCLUDING REMARKS

After the Lebanese civil war of 1975 to 1990, the Ministry of Education initiated major reform to update all aspects of the educational system. This major reform is owed to the fact that the Lebanese national curriculum was stagnant for decades, no longer addressing the needs of students. Now, in addition to addressing the needs of students as best as possible, it is also used as a vehicle to promote national belonging and strengthen social cohesion. This is included in the curricula because during the time of the civil war, the fragmentation of civil society was partially attributed to the national school curricula to which students could no longer relate. Much of this lack of ability to relate to the national school curricula is owed to the fact that private schools advocate the use of a foreign language as the language of formal instruction.

Unfortunately, the majority of Lebanese youth still attend private schools because public schools are not as reputable in terms of academic standards, teacher training, and student development, including extra-curricular activities. Consequently, one of the priorities for the soon-to-be formed government is to invest and capitalize in the public educational system at all levels; elementary, middle, and secondary.

Moreover, the current national middle school curriculum, should aim to further critical thinking skills among youth as alluded to in a recent study by UNESCO (2002). In fact, there is an awareness among many Lebanese educators and policy makers regarding the urgent need for the development of a national history textbook at the middle school level as a tool to promote national social cohesion.

It is believed that such a textbook will contribute to instill pride in belonging to Lebanon among youth who are from different social and religious backgrounds. In addition, extracurricular activities that teach student skills regarding peaceful conflict resolution, communication, and inter-personal dialogue in the spirit of celebrating the richness of diversity will play a part in bringing national pride to Lebanese youth. Educators and policy makers need to provide consistent quality education throughout all schools, be they public or private. The old elitist approach should be replaced by a more equitable and participatory platform, where all concerned (parents, students, teachers, universities) realize that they have a stake in the national educational system.

REFERENCES

Abu Rjeily, K. (1999). State expenditure on education in Lebanon. In M. Bashshur (Ed.). *The state and education in Lebanon* (pp. 185-243). Beirut, Lebanon: Lebanese Association for Educational Studies.

An-Nahar Staff. (May 6, 2008). The decisions of the council of ministers. *An-Nahar Newspaper,* p. 1

Atiyeh, N. N. (1970). Schools of Beirut. In Beirut College for Women (Eds.), *Beirut: Crossroads of cultures* (pp. 133-166). Beirut, Lebanon: Libraire du Liban.

Ayyash-Abdo, H. (2001). Individualism and collectivism: The case of Lebanon. *Social Behavior and Personality, 29,* 503-518.

Ayyash-Abdo, H. (2003). Adolescents' self-image in Lebanon: Implications for education. In F. Pajares & T. Urdan (Eds.), *International perspectives on adolescence, adolescence and education* (Vol. 3, pp. 173-197). Greenwich, CT: Information Age.

Ayyash-Abdo, H. (2007). Adolescence in Lebanon. In J. J. Arnett & U. P. Gielen (Eds.), *Routledge international encyclopedia of adolescence* (Vol. 2, pp. 583-590). New York: Routledge.

Ayyash-Abdo, H., Alamuddin, R., & Mukallid, S. (in press). School counseling in Lebanon: Past, present and future. *Journal of Counseling and Development.*

Bahous, R., & Nabhani, M. (2008). Improving schools for social justice in Lebanon. *Improving Schools, 11*(2), 128-141.

Bandura, A. (1997). *Self-efficacy: The exercise of control.* New York: W. H. Freeman.

Barakat, H. (1977). *Lebanon in strife: Student preludes to the civil war.* Austin: University of Texas Press.

Bashur, M. (2004). *Higher education in the Arab states.* Beirut: UNESCO.

Brand, L. A. (2007). State, citizenship, and diaspora: The cases of Jordan and Lebanon. *The Center for Comparative Immigration Studies* (working paper 146). San Diego: University of California.

Central Administration for Statistics. (2004). *Regions, nations and peoples (Lebanon) online.* Retrieved May 21, 2004, from http://www.cas.gov

Center for Educational Research and Development. (1994). *Plan for educational reform in Lebanon.* Beirut, Lebanon: Ministry of Education.

Center for Educational Research and Development. (1995). *El Haykalyah el Jadidah lil taaleem fi Lubnan* [The new framework for education in Lebanon]. Beirut, Lebanon: Ministry of Education.

Center for Educational Research and Development. (2008). Results of brevet official exams. Unpublished document. Beirut, Lebanon: Ministry of Education.

Chapman, E. (1964). *The educational system in Lebanon.* Washington, DC: American Association of Collegiate Registrars and Admissions Officers.

El-Amine, A. (1994). *El Taleem fi Lubnan* [Education in Lebanon]. Beirut, Lebanon: Dar El Jadeed.

El-Hassan, K. (1998). Relation of academic history and demographic variables to grade retention in Lebanon. *The Journal of Educational Research, 91*(5), 271 – 298.

Faour, A. (1998). *The silent revolution in Lebanon: Changing values of youth.* Beirut, Lebanon: American University of Beirut.

Haidar, N. F. (2002). Lebanon as a regional educational and cultural center. In K. C. Ellis (Ed.) *Lebanon's second republic prospects for the twenty first century* (pp. 140-145). Gainesville: University Press of Florida.

Inati, S. H. (1999). Transformation of education: Will it lead to integration? *Arab Studies Quarterly, 21*(1), 55-68.

Jarrar, S. A., Mikati, J. F., & Massialas, B. G. (1988). Lebanon. In G. T. Kurian (Ed.), *World education encyclopedia* (pp. 778-796). New York: Facts on File Publications.

Kashima, R., & Kashima, Y. (1998). Culture and language: The case of dimensions and personal pronoun use. *Journal of Cross-Cultural Psychology, 29*, 461-486.

Khalaf, M. C. (2002). Women in postwar Lebanon. In K. Ellis (Ed.), *Lebanon's second republic prospects for the twenty first century* (pp. 146-150). Gainesville: University Press of Florida.

Kobeissy, H. (1999). The state and public education in Lebanon. In M. Bashshur (Ed.) *The state and education in Lebanon* (pp. 105-183). Beirut, Lebanon: Lebanese Association for Educational Sciences.

Labaki, B. H. (1998). L'emigration depuis la fin des guerres a l'interieure du Liban (1990-1998). *Travaux et Jours, 16*, 83.

Mensch, B. S., Ibrahim, B. L., Lee. I. M., &. El-Gibaly, O. (2003). Gender-role attitudes among Egyptian adolescents. *Studies in Family Planning, 34*, 8-18.

Ministry of Education. (2006). *Education strategies in Lebanon.* Beirut, Lebanon: Author.

Ministry of Education. (1995). *Lebanese national curriculum.* Beirut, Lebanon: Author.

Oh, S. A., & Roberts, R. (2006). Palestinians and education in Lebanon. In R. Griffin (Ed.), *Education in the Muslim world: Different perspectives* (pp. 239-256). Oxford, England: Symposium Books.

Partners for Development, Civil Group, Khalidi, A., Nahhas, N., & Nuwayhid, I. (2004). *Gender, education and child labor in Lebanon.* Geneva, Switzerland: International Labour Organization.

Read, J. G. (2003). The sources of gender role attitudes among Christian and Muslim Arab-American women. *Sociology of Religion, 64,* 207-223.

Shaaban, K. (1997). Bilingual education in Lebanon. In J. Cummins & D. Corson (Eds.), *Encyclopedia of language and education: Bilingual education* (Vol. 5, pp. 215-259). Dordrecht, The Netherlands: Kluwer.

Shaaban, K., & Gaith, G. (1997). An integrated approach to foreign language learning in Lebanon. *Language, Culture, and Curriculum, 10*(3), 200-207.

Sharabi, H. (1998). *Neopatriarchy: A theory of distorted change in Arab Society.* New York: Oxford University Press.

United Nations Children's Fund. (2005). *The state of the world's children. 2006 excluded and invisible.* Retrieved June 15, 2008 from www.unicef.org/publications/index_30398.html

United Nations Development Programme. (2002). *Globalization: Towards a Lebanese agenda.* Retrieved May 30, 2008, from www.undp.org.lb

United Nations Development Programme. (2008) *UNDP in Lebanon.* Retrieved June 2, 2008, from http://www.undp.org.lb/WhatWeDo/MDGs.cfm

United Nations Educational, Scientific & Cultural Organization. (2002). *UNESCO. Education—Global monitoring report 2002.* Retrieved April 21, 2008, from http://portal.unesco.org/education/ev.php?URL_ID=11283&URL_DO=DO_TOPIC&URL_SECTION=201

World Bank. (2004). Retrieved May 15, 2008, from http://web.worldbank.org/WBSITE/EXTERNAL/COUNTRIES/MENAEXT/LEBANONEXTN/0, menuPK:294929~pagePK:141132~ piPK:141109~theSitePK:294904,00.html

CHAPTER 3

THE UNITED ARAB EMIRATES

Educating Young Adolescents

Toni Sills-Briegel, Sharon Lynne Bryant, and Wafa Abdul-Rahman Al Hashimi

The United Arab Emirates (UAE) has made remarkable progress toward establishing a strong and multidimensional education system. Today, education is compulsory and nearly 1,500 government and private primary (Grades 1-6), preparatory (Grades 7-9), and secondary (Grades 10-12) schools are in operation throughout the country. Government-funded education for national students, including monies for books, equipment, and uniforms is continuous from kindergarten through university. Boys and girls are educated separately after preschool, but follow the same prescribed curriculum. English is used in English, technology, science, and mathematics classes. Schools typically have social workers rather than trained guidance counselors. There is little or no interdisciplinary coordination among teachers. Activities and clubs are limited. Curriculum for the UAE is the responsibility of the Federal Ministry of Education. It appears to be well understood by specialists and consultants that different age groups have different needs. The concern, however, at this time is to broadly improve pedagogy.

An International Look at Educating Young Adolescents
pp. 47–72

47

CONTEXTUAL NARRATIVE

The United Arab Emirates, a Muslim country, was formed when the rulers of Abu Dhabi and Dubai decided to form a union between their two Emirates independently, prepare a constitution, then call the rulers of the other five emirates to a meeting and invite them to join. On December 2, 1971, at the Dubai Guesthouse Palace, four other Emirates agreed to join and enter into a union of six Emirates called the United Arab Emirates. Ras al-Khaimah joined as the seventh Emirate in early 1972. The United Arab Emirates (UAE), now a federation of seven independent states lying along the east-central coast of the Arabian Peninsula, formerly called the Trucial States (from the Perpetual Maritime Truce signed with Great Britain in 1853), and constituting, with Bahrain, Kuwait, and Qatar, the Persian Gulf States. The states making up the UAE are: Abu Dhabi, Ajman, Dubai, Al Fujayrah, Ras al Khaimah, Sharjah (or Ash Shriqah), and Umm al-Qaiwain. The states, occupying a vaguely defined area formerly known as the Pirate Coast, as well as 80 kilometers (50 miles) of coast on the Gulf of Oman, are bordered on the north by Qatar and the Persian Gulf, on the southeast by the Sultanate of Oman, and on the south and west by Saudi Arabia. The area of the UAE is 83,600 square kilometers (32,300 square miles). Its capital is Abu Dhabi. In 2006, the population of the UAE was 4.43 million with 20% Emirati nationals and 80% Asian, African, and European expatriates (Abu Dhabi Tourism Authority, 2008; King, 2008).

The United Arab Emirates, even though a young country, has high aspirations for playing an essential role in the global marketplace and is beginning to face some of the social issues that go along with rapid growth and the nationalization of the labor force. Women are entering the workforce in record numbers which creates the need for some adjustment to the once rigid division of labor in the household. The standard of living for Emirati nationals is very high with a gross national income public private partnership of $29,000 in 2004. Population is estimated at 4,600,000 people as of 2008 with a growth rate of 1.5%. Emirati national citizens make up less than 20% of the population. Other Arab nationalities and Iranians make up 23%, South Asians 50% and other expatriates including Westerners and East Asians 8%. The majority of nonnationals work in service or construction jobs earning low wages. Since a minimum salary level is required to sponsor families, most non-national workers do not make enough to bring their spouses or children. A requirement for citizenship is following the Muslim religion, and nationals wear traditional costumes to distinguish themselves from the large expatriate population.

UAE nationals live in extended families in large homes, sometimes walled-in compounds, designed to accommodate multiple branches of one family. Single parent families are rare, but are increasing in number and divorced or widowed women go back to their father's home with the children, or the father keeps the children and begins a new family with another wife or wives. Single parent families are also unusual in the expatriate sector as most nonresidents are male workers who have left their families back in their home countries. Marrying outside the UAE citizenship is discouraged to the point where national men and women are penalized if they choose to marry expatriates. Citizenship is an honor seldom awarded, even to spouses of national citizens. Nonnational workers and professionals at all levels are expected to fulfill their work contracts and go back to their home countries (Briegel et al., 2007).

The government provides assistance to native Emirates, including among other things, free education through university, low-cost excellent health care, assistance in buying a house, and access to a marriage fund to cut wedding costs and encourage citizens to marry each other. The Marriage Fund was established by the late Sheikh Zayed bin Sultan Al Nahyan to encourage UAE youth to marry national women and to curb the phenomenon of high dowries.

Males and females are brought up very differently in the same household. Boys are given more freedom and less responsibility than girls. Ideally, boys are required to attend and complete school and prepare to enter the work force and become responsible husbands and fathers. The lack of structure and responsibility in the home in addition to ample funds, however, often leads to misconduct of the males in the schools and a disregard for following rules in the community, particularly when driving. The death rate for young Emirati males involved in highway accidents is one of the highest in the Middle East. School children are not required or encouraged to work. The normal chores of running a house are given to maids or other females in the home. Boys often join their fathers on visits to friends and participate in numerous social events. They chaperone sisters and other women in the family and sometimes assist in shopping chores at the supermarket.

Females are expected to attend school and help the mother inside the home. They must look after younger brothers and sisters and assist the mother when she has guests. Girls are not expected to work outside the home as they become older, but are allowed to in some families if they desire. In the past, girls were not allowed to leave the home alone, but this is changing as more and more women move into the work force.

Rites of passage are predominately based on the Muslim religion. They are taught to pray at the age of seven and at ten are required to pray five times a day. When children reach puberty, they are required to fast during

Ramadan, but can do it earlier if desired. At puberty, girls begin wearing abayas (long black robes) and shaylas (black or colorful scarves). The hair and body must be completely covered. Levels of covering depend upon the desires of the girl and the traditions of her family or tribe. Variations of veiling or covering can be found in the same family as girls decide for themselves how they would like to appear in public. Once girls reach puberty, they must act more feminine. Women and girls form their own society as do men and each celebrate major events like weddings and graduations separately. After marriage, girls, now called women, are given more freedom, depending upon the level of conservatism of their husband. For example, they may leave the home alone to run errands, go shopping, or go to work (Briegel et al., 2007).

Emirates can earn their driver's license at the age of 18, but must renew it every year until they are 21. Females must get permission to learn to drive from their fathers or husbands or other guardian. Once a female has earned the license, however, it cannot be taken away.

The divorce rate among Emirates is one of the highest in the Gulf area, nearing 50%. Divorced women return to their father's home and are treated like girls again, but more strictly. The woman, as the caretaker of the home, is usually considered to be at fault. This attitude is changing, however, and depends upon the family and the reason for the divorce. The woman normally keeps the female children until they marry and the male children until they go to work. If the mother decides to remarry, then the father is awarded custody of the children. Divorce is normally much more difficult for the woman than the man, and it is much easier for him to remarry. Under Islamic law, men are allowed to have four wives at the same time. Children of divorce do not suffer social shame, but may have personal problems because their families have been broken up (Focus Group, 2006).

Every child born to an Emirati family gets 300 dirhams (about 82 U.S. dollars) a month from the government until the child gets a job or the girl gets married. Families with more than four children get priority for loans for government housing. Every citizen has the right to a free education through college. School is compulsory for boys and girls though grade nine. Currently, children are not required to attend kindergarten, but there are plans to change this soon. Children with disabilities are supported by the government and parents are becoming more open-minded about sending their children to schools.

The eldest son has responsibility for taking care of the elderly in the family. If there is no son, then the eldest daughter takes over. The rule is, the closest relative is responsible, but everyone in the extended family assists. Families living in the same house are often very large, including four generations. Sons marry and bring their wives to their parents' home to live, often for several years. Grandparents assist in taking care of young children, especially if the mother is attending school or working. Some nursing homes are beginning to accept patients, but this practice is considered shameful and families expect to take care of their elderly themselves.

Socioeconomic divisions are mainly tribal. Families are very close and children are expected to marry within the tribe. Often girls are expected to marry their first cousins, but this practice is slowly changing and depends upon the father's beliefs and family tradition. Every tribe has its sheiks or rulers. Women keep their own names when they marry. A wife keeps her tribal names and the husband keeps his. Children are given the tribe and tribal name of the father. Social strata are not clear cut, but some vague divisions may be made concerning levels of education, income, and religious beliefs. Tribe and reputation of the family and individuals within the family are very important. Families and young people seek to find marriage partners at the same or higher level, the key consideration for selecting a husband being can he afford the basic things for his family (Focus Group, 2006).

HISTORY AND ORGANIZATION OF SCHOOLING

Historical Background

According to Abdullah Al Taboor (2008) education in the UAE has gone through four distinctly different types of systems. The first type, called Mutawwa, was an informal system practiced by both males (mutawwa) and females (mutawaa). The intent of these teachers was to help their students memorize the *Quran* and the *Hadeeth* (sayings of the Prophet) along with learning writing and calligraphy. Schooling was informal and lasted for many years.

The second type of education, "Scientific Circle Education," was practiced by scientists, scholars, and intellectuals who were well versed in religious education, history, and grammar. Classes were held in the corners of local mosques or in the private home of the scholar himself. The most famous scientific circle included Najdian scientists who lived in Ras Al Khaima during the last British Expedition in 1819. The first UAE scholars were graduates of such scientific and religious circles. These learning groups started to disappear when developed schools began more structured classes with modern lessons and curriculum.

The third type of educational system, "developed education," in place during 1907 to 1953, began when pearl merchants (tawaweesh) were influenced by Arabid reform movements. These businessmen opened enlightened school in cities and brought in scientists to manage and supervise lessons. One of the most popular developed schools in Sharjah was the Talmia Mahmoudia in 1907 and the reformed school in 1935. Other developed-education schools came into being in the emirates of Dubai and Abu Dhabi in the 1920s and 1930s.

Modern systematic education, the fourth type, was started with the Al Qassemia School in Sharjah in 1953/1954. This was the beginning of organized modern or public education in the UAE. This education was organized and provided with schools, classes, and curriculum along with tests and certificates given to students at the end of every school year. Systematic education developed in the UAE in two stages. The first depended on local governments and knowledge departments that were founded in the 1960s. The second stage took place in 1971 when the seven Emirates were announced as a united country. Federal ministries were founded and the Ministry of Education and Youth was placed in charge of developing a federal education system (Al Taboor, 2008).

Barely into the fourth decade of its existence as a nation, the United Arab Emirates has made remarkable progress in establishing a strong and multidimensional higher education system to serve its young people. Education has been a priority for the United Arab Emirates since the founding of the country in 1971. Prior to establishing requirements for compulsory education, most children were taught household or occupational skills through their families in the home. Some children were also sent to religious schools called Madressahs where they learned to read the *Quran*. Still others were taught by religious leaders from their local mosque.

Today education is compulsory and nearly 1500 government and private primary, preparatory, and secondary schools are in operation throughout the country. Government-funded education for national students, including monies for books, equipment, uniforms, and in some cases boarding and transportation, is continuous from kindergarten through university (Education, 2008). At the conclusion of secondary school, national students who meet entrance criteria are eligible to attend at government expense the three government higher education institutions: United Arab Emirates University, Sheikh Zayed University, or the various campuses of the Higher Colleges of Education.

Organization and Structure

At the beginning of systematic education in the UAE, grades were divided into three levels: primary school (four grade levels), preparatory school (four grade levels), and secondary school (four grade levels). After

Table 3.1.   Grade Level Organization, Grades 1-12

Educational Stages		Educational Stages (Grade 1-12)	Educational Levels
	Cycle 3 (Secondary)	10/11/12	Five
Basic stage	Cycle 2 (Early Adolescence) (Middle School)	6/7/8/9	Three/Four
	Cycle 1 (Primary)	4/5	Two
		1/2/3	One

Source: Ministry of Education (2002).

that, the ministry reorganized the grade levels into primary school (Grades 1-6), preparatory school (Grades 7-9), and high school (Grades 10-12). In 2001, the current configuration came into existence. Table 3.1 shows the current division of cycles, stages and levels.

A parallel system of private education is also present at all levels. Nearly 40% of the students in the Emirates, including both nationals and expatriates, are enrolled in private schools (History, Education, 2008; Learning in United Arab Emirates, 2008). About 30% of the private primary, preparatory, and secondary schools follow the Ministry of Education Curriculum, while others follow curriculum from other countries, such as the United Kingdom, the United States of America, Pakistan, or India. Many UAE nationals send their children to private schools, because they desire that their children receive more English language teaching than they would receive in government schools. All private schools and private universities are funded by nongovernment sources. All private schools are licensed by the Ministry of Education (MOE) and operate under Ministry supervision. Government policy stipulates that private schools, in addition to their other curricula, must offer Islamic education, Arabic language, and social studies to all enrolled Arab students. These subjects are also offered as additional subjects for non-Arab students.

Government Schools for National Students

Boys and girls are educated separately after preschool education, but both sexes follow the same prescribed curriculum. Those students who choose technical secondary education enter a 6-year program following primary education (Cycle 1), choosing from technical, agricultural, or commercial strands. The language of instruction in Emirati schools has traditionally been Arabic, but English instruction begins in most kindergartens.

English is also used in English classes and in technology classes. A number of reforms are currently underway to increase the percentage of time allocated to English instruction in the primary school by implementing English instruction throughout science and mathematics classes and by increasing the number of English classes taught by native English speaking teachers and by nonnative teachers with near-native language fluency.

The Ministry of Education and Youth, the ministry previously responsible for school education, merged with the Ministry of Higher Education and Scientific Research in November of 2004 to create the current Ministry of Education (MOE) (Education Centre, 2008). Currently, many reforms are under consideration, including turning more decision making and prioritizing over to individual schools and school personnel.

Support Services in UAE Middle Level Schools

Trained guidance counselors are not available in UAE schools. School social workers whose duties include acting as administrative assistants to the principals and organizing social events for schools provide limited guidance services. Social workers do connect with families and work closely with mothers' and fathers' councils. The impact and organization of these councils vary from school to school. In some schools, parents come to school several days a week and work as volunteers to assist teachers and organize activities and events for teachers and students.

Each school has one or two social workers regardless of the number of students in the school. The social worker has the role of looking after the students and addressing the problems they encounter in the school. The social worker needs to know how to deal with different students and how to solve their problems and typically studies psychological courses at the university before working in schools. No special training is provided in dealing with young adolescents, but they try to develop their skills individually. Social work is an undergraduate degree in UAE colleges and universities.

Social workers deal with academic, social, economic, psychological, and behavioral issues. Each student is given individual attention. For example, if a student has behavioral problems, the social worker deals first with the student, then with the teachers, then with school administration, and finally with parents. On the other hand, if the student has social problems, the social worker deals directly with parents to collect information about the student's home and family.

Each social worker keeps a report book to record notes on all students in the schools. They often interact with students in the morning and at breaks and sometimes go into the classroom to observe students. The social worker collects information about student behaviors inside and outside the classroom and at home if necessary. A psychological advisor may be asked to come and work with a student if necessary (Al-Hwani, personal communication, June 24, 2008).

One of the duties of social workers is to develop consciousness programs for students. These programs include lectures, workshops, and activities. Lectures are done by experts from outside the school and they talk about psychological and biological changes that happen to young adolescents. Students are given the chance to ask questions and participate in discussions. Workshops are given about topics of interest to young adolescents including using the internet, how to use various computer programs, and leadership. Open days and sports days give student time to spend with friends practicing favorite sports and activities. Students can also volunteer to collect food, clothes, and money for poor people and help ill people. These activities help students play an important role in their community and feel confident about themselves (Al-Hwani, personal communication, June 24, 2008).

Advisors are academic advisors whose main role is to assess teachers and give workshops to develop teachers' skills. In the past, each was a subject area supervisor and was responsible for the quality of instruction in that subject in several schools. For example, a mathematics advisor would be responsible of the mathematics teachers in a number of schools and he/she would visit the teachers to evaluate them, help them if they need it, and provide professional development. Recently the system was changed and a site advisor is assigned to each school. The role of this "educational" advisor is to evaluate all the teachers in the school and to provide individual assistance and general professional development to teachers. In addition, the advisor is looking after teachers' activities inside and outside the classroom. The advisor also looks at the students' academic performance results and helps the teachers to decide how to enhance student achievement in the various subjects. This is particularly important when dealing with issues related to young adolescence. Some subject advisors continue to visit schools specifically to evaluate the academic ability of the teacher. For some subjects, such as English language, mathematics, science, instructional technology, and physical science, there are site advisors for each school, but in other subjects such as Arabic language, Islamic studies, history, social studies and art, the advisors visit the teachers one time each semester and do a limited number of workshops during the year. While Emirati schools do have "advisors," their mission is to improve the pedagogy of teachers, rather than directly assist students. No formal "advisory" program, by National Middle School Association (2003) definition, exists.

The typical Cycle 2 (Grades 6-9) school day begins with students assembling by class in the interior courtyard of the school. School buildings are usually designed in large squares around a central courtyard which is open to the air, but often covered by some sort of extended canopy to protect students from the desert sun. School begins in the courtyard with opening exercises including the national anthem, reading of the *Quran*, and skits or announcements. Students are dismissed and go with their teacher to their first class.

In government schools, students remain in the same classroom all day and teachers move from room to room. This system is followed from preschool to Grade 12, though changes are beginning to take place in lower levels. Middle level schools, called Cycle 2 or preparatory schools, have seven lessons a day. The length of time for each class is different from primary to preparatory to secondary school. Classes in preparatory school typically last for 45 minutes. Two short breaks are given, one after third period and one after fifth period. A lunch break may be given if students attend activity classes. Since students do not change classrooms between lessons, most schools do not provide a break between classes. Each teacher is responsible for maintaining the room to meet the needs of the lessons. In many government schools, students are not allowed to attach student work to walls and classrooms are kept clean, but bare of student work. Model schools, on the other hand, are often colorful and display a great deal of student work. Each classroom has recently been equipped with an instructional technology center consisting of a computer and power projector and professional development has been provided in their use. The Abu Dhabi Education Council (ADEC) is working on providing training in using the equipment to assist instruction.

Students typically study the following courses every day: English, Arabic, science, mathematics, social studies, Islamic studies. Teachers usually teach 12 to 21 hours a week in their given subject in comparison to American teachers who usually teach 25 hours or more a week—even in middle level schools. Teachers who have 12-hour class loads are usually assigned to additional duties such as school projects, committees, or as club sponsors. The school day lasts about six hours and the school year begins at the end of August and ends at the end of May for the students and at the end of June for the teachers. Holidays generally depend on the cycles of the moon and vary from year to year based on Islamic law. If the 29 to 30 days of Ramadan occur during the school year, then the school day is shortened to allow students to participate in family and religious events in the evening.

Schools typically have social workers rather than trained guidance counselors. Often, however, the school provides an on-campus medical doctor and dentist. Diabetes is a special problem in the Emirates due to the eating habits of UAE nationals. Efforts are being made to improve school lunches and provide better education in nutrition to children and families.

Table 3.2. Weekly Teacher Meeting Schedule (Al Mawaheb Model School Schedule, Abu Dhabi Zone, 2007/2008)

Day	Subject
Sunday	Islamic studies/Social studies
Monday	Arabic language
Tuesday	English language
Wednesday	Mathematics
Thursday	Science

Teachers are organized by departments and work together in offices by subject area. Weekly meetings are held for teachers of each subject area to discuss issues of planning, curriculum, and students. Sometimes teachers in the same subject from different schools meet for professional development workshops organized by the educational advisors or education zone.

Table 3.2 shows teacher meeting days for each subject area. This is a common schedule for all the teachers in government schools. Schedules in experimental schools and private schools will vary. The Muslim religious day is Friday, so the week runs from Sunday through Thursday, with a Friday/Saturday weekend.

There is little or no interdisciplinary coordination among teachers. Activities and clubs are limited. There are simple activities for the students in primary school, but there are more activities and different clubs for Cycle 2 students. The activities and clubs are different from one school to another. For example, student council is a committee that includes leader students in the school who are able to plan activities for the school and make decisions that related to students. The media committee is another activity for the students who like activities such as taking photographs, writing reports, and recording video. There is also a science club for students who have the ability to do science projects. And the students who have the ability to act can be a member of the theater club. In addition to these clubs and committees, there are some activities for the students such as writing short stories, writing poems, and competitions for mathematics and science.

Curriculum, Instruction, and Assessment Practices

Curriculum for the UAE is the responsibility of the Federal Ministry of Education (MOE). The following is the current list of MOE Strategic Objectives:

1. To organize the ministry as an active educational system with national experts and capabilities that depends on policies and practices when making decisions with a clear definition for the relationship among the educational committees, educational councils, and educational zones that guarantees school to be the base for educational development.

2. To provide modern curriculum accompanied by evaluation tools and procedures that rely on universal academic standards and contributes to the creations of an educational environment which makes the student the turning point of the educational process.

3. To provide an infrastructure that relies on modern techniques through all educational levels and to employ that structure in the educational process to allow schools to utilize it in management and work achievement.

4. To promote policies and regulations for human resources to contribute to improving and developing the quality of performance of working committees in the educational system (administrators, teachers, and other employees.)

5. To develop and improve school buildings and utilities, provide them with equipment and tools that harmonize with modern educational standards and in a way that enables schools to lay out and execute developed curricula and activities.

6. To promote professional development programs and systems for all educational staff in ways that achieve the ministry's strategic objectives.

7. To develop systems that enable parents to contribute in following their children's academic performance and provide concerned people in the community with information about the educational progress and performance of students (Ministry of Education, 2008).

Current Assessment System in Grades 6-9, Cycle 2, Levels 3 and 4

The school year includes two semesters. In the first semester there is ongoing monthly assessment in September, October, November, and the first half of December. In the second half of December there is a final exam of the first semester. At the end of the first semester, the grades of the students are the average of the ongoing assessment and the final exam of first semester. In the second semester there is monthly ongoing assessment in February, March, April, and the first half of May. In the second half of May there is a final exam of second semester. At the end of the second semester, the grades of the students are the average of the ongoing assessment and the final exam of second semester. Each student's final grade is the average of first semester and second semester grade.

In the UAE Ministry of Education, a special department is responsible for analyzing students' grades for all age groups, specifically the middle group level (Cycle 2), in order to identify learning problems and allow a search for solutions (see Figures 3.1, 3.2, and 3.3). The percentage of failed male students is greater than that of girls who fail, but is not considered to be a high percentage. On the other hand, current government statistics indicate that the overall literacy rate for UAE males is about 84% and for UAE females 91%. The government is aiming for 100% literacy by the year 2010 at the latest (Fahem, 2006).

The Federal Ministry of Education has revised curriculum for 14 subjects taught in various grades. Director of Curriculum, Kholoud Al Qasimi (Shammaa, 2008) said that the new curriculum was more visual, developed, and modern, and in-line with international standards." In the past, said Qasimi, teachers were given full responsibility for student achievement. Now students will be monitored more closely and asked to take responsibility for their learning. They will also be required to participate in community work. MOE curriculum changes taking place in September 2008 include the following subjects and grades: Islamic Studies and music

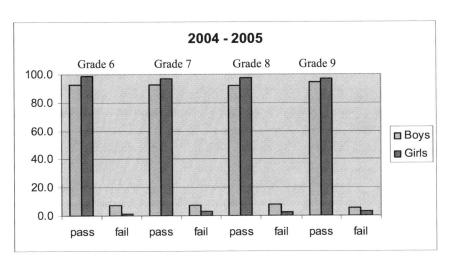

Source: Department of Statistics (2006-2007).

Figure 3.1.   Assessment data, 2004-2005, from Ministry of Education yearly examinations.

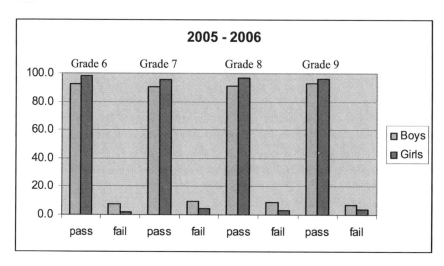

Source: Department of Statistics (2006-2007).

Figure 3.2.   Assessment data, 2005-2006, from Ministry of Education yearly examinations.

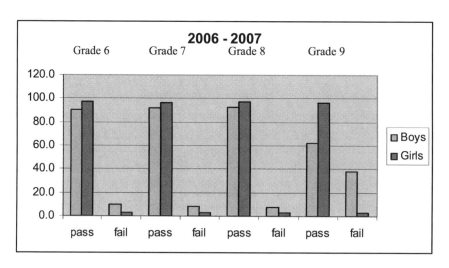

Source: Department of Statistics (2006-2007).

Figure 3.3.   Assessment data, 2006-2007, from Ministry of Education yearly examinations.

and fine arts: 7, 8, 9, 11, 12; Arabic language: 6 and 12; science and social studies: 7; geography and history: 11; mathematics: 7 and 9; English, geology and psychology: 12, economics: 11 and 12, social studies; 7; anthropology: 11.

New textbooks in middle levels classes will be introduced for Grade 6 Arabic, Grade 7 science and social studies, Grades 7 and 9 mathematics, and Grades 7-12 Islamic studies. "The new curriculum concentrates on thinking skills" said Shaikha Khulood. "It's more than just memorizing content. With the old curriculum, the student was dependent totally on the teacher. Now the student can learn with the textbook and the teacher is only guiding him" (Lewis, 2008a).

By special request, however, individual Emirates may choose to develop their own curriculum. As an example of such a curriculum, we have included an overview (Table 3.3) of the curriculum standards being designed and implemented by the Abu Dhabi Education Council (ADEC). Curriculum for courses that are Arabic-language based currently follow the MOE requirements and standards. These courses include Arabic language, Islamic studies, social studies, and business studies (Abu Dhabi Education Council, 2008).

In Abu Dhabi, 305 government schools are divided into four categories:

1. 24 model schools;
2. 13 al Gatz Schools (MOE schools) that ADEC will take over next year;
3. 118 public private partnership (PPP) schools, KG, Cycles 1, 2, 3. The first 30 were set up basically by private schools. Thirty more PPP schools were added during the 2007/2008 school year and 57 more were launched the following year.
4. Regular government schools.

OUTCOMES OF THE SCHOOLING OF YOUNG ADOLESCENTS

ADEC developed a strategic plan that will be launched in the fall of 2008 to redo education in Abu Dhabi:

1. Student-centered, outcomes-based curricula have been written for English, mathematics, science, and information technology.
2. Textbooks are being rewritten for mathematics and science to match new standards. Textbooks will be in English and will be culturally sensitive.

3.   Standards will be given to all concerned parties, including parents, administrators, teachers, and members of the educational community.

One hundred and eighteen public/private/partnership (PPP) schools are using private expertise to help improve schools, upgrade computers, wireless connectivity, video conferencing, and interactive technology. "The new curriculum drives everything, including resources," said Paul Doorn (2008), PPP school manager. New curriculum will be in place in the fall of 2008 for the following subjects: English, mathematics, science, health and physical Education, music, art, and information and communication technologies. Table 3.3 provides a brief description of each learning area and the strands that make up each area.

The Emirate of Dubai is served by the Knowledge and Human Development Authority, an organization similar to ADEC in Abu Dhabi. Their focus has been primarily on developing standards and assessments for private schools as there are fewer government schools in Dubai. Other Emirates are much smaller than Dubai and Abu Dhabi and depend predominately upon the federal Ministry of Education for guidance and support in improving their school systems. As a whole, however, the interest in improving education throughout the United Arab Emirates is of primary importance. Education, primary through Grade 12, is being examined in every Emirate and professional development and assistance is being provided at every level. No organization, however, exists that can be compared to the National Middle School Association. The needs of the entire UAE school system are so great and change is taking place so swiftly that it is difficult to place more emphasis on one group than another.

Research Supporting Academic Performance and Other Outcomes

Assessment has always been of particular interest to directors of the education system in the UAE. Currently, federal Ministry of Education examinations are given twice a year to every grade level. Scores on these tests determine if students pass their classes, help evaluate teachers, and determine whether individual students may remain in model schools. Model schools are open to students who score 70% or over on their semester tests. Dropping below this score for two consecutive semesters causes students to be moved to government schools where resources are fewer and teachers are paid less. Ministry tests are created by the federal Ministry of Education and are administered to all students in all levels of government schools in the UAE.

Table 3.3. Abu Dhabi Education Council Subject Area Curricula

Subject Area	Description	Strands
English language	Students will extend their ability to talk, listen, read and write, using English in real-life situations.	• Talking and listening • Reading • Writing
Mathematics	Students will learn mathematical knowledge, skills and understanding. They will learn to reason and communicate using the language of mathematics and to appreciate mathematics as a tool for life.	• Numbers • Patterns and algebra • Measurement and data • Space and geometry
Science	Students will extend their scientific understanding of their world and develop an appreciation for science as an evolving body of knowledge and an important and exciting field of study.	• Matter • The physical world • The living world • Earth and space
Health and physical education	Students will learn about maintaining a healthy lifestyle. They will learn about the importance of participating in physical activity and being active and about issues such as self-esteem and safety.	• Healthy choices • Self and relationships • Games, sports, and movement • Active lifestyle
Music	Students will learn to link the world of music in the UAE with the international music scene. They will listen to, compose and perform music that connects with their community, nation and culture, as well as with other cultures in the world.	• Performing • Composing • Listening
Art	Students will learn to communicate ideas about the world and to understand art in contemporary and historical cultures.	• Creating • Appreciating
Information and communication technologies	Students will learn to use technology confidently and will prepare for a future in a world of increasing social, economic and technological change.	• Issues • Enquiring • Core operations • Communicating and producing

Source: Abu Dhabi Education Council (2008).

ADEC, in concert with developing a new curriculum for the Emirate of Abu Dhabi, is working to develop a new system of assessment. A consulting firm will be hired in 2008/2009 to develop a standardized test, establish a baseline, and provide objective data. In the mean time, the federal tests will continue to be administered twice a year. It is expected that the new test will be given once a year to all grade levels. In the more distant future, there is the desire to move to international tests as the school system continues to improve and eventually reaches its goal of meeting international standards for education.

Tracking student performance is a key component to the success of the entire program. Based on results of the Center for Education Testing, Measurement, and Evaluation located in the Federal Ministry of Education (P. Doorn, personal communication, July 16, 2008), students are performing about two years below national standards in English and math. Scores in Arabic are just slightly better. Results show that as students get older, they get farther and farther behind. In November and February of coming years, all students in grades 3-12 in all schools (model, PPP, and regular government schools) will take benchmark tests in Arabic, math, science, and English. This evidence is needed to check progress of innovations, hence the twice a year administration (P. Doorn, personal communication, July 16, 2008).

The intent of the general and twice yearly evaluation by the Emirate Educational Zone and ADEC is to enable comparisons including, but not limited to private providers, city versus country progress, male versus female results. Change happens very quickly in the UAE. Frequent testing allows for prompt removal or expanded implementation of programs. It also identifies program weaknesses and can serve as a guide for professional development. Progress of every student will be tracked from Grades 3-12.

As tests are administered and graded by teachers, however, data are expected to have some irregularities. Teachers and administrators have expressed their concern about the use of data to assess teachers and schools. Tempting as this might be, ADEC is working hard to ensure that the data remain confidential and are used for systemic changes.

The PPP schools are about working with teachers to help them improve their methods of working with students. Eight providers from outside the UAE are currently providing services to 118 PPP schools: three from the Great Britain, two from the United States, one from New Zealand, one from Lebanon, and one from Canada. The overall school improvement plan has been outsourced to these eight providers. They are required to use the provided curriculum, resources including libraries and technology infrastructures, and assessment schedule and tests to enable comparison of programs. Pedagogy and professional development are the major variables. An external monitoring agency has been hired to assess all programs and elements of the education program (P. Doorn, personal communication, July 16, 2008).

CURRENT ISSUES RELATED TO THE SCHOOLING OF YOUNG ADOLESCENTS

The Abu Dhabi Education Council's (ADEC) purpose is school reform. It was established in 2005 though a memo of understanding and a decree to find things that lead to school reform in English, mathematics, science, IT, PE, and health. Standards have recently been developed for these subjects by ADEC. A second memorandum of understanding was signed in December 2007 that increased the responsibilities of ADEC.

Model schools were established in 2000 and are now under ADEC's wing. One hundred native English-speaking staff have been hired as educational advisers and placed in model schools to change pedagogy, provide professional development, and introduce the newly developed standards. Their major goal is to move instruction in key areas from Arabic to English. A key problem is that mathematics and science teachers do not speak English well and are having difficulty shifting instruction from teacher-centered, more traditional methods to more student-centered methods. There is also a movement toward using computers as tools of instruction in classrooms. In the future, professional development will be assisted by interactive technology.

Currently many Abu Dhabi schools are caught between the older system of Educational Zones and the new ADEC rules. Educational Zone supervisors currently evaluate all teachers, but their responsibilities for professional development of subjects served by ADEC Educational Advisers are reduced. Zone supervisors will work closely with Arabic and social studies teachers and with teachers of other subjects whose language of instruction is predominantly in Arabic. Gradually, it is expected that ADEC will take over responsibility for all schools in the Emirate of Abu Dhabi. The federal Ministry of Education will continue to influence education through the Emirates.

At this time, there is no specific emphasis or panel looking at instruction in Cycle 2 or preparatory schools (Grades 6-9). School improvement is underway across all grade levels, preschool through Grade 12. Evaluation is of special concern to ADEC. Past reviews have shown that UAE students were underperforming (L. B. Pierson, personal communication, July 9, 2008). Several things contributing to this including the short school day and school year and extreme weather conditions which causes many schools to be closed down during the hottest months of the year when parents often take their children to cooler climates for extended holidays. Teachers have been underpaid in comparison to other service professions, which has caused, in many cases, less well-trained people to be hired. Recent advances in salary have helped alleviate this somewhat, but many teachers are still using traditional methods of memorization rather than more sophisticated methods requiring critical thinking. UAE girls have consistently outperformed boys in the country. Boys have more life choices than girls and frequently choose paths requiring less education or training or go into a profession such as the military or the police where training is provided after hiring. Job opportunities are often limited for girls and many choose to continue their studies in order to find careers in teaching or other professions requiring higher levels of education. The late President, Sheikh Zayed, believed in the education of women and encouraged education for girls through college. Sheikh Zayed University was established in 1998 as a higher learning institution devoted to the education of UAE women. The university opened its doors to men for the first time in the 2007/2008 academic year (L. B. Pierson, personal communication, July 9, 2008).

ADEC is not concentrating specifically on middle school (Cycle 2), but is trying to overhaul the whole system (P. Doorn, Personal Interview, July 16, 2008). Prior to designing reforms, ADEC surveyed major government departments, banks, manufacturing companies, Abu Dhabi National Oil Company (ADNOC), universities, and others. The main question asked was: How did each organization perceive UAE high school graduates? All agreed upon the following:

1.   Memory and rote learning did not prepare students for anything.
2.   Emiratis had a poor work ethic. Companies said it was difficult to motivate nationals to want to work.
3.   A need existed to provide training in interactive skills, both computer and personal.

REFORM INITIATIVES AND NATIONAL POLICIES

One of the big changes ADEC has made is to assign teachers to classrooms and make students change rooms for each class period. In the past, students stayed in the same room all day—even through high school—and teachers moved from room to room. The new system allows teachers to make fuller use of facilities and develop more complex projects as materials can remain in the room over time.

Since most instruction takes place in a second language, English, students are loosely grouped by level of English in some classes, especially

Grades 6-9 in mathematics and science. Some peer tutoring and cross-grade work takes place.

Pedagogy is a major problem in the school system as teacher certification does not exist. Completion of a college degree in many cases is enough to be offered a position. Many programs are being developed and implemented to assist teachers in improving their English and techniques for teaching their subject in English. This is a particular concern in mathematics and science courses as they have only recently been converted to all English courses. Arabic speaking teachers, even with years of experience, are struggling with the language barrier and the new student-centered pedagogy. These challenges are partly to blame for the current teacher shortage. ADEC has created a new college, the Emirates College of Teacher Education, to train teachers in the new systems being designed for the Abu Dhabi system. The college is also targeting retiring military and police who would like to retrain to become teachers. There is a real need for male teachers in the schools. Male and female students study together only during preschool and kindergarten (Cycle 1). From first grade on, boys and girls attend separate schools. Women are the main teachers for both genders through elementary, then men begin to take over education of middle level through high school students. Male Emirate teachers, however, are in very short supply. UAE males tend to go into business or join the military or the police force. Currently the low pay for teachers does not compare with these other professions.

Change is the name of the game in the UAE in every area including education. Principals, as the public face of local institutions, need special support as they face concerns of parents, students, teachers, and community. The first year PPP schools were introduced, most feedback from concerned parties was negative. "Now parents are trying hard to get their children accepted into the PPP schools" (P. Doorn, personal communication, July 16, 2008).

RESEARCH

In the Ministry of Education there is a research department which aims to collect the research done about education yearly and create a booklet that includes the topics and the summary of all the research. The research not only related to the UAE, but also to other Gulf and Arabic countries. There are a variety of topics related to teachers, students, parents, subjects, teaching strategies, behaviors, and education system. There are many topics about student achievement, behaviors, and professional development. But there are few topics about specific groups or age of students. Some of the studies implemented in Gulf countries may have the same results as the UAE because they have almost the same environment.

The Ministry of Education intends to improve education for all grade levels. There is a special focus on the primary level to build the main learning skills and attention is also given to the high school level to prepare the students for university level. At the current time, there is a planning for middle grade level to reform the assessment and evaluation system and to prepare this group of students for higher grade levels. For example, the development planning is implemented in model schools for Cycle 1 then for Cycle 2 (L. B. Pierson, personal communication, July 9, 2008).

FUTURE DIRECTIONS

Currently, many students graduating from high school are required to undergo one to two "foundation" years of intensive study before entering a 4-year college system. For example, students entering Zayed University must score 500 on the TOEFL (Test of English as a Foreign Language) or reach Band 5 on the IELTS (International English Language Testing System), before entering their freshman year. Up to 2 years of "readiness" may be required to assist students in reaching this goal. All courses at Zayed University are taught in English, with the exception of Arabic and Islamic studies.

Grade 10 is going to be the focus of the new "Foundation" program. In the UAE, most colleges and universities require students to enter a precollege "foundation" program to reinforce their language and basic learning skills. At Zayed University, for example, students are required to score at the Band 5 level on the IELTS test before they are allowed to enter their freshman year. The Grade 10 Foundation program will have a heavy English concentration, but will not be culturally insensitive. Arabic will be used in Arabic studies, Islamic studies, and other Arabic-focused classes. Math, science, English, and instructional technology will be taught in English. All classes will use student-centered, upgraded pedagogy. The goal is to have students scoring Band 5.5 on the IELTS by the end of Grade 12, allowing them to directly enter their freshman year in university (P. Doorn, personal communication, July 16, 2008).

There is a desire to push foundation year studies back to the 10th grade and even earlier than that, so that students can pass their language tests and enter freshman college courses straight from high school. As students are pressed to improve their English skills, however, a movement to protect the Arabic language and UAE culture is gaining force. The goal of education in the future will be to produce highly qualified students who are bilingual in English and Arabic and have a deep appreciation and understanding of their own and global cultures.

The Ministry of Education in the UAE is implementing new plans to develop the level of education in all grade levels and to achieve the international standards. So, there are educational organizations that support the Ministry of Education in some emirates such as: Abu Dhabi Educational Council, Knowledge and Human Development Authority (Dubai) and Sharjah Educational Council.

Principals at government schools in the UAE will be required to prove they are qualified when the 2008 Ministry of Education standards for education are introduced. Newly hired assistant principals must have a bachelor's degree and have at least 6 years of teaching experience. They must all score at least 500 on the TOEFL test or at least Band 5 on the IELTS test. The Ministry of Education is also redefining the job of principal to make them instructional leaders in their schools rather than managers who monitor the budget and order supplies. Principals will be trained to hire good teachers and to recognize good pedagogy in the classroom. Currently, instruction is primarily teacher-focused and reforms are encouraging a more student-centered type of instruction (Lewis & Bardsley, 2008)

In 2008, the UAE government issued a set of bylaws to ensure that every child in the UAE receives a quality, uniform education. Schools, including private schools, will have to undergo a process of accreditation to ensure they meet minimum standards to be set by the ministry by the end of 2009. Prior to this time, schools were issues licenses to practice, but there were no common standards that schools had to follow (Lewis, 2008b).

CONCLUDING DISCUSSION

It is difficult to emphasize strongly enough how quickly change is taking place in education in the United Arab Emirates. In the United States, it has taken over 30 years to develop a focused interest on the educational needs of young adolescents. In that same 30 years, the UAE has developed an entire school system from preschool through university. This has been done by pouring money into examining and experimenting with as many international programs as possible. Many programs were brought in as "packages" and others were developed by international specialists within the country. What did not work immediately had a limited life span. Sometimes good programs that needed longer times to develop were abandoned and other programs with quicker, but more limited results were kept. The goal of each one has always been to develop an international quality school system and produce UAE citizens who could complete on a global scale. The school system as a whole is well on its way to achieving those goals. Flexibility and the ability to adapt to change are absolute requirements for working in this rapidly developing country.

While "true" middle level schools do not exist, with the exception of one school in Abu Dhabi, The American Community School, and one or two possible schools in Dubai, there is definite concern for the improvement of education at every grade level. There is no special emphasis on primary or high school to the detriment of middle level grades. It appears to be well understood by specialists and consultants that different age groups have different needs. The concern, however, at this time is to broadly improve pedagogy. Teachers need training in English in order to teach mathematics, science, and technology using the best resources. They need training in student-centered methods of instruction and need to be moved away from rote learning and teacher-centered lectures and worksheets. Books must be rewritten to be culturally sensitive. Curriculum has to be and is being totally revised to reflect the needs of this growing country. Schools are being torn down and rebuilt with appropriate wiring to support computers and other technology. Scholarships are being offered to send promising students to study internationally. Certification requirements for teachers and administrators are being devised.

The assessment program appears to be too intense and time-consuming. Teachers spend much of the school year preparing students for and administering the high stakes tests given twice a year to every grade level. On one hand, assessment this frequent slows down learning, but on the other hand, change is taking place so fast that frequent assessment is needed to help authorities determine the next steps to take as soon as possible. Innovations that take 20 years in other countries, may literally take 2 years or a few months in the UAE. For example, one day it was announced in the newspapers that the weekend would no longer be Thursday and Friday, but would change to Friday and Saturday. Businesses and schools adapted immediately. That is the way it is done in the UAE.

There is definitely concern about the education of young adolescents as a part of the larger picture of educational reform in the UAE. The current system could be compared to the junior high school system common in the United States a decade or two ago. The name "preparatory school" even evokes a similar mental image—preparing for high school. High school teachers normally begin as preparatory school teachers and are then "promoted" to high school. The needs of the children remain the same. Young adolescents need special programs and special teachers. The awareness of this is there. As the UAE reaches its goal of international competitiveness, it will continue to refine its system and at that point will be ready to look at what works specifically for its 10- to 15-year old students.

REFERENCES

Abu Dhabi Education Council. (2008). *6-9 curriculum standards*. Abu Dhabi, United Arab Emirates: Abu Dhabi Education Council.

Abu Dhabi Tourism Authority. (2008). *Abu Dhabi: About the UAE*. Retrieved July 20, 2008, from http://www.visitabudhabi.ae/en/uae.facts.and.figures/about.uae .aspx

Al Taboor, A. (2008). *History of education*. Retrieved July 20, 2008, from http://www.moe.gov.ae/English/Pages/HistoryofEducation.aspx

Briegel, T., Jongsma, K., Bryant, S., Adam, K., Tennant, L., Engelbrecht, G., et al. (2007). The United Arab Emirates. In G. H. Talham (Ed.), *Greenwood encyclopedia of children's issues worldwide: North Africa and the Middle East* (pp. 311-330). Westport, CT: Greenwood.

Department of Statistics. (2006-2007). *Results of yearly school testing program*. Dubai, United Arab Emirates: Ministry of Education.

Education. (2008). *Population*. Retrieved July 20, 2008, from http://countrystudies .us/persian-gulf-states/82.htm

Education Centre. (2008). Retrieved July 20, 2008, from http://www.uaeinteract .com/education/

Fahem, F. (2006, January 11). Dh9.52 billion allocated to UAE education. Sector. *Khaleej Times* [online].

Focus Group. (2006, May). *Zayed University students respond to questions based on family issues in the UAE*. Abu Dhabi, United Arab Emirates.

History, Education. (2008). Education. Retrieved July 20, 2008, from http://www.sheikhmohammed.co.ae/vgn-ext-templating/v/index.jsp?vgnextoid= 1e8c4c8631cb4110VgnVCM100000b0140a0aRCRD

King, D. C. (2008). *Cultures of the world: United Arab Emirates*. Tarrytown, NY: Marshall Cavendish Benchmark.

Learning in the United Arab Emirates. (2008). Retrieved July 20, 2008, from http://www.cp-pc.ca/english/uae/learning.html

Lewis, K. (2008a, July 9). State schools to introduce 14 new textbooks. *The National*, p. 6. Retrieved July 20, 2008, from http://www.thenational.ae

Lewis, K. (2008b, July 11). Private schools to face regulation. *The National*, p. 1. Retrieved July 20, 2008, from http://www.thenational.ae

Lewis, K., & Bardsley, D. (2008, July 17). Principals must hold degrees. *The National*, p. 2. Retrieved July 20, 2008, from http://www.thenational.ae

Ministry of Education. (2002). *Documentation for developing primary and secondary education in the UAE*. Dubai, United Arab Emirates: Author.

Ministry of Education. (2007, September). *The National Report for Education for All United Arab Emirates EFA/UAE: 2000-2005*. Dubai, United Arab Emirates: Author.

Ministry of Education. (2008, February). *Ministry of Education strategic objectives.* Retrieved July 20, 2008, from http://www.moe.gov.ae/English/Pages/ StrategicObjectives.aspx

National Middle School Association. (2003). *This we believe: Successful schools for young adolescents.* Westerville, OH: Author.

Shammaa, D. E. (2008, July 9). Improved school curriculum to take effect in September, *Gulf News*, p. 5.

CHAPTER 4

PLAYING CATCH-UP

Leveling Education for Young Adolescent Students in India

Supriya Baily

Middle school education in India languished due to a greater emphasis on developing primary and higher education systems. Rapid development has meant the focus until now has been on providing basic needs. Young adolescence as a separate phase of human development was also not given much merit. Yet all this is changing as an increased demand for middle school education in India has led the Central Advisory Board of Education to explore redesigning secondary education (where the middle school years fall) to be accessible, increase focus on equality and social justice, and remain relevant. Challenges facing students between the ages of 10-15 are varied depending on income, gender, caste, and geographic location, but the growing body of research is exploring many aspects of education for young adolescents and a fresh perspective on reframing education is in the making, setting the stage for a dynamic time to be looking at young adolescent education in India.

An International Look at Educating Young Adolescents
pp. 73–96

CONTEXTUAL NARRATIVE

In the current climate, it is easy to say that there is nothing about India that is simple. It is a country of contradictions—a country, which on one hand is on the cutting edge of science and technology, yet on the other hand faces immense poverty. In the geopolitical context, India has shaped itself to be a regional superpower and is setting the stage to be a dominant world player. In the social context, its population is shifting its philosophies and traditions to meld with imported cultures and ideas. In an academic context, the education system is being shaped and reshaped to move from a postcolonial hierarchical system to meet the needs of a globally connected world. Yet, the contradictions continue—while India exports vast numbers of science and technology graduates, the country is also just coming to terms with providing basic education for most of its children.

Having a long history of revering education, it has been relatively easy for this country of over one billion people to recognize that with education will come development, with development will come economic success, and with economic success will come power. Hungry to be considered a force to contend with on the international stage, the Indian government has been quick to recognize that education is a primary investment for future gain. Over the last few decades, the primary and higher education systems have seen the greatest growth, but it is evident that secondary education planning and implementation has been less extensive and as a result adds another layer to the inconsistencies that exist in the country.

So where does India stand in terms of its vital statistics? India is the world's largest democracy and the second-most populous nation after China (U.S. Department of Agriculture [USDA], 2003). Located in South Asia, India ranks 126th out of 177 countries on the Human Development Index scale of the United Nations Development Program ([UNDP] 2006). Poverty is high and a history of self-reliance did not produce the social, political, and economic gains that were expected 50 years ago when the country was newly independent (Abadzi, 2002). Furthermore, the country faces various challenges with its neighbors, having fought two wars with Pakistan and one with China (Central Intelligence Agency, 2006) over boundary issues. India's economy is Asia's third largest, after Japan and China, but with a per capita annual gross domestic product of only $380, India is also among the lowest income countries in the world. Nearly three-fourths of the population live in rural areas and derive their livelihood from agriculture. An estimated 250 million people, or a quarter of the population, fall in the middle-income and upper-income groups (USDA). India's economy encompasses software development, medicine, and engineering as well as traditional village farming, modern agriculture, handicrafts, industry and support services. The life expectancy for women is 63 years and for men, 61 years (World Heath Organization [WHO], 2006). Familial relationships show a strong preference for males which has drastically affected education in rural areas (Abadzi) where the literacy rates for females is half that of males, with the males at 65.5% and the females at 37.7% (CIA).

Historically, education in India has been the bastion of the elite. The Brahmin and Kshatriya castes, for example, have maintained a hold on education at all levels, but especially at the higher education levels (Library of Congress, 2003). The twin legacies of colonialism and casteism influence the status, reach, and power of education in India today.

The colonial interests in education were designed to provide English bureaucrats and officers with a cadre of low-level clerks and other government servants to help move the work of the nation forward (Banya, 1993). To support this, colonial rulers focused attention on the development of urban, higher educational institutions to meet those needs. This imbalance continues today, with rural education still languishing. Educational neglect under colonial rule occurred simultaneously with the destruction of many indigenous forms of learning embedded in the social and economic lives of Indians (Singh, 2001). One alteration emerging in the post-colonial era is the quota system, similar to affirmative action in the United States, which aims to bridge the gap for those who have been historically deemed as "lower caste."

The caste system is a complex web of social relationships, which was used to determine the occupation, education, and interactions of people leading to a highly stratified society based on rules and classifications. Initiated to maintain professional hierarchies, it quickly evolved into a system based on boundaries and social separations (Keay, 2000). In fact, "caste membership conferred important rights of participation in the economic and political processes … it was as much about being a citizen as being a subject" (Keay, p. 189). This changed sometime during A.D. 400-500 where caste became much more situated within a hierarchical system of privilege and power and the majority who were deemed the lower castes faced centuries of hardship, discrimination, and inhumane treatment (Seenarine, 1998).

The context of India's growing modernity, its colonial past, and the influence of caste in the structure of society plays an important role in understanding how education has both thrived in the face of significant challenges and languished amidst vast resources. From 1947 and India's independence, the Constitution of India required free and universal primary education (World Bank, 1997). The responsibility to implement the mandate on the part of the Constitution is one that is shared by the

Central and State governments (Ministry of Human Resource Development, Government of India, 2008). Yet some of the primary challenges against reaching universal education goals include: high dropout rates ranging up to 60%; large numbers of out-of-school children (about one third); shortage of schools in close vicinity to homes; and wasted time in terms of children taking just over seven years to complete what should be 5 years of primary schooling (Government of India, 2003). There is also low achievement and participation of girls, Scheduled Castes, Scheduled Tribes and other disadvantaged groups. Coupled with these factors are various systemic issues relating to the effectiveness and efficiency of primary education such as poorly functioning schools, inadequate school infrastructure and facilities, high teacher absenteeism and vacancies, and inadequate funds (Government of India, Ministry of Education, 2003).

Within this contextual framework there is a sense that India, a relatively young country with a rich and complex past, is cognizant that education plays a vital role in individual and national development. It has succeeded in building a system that addresses the needs of the young child and the university student, but the bigger question lies in what the country has done and plans to do with its young adolescent learners who are fast becoming one of the largest segments of the Indian population.

HISTORY AND ORGANIZATION OF
SCHOOL FOR YOUNG ADOLESCENTS

India, like other Asian nations, is predominantly focused on the collective rather than the individual (Reddy & Gibbons, 1999), and has not necessarily recognized young adolescence as a specific category of human development for much of its history. In fact, young adolescence in India is a time where a person is neither child nor adult, and India is a country that has been resistant to the concept of young adolescence, which can be "explained by delay in the onset of puberty (due to poor nutritional status) and prevalence of early marriage (signifying adulthood). It may further be noted that in India the generation gap cited in the West does not exist. However, with the changing economic and social profile, generational differences in India are becoming increasingly important" (United Nations Population Fund, n.d., p. 4).

The lack of a cohesive belief in the term leads to a certain elusiveness in determining the population figures that cover the age range between 10 and 15. To estimate the figure as a total or as a percentage of the entire population can be extrapolated from other statistics monitored in a number of United Nations databases. The United Nations Educational, Scientific and Cultural Organization (UNESCO) estimates that a fifth of India's population falls into the age group between 10-19 (UNESCO, 2006) while the World Health Organization (WHO) has estimated that India's population below the age of 15 makes up approximately 33% (WHO, 2008). Another key statistic highlighting the youthful nature of India is that the median of the country is 24 (WHO, 2008). From these figures we can infer that India has a large population between the ages of 10-14 and could range between 20% to 25% of the population. For this relatively young population, the history of education has been a series of steps and challenges.

Historical Background

The systems of education that cater to the age range between 10-15 lies under the auspices of upper primary and secondary school systems. Most children start school between the ages of 4 and 6, leading those between the ages of 10-15 to be in Classes Five through Ten. Therefore, to focus on education for young adolescents in India, is to also focus attention on the historical nature of both primary and secondary schooling as this population could be immersed in both systems.

Because India has established a broad national policy to provide free and compulsory education to those under the age of 14, the focus has been weighted on early primary education, (Classes One through Four) with Classes Five through Nine reflecting overall less importance. The strength of the primary education system is evidenced by the series of programs launched by the Government of India from the 1980s to improve education. The National Policy on Education was framed in 1986 and initiated Operation Blackboard, which launched a drive for additional classrooms, teachers, and teaching materials and aids (Dyer, 2000). District Institutes of Education and Training were established under a centrally sponsored scheme in 1988 to address teacher training. The Total Literacy Campaign was also launched in 1988 to eradicate illiteracy. The Minimum Levels of Learning program began in 1991 to identify basic competencies in language, mathematics and other subjects and to develop new textbooks (Government of India, Ministry of Education, 2003). All of these programs set the stage for the ambitious District Primary Education Program (DPEP), the world's largest primary education program (Alexander, 2000).

Initiated in 1994 by the Government of India, the DPEP is a program to universalize primary education across the country. It aimed to universalize access, increase enrollment, maintain attendance, and raise achievement in primary education with a special emphasis on improving access to those who have historically been denied such educational advantages; namely, girls, the disabled, and those in scheduled castes and tribes. The DPEP was one of the largest educational programs in the world, with funding primarily from the World Bank, UNICEF, the governments of the United Kingdom and the Netherlands. The key populations targeted were children between the ages of 6 and 14 with a goal to provide at least 5 years of quality primary education in 149 districts covering 14 states (World Bank, 1997). India has youth literacy rates that are on par with its regional neighbors but with the BRIC Group (Brazil, Russian Federation, India, and China) that it is often compared with, India is lagging behind. Youth literacy rates are only 76.4% for India, as compared to Brazil at 96.8%, the Russian Federation at 99.7%, and China at 98.9%. The world youth literacy rate is 87.3% (Kingdon, 2007).

The demand for secondary education is rapidly rising. Improving access to secondary education has been defined as one of the main goals of the Department of School and Literacy (Ministry of Human Resource Development, Government of India, 2008). Researchers have shown that secondary education is a relatively "lucrative level of education" (Kingdon, 2007, p. 172), where the returns on investment to individuals with secondary education is higher that any other forms of education. Yet, participation in secondary education remains relatively low at 47%.

Curriculum, Instruction, and Assessment Practices

India's school system is made up multiple parallel systems that sometimes overlap, while at other times engender the inequalities of class, gender, religion, and/or caste. Each system is overseen by a board, which sets curriculum and designs assessment practices. The most privileged students can attend any number of private schools ranging from exclusive boarding schools, on par with any prep school in the West. These private schools require fees and the students who attend usually come from upper, upper-middle or aspiring middle class families who can afford not only the fees but also the costs of uniforms, textbooks, and transportation. Another segment of private schools are small neighborhood schools, often in slums (Gupta, 2007), and sometimes run by missionaries or other religious figures. The Central Government also controls a segment of schools that are usually reserved for the students of civil workers with the government, children of military families, and others engaged in central government work. Finally, since states are also tasked with meeting the needs of free and compulsory education, there are a number of state-sponsored schools, usually attended by the less privileged. Each school is certified by one of the boards and differs in terms of the opportunities offered to the students, the caliber of teachers they attract, and long term potential for careers and growth.

India's education system is centered on the annual year-end examinations that determine a student's progress from class to class. Often as early as Class One, students face a final exam in every subject that they are taught. Beyond the yearly exams, the Class Ten exam is a compilation of at least three years of material. The commonality between the schools is the examination system, but what might be different is the content and quality of coursework covered.

Students in India, whether they attend a private or public schools follow the Ten plus Two system, where the majority of subjects up to Class Ten are considered mandatory with only the choice to exercise an option allowed for one or two subjects. Mandatory subjects at the upper primary and secondary school level include:

1. Grammar and Composition—usually in the language of instruction in the school—which could include English (especially in the urban, middle class private schools), or Hindi, the national language, or the state language (India has over 26 recognized languages and since states are equally responsible for implementing the free and compulsory education policies up to age 14, the public schools might primarily operate in the state language);

2. Literature—again this would be in the language of instruction of the school;

3. A second language—which would be another language besides the language of instruction and will include grammar, composition, and literature;

4. Mathematics;

5. Algebra, geometry and trigonometry;

6. Geography;

7. History and civics;

8. Physics (all of the sciences are made up of a practical and a theoretical component);

9. Chemistry;

10. Biology; and

11. Optional subjects include computer science, home economics, and business management, among others.

The language of instruction differs from school to school, from state to state, and from system to system. Some use English, and this is true of many private and national schools, while the state language might be more popular in state schools. The national language of Hindi is also a popular language of instruction especially in the northern part of the country. Singha (1991) pointed out that the students in the English language schools are not always the richest or most affluent, but they are simply the children of parents who recognize the value of school and are willing to invest in their children's education.

Assessment can be seen as both ambitious and unwieldy where a great deal of pressure is exerted on young adolescents. With the broad curriculum that focuses on knowledge retention and the need for rote memorization to pass examinations, instruction and teacher preparation is increasingly becoming more important in India. One of the most direct challenges to instruction in schools is the high stakes examinations which students are expected to excel at, leading to teaching styles that are focused on "the student's ability to reproduce facts and information" (Verma, Sharma, & Larson, 2002, p. 500). Textbooks remain the central focus of teaching and much classroom time is spent asking students to underline pertinent points, which teachers have learned are examination "favorites."

Students are assessed in a series of examinations, predominantly of an essay style, usually lasting about 2 hours, at the end of each school year in the middle-school years (Verma et al., 2002). The subject area teacher grades these exams and students usually will be retained in their current class, if they score below 50% in two or more subjects. At the end of their tenth year in school they are assessed in a grueling examination that occurs over a span of 10 to 14 days and covers most of their syllabi over the course of Classes Eight, Nine, and Ten. These exams are usually not graded by in-school teachers, but are sent, with only identification numbers, to a subject area teacher in another part of the state or the country for grading. Assessments are very important and the grades students receive can have a life changing impact on career and future goals as will be explored in later sections of this chapter.

OUTCOMES OF THE SCHOOLING OF YOUNG ADOLESCENTS

In her essay on the role of education in Indian society, Khar (2007) stated the development of an individual requires a high quality education to ensure "the context of an educational system which integrates all sectors of life. Thus education viewed as a life-long process is concerned with the task of creating healthy homes, schools and society, and this task is to make the society in its entirety a learning society" (Khar, p. 59). This overarching aim initiated the incremental steps being taken by the Government of India to address the broader outcomes for the education for young adolescents.

Until recently, the main goals for Indian education were to increase enrollment, standardize curriculum, and engage teachers to meet the needs of a large school population. The government worked on universal primary education and creating a higher education system that would allow the country to compete on a global stage, but for young adolescents the anticipated outcomes were to get through and get on. Go to college, go to vocational training programs, or go to work was how education might have been characterized for students at the upper primary or lower secondary levels.

As the success of the universal primary education program will attest, the new reforms presented to expand secondary education, and the renewed interest in new directions for research, the anticipated outcomes for young adolescents is dramatically changing. This is especially true since the Seventh All India School Education Survey came back with statistics showing growth in every area studied from enrollment to access (Sharma & Singh, 2007). India is in a critical place to begin to set the stage to shape new outcomes for young adolescent learners.

Academic Performance Outcomes

Middle school education and secondary education in India is said to serve as a bridge between the primary and higher education systems and prepare students for either the world of work or the path leading to higher education. It is also seen as a time to expose students to the "differentiated roles of science, the humanities and the social sciences" (Singha, 1991, p. 12). As early as 1955, educators were starting to understand the need for secondary education to cater to the diverse needs of students, and "with the advent of adolescence, boys and girls begin to develop different skills, aptitudes and taste. There must be, therefore a diversity of courses to meet their different needs" (Kabir, 1957). There is growing recognition of adolescence as a time for change and the need for options to meet the growing independence of this population.

Since India does not participate in the Trends in International Math and Sciences Study (TIMSS) or the Progress in International Reading Literacy Study (PIRLS) there is little opportunity to compare India's performance with other developed or developing countries (Kingdon, 2007). Nevertheless, national surveys have been conducted to assess reading, mathematics and writing comprehension and learning. Class Five students performed poorly where 47% could not read a story at the Class Two level and 55% could not solve a long division problem (Kingdon). As mentioned earlier, Indian youth are performing below other countries with whom they are often compared, and since the examination system is set and assessed by different boards, there is very little standardized data to evaluate at a national, let alone international level (Kingdon).

Other Important Outcomes

Recently, the National Council for Educational Research and Training (NCERT) determined that there had not been a comprehensive survey of the basic competencies in language, mathematics and environmental studies since the 1990s (NCERT, 2007) and in 2007 they conducted the *Seventh All India School Education Survey*. Though the survey did look at the entire K-12 system, the report focused to a great extent on secondary education, in part due to the fact that it is the next sector of national focus for education. The survey addressed, primarily in statistics, the state of education, and the predominant outcomes addressed were:

1. The availability of facilities for all Classes and for all populations;
2. The types of facilities available for students and teachers in the schools including classrooms, drinking water, electricity, health monitors, and bathrooms;
3. Enrollment in all schools;
4. The extent of disability in the student population;
5. The subject-wise enrollment by gender in the academic streams; and
6. The availability of teachers for secondary school.

As the most recent extensive survey on Indian education, the outcomes are clearly still on developmental milestones and highlight the parameters within which education operates.

Research Supporting Academic Performance and Other Outcomes

At the middle school level research on outcomes in education focuses attention on the ability of the system to support the outcomes designed by the government and education boards. Starting to look at innovative middle schools, Sharma (2005) found three aspects of education critical to the success of academic performance in schools and cited leadership, an extensive network with parents and community, and innovative teacher training as the primary successors in performance. Chirayath and Khalique (2005) studied how principals and other administrators were meeting their responsibilities for academic outcomes. Agarwal and Goswami (2005) also conducted an extensive study on secondary school principals, initiating the idea that the onus was more on the administrators and principals to meet the academic outcomes.

In other areas, research on curriculum appraises the system as to whether it meets the needs of the students (Bhuyan, 2005). State studies may be the first step toward collecting national level data on the outcomes of education that emerge from the various boards but with the complexity of systems, and the necessity to redesign secondary schools, understanding how the curriculum addresses outcomes in schools is still unclear. Gender and young adolescence is an emerging topic as well, where the greater intermingling of boys and girls in middle school is leading researchers to delve into understanding the role of motivation, stereotypes, and home environment on the outcomes of education for adolescent boys and girls (Rani & Kaushik, 2005). Finally, at the middle school level, students are gearing up to be more independent in their studies and some research is starting to focus on study skills to meet the academic outcomes demanded in upper secondary and higher education (Vaish, 2004).

CURRENT ISSUES RELATED TO THE SCHOOLING OF YOUNG ADOLESCENTS

Understanding the system of education and the effects on the academic performance of young adolescents in India opens the picture up to address the challenges and benefits of such a system on and for young adolescents. Due to the vast differences between the rural and urban areas, the poor and the wealthy populations, and the high caste and the scheduled castes and tribes, the challenges and benefits are much more nuanced and complicated. There is a sense of fluidity where the benefits for one group might in turn challenge another group, and the education system must play a role in balancing the successes on one side, while designing improvements on the other. In discussing the challenges and the benefits below, "real life" vignettes are presented to highlight a selection of the most important challenges addressing education for young adolescents.

Concerns About the Current Educational System

Vignette #1: Shanti has had lived in Thira village her whole life. Her parents have educated her and her twin brother, Sachin, knowing that the opportunities for them to earn a living are greater if they can read and write.

Shanti and Sachin have been good students, and the local primary school teacher has been excited about the fact that the parents are willing to commit extra money to pay the fees for the middle school. Unfortunately, their mother became sick and was unable to handle the responsibilities at home. As a result Shanti gave up school to help her mother look after her younger siblings. Sachin was willing to come home and share what he learned from school with his sister, but after three weeks of walking sixteen kilometers a day back and forth to the school, a drunk truck driver nearly sideswiped Sachin, and now Sachin is too scared to walk the highway to school. Now, he is also home helping his father in the fields.

In rural areas, the challenges affecting young adolescents are varied with access and quality being two of the primary ones. In 2007 the Central Advisory Board on Education (CABE) submitted a report detailing the problems with the delivery of secondary education to Indian students. Highlighted in the report is the fact that nearly two thirds of the population of middle school age students, are not in school, and that only two out of every ten students in Class One, actually reach Class Ten ("Government Stalling," 2006). A major part of the problem is that though the lower primary schools are in close proximity to student's homes, higher primary and secondary schools are far more spread out, causing tremendous difficulties for students to reach the schools. Improving access leads to the challenge of resources and the CABE report estimates that over 88,000 new classrooms and over 130,000 new teachers would need to be added to maintain adequate access to the population currently out of the secondary school system (CABE, 2007). Additionally, though girls are increasingly present in primary schools, and though the population is rapidly recognizing that there is a great deal of value in educating girls, when there is a family crisis, when the income of the family is endangered, or if there is any thought of improper behavior, girls are quickly withdrawn from schools. There is rising gender equity, but with girls of middle school age, there are multiple reasons cited to keep them at home.

Vignette #2: *Dinesh lives in a lower-income neighborhood, but his parents have been impressed with his strong intellect. His father, a peon in a government office has seen other people, less intelligent than his son succeed in high positions, because they knew English. Working an extra job, he has enrolled Dinesh in an English-medium school, but Dinesh is miserable. It is not the academics that affect him – in fact, he can easily complete his assignments, it is the fact that at school, the wealthier boys tease him about his traditional name, the religious dot on his forehead, and the accent with which he speaks, which shows he does not speak English at home. When he comes home to play with the neighborhood boys, they alienate him as well, since they feel he* *thinks he is "above" them because he does not go to the local state school, where they all go. Fitting in neither here nor there causes Dinesh a great deal of anxiety, making him lonely and confused.*

Another challenge facing the country today is the difference between the private and public schools, where the private, usually English-language schools and the state-language schools are considered to be two poles opposing each other and building two cultures in contrast to each other (Singha, 1991). The rising middle class see English-language schools as a pathway to the continued economic success of a family, and parents aspiring for their child to begin to take their share of the international job opportunities and experiences being offered to the newly modernizing country would seek to invest in an education where English is the medium of instruction. These schools require parents to pay fees and other costs related to education, which is not a burden the subsidized public schools face, where the medium of instruction is the language of the state. Singha argued that the economics of the country speak to the growth of these schools, and yet there are challenges that address the inequities and the confusion young adolescents face as they begin to navigate their place in the world.

Vignette #3: Fifteen year old Radha is starting Class Ten, at a private school in a large city. She knows she will be attending college, but is unsure if she wants to work in graphic design or as a dentist. She is a middle of the road student, usually in the top 20% of her class, but has also participated in extra curricular activities where she plays sports and performs in plays. Before the year-end, she needs to decide whether she plans on seriously pursuing the degree in dentistry, which would require extremely high scores in the sciences to get admission to a "science stream" program in Class 11 and 12, leading her to apply ultimately for a dentistry program. If she doesn't score above 90% in the sciences, but does reasonably well in the social sciences and languages, she will have no problem getting into the "fall back" position in a "arts stream" program, often seen as the third choice for students who did not make it in either the science or commerce streams. Radha studies hard so she has options, but the night before her final mathematics exam she comes down with a terrible stomach virus, and is unable to complete her paper. This causes her to receive only 60% in the subject, rejecting much of her hope that she would get into the science stream, and she has no choice but to start an arts stream to study graphic design.

Two more challenges facing Indian education for young adolescents is the role of high-stakes examinations which can determine the course of a career, and the relative youthfulness of the student to actually know and understand what sort of career they are interested in exploring. In the United States it is common for college freshmen and sophomores to still be unclear about their career goals, but in India, students are expected to have a pretty firm idea and commitment to a career by a young age. Since higher education is the next stage for a student in the secondary education system, and since it is parceled out into categories related to the arts, sciences and commerce, young adolescents are required to know by age 15 what career they plan to follow, submit themselves to grueling examinations, and based on the results of those exams, be allotted a seat in a higher educational institution for the subjects they may or may not be interested in studying.

Additionally, the social stress on students is extremely high. Students have a great deal of pressure to perform in multiple examinations, and monthly quizzes, and there is a high level of mental health problems among adolescents. Suicide at the extreme, Verma et al. (2002) pointed out the high incidence of young adolescents referred to "hospital psychiatric units for school-related distress, exhibiting symptoms of depression, high anxiety, frequent school refusal, phobia, physical complaints, irritability, weeping spells, and decreased interest in school work (p. 501). Researchers and policy makers are finding that including more creative teaching methods and engaging students in multiple ways will have little merit as long as the examination system remains so important, since students tend to continue to fill the leisure hours with more studying but are increasingly unhappy doing so (Verma et al, 2002).

Benefits of the Current Educational System

Gupta (2007) points out that India has the "largest pool of skilled person-power" (p. 101), with a large middle class that is increasingly educated and skilled. The history of revering education, the value of learning and its effects on continuing to grow a middle class show that education in India is also working. Though the previous section shows that access to secondary education might still be predominantly available to those who have resources to begin with, the fact remains that the middle class is estimated to grow from approximately 350 million in 2007 to over 550 million by 2025 (Gupta, 2007). This means that the curriculum has had meaning for the skilled and educated workers who are becoming the mainstay employees of growing Indian and multinational companies.

Another strength of this mammoth system that caters to large numbers of students is the three-language formula. By middle school, young adolescents are exposed to a minimum of three languages, usually English, Hindi, and the state language. At other times those in more elite schools have the opportunity to learn a European language or Sanskrit. Maintaining cultural diversity was the initial goal for the multiple languages (Singha, 1991), but in the growing and mobile economy that is India today, the opportunity for middle school students to be exposed to multiple languages has assisted in the ability for people to migrate for work as they got older. In this land of comparisons, there is also the urban, dynamic side to India that has young people excited about the direction the country is headed. In this environment and from the educational system, there is a lot of hope that people will succeed. Tied into this is the realization that innovative thinking is helping many of India's new ventures to succeed and some researchers are starting to look at the secondary system as one that builds a foundation for such entrepreneurship (Arora & Athreye, 2002).

For the lasting benefits of a growing economy and increasing wealth for a large population, the curriculum where the upper primary and secondary schools stress the importance of less choice and a more grounded educational foundation might be one of the benefits of the educational system. Literature to physics, botany to geography, Indian students are exposed to a broad spectrum of knowledge all with an aim to continue to challenge the learner. What is currently exciting about the prospects for middle school education is that with the success of near universal primary education, the demand for high quality middle school education is coming from lower income families and there is growing discernment on what ensures a high quality education. This groundswell of demand will be one of the most positive aspects of middle and secondary education for the future.

REFORM INITIATIVES AND NATIONAL POLICIES

The Government of India has a long history of embracing education reform where the scope has been both large-scale and on the national stage, as well as small, localized and at the grassroots level. The primary government initiative to get all primary age children into schools, or the Sarva Shiksha Abhiyan (SSA) scheme was found to be extremely successful, therefore the government launched a plan for secondary education entitled Scheme for Universalization of Access to Secondary Education or SUCCESS. The main goals of the program are to make secondary education of good quality available, accessible, and affordable to all young students; promote retention; provide infrastructure; and work more with previously marginalized populations including girls, rural children, and students belonging to the scheduled Castes and Tribes (Ministry of Finance, Government of India, 2007).

The government has designated that the constitutionally mandated eight years of education is no longer adequate for a country like India and therefore a committee of the Central Advisory Board of Education was tasked with exploring the universalization of secondary education in India (CABE, 2007). This board is the "highest advisory body relating to policy making in education in India" (CABE, p. 10) and allows a forum for the concurrent responsibilities of education at the central and state level to evaluate and envision policies and programs for future implementation. The committee's recommendations focused on the need for four main issues:

1. Universal access—Interweaving physical, social, cultural and economic aspects of access where the creation of a "new cultural ambience and a child friendly curriculum" (CABE, p. 15) is at the heart of access;
2. Equality and social justice—Empowering children to understand, act, and deconstruct injustice;
3. Relevance and development—Recognizing the full potential of students and linking development of the individual with society focusing on citizenship, critical thought, skills and technology; and
4. Structural and curricular considerations—Reducing the gap between the "world of work" and the "world of knowledge" (CABE).

The extent of improvements in secondary education depends on a number of key issues, including the economic backing, political will, and greater understanding of how secondary education can bridge the education needs of a population with rising primary school attendance and a higher education system that meets the needs of the Indian workforce. At the secondary level, the National Policy on Education has focused on improving access for girls and the scheduled castes and tribes in areas such as science, commerce and vocational training (Ministry of Human Resource Development, Government of India, 2008). The primary push to ensure girls have a fair share of resources came after the initial reforms for education, but with the reforms for secondary education expected to make its full effect in the next decade, the education of girls is playing a prominent role in the planning stages.

RESEARCH

Research in education in India is multifaceted and relatively extensive. Within the broad parameters of a strong higher education system with a cadre of scholars, and a well-respected center for research in education, namely the National Council of Educational Research and Training, research in India is growing. Topics in education cover everything from student achievement, women's education, sports education, management and administration of educational institutions, and the philosophies of education.

Current Research Topics

Overwhelmingly, academic achievement dominates the research agenda for young adolescent learners. Whether the authors are discussing teachers attitudes toward students and the resulting self-perception leading to achievement (Sahu & Sood, 2005), or the involvement of parents affecting adolescents performance at school (Rani & Kaushik, 2005; Vamadevappa, 2005), the key seems to be academic achievement most probably stemming from the critical importance placed on examinations. The research on achievement is multifaceted with forays into physiological aspects of learning, like the role of memory and it's effect on learning, especially as students emerge to sit for these high-stakes examinations (Rana & Kumar, 2000; Vyas, 2002), and television viewing patterns among adolescents and it's effects on achievement (Anuradha, Bharthi, & Jayamma, 2006). As described earlier, the competitive environment of middle schools can affect career decisions, and India's articulation of a clear vision to build a skilled and educated populace is spilling over into how academic achievement is perceived and how the multiple factors affecting achievement can be manipulated to help the most students succeed.

Other areas of research address how subject content is absorbed by students, where research focuses on how secondary students address physics, chemistry or mathematics (Sidhu & Singh, 2005; Thillaka & Pramilla, 2000; Vaish, 2004) as well as newer topics in education like computer science (Sarupria, 2005) and the role of the environment in their lives (Sahaya & Paul, 2005).

There is also growing interest in how minority students are coping as both young adolescents and students in the school system. Vijayalakshmi (2003) explored the problems faced by tribal children in secondary schools and other researchers have looked at how Muslim middle school students are faring in schools in India (Alam, 2001). Another group that has been relatively marginalized as learners are those students who learn in schools where the medium of instruction is different from their native tongue (Dwivedi & Gunthey, 2005). In a country where English-language schools are a matter of prestige for middle-class bound ambitions, academic achievement and student anxiety of a different language play a role in engaging students as learners.

Finally, another broad area of research that has direct relevance to young adolescent learners is the role of academics, career development, and vocational and technical training. In 2000, Yadav studied the relationship of vocational preferences with young adolescents based on levels of intelligence and achievement. He followed this with a study on the needs of adolescent learners in selecting a vocation of choice (Yadav, 2005).

Methodologies

The *Indian Education Review* or the *Journal of Indian Education*, major educational research journals in India, show a preference for quantitative research where the dominance of questionnaires, random sampling, and correlations remain popular. Most of the research cited above is weighted heavily toward quantitative research, where seeking out significant relationships between the research hypothesis and the data collected highlights the evidence. For instance, in Sindhu's (2005) study on teachers' motivation, student adjustment and academic achievement, the researchers used a normative testing survey method and cross-sectional approach to collect data. In a study on achievement and the influence of the home environment between parents and young adolescents, Rani and Kaushik (2005) collected data from 200 young adolescents using a stratified random sampling strategy and used a number of inventories to analyze data collected the mean, standard deviation, t values and correlation analysis to discover the relationship between the variables.

Though some of the studies have a qualitative dimension, the majority of the research for young adults appears to be quantitative in nature. NCERT is beginning to call for qualitative studies with a need for "further in-depth qualitative analysis and research support to see the effectiveness in teaching-learning process in the schools" (Yadav, 2006, p. 36).

Important Research Findings

Since the topics surrounding young adolescent learning in schools is quite broad, the important findings are synthesized to explore the overarching themes of how young adolescents are coping in schools especially related to the challenges outlined in the previous sections. Instruction in schools for young adolescents focuses on preparing students for the comprehensive high-stakes examination in Class Ten. A burgeoning area of research focuses on the tools used to plan lessons including textbooks other instructional technology tools. Sinha and Tripathy (2005) studied the impact of the science curriculum teaching though the textbooks and found that many concepts were repetitive, students were not given a chance to enjoy the learning, and the process was increasingly mechanical especially as the students got closer to the exam. Close to the ages of 14 and 15, the focus was more on finishing the curriculum so the students could sit for the exams.

Developing an effective school for secondary schools students is another pertinent area of research. Though the findings are not a surprise, it is important to highlight that Indian researchers are looking at all the factors related to successful education at the secondary school level. Agrawal, Jain, and Chandrasekhar (2004) looked at secondary schools in the capital of India, New Delhi, and found that young adolescent learners succeeded in schools where teachers' had positive attitudes and high expectations for the students. Success was also linked to student participation in extra-curricular activities, sports, and games. Parental involvement in the schools also influenced learning achievement.

Research around vocational and alternate education for students supports two predominant arguments. The first argument is that non-formal education, or those education programs that lie outside the organized, systematic, education activity which might provide selected types of learning to particular subgroups in the population, is somewhat less prestigious than the formal education system which is education is characterized by the institutionalized, "chronologically graded and hierarchically structured system" that spans education from primary to university level schooling (Coombs & Ahmed, 1974, p. 8). The prestige attached to certifications, degrees, and diplomas that are tickets to increased social status and rank hold an inherent and increased value than those who are availing themselves of skills-based, technical, vocational or non-formal education (Fershtman, Murphy & Weiss, 1996). Additionally, income, education and occupation are clear indicators of socioeconomic status (Bradley & Corwyn, 2002), and in a competitive system like India, education can determine occupation and subsequently income, therefore, it becomes more critical for the "value" placed on education to be equitable for those with either extensive or limited means. This research has been critical to young adolescents since they are the ones getting ready to make decisions about career and livelihoods.

Finally, another area of research that is emerging around young adolescents in India is the role of school stress and its impact on time and emotions. The context of stress is one of the challenges mentioned in earlier sections, and the extra classes, the burden of homework, the high expectations of parents, and the lack of leisure time all affect a young adolescents stress levels. Verma et al. (2002) found that the conflict faced by young adolescents to choose how they spent their leisure time resulted in greater anxiety for students. Having to choose between rigorous academic work with little to no time for leisure or extra curricular activities or vice versa, where they risked lower achievement in school while allowing greater time to relax or participate in nonacademic related activities was a trade-off that in itself caused greater levels of stress in their lives. Additionally, the negative experiences around school led to greater feelings of unhappiness, irritability, worry or boredom affecting the overall positive adjustment for Indian adolescents (Verma et al.).

FUTURE DIRECTIONS

In trying to set the context of India's education in the Annual State of Education, Kaushik (2006) said "In recent years, there has been much discussion about the age profile of the Indian population, with great emphasis on its youth. But while this significant proportion of young people represents an emerging market for business, it is frightening to think of many of them reaching maturity without acquiring the basic skills of literacy and numeracy" (p. 15). Fortunately, India shows signs of recognizing the scope of the population, the long term dimension of setting goals for middle school education, and the political will to follow it's successes with primary education to the upper primary and secondary school level.

In the national plan for education, the budget shows considerable growth, where there has been almost an almost 67% increase from 2003 to 2008 (Ministry of Human Resource Development, 2008) for middle school growth. Looking back at the influential CABE report which is setting the stage to expand secondary education for young adolescents, the focus on the universal access, equality and social justice, relevance and development, and structure and curriculum remain at the forefront of where India is seeking to go in educating young adolescents.

With 25% of the country's most affluent students in private middle schools, the challenge also exists to address education for those who have historically been neglected by the school system (Kingdon, 2007). Additionally, any plans to implement the secondary school plans (where middle school students would fall) would also have to devise alternate arrangements for the young adolescents who slip through the cracks. Right now, there is a large population of out of school youth who have sought work in both the rural and urban areas since middle school education might have been out of reach. If the plans to expand secondary education proceed quickly as the CABE report is requiring, there will still be a population of young adolescents who will have to be encouraged to engage in alternate learning, if the middle school option is untenable for them.

Additionally, India is recognizing that government initiatives are critical to fill the gap between those previously marginalized in middle schools. Teacher outreach, recruitment, and retention is another focus for the future for India, and the CABE report has stressed the need for the country to depend on fully qualified teachers for the middle school level and reduce the dependency on para-professionals (CABE, 2007).

CONCLUDING DISCUSSION

This chapter began by describing the contradictory nature of India, with modernity intermingling with tradition, with science standing alongside superstition, and where the challenges and successes of the school system have promoted exponential opportunities for young people in India. For students between the ages of 10 and 15, education has to be convenient, accessible, relevant, and goal oriented. In the current climate, high levels of poverty prevent middle school education to be seen as valuable when the child can bring home a daily wage to add to the family's income. Distance to schools and the fees spent on uniforms and textbooks make middle school education less appealing in the rural and poorer areas of the country. For young adolescents in urban areas, the value of education is not questioned, but the limited access to lucrative higher education opportunities makes for a competitive environment. The extra tutoring and extensive studying is putting too much pressure on students too young to handle the burden.

The challenge for the system is to meet the needs of students in both environments and broaden the scope of opportunity for work so decisions made at the middle school level will not be so specific and rigid. The positive aspect here is that research on Indian middle school students is also growing. The idea that young adolescence is a separate time of growth and development for individuals, requiring different needs from those in the primary and higher education systems, is a good sign that there is still a shift.

The India of the twenty-first century is very different from the India of 50 years ago. Education for young adolescents did not have a unique place in India's education systems and there was little demand from the grassroots and rural levels for more than an early primary education. The challenges that face young adolescents spill over into spheres of their lives. In education, contrasting the haves with the have nots will be the larger story of how India begins to address its next phase of academic development reaching this immense population of young adults.

REFERENCES

Abadzi, H. (2002). *India: Education sector development in the 1990's: A country assistance evaluation.* Washington, DC: World Bank.

Agarwal, R., & Goswami, M. (2005). Academic performance of principals. *Journal of All India Association for Educational Research, 17*(3-4), 23-25.

Agrawal, M., Jain, V. K., & Chandrasekhar, K. (2004). *Factors influencing effectiveness of secondary schools of Delhi.* New Delhi, India: NCERT.

Alam, M.M (2001). *Academic achievement in relation to socio-economic status, anxiety level and achievement motivation: A comparative study of Muslim and non-Muslim school children of Uttar Pradesh.* Unpublished doctoral dissertation, Aligarh Muslim University, Uttar Pradesh.

Alexander, R. (2000). *Culture and pedagogy: International comparisons in primary education.* Malden, MA: Blackwell.

Anuradha, K., Bharthi, V. V., & Jayamma, B. (2006). Television viewing behavior of adolescents—Its impact on their academic achievement. *Edutracks, 6*(7), 27-31.

Arora, A., & Athreye, S. (2002). The software industry and India's economic development. *Information Economics and Policy, 14,* 253-273.

Banya, K. (1993). Illiteracy, colonial legacy, and education: The case of modern Sierra Leone. *Comparative Education, 29,* 159-170.

Bhuyan, S. (2005). *General science curriculum and its teaching in the secondary schools of Assam: An appraisal.* Unpublished doctoral dissertation, Dibrugarh University, Assam, India.

Bradley, R. H., & Corwyn, R. F. (2002). Socio-economic status and child development. *Annual Review of Psychology, 53,* 371-399.

Central Advisory Board on Education. (2007). *Universalization of primary education.* New Delhi, India: Ministry of Human Resource Development.

Central Intelligence Agency. (2006). *World factbook 2006.* Washington, DC: Author.

Chirayath, S., & Khalique, A. (2005). A study of the relationship between leadership style of the headmasters and organisational climate of secondary schools of Kerala. *Ram-Eesh Journal of Education, 2*(1), 32-46.

Coombs, P. H., & Ahmed, M. (1974). *Attacking rural poverty: How non-formal education can help.* Washington, DC: World Bank.

Dwivedi, N., & Gunthey, R. (2005). Influence of medium of instruction on level of academic anxiety among school students. *Edutracks, 5*(12), 31-32.

Dyer, C. (2000). *Operation Blackboard: Policy implementation in Indian elementary education.* Manchester, United Kingdom: Symposium Books.

Fershtman, C., Murphy, K. M., & Weiss, Y. (1996). Social status, education and growth. *The Journal of Political Economy, 104*(1), 108-132.

Government of India, Ministry of Education. (2003). *DPEP guidelines.* Retrieved February 20, 2003, from http://www.education.nic.in/htmlweb/eleedu4.htm

Government stalling secondary school reforms. (2006, August 24). *India Together.* Retrieved June 15, 3008, from http://www.indiatogether.org/2006/aug/edu-secschool.htm

Gupta, A. (2007). *Going to school in South Asia.* Westport, CT: Greenwood Press.

Kabir, H. (1957). *Education in new India.* New York: Harper.

Kaushik, A. (2006). *Annual status of education.* Mumbai, India: Pratham.

Keay, J. (2000). *India: A history.* New York: Grove Press.

Khar, M. (2007). Education—Our expectations. *Journal of Indian Education, 33*(1), 57-61.

Kingdon, G. G. (2007). The progress of school education in India. *Oxford Review of Economic Policy, 23,* 168-195.

Library of Congress. (2003). *Country reports: India.* Washington, DC: Author.

Ministry of Finance, Government of India. (2007). *Economic survey, 2007-2008.* New Delhi, India: Author.

Ministry of Human Resource Development, Government of India. (2008). *Secondary education.* Retrieved March 24, 2008, from http://education.nic.in/secedu.asp

National Council of Educational Research and Training. (2007). *Seventh all India school education survey: National reports.* New Delhi, India: Author.

Rana, M., & Kumar, P. (2000). Factors associated with immediate memory recall in young adolescents. *Journal of Educational Research and Extension, 37*(3), 8-16.

Rani, S., & Kaushik, N. (2005). A comparative study of achievement motivation, home environment and parent-child relationship of adolescents. *Journal of Psychological Researches, 49,* 89-94.

Reddy, R., & Gibbons, J. L. (1999). School socio-economic contexts and adolescent self-descriptions in India. *Journal of Youth and Adolescence, 28,* 619-631.

Sahaya, M. R., & Paul, R. I. (2005). Environmental awareness among high school students. *Edutracks, 5*(4), 33-35.

Sahu, L. P.,& Sood, R. (2005). Impact of students' perception of their teachers' attitude towards them and its relationship with their self-perception and academic achievement. *Ram-Eesh Journal of Education, 2*(2), 53-57.

Sarupria, S. (2005). *Status, issues and future perspectives of computer education in senior secondary schools.* Unpublished doctoral dissertation, Vidya Bhawan G. S. Teachers College, Rajasthan, India.

Seenarine, M. (1998). *Voices from the subaltern: Education and empowerment among rural Dalit (untouchable) women and girls.* Unpublished doctoral dissertation, Columbia University, New York.

Sharma, R. (2005). Identifying a framework for initiating, sustaining and managing innovations in schools. *Psychology and Developing Societies, 17*(1), 51-80.

Sharma, S. K., & Singh, V.P. (2007). Seventh all India school education survey: A statistical profile on selected parameters of school education. *Journal of Indian Education, 32*(1), 81-92.

Sidhu, R. K., & Singh, P. (2005). Comparative study of concept attainment model, advance organizer model and conventional method in teaching of physics in relation to intelligence and achievement motivation of Class IX students. *Journal of All India Association for Educational Research, 17*(1-2), 89-92.

Sindhu, I. S. (2005). A study of teachers' motivation, student adjustment and their academic achievement. *Ram-Eesh Journal of Education, 2*(2), 19-23.

Sinha, M. P., & Tripathy, H.H. (2005). A study of correlation of the curriculum load in science for classes IX and X. *Indian Educational Review, 41*(1) 59-64.

Singh, M. (2001). Reflections on colonial legacy and dependency in Indian vocational education and training: A societal and cultural perspective. *Journal of Education and Work, 14*, 209-225.

Singha, H. S. (1991). *School education in India: Contemporary issues and trends.* New Delhi, India: Sterling.

Thillaka, S., & Pramilla, K. S. (2000). Use of computer multimedia program in learning trigonometry among high school students. *Journal of Educational Research and Extension, 37*(2), 1-10

United Nations Development Program. (2006). *Millennium development goals.* Retrieved June 11, 2006, from http://www.wunrn.com/news/04_16_06/042406_unesco_education.html

United Nations Educational, Scientific and Cultural Organization. (2006). *Statistics in brief: Education in India.* Retrieved March 21, 2007, from www.uis.unesco.org/profiles/EN/EDU/3560.html

United Nations Population Fund. (n.d.). *Adolescents in India: A profile.* New York: Author.

U.S. Department of Agriculture. (2003). *India—Country reports* Washington, DC: Author.

Vaish, R. (2004). Self-study skills in learning science at the middle school level. *Primary Teacher, 29*(1), 18-27.

Vamadevappa, H. V. (2005). Study of the effectiveness of parental involvement on academic achievement among higher primary students. *Journal of Educational Research and Extension, 42*(2), 23-32.

Verma, S., Sharma, D., & Larson, R. W. (2002). School stress in India: Effects on time and daily emotions. *International Journal of Behavioral Development, 26*, 500-508.

Vijayalakshmi, G. (2003). Problems of secondary school tribal children. *Edutracks, 3*(3), 32-35.

Vyas, A. (2002). *A study of learning style, mental ability, academic performance and other ecological correlates of undergraduate adolescent girls of Rajasthan.* Unpublished doctoral dissertation. Charan Singh University, Meerut, India.

World Bank. (1997). *Staff appraisal report.* Washington, DC: Author.

World Health Organization. (2006). *India.* Retrieved March 15, 2007, from http://www.who.int/countries/ind/en/

World Health Organization. (2008). *Statistical indicators.* Retrieved July 1, 2008, from http://www.who.int/whosis/data/Search.jsp?countries=[Location]

Yadav, R. (2000). The vocational preferences of adolescents in relation to their intelligence and achievement in relation to their intelligence and achievement. *Journal of Educational Research and Extension, 37*(3), 36-45.

Yadav, R. K. (2005). A study of relationship between needs and vocational preferences of adolescents. *Journal of Educational Research and Extension, 42*(3), 12-22.

Yadav, S. K. (2006). Implementation of the school curriculum in the upper primary stages in different states. *Journal of Indian Education, 32*(1), 22-37.

CHAPTER 5

THE AWAKENING OF YOUNG ADOLESCENT EDUCATION IN THE PEOPLE'S REPUBLIC OF CHINA

Lisa Hervey, Hiller A. Spires, and Junzheng Zhang

Fueled by a booming economy and increased interest from international markets, China is breaking all records as it emerges as a dynamic developing country. Because of its vast population, rapidly growing economy, and large research and development investments, China is considered by most an emerging superpower. In the context of dramatic change, the Ministry of Education has created new educational policies impacting young adolescent education that attempt to embrace modernity while simultaneously preserving and honoring the best of Chinese tradition. Currently, the dominant teaching approach is based on the *transmission-acceptance model,* where teachers transmit knowledge to students through exhibition and clarification. In light of China's new goal of becoming an *innovation oriented society,* teachers are beginning to entertain more student-centered models such as *quality oriented education, inquiry learning,* and *cooperative learning.* As new policies and constructs for teaching and learning unfold, opportunities for purposeful cultivation of young adolescent education are emerging.

An International Look at Educating Young Adolescents
pp. 97–114

CONTEXTUAL NARRATIVE

It has been reported that in the early 1800s, Napoleon Bonaparte compared China to a "sleeping dragon" and predicted, "when it awakes, the world will shake" (Forbes, 2004). China *has* awakened and the tremendous change that is taking place has affected many aspects of the global economy. Fueled by a booming economy and increased interest from international markets, China is breaking all records as it emerges as a dynamic developing country. Because of its vast population, rapidly growing economy, and large research and development investments, China is considered by most an emerging superpower. Based on a recent report by the Chicago Council on Global Affairs (2006), China has become a global manufacturing power and is already displacing the United States as the primary trading partner for many nations. China's economic and political clout is also increasingly felt well beyond Asia, especially in countries and regions that China regards as important for its growing energy needs.

The People's Republic of China (PRC), commonly referred to as simply China, is the largest country in East Asia and the most populous country in the world. The Communist Party of China (CPC) has led China under a single-party system since the state's establishment in 1949. As a point of clarification, the People's Republic of China is different from the Republic of China, commonly known as Taiwan. Due to the persistent diplomatic pressure from China, which does not recognize Taiwan as a sovereign nation, the international community frequently avoids the use of "Republic of China" or "Taiwan" so as to avoid offending the Chinese government. The PRC is involved in a long-running dispute over the political status of Taiwan. The CPC's rival during the Chinese Civil War, the Kuomintang (KMT), fled to Taiwan and surrounding islands after its civil war defeat in 1949, claiming legitimacy over China, Mongolia, and Tuva while it was the ruling power of the Republic of China (ROC). The term "Mainland China" is often used to denote the areas under PRC rule, but usually excludes its two special administrative regions: Hong Kong and Macau.

China's rapid economic growth has led to dramatic improvement in the lives of an increased percentage of Chinese citizens. In 1980, China's per capita income was approximately $300—less than that of countries such as Chad, India, Ghana, and Nigeria. Today China's per capita income has more than quadrupled to about $1,100. Along with a growing economy, the Chinese Ministry of Education has created an ambitious agenda to modernize the educational system with a goal of educating all the people of China. Several key social issues are critical to understanding China's education system, and specifically how the country educates its young adolescents, 10 through 15 years of age. These issues include population, aging, urban-rural divide, and the environment.

First, China is the most populous country in the world with more than 1.3 billion people, about 20% of the world's total population and nearly 4.3 times more people than in the United States. The population density in China is 134 people per square kilometer; whereas, the density in the United States is 31.17 people per square kilometer. In 1979, a strict family planning policy was enacted that directed families to have one child per couple. The policy has had mixed results and has been revised to allow married couples, only children themselves, to have two children. The UN Population Fund is encouraging government officials to use a voluntary, noncoercive approach to family planning. The government's goal is to stabilize the population early in the twenty-first century, although some current projections estimate a population of 1.45 billion by 2025.

Second, according to UN projections, China will experience a dramatic aging of its people in the next few decades. By 2050 almost half of the population will be 45 years and older and 23% will be 65 and older. The number of Chinese people older than 60, accounting for more than 12.38% of the country's population, is increasing at a rate of 3.2% per year. This age group exceeded 154 million at the end of 2004, accounting for about one half of Asia's and one fifth of the world's total population over 60. According to United Nations Educational, Scientific and Cultural Organization's World Education Report (2000), since the 1970s, average life expectancy in China has risen from 65 to 72. The increase in aging and life expectancy brings various social and economical challenges to China. Housing, health costs, retirement income, and the need for care giving are among the services that need to be addressed.

Third, there is an increasing rural-urban income gap. According to recent estimates by the UN Population Division, China's urban population increased from some 70 million in 1950 to roughly 530 million in 2005. By 2015, the urban population will surpass the rural population; and by 2030 China will have an urban population of some 875 million people—far larger than that of Europe and the United States combined. "Rurality" and illiteracy are highly related in China. At the turn of the twentieth century, China's illiteracy rate was about 85-90% of the total population. It was not until the communist revolution in 1949 that China embarked on a comprehensive effort to eradicate illiteracy. In 2004, the adult illiteracy rate was 17.8% or 164.3 million, for those over 15 years old. This rate compares with India's 45.1% or 274.1 million. The rural-urban economic gap appears to be widening.

Fourth, there is rapid environmental degradation. As China becomes more industrialized, the country faces increased environmental challenges. Most of China's bodies of water are polluted with seven of the country's major bodies of water documented as having serious pollution. Over half the population lack access to clean water with only about 5% of household waste and about 17% of industrial waste receiving any treatment before entering local irrigation ditches, ponds, lakes, and streams. Likewise, air pollution in some cities is among the highest ever recorded, averaging more than ten times the standard proposed by the World Health Organization. Six of China's largest cities—Beijing, Shenyang, Chongqing, Shanghai, Xian, and Guangzhou—rank among the most polluted in the world. Beijing's winning bid for the 2008 Olympics forced China to engage in measures to address water and air quality issues.

The Chinese leaders have understood that in the twenty-first century China can no longer survive as a closed and self-sufficient nation that develops by its own rules. To flourish, it must be an open society with links to worldwide finances, resources, skilled labor, technical expertise, and mass communication. As any other country in the world, China will have to cope with international standards and regulations, will have to adapt to the scrutiny of international mass media, will be subject to global environmental changes, and will depend on international political alliances. When China recently joined the WTO she finally became a global player with the same opportunities and problems as any other internationally relevant nation.

HISTORY AND ORGANIZATION OF
SCHOOLING FOR YOUNG ADOLESCENTS

Historical Background

A well-known Chinese proverb claims, "If you are planning for a year, sow rice; if you are planning for a decade, plant trees; if you are planning for a lifetime, educate people." This adage captures the momentum and direction that China's Ministry of Education (MOE) has embraced in recent years as they chart the course of modernizing the Chinese educational system. Of particular importance to the MOE is the capacity to embrace modernity while simultaneously preserving and honoring the best of Chinese tradition.

China's education system has a longstanding ritual of philosophical thought in education. Further, educational philosophy has been a major characteristic of Chinese traditional philosophy. Great thinkers such as Confucius, Zhu Xi and many others advocated the cultivation of virtues through education. The content of education was in the Confucian classics, which dealt with family relations and, by extension, human relations throughout the whole empire. At the center of Confucian teaching is the value of learning and social mobility, which are achieved through intellectual development. Education was informal and used as a tool for social mobility and acquisition of personal power. Upward mobility was gained through administrative examinations organized by the government. Exceptional male students who passed examinations were selected for valued government posts. *The Great Learning* formed the content of the examination (Tuner & Acker, 2002). *The Great Learning* is based in part on the introduction of the Dà Xué (or the Ta Hseüh), written by Confucius and his pupils between the fifth and second centuries B.C. and translated by the poet Ezra Pound.

The indigenous education system of China came to a close with the end of the Opium Wars (1839-1842), with China relinquishing territories to Great Britain. This resulted in an infiltration of foreign missionaries who founded missionary schools and with them foreign educational ideals. Missionary schools provide open access to both men and women, facilitating increased opportunities for students to study abroad. Only after the 1911 revolution did modern scientific knowledge and a Western system of education begin to be introduced and some elements of Chinese classical learning were removed from school curricula (Chen, 1999). Initially, the content of education mimicked Japanese curriculum and consisted of the classics, history, geography, morals, and the natural sciences.

Throughout the twentieth century, many leaders experimented with various approaches to education, mostly modeled on Western systems (Chen, 1999). However, no successful education system was sustained until the creation of the People's Republic of China (PRC) in 1949. When the Chinese communists took power, school curriculum planning was conducted wholly on the Soviet "encyclopedic" knowledge basis, paying special attention to rationality and universality (Chen). The Chinese encyclopedist ideal of universality affirms that all students should reach minimum standards of attainment in the acquisition of a standard body of *intellectual knowledge* which contributes to their intellectual, moral, physical and aesthetic development. This approach was heavily influenced by Marxist views, specifically gearing for the reconstruction and modernization of China upon a socialist theme. The education system was established, promising primary education for all, but fell short of that target. The intellectual knowledge focus of education in China created a vacuum for criticism and creativity, that stills endures today.

Organization

In China, government is the primary investor in education, although private educational investment has been increasing rapidly since 1978. As a result of the reform, decision making in the area of education has become much more decentralized. Local government is playing a key role in compulsory education, while central and provincial governments are dominant in higher education. In occupational and adult education, nongovernmental entities including industrial organizations, businesses and public institutions play an important role (Liu, 2002).

China's basic education system involves preschool, 9-year compulsory education from elementary to junior high school, standard senior high school education, vocational education, special education for disabled children, and education for illiterate people. An estimated 250 million Chinese attend the three levels of basic education: elementary, junior and senior middle schools (Chinese Ministry of Education, 2003). Since 1950, China has implemented a nine-year compulsory education system in and around China's major cities. By 1986 universal secondary education was part of the 9-year compulsory education law that made primary education (6 years) and junior-middle-school education (3 years) mandatory throughout the entire country (see Table 5.1). Nine-year compulsory education operates in 90% of China's populated areas. For compulsory education, school enrolment has reached 98.9%, and the gross enrollment rate in junior high schools reached 94.1% (The Central People's Government of the People's Republic of China, 2006).

Chinese secondary schools are called middle schools and are divided into junior and senior levels. Junior, or lower, middle schools offers a 3-year course of study, which students began at 11 to 12 years of age. According to the Chinese Ministry of Education (2002), in 2001 there were 66,600 junior middle schools, with 65,143,800 students enrolled, and 3,385,700 teachers. There were 14,907 senior middle schools, with 14,049,700 students enrolled and 840,000 teachers. The desire to consolidate existing schools and to improve the quality of key middle schools was, however, under education reform, more important than expanding enrollment.

Secondary education in China has a complex history. In the early 1960s, education planners followed a "two leg" approach that established both regular academic schools and separate technical schools for voca-

Table 5.1.   School levels in China

School Level	Ages	Compulsory
Primary school	6-12	Yes
Junior middle school	12-15	Yes
Senior middle school	15-18	No
University or college	18-22	No

tional training. The rapid development of secondary education during Mao Zedong's Cultural Revolution, 1966-1976, created serious problems. First, existing resources were stretched beyond capacity causing a decline in educational quality. Secondly, this growth was limited to only regular secondary schools; technical schools were eliminated during the Cultural Revolution because they were viewed as an attempt to provide inferior education to children of worker and peasant families.

Rural secondary education has undergone several reorganizations since 1980, when county-level education administrators closed some schools and took over certain schools run by the people's communes. In 1982 the communes were eliminated. In 1985 educational reform legislation officially placed rural secondary schools under local authorities. There was a high dropout rate among rural students in general and among secondary students in particular, largely because of parental attitudes. All students, however, especially males, were encouraged to attend secondary school if it would lead to entrance to a college or university (still regarded as prestigious) and provided an escape from village life.

In China, a senior-middle-school graduate is considered an educated person, although middle schools are viewed as a training ground for colleges and universities. And, while middle-school students are offered the prospect of higher education, they are also confronted with the fact that university admission is limited. Middle schools are evaluated in terms of their success in sending graduates on for higher education, although efforts persist to educate young people to take a place in society as valued and skilled members of the work force.

Curriculum, Instruction, and Assessment Practices

There are few studies of the classroom environment for secondary schools in China. In general, it is believed that class size ranges from 40 to 50 students, and can be as high as 70 students (Salili, Zhou, & Hoosain, 2003). Generally, middle school classrooms consist of long rows of desks, with desks bolted to the floor. In most cases, as suggested by Chinese educators, the atmosphere remains teacher-focused, prescribed and undisputed (Spires, Morris, & Li, 2008). This traditional model used in secondary schools is know as the *transmission-acceptance model* (Wu, 1993) where teachers transmit knowledge to students through exhibition and clarification. This widely used model is deemed most effective for delivering a large amount of content knowledge to students in a relatively short time. As a consequence, active student involvement is stifled. Universal criticisms for this traditional model have emerged, leading government officials and educators to explore new models for education.

The encyclopedist tradition in the curriculum of Chinese schools has been challenged in several ways. China has one of the most centralized curriculum systems in the world. Not only is there a national curriculum laid down, but until the late 1980s all students in China used the same set of textbooks developed by a quasi-official publisher, the People's Education Press. In the 1990s, the Chinese Government attempted to relax this system. Instead of only allowing the People's Education Press to publish school textbooks, more publishers have been permitted to produce textbooks. However, the Chinese Ministry of Education (2002) policy states:

> To ensure the quality of textbooks and other teaching materials produced, a system of examination and approval of textbooks has been established in China. All textbooks for obligatory subjects taught in primary and secondary schools have to be examined and approved by the State Textbooks Examination and Approval Committee before publication in terms of ideological content, scientific spirit and adaptability to classroom instruction. The textbooks approved are allowed to be used by the local educational departments. However, supplementary teaching materials with local figures are to be examined and approved by a provincial-level School Textbook Examination and Approval Committee and allowed to be used within the province concerned. (www.moe.edu.cn/edoas/website18/info405.htm)

In 1993, the State Council issued the "Educational Reform and Development Outlines" (State Education Commission, 1993). This document urges the education system to move away from an "examination-oriented education." One such innovation, know as a *quality-oriented education*, is an attempt for a more well-rounded education. Quality-oriented education reform has led educators to explore many models for curriculum delivery. The *inquiry learning* model is one example, used with subjects such as chemistry, physics and mathematics (Salili et al., 2003). The *cooperative learning* method is also being applied to many subjects. As a result, learning environments for young adolescents are changing.

Generally, the junior middle school year has two semesters, totaling nine months. In some rural areas, schools provide unique school schedules that match agricultural cycles. Basic academic curriculum consists of Chinese, mathematics, physics, chemistry, biology, geology, foreign language, history, geography, politics, music, fine arts, and physical education. Some junior middle schools also offer vocational subjects. There are 30 or 31 class periods a week in addition to self-study and extracurricular activity. Curriculum at a junior middle school focuses on Chinese, mathematics, and foreign languages. Much of the teaching at a senior middle school is in natural sciences and mathematics. Secondary education is divided into regular secondary education, occupational and polytechnic secondary education. Regular secondary education consists of junior middle school and senior middle school. Senior middle schools are for students who want to go on to higher education. Occupational and polytechnic secondary education generally lasts from 2 to 4 years, and trains medium-level skilled workers, farmers, managerial, and technical personnel. Upon graduation from junior middle school, students either go to a senior middle school or an occupational and polytechnic school, depending on their aspirations and other considerations.

Recognition that all students, particularly young adolescents, are different and require unique knowledge for a variety of occupational futures has been an increasing obstacle to the Chinese Ministry of Education's development and implementation of a fixed curriculum. Ultimately, teachers still widely use traditional teaching methods geared toward preparing students for examinations, with an emphasis on repeated practice and rote memorization. Where junior middle school education is basically universal, students who have graduated from primary schools may, without examination, advance to the appropriate junior middle schools. Junior middle school graduates may enter senior middle schools after passing examinations set by the local education authorities.

OUTCOMES OF THE SCHOOLING OF YOUNG ADOLESCENTS

The intense pressure to achieve academically, particularly in the later years of junior and senior middle schools, is one of the most pervasive trials that Chinese young adolescents endure in their lives. Young adolescents who are unsuccessful in achieving school standards often receive harsh reprimands from parents and teachers and receive minimal respect and acceptance in their peer group. Children's academic achievement has traditionally been considered important in Chinese culture. School achievement, for young adolescents, makes accessible higher levels of education and ultimately increased social and occupational, and perhaps economic, status. However, due to limited opportunities to receive a higher education in China, there is strong academic competition at almost every level from primary to senior middle school. A number of cross-cultural studies have been carried out in the past decade comparing Chinese children with children in other countries on academic achievement (e.g., Stevenson et al., 1990). It was found that Chinese children and young adolescents, on average, outperformed their North American peers in various academic areas. The high achievement of Chinese children and young adolescents may be associated with effective strategies of classroom instruction (e.g., Stevenson, Chen, & Lee, 1992), students' high achievement motivation (Chen & Stevenson, 1995), and positive family influences such as parental involvement (Stevenson et al., 1992, 1993).

CURRENT ISSUES RELATED TO THE
SCHOOLING OF YOUNG ADOLESCENTS

Over the last several years, Chinese education has undergone spectacular development in compulsory education and higher education. As previously mentioned, 9 years of education was made compulsory for all students in 1986 and higher education expansion has created enormous opportunities for senior middle school graduates. Unfortunately, a predicament has materialized with the development of secondary schools falling behind. The great expansion in both primary and higher education has created a narrowing effect in the middle: there are not enough junior secondary schools to house the primary school graduates, and there is a serious shortage of senior high schools. In rural areas where more than 60% of China's population resides, the number of junior high schools is far from meeting the requirement of the Compulsory Education Law (Lin & Zhang, 2006). Local counties do not have the facilities to provide junior high education for all students. In the country, the estimation is that only 75% of students can advance to junior high schools and the majority of those rejected are rural students (Lin & Zhang). Enrollment in junior high schools is nearly universal in urban areas, but this is far from standard in rural areas, which creates a dire shortage of opportunities for young adolescents that may hinder their ability to meet the increasing demands of society and the needs of a quickly developing economy in China. This issue has attracted the attention of policy makers in the Ministry of Education, which urged for the rapid expansion of high school enrollment. However, doubts have been voiced: besides lack of funding and shortage of schools, teacher shortage is another serious concern. It is estimated that China needs 1.16 million more teachers, which means adding 240,000 more teachers each year in the next 5 years (Lin & Zhang).

This "bottle-neck" puzzle presents a big challenge to the Chinese education system overall (Lin & Zhang, 2006). Educational funding has been low. In 2000, the standard average governmental funding nationally per student was 77 yuan (U.S.$11) per year per junior high school student and 277 yuan (U.S.$1,060) per year per senior high school student, as announced by the National Statistic Bureau and Chinese Ministry of Education.

Encouragingly, United Nations International Children's Emergency Fund (2004) research shows that as a group, Chinese young adolescents are better educated, better informed, and healthier than ever before. But because young adolescence is usually perceived as a transition from one life stage towards the more desired state of adulthood, it is often not valued or recognized in its own right. In some ways, adolescents are a neglected group: their vulnerabilities unrecognized, their potential contributions undervalued; noticed only when they present the Chinese society with a problem. For example, young adolescence is a time of sexual awakening, but in China, sex education has for many decades, been taboo. This is changing. Educators are advising the self-conscious Chinese to talk more with their children about sex, and new textbooks that discuss sex frankly are being introduced on a limited basis in Chinese schools. Nevertheless, there remains a need for education about sexuality and reproductive health. Curriculum is beginning to emphasize the need to give young adolescents the knowledge they need to protect themselves against a variety of threats facing them as they approach maturity. These include knowledge of how to prevent sexually transmitted diseases and infections, particularly HIV/AIDS.

REFORM INITIATIVES AND NATIONAL POLICIES

Recent reforms that have had a significant impact on the quality of education for young adolescents include Project Hope, the Spring Bud Project, the Millennium Development Goals, and the Ministry of Education's recent *Reforms of Evaluation and Assessment Systems in Elementary and Secondary Schools*. Project Hope was initiated by the China Youth Development Foundation in 1989 and is aimed at mobilizing domestic and overseas resources to help young adolescents from poor counties continue their education, improving education conditions, and assisting the government in realizing universal nine year compulsory education in these regions. In 1995, a national teacher-training center was established in Zhejiang province. In 1997, the Star of Hope Scholarship was established. However, due to the huge demand for improving the physical conditions of schools in these poor counties, building Hope Schools remains an important part of the project. By the end of 2001, funds donated to the project reached 2 billion Yuan (U.S.$242 million); 2.49 million drop outs returned to school; 8,890 Hope Primary Schools were established; and more than 6,000 teachers received training (Liu, 2002). Its success demonstrates the increasingly important role of nongovernment organizations (NGOs) in China's educational development. Since 1999 the International Community Foundation, through the Robert and Joyce Chang Fund, has built 12 hope schools in the poor counties of Yunnan province and Hubei province and provided hundreds of scholarships to students. A significant portion of the funds is also used towards the improvement of school facilities, such as the construction of a science building at Guangnan First Middle School, Yunnan province (Liu).

The Spring Bud Project was launched 1989 and carried out by the China Children and Teenagers Fund (CCYF), another major nongovernmental agency active in the education arena. The goal is to assist young adolescent girls from poor areas of China to return to school and also help them to master practical skills to give them a better standing in society. At present, the project has been carried out all over China. 300 million Yuan (U.S.$36 million) have been donated and 1.15 million dropout girls have been helped back to school. In 1996, Spring Bud Practical Skill Training Fund was set up to provide girls with vocational education. Besides studying regular textbooks, they are taught to master one or two basic skills. These skills are helpful in lifting them out of poverty. An estimated 1.7 million girls have taken the Spring Bud Training Classes (China Children and Teenagers' Fund, 2008).

At the September 2000 United Nations Summit, 149 heads of state and government from 189 member countries adopted the Millennium Declaration, a document outlining a universal set of Millennium Development Goals (MDGs) (see Figure 5.1). To meet one educational goal, the Chinese government is consolidating its policy of 9-year compulsory education by focusing on poor and ethnic minority areas. The following reforms are underway: increase middle school enrollment; promote quality and relevance of education; encourage innovation and job skills; reform curricula and textbooks to replace the traditional teacher-centered and rote learning methodology in Chinese schools with qualitative, student-centered methods; require full-time teachers in primary and junior middle schools to attain associate bachelor and undergraduate degrees respectively; and improve teacher training curriculum that emphasizes essential *quality-oriented education*.

More recently, the Chinese Ministry of Education (2002) issued a policy entitled *Ministry of Education's Notice Regarding Furthering the Reforms of Evaluation and Assessment Systems in Elementary and Secondary Schools.* In stark contrast to the current NCLB policy in the United States, China's policy calls for new ways of assessing academic knowledge and forbids ranking schools, school districts, or individual students based on test results. According to Zhao (2007), the 2003 Chinese Ministry of Education plan for curriculum reform emphasized creativity, the spirit to innovate and life skills. Strategies include encouraging more flexibility and autonomy for students and schools in what content to learn, more courses outside traditional disciplines, and a more authentic assessment and evaluation scheme. The policy also includes a strong community service and experience component and requires English as a second language beginning in third grade.

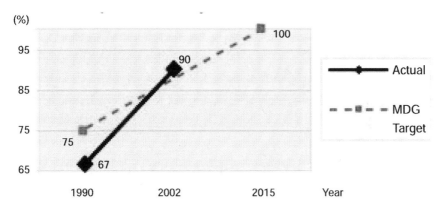

Source: United Nations Development Programme: Millennium development goals China's progress: An assessment by the UN country team in China (2004).

Figure 5.1. Enrollment goal for middle grades education for 2015.

RESEARCH

Important Research Findings

China is noticeably absent from the multinational research studies like Trends in International Mathematics and Science Study (TIMSS) and Programme for International Student Assessment (PISA) and this absence limits the capacity to compare the performance of young adolescents in China to those in other countries. Two areas of research that are significant to the social changes that China is undergoing relate to (1) the paradox of the Chinese young adolescent learner, and (2) young adolescent use of technologies in and out of school.

Paradox of the Chinese learner. Watkins and Biggs (2001) coined the phrase the "paradox of the Chinese learner" to reflect the image of students from Asian cultures as rote memorizers being taught by authoritarian teachers. Asian students consistently outperform Western students although Chinese school environments do not appear to be engaging by Western standards. For example, in middle secondary schools, China has large classes, didactic instruction, exhaustive testing, and a teacher-centered classroom environment. On multinational assessments such as

TIMSS and PISA, middle school students from Japan, Korea, Singapore, Chinese-Taipei, Hong Kong-China, and Macao-China (to date, the PRC has not participated) all demonstrate deeper content knowledge and better conceptual development than American students of similar age and grade levels (Tatsuoka & Corter, 2004).

Two hypotheses have been set forth to account for this apparent paradox. One hypothesis is that Chinese students learn at early ages how to actively memorize—how to use memorization as a tool for concept development (DeHaan, 2006). Students at Nanjing University who were queried about their conceptions of learning, did not see memorization as a barrier to conceptual understanding. Rather they were able to distinguish between mechanical memorization versus memorization with understanding (Wong & Wen, 2001). Chinese parents tend to place greater emphasis on mastery of practical knowledge by their preschoolers than do U.S. or Australian parents. There is some evidence that these early language-learning experiences may influence a child's problem-solving and theory formation capacities later in life (Wellman, Fang, Liu, Zhu, & Liu, 2006).

A second hypothesis pertains to the image of the Chinese instructor as authoritarian, which may be interpreted differently by Asians. Based on a review of current literature on authoritarian instruction, Ho (2001) suggested that Westerners focus on the restriction of freedom of choice, whereas Asians interpret the situation as the person in authority caring for students. Where strictness in Western classrooms may be viewed negative and limiting, it is seen in the Chinese context as nurturing and motivational for students.

The importance of context and motivation in learning is made clear from experiences of students displaced from their countries of ethnic origin. In the United States, for example, ethnic Korean students are usually found among the "Asian model" group of high-achievers. In Japan, in contrast, Korean families often occupy lower socioeconomic levels and their children perform poorly in school (Park, 2007). The inadequate performance of Korean students in the Japanese schools, like that of many African American students in U.S. schools, may result from factors such as language differences, low level of school engagement, lack of educational motivation, and social identity threat (Walton & Cohen, 2007). But much more research is needed to understand causal relationships in this area.

Technology use in and out of school. Based on a recent study conducted by Spires et al. (2008), there appears to be less technology use in school than there is out-of-school in both America and China. This perspective was underscored in a recent study conducted by Internet Access Coalition and J. Walter Thompson, called *Young Digital Mavens* ("China Leads," 2007). The study aimed to explore how attitudes toward digital technology are changing among Chinese and American youth at a time when people are spending less time with traditional media and more with online technologies. The study reported that 80% of Chinese respondents agreed that digital technology was an inherent part of their lifestyle, compared with 68% of Americans. Chinese youth reported they are twice as likely as young Americans to say they would not feel comfortable without Internet access for more than a day. More than twice as many Chinese youth admitted they sometimes feel "addicted" to living online. This finding is not surprising since China is emerging from being a closed society; the new-found freedom of expression associated with using the Internet to communicate may produce a more intensified experience for Chinese users. In a recent survey conducted by Spires et al. (2008), Chinese teachers reported that their students spent on average 1.3 hours per week on a computer in class; there appears to be a greater disconnect between in-school and out-of-school technology use by Chinese students than their American counterparts.

In December 2008, the China Internet Network Information Center (CINNC) reported that 210 million Chinese age 6 and above have used the Internet in the past half-year. They also reported that 157.4 million Internet users lived in cities and towns, while 52.6 million lived in rural areas. By December 2007, the total of Internet users in China had increased to 210 million, with a sharp increase of 73 million in the year of 2007, at an annual growth rate of 53.3%. The Internet is gradually diffusing among residents at different levels. Out of the new users in 2007, people below 18 and above 30 showed a relatively fast increase. People with the education background of secondary school and below grew relatively fast and low-income groups have started to accept the Internet increasingly. In view of regions, Beijing and Shanghai have a higher Internet penetration rate, being respectively 46.6% and 45.8%.

FUTURE DIRECTIONS AND CONCLUDING DISCUSSION

Early in 2006, U.S. President George W. Bush called on the American people to bolster mathematics and science education and to nurture corporate innovation. In the same month, Chinese President Hu Jintao outlined major strategic tasks for building an innovation-oriented society." Clearly, China is benefiting from a robust economy and modernization, and new educational policies are being created to support accelerated growth. Despite a trend toward social modernization, traditional cultural values continue to have major influence on the practice of educating young adolescents in China. Future directions for young adolescent education must include attention to the educational infrastructure to accommodate the influx of students transitioning from primary school to middle school. More research needs to be conducted on the social, emotional, and academic needs of young adolescents as they negotiate the pressures and demands associated with the rapid economic and social changes occurring in China. With regard to teacher pedagogical approaches, extensive research needs to be conducted on how to provide teachers with professional development opportunities as they transition from the *transmission-acceptance model* of instruction to more student-centered approaches. Making instructional changes is difficult for most teachers. Chinese teachers are particularly challenged since proposed changes will require a redefinition of a basic value system ingrained in Chinese traditional culture. While these shifts in educational practice will be difficult, change is essential in order for China's young adolescents to embrace their country's evolving innovation-oriented society and become century learners and workers.

REFERENCES

The Central People's Government of The People's Republic of China (2006). *Basic education.* Retrieved June 9, 2008, from http://english.gov.cn/2006-02/08/content_182558.htm

Chen, Y. (1999). Tradition and innovation in the Chinese school curriculum. *Research in Education, 61,* 16-28.

Chen, C., & Stevenson, H. W. (1995). Motivation and mathematics achievement: A comparative study of Asian-American, Caucasian-American, and East-Asian high school students. *Child Development 66,* 1215-1234.

Chicago Council on Global Affairs. (2006). *The United States and the rise of China and India: Results of a 2006 multination survey of public opinion.* Chicago: The Chicago Council on Global Affairs. Retrieved July 12, 2008, from http://www.thechicagocouncil.org/taskforce_details.php?taskforce_id=5

China Children and Teenagers' Fund. (2008). *The spring bud program.* Retrieved July 12, 2008, from http://en.cctf.org.cn/?q=node/23

China leads the US in digital self-expression. (2007). *CNNMoney.* Retrieved November 23, 2007, from http://money.cnn.com/news/newsfeeds/articles/prnewswire/NYF007231120071.htm

China Internet Network Information Center. (2008). *Statistical survey report on the internet development in China.* Retrieved March 14, 2007, from http://www.cnnic.cn/uploadfiles/pdf/2008/2/29/104126.pdf

Chinese Ministry of Education. (2002). *Ministry of Education's notice regarding furthering the reform of evaluation and assessment systems in elementary and secondary school.* Beijing: China: Author. Retrieved July 12, 2008, from www.moe.edu.cn/edoas/website18/info405.htm

Chinese Ministry of Education. (2003). *Report of Education Statistics, 1*(26). Retrieved June 7, 2008, from http://www.moe.edu.cn/english/planning_s.htm

DeHaan, R. L. (2006). Education for innovation: A look at China & the U.S. *China Currents, 5*(3). Retrieved September 26, 2007, from http://www.chinacenter.net/China_Currents/fall_2006/cc_dehaan.htm

Forbes, K. J. (2004) China's economic outlook: Moving towards a market economy. *Council of Economic Advisers.* Retrieved August 26, 2008, from http://www.whitehouse.gov/cea/chinabusinesssummit-20041014.html

Ho, I. (2001). Are Chinese teachers authoritarian? In D. A. Watkins, & J. B. Biggs (Eds.), *Teaching the Chinese learner: Psychological and pedagogical perspectives* (pp. 99-114). Hong Kong: Comparative Education Research Centre, University of Hong Kong.

Lin, J., & Zhang, Y. (2006). Educational expansion and shortages in secondary schools in China: The bottle neck syndrome. *Journal of Contemporary China, 15*(47), 255–274.

Liu, X. (2002). *Overview of educational needs & philanthropic opportunities in China.* San Diego, CA: International Community Foundation.

Park, H. (2007). Japanese and Korean high schools and students in comparative perspective. *European Forum.* Retrieved September 7, 2007, from http://www.eui.eu/RSCAS/e-texts/EF200706-Park.pdf

Salili, F., Zhou, H., & Hoosain, R. (2003). Adolescent education in Hong Kong and mainland China. In F. Pajares & T. C. Urdan (Eds.), *International perspectives on adolescence* (pp. 277-302). Charlotte, NC: Information Age.

Spires, H., Morris, G., & Li, D. (2008, April). *US and Chinese teachers have their say about new media literacies.* Paper presented at the Asian/American Summit on Global Partnerships, Phoenix, AZ.

State Education Commission. (1993). *The development and reform of education in China.* Beijing, China: Author.

Stevenson, H. W., Chen, C., & Lee, S. (1992). Chinese families. In J. L. Roopnarine & D. B. Carter (Eds.), *Parent-child socialization in diverse cultures* (pp. 17–33). Norwood, NJ: Ablex.

Stevenson, H. W., Chen, C., & Lee, S. (1993). Mathematics achievement of Chinese, Japanese, and American children: Ten years later. *Science, 259,* 53-58.

Stevenson, H. W., Lee, S., Chen, C., Stigler, J. W., Hsu, C., & Kitamura, S. (1990). Contexts of achievement. *Monographs of the Society for Research in Child Development, 55,* 1-116.

Tatsuoka, K. K., & Corter, J. E. (2004). Patterns of diagnosed mathematical content and process skills in TIMSS-R across a sample of 20 countries. *American Educational Research Journal, 41*(4), 901-926.

Turner, Y., & Acker, A. (2002). *Education in the new China: Shaping ideas at work.* Hampshire, United Kingdom: Ashgate.

United Nations Educational, Scientific and Cultural Organization. (2000). *World education report: The right to education, towards education for all throughout life.* Retrieved July 12, 2008, from http://www.unesco.org/education/information/wer/index.htm

United Nations International Children's Emergency Fund. (2004). *The children: Adolescence.* Retrieved June 7, 2008, from http://www.unicef.org/china/children_877.html

United Nations Development Programme. (2004). *Millennium development goals China's progress: An assessment by the UN country team in China.* Retrieved June 9, 2008, from http://www.undp.org.cn/modules.php?op=modload&name=News&file=article&catid=18&key=mdgrs&sid=64

Walton, G. M., & Cohen, G. L. (2007). A question of belonging: Race, social fit, and achievement. *Journal of Personality and Social Psychology, 92*(1), 82-96.

Watkins, D. A., & Biggs, J. B. (Eds.). (2001). *Teaching the Chinese learner: Psychological and pedagogical perspectives*: Hong Kong: Comparative Education Research Center.

Wellman, H. M., Fang, F., Liu, D., Zhu, L., & Liu, G. (2006). Scaling of theory-of-mind understandings in Chinese children. *Psychological Science, 17*(12), 1075-1081.

Wong, K., & Wen, Q. (2001). The impact of university education on conceptions of learning: A Chinese study. *International Education Journal, 2*(5), 138-147.

Wu, Y. X. (1993). *Major teaching methods used in primary and secondary schools in China.* Chengdu: Sichuan Education Press.

Zhao, Y. (2007). Education in a flat world: Implications of globalization on education. *Edge Magazine, 2*(4), 3-19.

CHAPTER 6

EDUCATION FEVER AND EXAM HELL

The Current Educational Systems and Issues in South Korea

Bogum Yoon

Based on the personal observations, experiences, and the relevant literature, this chapter introduces the current educational systems, policies, and
issues with regard to educating young adolescents in the Republic of Korea.
The historical, cultural, and social contexts help us understand how the
educational systems and policies operate and are interpreted in this
dynamic and unique society. The 2 phrases *"Gyo-yuk-yul-bung"* (education
fever) and *"Si-hum-ji-ok"* (exam hell), which portray the current schooling of
South Korean young adolescents, are examined. By focusing on these social
phenomena, this chapter addresses how young adolescent students in South
Korea are forced into the role of passive learners under the current educational systems and policies.

An International Look at Educating Young Adolescents
pp. 115–133
Copyright © 2009 by Information Age Publishing
All rights of reproduction in any form reserved.

CONTEXTUAL NARRATIVE

Education has always been one of the most heated discussion topics in the Republic of Korea. The characteristics of South Korean education are well represented by this quote: "No nation has a higher degree of enthusiasm for education than Korea, and nowhere are children under more pressure to study" (Diem, Levy, & VanSickle, 1997, p. 87). *"Gyo-yuk-yul-bung"* (education fever) and *"Si-hum-ji-ok"* (exam hell) are the phrases that reflect the current Korean schooling that young adolescents experience. Academic elitism has been prevalent in the South Korean society and entering prestigious colleges has become an end goal of education for many students. Proof of educational accomplishments such as diplomas from first-rate universities greatly affects a person's acceptability in employment, marriage, and even interpersonal relations. Many researchers view these social phenomena as needing to be examined through the lens of Confucianism (Seth, 2002), which places a value on education and deeply influences the way that the Korean people think and interact.

The Republic of Korea's high zeal for education is often regarded as a positive feature—a driving force of its remarkable economic growth (Lim, 2007). By developing human resources through formal education (Morris, 1996), South Korea accomplished an economic "miracle" in a half century. From 1962 to 2007, the nation's gross domestic product (GDP) increased from U.S.$2.3 billion to U.S.$969.9 billion, with its gross national income (GNI) per capita soaring from U.S.$87 to about U.S.$20,045 (Korean Culture and Information Service, 2008). Today, South Korea's major products are related to information and technology (IT), which include computer chips and mobile phones produced by the companies such as Samsung and LG. Those products are over 30% of the nation's total exports. Almost every South Korean over the age of 12 owns one mobile phone (Korean Culture and Information Service, 2008). Moreover, nearly every house has Internet service and every other household has broadband connection.

After the Korean War (1950-1953), the major interest and concern in the Republic of Korea was economic development. Education and human resources development have been regarded as the highest priority to accomplish this goal. The fact that South Korea has a lack of natural resources prompted the nation to be more dependent on human resources. Since its first Five-Year Plan for Economic and Social development after the Korean War, the Korean government has consistently focused on the development of scientific and technical manpower. The cultivation of these human resources served as the strongest driving force for the nation's economic development. To date, the government's emphasis on gifted children programs in the field of science and math has been continuous toward the goal to be one of the strongest IT societies in the world.

With its quantitative expansion in the 1960s and 1970s and its qualitative expansion in the 1980s, the Korean government has changed its major educational policy seven times to improve the curriculum and to reform the educational system (Ministry of Education and Human Resources Development [MOE], 2006a). Currently, 16.5% of the Korean government spending goes to education, which is almost three times more than that of the United States (United Nations Educational, Scientific and Cultural Organization, 2006). In spite of the Korean government's investments and efforts on education, the educational system seems to have failed to satisfy Korean parents and simply increased concerns for their children's education (Y. H. Kim, 1999). Many parents do not depend only on public education and spend lots of money for their children's tutoring outside of school. This phenomenon is culturally grounded: The more you study, the better you do. It is common that many youngsters, including primary school students, receive lessons in their content areas for a few hours a day from private tutoring institutions.

Furthermore, many parents who feel that their children might not be able to succeed in entering esteemed colleges tend to send their young children to other countries to avoid the fierce competition at home (MOE, 2006a). They also send their children to other English-speaking countries to have them learn the English language, which is regarded as a critical instrumental skill for their children's college entrance and employment in the future. According to the report by MOE (2006b), the number of students leaving South Korea to study abroad increased from 4,397 in 2000 to 16,446 in 2004. This trend may continue until public education meets the needs of the Korean parents who have great aspirations for their children's educational success.

As discussed above, South Korean education is currently characterized by very complicated dynamics, which are intertwined with historical, cultural, and social contexts. These educational phenomena are rarely found in other countries (Lim, 2007). In this respect, it would be limiting to discuss the Korean education system by excluding these unique and complex contexts. As a person who grew up for a few decades in South Korea, raised two children both in the home country and in the United States, and taught Korean middle school students, this general picture of the dynamics plays a vital role in understanding the schooling for young adolescents in South Korea.

HISTORY AND ORGANIZATION OF
SCHOOLING FOR YOUNG ADOLESCENTS

Historical Background

Today South Korea has one of the highest literacy rates in the world (Korean Culture and Information Service, 2008). Formal education in Korea started during the Three Kingdoms' period between 57 B.C. and A.D. 668. During this period, ethics education was emphasized in order to cultivate the morals of students based on Confucianism and Buddhism. From the late seventeenth century, there was a strong movement for modernization in South Korea. In the nineteenth century, modern schools were first introduced through Christian missionaries from Western countries, including the United States. During this era, the Western missionaries founded several private schools across the nation.

More systematic public education was established in the beginning of the 1950s after the liberation from 35-year Japanese colonial occupation. In order to lay the foundation for democratic education, the South Korean education policies for young adolescents focused on the reform of the school system and the implementation of compulsory education. The reformed school system which was put into practice in 1951 was a 6-3-3-4 pattern: 6 years of elementary school (Grades 1 through 6), 3 years of middle school (Grades 7 through 9), 3 years of high school (Grades 10 through 12), and 4 years of college. The current Korean schools still follow this single-track system.

Although compulsory education for primary schools was implemented in 1945, it began in 1985 for middle schools (Grades 7 through 9). By 2004, middle school compulsory education started from remote island areas and expanded to all cities. Before 1974, elementary school graduates had to take an entrance examination to advance to middle schools. However, in the beginning of 1974, the entrance examination was abolished to relieve students' examination pressures and to lower the achievement gap between schools. Candidates whose residence is in a cluster are assigned to one of the middle schools in the area.

The number of middle school students increased rapidly in a few decades. The percentage of primary school graduates progressing to middle school for Grades 7 through 9 increased from 58.4% in 1969 to 99.9% in 1997. There were about 1,600 middle schools and 13,000 students in the 1970s. As of 2005, there are approximately 3,000 middle schools and 2 million middle grades students in South Korea (Korea Educational Development Institute [KEDI], 2005).

Curriculum, Instruction, and Assessment Practices

The school curriculum is designed by the ideal of *"Hongik-ingan"* (contributing to the overall benefit of mankind), which was the foundation spirit of the first Korean kingdom. The objectives of South Korean education are to assist all people to develop their individual character, to develop the ability to achieve in independent life, to acquire the qualifications of democratic citizens, to be able to participate in the construction of a democratic state, and to promote the prosperity of all humankind (KEDI, 2008).

The middle school curriculum is guided by the general framework of education as follows: (a) design the curriculum to help the students acquire basic abilities which will enable them to lead the trends of social change; (b) introduce a system of national common basic curriculum and elective-centered curriculum; (c) optimize the volume and level of the content of learning and introduce the differentiated curriculum so as to provide students with in-depth education; (d) diversify the contents of the curriculum and methods of instruction in consideration of each student's ability, aptitude, and career choice; (e) broaden the autonomy of individual schools in organizing and implementing their own curriculum; and (f) reinforce the quality control of education by establishing a curriculum evaluation system. This curriculum is designed to accomplish the goals of middle school education that the South Korean government pursues which focuses on developing well-rounded citizens (KEDI, 2008).

South Korea has a national curriculum, which is developed and standardized by the Ministry of Education and Human Resources Development (MOE). All the textbooks are guided by the national curriculum and there are three different types: *"il-jong"* (Type one), those which copyrights are held by the MOE; *"e-jong"* (Type two), those which are authorized by the MOE and published by private publishers; and *"sam-jong"* (Type three), those which are recognized by the MOE as relevant and useful. The national curricula underwent many revisions since its first implementation in the 1980s. The Seventh Curriculum, which was introduced on December 30, 1997, is currently in practice. According to the MOE, unlike the curricula of the past, the Seventh Curriculum is a student-oriented curriculum emphasizing individual talent, aptitude, and creativity. However, the curriculum has been criticized since it has been operated with rigid restrictions and uniform control, and has not been responsive to the diverse needs of local schools and students (Y. H. Kim, 1999).

The curriculum in middle schools is similar across the nation. It consists of 10 required subjects, optional activities, and extracurricular activities. The required subjects are: Korean language arts, moral education, social studies, mathematics, science, practical arts, physical education, music, fine arts, and English as a foreign language. Among others, Korean language arts, English, mathematics, science, and social studies are generally considered to be the most important subjects. This emphasis can be identified through the hours that the students are required to take. Optional activities are divided into elective subject matter activities and creative elective activities. Extracurricular activities consist of student government activities, adaptive activities, self-development activities, social-service activities, and event activities. For middle schools, the total class hours are 1,156 during the 34 weeks that constitute a school year (see the specific hours on each subject and each grade in Appendix A).

Although it varies based on their subject content area, most South Korean teachers' instructional practices are lectures. Teacher-centered teaching that focuses on rote learning and memorization is evident throughout the classrooms (J. C. Kim, 1985; McGuire, 2007; Organization for Economic Cooperation and Development [OECD], 1998). Teachers are viewed as authority figures that possess knowledge. Teachers usually "talk" and students listen in the classroom. Students are rarely provided with the opportunities to develop their critical thinking ability, creativity, or aesthetic sensitivity. They focus on drills and on the content areas, which are included in the college entrance examinations (Y. H. Kim, 1999). Extracurricular activities are usually ignored. Students who are successful at core subjects such as English, math, or science are more respected than those who are talented at arts or athletics.

The major assessment instrument of students' academic performance is a test on each subject. Most of the tests, which typically consist of multiple choice items, require students' memorization skills. This assessment tool is based more on product, rather than process. At the end of each semester, the test results are recorded on each student's school transcript. Each student's rank standing is indicated for each subject area on the transcript. Letter grades are given to the middle school students based on the percentage group in which they fall (MOE, 2007). For example, "Soo" for 90% and higher, "Woo" for 80-89%. "Mi" for 70-79%, "Yang" for 60 - 69%, and "Ka" for lower than 60%. These letter grades are similar to the United States's grading system A, B, C, D, and F. There is no failing grade, so all of the middle school students can advance to high schools as long as they meet the minimum attendance requirements. See the standard middle school transcripts form in Appendix B.

Organization and Structure

The South Korean education system has been organized and operated with strict restrictions and uniform control (Y. H. Kim, 1999). The Ministry of Education and Human Resources Development administers the system. Before 2001, it was named the Ministry of Education. However, to reflect the importance of human resource development, it was renamed and its head was elevated to the level of a deputy prime ministerial office on January 29, 2001. The ministry is the government body which is responsible for the creation and implementation of educational policies related to public education including middle schools. The MOE publishes and approves all of the textbooks for elementary, middle, and high schools. Schools do not have much choice to select the materials.

The ministry administers each district, which supports each school within the district. Regardless of its size, most of middle schools have one "Kyo-jang" (school principal) and one "Kyo-gam" (vice-principal) as administrators. Under the public school system, these administrators do not have authority to hire or fire teachers. The education department in each "Do"—similar to a state in the United States—is in charge of this. Candidates undergo extremely competitive and rigorous screening procedures to be teachers in Korea. They first have to pass the entrance examination for teacher education programs. Upon completion of the programs, they obtain a teaching license which allows them to work in private schools. To obtain a teaching job in the public schools, which guarantees tenure, prospective teachers take another competitive test, the National Teacher Employment Test (NTET). After they are hired for middle school teaching, teachers work with students 570 hours per year, organized into three to four class periods per day. The ratio of teachers to middle school students is 1 to 20.8. The average number of the students in one classroom is 36, which is larger than that of the United States (24.9) and many other countries (13.7) (OECD, 2007).

A typical school day starts from 8:30 A.M. and finishes at 3:30 P.M. Every morning "Dan-im" (the homeroom teacher) comes into the students' classroom, checks their attendance, and documents it. Students have their own classrooms and they do not change rooms during the academic year. That is, the students who are randomly assigned to a certain classroom have the same classmates throughout the year. These young adolescents usually have six to seven 45-minute class periods each day. The students stay in the classroom while subject teachers move from classroom to classroom to teach.

According to school calendars, Korean middle school students go to school no less than 220 days. The school semester starts in March and ends in February. The first semester starts in March and ends in August while the second semester spans from the beginning of September to the end of February. There are summer and winter breaks between these semesters. Summer break extends from the middle of July to the end of

August. Winter break is longer than summer break, which begins from the end of December and finishes at the end of February.

OUTCOMES OF THE SCHOOLING OF YOUNG ADOLESCENTS

Academic Performance Outcomes

The results based on the data from both the 2003 Programme for International Student Assessment (PISA) by Organization for Economic Cooperation and Development (OECD) and the 2003 Trends in International Mathematics and Science Study (TIMSS) suggest that South Korean middle school students excel in many academic fields. For example, the PISA data show that the students achieved the highest ranking in problem solving skills, the second highest in reading skills, the third in the mathematics skills, and the fourth in science, among the 41 participating countries. Among the top 5% of the students, South Korea ranked third, seventh, third, and second, respectively, in the areas of problem solving, reading, mathematics, and science. The 2003 PISA results show that Korean male students outperform female students in all content areas, but the gender gap has been gradually narrowing. In addition, the 2003 TIMSS data also confirm the South Korean students' outstanding academic performances. They ranked second in both mathematics and science among 46 countries.

Although the international data show that South Korean middle students' academic performance is outstanding, their motivation to study is very low. The international data show that the students' academic performance is not related to the degree of their motivation. Among the 41 participating countries, South Korea ranked the 31st in the section of the "Interest in Mathematics." Moreover, their anxiety in mathematics is very high compared to the students in other countries. South Korea ranked the 39th in the "Motivation for Learning" section, which is almost the lowest among the participating countries. This result also provides evidence that South Korean students' performance is not associated with the level of anxiety.

Other Important Outcomes

Due to the heavy focus on academic performance outcomes, the social and emotional development of young adolescents has not been considered as important in the South Korean society. The students who excel in academic content areas such as math, science, and English are usually recognized as outstanding students by their peers, teachers, and parents. No matter how artistic and athletic the students are and how good personalities and social skills they have, it is difficult for them to be recognized as excellent students if the students do not perform well in those academic areas. It appears that society's main emphasis on academic performance outcomes takes away the opportunities for the students' social and emotional development.

Research Supporting Academic Performance and Other Outcomes

There are many different perspectives on the Korean students' high academic performances, which were identified through the international data, TIMSS and the PISA. First, KEDI, which is administered by the MOE, claims that the middle school students' outstanding performance is related to educational policies. It summarizes that the key factor is the continuous implementation of innovative educational policies, introduced in the Educational Reform Plan in 1995, which emphasize students' creativity. The KEDI also claims that the Korean government's continuous efforts on the improvement of classroom conditions ensure the students' remarkable performance.

Another point is that the students' excellent performance is associated with the teacher workforce in South Korea. Akiba, LeTendre, and Scribner (2007) noted that the outstanding achievements by the students are based on the teachers' high quality. They argued that, in the Republic of Korea, there are more qualified teachers compared to other countries. For instance, the TIMSS data show that only 4.8% of teachers taught mathematics without a specialization in mathematics compared to the percentage of the United States (29. 7%).

Although Kang and Hong (2008) concurred with these arguments by Akiba et al. (2007), which focused on the teachers' quality, they added another significant factor related to the students' remarkable performance—the extra number of hours that the students spend on their learning. For example, approximately 75% of South Korean middle school students received tutoring from private institutions in 2003. Their total afterschool time with regard to math is 4.6 hours per week, which is three times more than the average hours of other OECD countries including the United States (1.5 hours per week).

As presented above, the different views provide us with multiple factors relating to the South Korean middle school students' academic success. However, it does not seem to be sufficient unless it explains the discrepancy between the students' high performance and their low motivation. It is a commonly accepted view that students' performance is correlated to their motivation—the stronger the motivation, the higher the performance. However, this point does not seem to apply to the South Korean students. As shown in the PISA data, the middle school students' motivation is quite low, but they have performed well. To help us better understand the complexities of the South Korean students' academic performance, this remaining issue needs to be explored in-depth.

CURRENT ISSUES RELATED TO THE
SCHOOLING OF YOUNG ADOLESCENTS

Concerns About the Current Educational System

There are several major concerns about the current educational system. First, college entrance examination is a critical issue. The structure of Korean education facilitates boundless competitions toward the goal of entering prestigious colleges. Even middle school education has fallen into functioning as simple preparatory courses for the examination. It is commonly known that middle grades students go directly to their private tutoring institutions right after school to prepare themselves for the rigorous college entrance examination. The students are frequently enrolled in English and mathematics at the afterschool tutoring institutions. Since the college entrance examination is based on the national curriculum, most of the tutoring instructions focus on the preview or the review of the content of the school curriculum. The students who do not go to a private tutoring institution take lessons at home from the private tutor who visits a student's house once or twice a week for 1 or 2 hours per lesson.

Predictably, students are physically and mentally overstrained with the amount of work they have to complete. They have to finish their school assignments everyday and private tutoring homework as well. Although the South Korean government proclaims that it works for the genuine education goals focusing on the development of well-rounded individuals, it may not be able to accomplish the goals under this situation that the students face. As Lim (2007) pointed out, "Public education is now such in name only" (p. 83).

Second, parents suffer from the heavy burden of expenses they must pay for their children's private tutoring. The cost varies from 100,000 won (U.S.$100) to 1,000,000 won (U.S.$1,000) and even more per subject per month. According to the report by the MOE (2006b), the total private education spending in 2003 was approximately 13 trillion won (U.S.$13 billion). High-income households spend approximately seven times more than low-income families. Furthermore, home tutoring costs more than private tutoring at institutions. Given that Korean's GNI per capita is about $20,000 (Korean Culture and Information Service, 2008), the expenses are a burden to most of the Korean parents who have two children. However, this burden does not seem to hinder the parents' desire to provide their children with the best educational opportunities. Korean parents are willing to sacrifice their personal lives for their children and work extra to earn money for *"kwa-wae-bi"* (tutoring fee). Some housewives work as housemaids to pay high tuition fees for their children (Lim, 2007).

Third, there is a huge discrepancy between the school curriculum and the current teaching practices in the classroom. The MOE (2006b) ensures that the ultimate goal of the curriculum is to cultivate creative human resources who will lead the new society. It also ensures that the current curriculum focuses on learner-centered education to meet students' various needs. However, researchers view that there is little room to promote students' critical and creative thinking under the structure of Korean education (McGuire, 2007; Seth, 2002). For decades, Korean education has been criticized due to its excessive emphasis on memorization of isolated information (OECD, 1998). One of the critical weaknesses of the system is "its over-reliance on teacher-centered instructional methodologies involving rote-memorization" (McGuire, 2007, p. 230). In spite of the MOE's efforts, the majority of the classroom instructions focus on the transmission of knowledge, rather than the creation of knowledge. Seth (2002) argued that the entire educational system is driven by the college entrance exam and the South Korean students are mainly prepared for multiple-choice exams.

Finally, "English education fever" is another issue in the South Korean society. In curriculum, English is the only required foreign language and is considered as one of the most important subjects. Following the new revised curriculum by the MOE, the current emphasis on English education and its focus on speaking and listening skills reveal many educational and social issues. There are many English teachers who do not feel competent to teach these new skills. They are more familiar with grammar-translation methods based on decoding skills. South Korean parents, who are unsure about this current English education system, tend to send their children to other English-speaking countries such as the United States, Canada, New Zealand, and Australia. In addition, the emphasis on English education results in this unique social phenomenon: *"ki-ru-ki-a-ppa"* [a wild goose]. This symbolizes a father who lives in Korea to financially support his wife and children who stay in other countries and sees them only once or twice a year.

Benefits of the Current Educational System

The MOE's continuous investment and development of educational technology contributed to the equal access to many students for their learning opportunities. With the establishment of infrastructure for digitalization, students could learn computer literacy for 1 hour per week. Since 2002, all schools across the country are provided high-speed Internet services. Cyber home-schooling programs help students from remote areas and low-income families obtain access to learning opportunities. In addition, as a means of reducing high private tutoring costs, the MOE is making good use of e-learning system. The MOE conducts online lectures through the public Educational Broadcasting System (EBS).

In sum, the relevant literature indicates that the current issues outnumber the benefits of the educational system in South Korea. The government has been developing many strategies to solve the issues by continuously revising its national policies. In the next section, the government's reform initiatives and national policies will be discussed in detail.

REFORM INITIATIVES AND NATIONAL POLICIES

The South Korean government has changed its national policies several times, every 5 to 6 years since the 1980s. These policy changes reflect the government's attempts to respond to the society's high demands on education. The major reform initiatives and national policies for middle schools that MOE (2006a) provides are as follows.

First, to keep abreast of society's fast change, the curriculum policy is to be changed to an "on-demand" system. That is, whenever there is a call, school curriculum will be revised. The Ministry believes that this helps deliver "new" knowledge to students. For middle school textbooks, the ministry plans to change from the current government-publishing system to a government-appraisal system. In other words, private publishers produce textbooks and the government gives official approval after close examination. By doing this, schools are given more autonomy and a wider choice of textbooks.

Second, the 5-day school week system was introduced. Since 2006, middle school students have taken off every other Saturday. Before 2006, all of the middle school students, including elementary and high school students, had to go to school every Saturday, staying until noon or 1 P.M. One of the major purposes of this new system is to provide the students with more social learning opportunities by interacting with their parents, siblings, and peers.

Third, the new afterschool program was introduced in order to alleviate the parents' heavy financial burden due to their children's private tutoring fees. One of the main goals for this program is to provide learning opportunities to the students from low-income families. Since 2006, classroom teachers, preservice teachers, and volunteers work after school to provide students with various learning programs including arts, sports, English, and other regular subjects. Surveys, which were conducted by the MOE, show that 29% of middle school students turned away from private education institutes due to this afterschool program.

Fourth, the Ministry plans to focus more on teacher education. The process of teacher selection, training, and evaluation will be reformed. Stricter criteria will be applied to teacher selection, and professional development programs will be more tailored to teachers' needs. A new teacher evaluation system will be introduced, and it has three major features: (a) the principal and vice principal will be evaluated. In the past, the principal evaluated teachers and utilized the evaluation results for their promotion; (b) students, parents, and peers will evaluate teachers on their teaching practices; and, (c) teachers will make use of the evaluation results to improve their class instruction.

In this society, where Confucian tradition is deep-rooted and people have a high respect for the teaching profession, this new evaluation system is shocking to many people. It is unclear at this point whether this system will be implemented. Survey results indicate that South Korean teacher unions disagree with this system, but most parents are in favor of the system.

Finally, the school curriculum is revised to prepare for the "knowledge era" of the twenty-first century and to meet students' individual needs based on their ability. Education on information and communication technology (ICT) will be strengthened and educational ICT usage is to comprise at least 10% of the teaching in each subject. "Step-by-Step" curriculum will be applied to the core subjects of mathematics and English language arts. Mathematics will be taught with a curriculum, which is divided into 20 different levels for middle school students, along with primary school students. The new English curriculum is divided into eight levels to meet the students' different needs.

RESEARCH

Current Research Topics

The educational systems and policies are major research topics in South Korea. The study by K. S. Kim et al. (2005), which analyzed the educational trends of four different countries (South Korea, Japan, the United States, and the United Kingdom), suggested that Korean scholars explore these topics. Compared to the United States, which focuses on research on academic achievement, South Korea's focus on these educational systems and policies reflect the current issues that Korean education faces.

In South Korea, the research topics regarding middle school students are so broad that it is hard to define what research has been conducted. The general topics include the comprehensive middle school evaluation system, the policy on gifted and talented education, and the current middle school students' schooling issues. It appears that the outcomes of the implementation of certain educational systems and policies are major focuses. For example, the effect of the policy "five school days a week" (Monday through Friday, rather than Saturday) on the students' academic outcomes, or the influence of the "English Immersion" policy on the students' English proficiency, have been the important topics. As we can see from these examples, the research topics are not as specific as those in the United States which cover more detailed topics such as "reader response" in the literacy field.

The Korean Educational Development Institute, a quasi-governmental think tank, plays a major role in conducting researches in South Korea. About 50% of its budget comes from the preset government funds (M. Kim, 2006). Sometimes, KEDI conducts research by having a partnership with university research institutions. It is not common that individual scholars, professors, or teachers go to the field for their empirical studies. The data are often collected nationwide or districtwide by using survey or questionnaire research methods.

Methodologies

The extensive review of current major educational journals including *Journal of Educational Policy* in South Korea suggests that various research methodologies including qualitative, quantitative, and mixed methods are used. However, the quantitative method is the most commonly used. More than 70% of studies were conducted using this method. Research in the field of mathematics, science, and English education with the topics of gifted and talented programs and policies are often published in the current educational research journals. These research topics show the emphasis on those academic fields.

Among the traditions of quantitative method, survey or questionnaire is a major instrument to explore the issues of educational systems and policies. The history of qualitative research in South Korea is relatively short. Before 1990s, the qualitative methods were virtually absent in South Korea due to the lack of the human resources to teach this approach to research. However, as the Korean people who studied in western countries such as the United States began to use this method for their empirical studies in their home country, qualitative methods became recognized in the educational field. In addition, mixed method designs are new to most Korean researchers and it is very rare to use this method in South Korea. Again, this is mainly due to the lack of teacher educators and researchers who have a deep understanding of this method and who teach students in their graduate programs.

Critics view that Korean educational phenomena need to be examined through various methodological approaches rather than focusing only on one approach (Chung, 2002). That is, more diverse research methods including qualitative and mixed methods are essential to discuss the complex issues of Korean education as well as to gain insights from the issues.

Important Research Findings

There are several important research findings which depict the current picture of middle school students in South Korea. These studies were mostly conducted by survey or questionnaire. For example, the study by M. Kim, Cho, Yoon, and Jin (2004) suggested that the students are not happy with their school life in general. The phenomena of increased drop out (13.6%), class avoidance (8.8%), and interference with other learners (11.3%) (Lee at al., 2001) indicate that students suffer from the current classroom setting which consists of the lack of autonomy, and ineffective and test-driven teaching methods (M. Kim, 2003).

The other interesting finding is from the study by Y. B. Kim and Namgung (2007), which suggests that the achievement gap between schools is different according to different subjects. For instance, the variation of academic achievement among the schools in urban, suburban, and rural areas was 5.5% in Korean language arts, 10.0% in math, and 12.3% in English language arts. It shows that the academic achievement gap in English is higher than that of Korean and math. The study also indicates that the students who are in the schools which are located in more affluent areas (small- and medium-sized cities) achieve better than those who are in rural or suburban areas.

FUTURE DIRECTIONS

The reports by MOE (2006b) and KEDI (2008) well document the possible future directions in the education of young adolescents in South Korea. These directions are particularly shown through the current national policies. The government of the Republic of Korea will propel all the educational systems to prepare students for the twenty-first century, the era of globalization and knowledge-based society. *"Se-ke-wha"* (globalization movement), *"Ji-sik-jung-bo-wha"* (knowledge-information movement) *"Kuk-je-wha"* (internationalization movement) are commonly heard in the Korean society. The South Korean government seems to focus on the movement *forward* to the "new world." That is, it focuses more on the *future*.

Along with these movements, the key points of the current educational policies are to develop students who seek individuality and exhibit creativity. By employing a student-oriented curriculum, which emphasizes individual talent, aptitude, and creativity, the government seeks to accomplish educational success for all students. For this purpose, the gifted programs which for the students who show strong potential in the field of science, math, and foreign language (English, in particular) will be more emphasized. Special high schools for these students are being operated across the nation. It is widely known in Korean society that students have a better chance to enter prestigious universities, if they study at one of these schools. Since students are selected through rigorous screening procedures including written tests and interviews, fierce competition among potential students is evident.

CONCLUDING DISCUSSION

South Korea's national curricula and policies on students' individuality and creativity seem to speak for themselves. The close link to classroom practices is missing. Researchers, along with classroom teachers, parents, and students are skeptical about the government's educational approach. In the classroom where students are instructed to select only "right" answers for the preparation of the college entrance examination, there is little room to meet the students' different needs and to develop their creativity. As long as the social phenomena of the "education fever" and college entrance "exam hell" continue, it would be impossible to achieve the eventual goal of education. It appears that these social features guide the Korean education, rather than the national curriculum and policies.

In conclusion, based on the relevant literature and my experiential knowledge, the issues that the Korean society encounter are not within the educational system itself, but how these issues are interpreted and operated under the complex historical, cultural, and social contexts. South Korean's education fever cannot be evaluated as positive or negative without closely looking at these contexts. As education itself is a complicated multifaceted concept, so is Korean education. Along with the reform of the educational systems and policies, South Korea's social issues need to be explored through diverse research methodologies for the benefits of all students.

APPENDIX A: CLASS HOURS BY SUBJECT AND GRADE LEVEL

Column groups: grades 1–6 = Elementary School; grades 7–9 = Middle School; grades 10–12 = High School.

Subjects \ Grades	1	2	3	4	5	6	7	8	9	10	11	12
Korean Language	Korean Lang. 210	238	238	204	204	204	170	136	136	136	Elective	Courses
Moral Education			34	34	34	34	68	68	34	34		
Social Studies	Mathematics 120	136	102	102	102	102	102	102	136	170 (Korean History 68)		
Mathematics	Disciplined Life 60	68	136	136	136	136	136	136	102	136		
Science	Intelligent Life 90	102	102	102	102	102	102	136	136	102		
Practical Arts					68	68	68	102 (Technology / Home Economics)	102	102		
Physical Education			102	102	102	102	102	102	68	68		
Music	Pleasant Life 180	204	68	68	68	68	68	34	34	34		
Fine Arts			68	68	68	68	34	34	68	34		
Foreign Languages (English)	We are the first graders 80		34	34	68	68	102	102	136	136		
Optional Activities	60	68	68	68	68	68	136	136	136	204		
Extracurricular Activities	30	34	34	68	68	68	68	68	68	68	8 units	
Total Hours	830	850	986	986	1088	1088	1156	1156	1156	1224	144 units	

Source: Ministry of Education and Human Resources Development (2006a).
Note: Based on 34 school weeks a year.

APPENDIX B: MIDDLE SCHOOL TRANSCRIPT FORM

Subject	Grade	Rank standing (number of students who are placed in the same rank) / total number of students enrolled in the subject	Grade	Rank standing (number of students who are placed in the same rank) / total number of students enrolled in the subject	Note

Source: Ministry of Education and Human Resources Development (2006a).

REFERENCES

Akiba, M., LeTendre, G. K., & Scribner, J. P. (2007). Teacher quality, opportunity gap, and national achievement in 46 countries. *Educational Researcher, 36,* 369-387.

Chung, K. C. (2002). *Han-kuk-kyo-yook-hak-eu yun-gu-bang-bub-ron soo-yong-kwa kwa-je* [The Issue of Educational Methodologies in Korea]. Youngnam, Korea: Author.

Diem, R., Levy, T., & VanSickle, R. (1997). Korean education: Focusing on the future. *Social Education, 61*(2), 83-87.

Kang, N. H., & Hong, M. (2008). Achieving excellence in teacher workforce and equity in learning opportunities in South Korea. *Educational Researcher, 37*(4), 200-207.

Kim, J. C. (1985). *Education and development: Some essays and thoughts on Korean Education.* Seoul, Korea: Seoul National University Press.

Kim, M. (2003). Teaching and learning in Korean classrooms: The crisis and the new approach. *Asia Pacific Education Review, 4*(2), 140-141.

Kim, M. (2006). *Educational research at KEDI and its relations to policy and practice in Korea.* Seoul: Korean Educational Development Institute.

Kim, M., Cho, S., Yoon, C., & Jin, S. (2004). *Cognitive and affective characteristics of and teaching strategies for the Korean junior high school gifted students* (Research Report CR 2004-40). Seoul: Korean Educational Development Institute.

Kim, Y. B., & Namgung, J. (2007). *The study on the level and status of the quality of school education (in high, middle, and elementary schools)* (Research Report RR 2007-21). Seoul: Korean Educational Development Institute.

Kim, Y. H. (1999). Recent developments in Korean school education. *School Effectiveness and School Improvement, 10*(1), 55-71.

Kim, K. S., Kwon, M. S., Kim, B. G., Park, H. J., Song, S. M, & Hwang, J. H. (2005). Kyo-yuk-sa-hoe-hak-oi dong-hyang-bun-suk [The research trend analysis of sociology of education]. *Secondary Educational Research, 53*(3), 89-114.

Korea Educational Development Institute. (2005). *Brief statistics on Korean education*. Retrieved June 30, 2008, from http://eng.kedi.re.kr/

Korea Educational Development Institute. (2008). *Education in Korea 2007-2008*. Retrieved July 14, 2008, from http://eng.kedi.re.kr/

Korean Culture and Information Service. (2008). *Facts and figures*. Retrieved July 13, 2008, from http://korea.net

Lee, C. J., Lee, Y. M., Kang, T. J., Kim, S. Y., Baik, S. K., Lee, C. Y., et al. (2001). *Current situation of school education and some strategies for improvement* (Research Report CR 2001-32). Seoul: Korean Educational Development Institute.

Lim, H. (2007, Summer). A religious analysis of education fever in modern Korea. *Korea Journal*, 71-98.

McGuire, J. M. (2007). Why has the critical thinking movement not come to Korea? *Asia Pacific Education Review, 8*(2), 224-232.

Ministry of Education and Human Resources Development. (2006a). *Education in Korea 2005-2006*. Seoul, Korea: Author.

Ministry of Education and Human Resources Development. (2006b). *Korean educational policies and current issues*. Paper presented at 2006 AEF professional development workshop, Chungbuk, Korea: Author. Retrieved June 20, 2008, from http://english.mest.go.kr

Ministry of Education and Human Resources Development. (2007). *Korea's secondary school grading system*. Seoul, Korea: Author.

Morris, P. (1996). Asia's four little tigers: A comparison of the role of education in their development. *Comparative Education, 32*, 95-109.

Organization for Economic Cooperation and Development. (1998). *Reviews of national policies for education*. Paris: Author.

Organization for Economic Cooperation and Development. (2007). *Education at a glance, 2007: OECD indicators*. Paris: Author.

Seth, M. J. (2002). *Education fever: Society, politics, and the pursuit of schooling in South Korea*. Honolulu: University of Hawaii Press.

United Nations Educational, Scientific and Cultural Organization. (2006). *UIS Statistics in brief: Education in Republic of Korea*. Retrieved July 2, 2008, from http://stats.uis.unesco.org

CHAPTER 7

MIDDLE SCHOOLING
IN NEW ZEALAND

Tony Dowden, Penny Bishop, and C. J. Patrick Nolan

Schooling for young adolescents in New Zealand (NZ) is problematic. Although NZ education has an enviable international reputation, the bipartite primary-secondary system has responded poorly to many young people who struggle to negotiate the transition between the 2 types of schooling. In this chapter we discuss the emergence of an indigenous middle schooling movement in NZ. We trace the history of middle level schooling from the first middle school in 1894, to a dalliance with a junior high school model in the 1920s, to the founding of the ubiquitous "intermediate" school in the 1930s and, recently, the development of a handful of middle schools in the 1990s. We then evaluate current research and practice pertaining to middle level schooling in NZ. In particular we focus on current indictments on middle level schooling and recent reform efforts. We conclude by suggesting future directions for the education of young adolescents in NZ.

CONTEXTUAL NARRATIVE

The bipartite primary-secondary school system of England, which British colonists brought to New Zealand (NZ) in the mid-1800s, has shaped the nature and structure of schooling in NZ to the present day. Consider-

An International Look at Educating Young Adolescents
pp. 135–156
Copyright © 2009 by Information Age Publishing
All rights of reproduction in any form reserved.

ations of physical geography, changing demographics, political economy and ethnicity have all modified the colonial system to produce schools adapted to NZ's distinctive landscape and South Pacific society.

NZ is a relatively stable social democracy whose social context has been shaped by a bicultural discourse between indigenous Maori and Pakeha (New Zealanders of European descent). Over the last 30 years, biculturalism has been cemented by the willingness of Maori and Pakeha to honor the Treaty of Waitangi, signed between the British crown and Maori tribes in 1840 to record the ceding of Maori land rights to the crown (King, 2003). English and Maori translations of the document were at variance, however, allowing multiple interpretations; ultimately leading to a process of reconciliation and reparation between Maori and Pakeha enshrined in legislation at the end of the twentieth century.

NZ, the first country in 1893 to adopt universal suffrage for men and women, also granted voting rights to Maori at the same time as Pakeha; in contrast, indigenous Aborigines in neighboring Australia gained the right to vote only as recently as 1967. It is noteworthy, too, that in the last 20 years women have filled almost every conceivable leadership role in NZ society. Notably, Helen Clark has been prime minister (the nation's political leader) for the last 9 years.

The colonists of the 1800s who brought British schooling to NZ also brought Christianity, which played a role shaping NZ's political and social institutions, including schools. While the state school system, which predominates, is secular, private and state-integrated church-aligned schools also exist alongside it. Today, religion plays a less dominant role in NZ culture, and in education, than the past. The wider trend is towards a lack of church affiliation, although the Christian heritage is still strong in Maori and Pasifika (people from South Pacific nations) communities.

The landscape in many ways defines NZ. One of the last and most remote landmasses to be inhabited, the two main islands—North Island and South Island—and several minor islands stretch over 2,000 kilometers in a north-south direction. Shaped by a meeting of two tectonic plates, the NZ landscape features sharply rising mountain ranges and alluvial plains in South Island, and volcanoes and other spectacular geothermal activity in North Island. The temperate, maritime climate with its plentiful rainfall gives rise to lush vegetation with verdant farmland and remnant rain forest harbouring ancient flora and fauna.

The NZ economy, dominated by agriculture, tourism and service industries, generates a GDP of about U.S.$125 billion. The workforce is 99% literate and relatively well educated. NZ has two official languages: English and Maori. According to Organization for Economic Cooperation and Development (OECD) figures in 2004, the NZ infant mortality rate was five out of 1,000 live births (OECD, 2008). In addition, the 2004

OECD figures for NZ life expectancy were 81 years for women and 77 years for men.

NZ has a relatively small population of 4.2 million people comprised of 67.6% NZ European, 14.6% Maori, 9.2% Asian, 6.9% Pasifika, and 1.7% other. NZ culture is becoming more multicultural, due to a steady flow of immigrants from the United Kingdom, the South Pacific, East Asia, and South Africa as well as refugees from South East Asia and Africa.

HISTORY AND ORGANIZATION OF SCHOOLING

Schooling in New Zealand starts at age 5 and is compulsory from age 6 to 16. The school structure is two-tiered: primary schooling (Years 1-8) and secondary schooling (Years 9-13). Young adolescents (Years 7-10) are distributed in various permutations of primary and secondary school type: full primary (Years 1-8); intermediate (Years 7-8); restricted composite (Years 7-10); composite (Years 1 to 13); and secondary (Years 9-13 and 7-13). As shown in Figures 7.1 and 7.2 (adapted from Durling, 2007), most Years 7-8 students (83%) are educated in full primary and intermediate schools while nearly all Years 9-10 students (95%) attend secondary schools.

Yet, the data depicted in Figures 7.1 and 7.2 do not fully reveal the extent of the pedagogical and cultural divide between primary and secondary schooling in NZ. Students in Years 7-8 are taught by primary teachers and almost all Years 9-10 students are taught by secondary teachers. The pri-

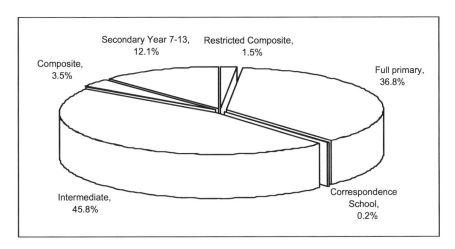

Figure 7.1.   Distribution of students in Years 7 and 8 by school type in 2006.

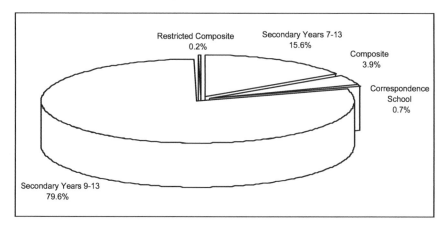

Figure 7.2.   Distribution of students in Years 9 and 10 by school type in 2006.

mary and secondary schooling division is further accentuated by the conflicting interests of the influential national teachers' unions: the secondary teachers' union, the Post Primary Teachers Association (PPTA) and the primary teachers' union, the New Zealand Educational Institute (NZEI).

Over the last century, schooling for young adolescents in NZ has been shaped by an awkward transition—plumb in the middle of young adolescence—between primary schooling (Years 1-8) and secondary schooling (Years 9-13), and a political struggle concerning the type of school structure in which these students should be accommodated and taught. Also traceable, but almost imperceptible outside official documents, is the development of an increasingly robust discourse concerning the educational and developmental needs of young adolescents in NZ.

Origins of the New Zealand Middle School

Advocates of middle schooling in NZ, such as the New Zealand Association for Intermediate and Middle Schooling (NZAIMS) and a few academics argue for a unique pedagogy in Years 7-10 (Nolan & Brown, 2002; Stewart & Nolan, 1992), yet they do so in a political context that has not historically recognized middle schooling as a distinct tier in the structure of NZ education.

Early Middle School Types

Philosophical differences and political rivalry has typified the debate concerning how to best educate young adolescents ever since the 1890s (Hinchco, 2004). Two acts of parliament, the 1877 Education Act and the

1877 Education Reserve Act, established primary and secondary schooling in NZ. The 1877 Acts remained the guide for national policy on schooling (Hinchco). This was despite the fact that as early as 1885, Minister of Education Robert Stout expressed concern about the "disjunction" between primary and secondary schooling (Watson, 1964); and in 1925 Frank Tate, director of education in Victoria, Australia noted the "general lack of articulation" between primary and secondary schooling in NZ (Butchers, 1932 cited in Hinchco). In between these criticisms, however, the establishment of Nelson Central School (Years 5-9) in 1894 at the top of South Island became the first NZ experiment with middle schooling. The experiment echoed the "central" school movement in England and Scotland. It provided primary schooling with access to early secondary specialization. The experiment did not spread beyond the Nelson district, however, and it finished in 1911 (Hinchco).

Nonetheless, from about the time of John Dewey's Laboratory School in Chicago at the turn of the twentieth century and especially during the first flush of the progressive "New Education" movement in the 1920s, NZ educators sought to establish middle schooling. Reciprocal visits between NZ and the United States by educational leaders catalyzed change. Frank Milner, a long-serving secondary school principal, and primary school principal Thomas Wells visited the United States. They were followed by Clarence Beeby—director of education (1940-1960)—who was the architect of major educational reform in NZ. The school practices the three observed in the United States, particularly the ideas advanced by Dewey and other progressives such as Abraham Flexner and Isaac Kandel, strongly influenced their thinking (Dowden, 2007a). In particular, all three articulated the notion that young adolescence is a unique developmental stage requiring a distinctive approach to middle level schooling.

The educational ferment of the 1920s saw an ambitious attempt to bring about structural change to the bipartite NZ school system with the introduction of junior high schools (Years 7-9 and Years 7-10). The junior high was based on the American model where exploration of subject areas and early specialization of subjects were intended to sit together. The first, Kowhai Junior High School (Years 7-9) opened in 1922. The others were attached to existing high schools as junior departments, thus Kowhai Junior High was the only stand-alone junior high school (Hinchco, 2004).

The Intermediate School

In 1932 the government changed the legislation and established the Years 7-8 "intermediate" school (Watson, 1964). With the exception of Kowhai Junior High, that continued to accept Year 9 students until 1957, the junior high experiment ended. Hinchco (2004) argued that junior high advocates failed to recognize that a forced marriage of (primary-oriented) exploration and (secondary-oriented) early specialization was always likely to lead to conflict. The 1932 decision was also influenced by the Great Depression which dictated a need for major cuts to the national budget. For instance, in a parallel austerity measure, the government excluded all 5-year-old children from state-run schools in 1932 (Alcorn, 1999).

The outcome of the effort to develop middle schooling in the 1920 and 1930s was, therefore, the establishment of the intermediate school (Stewart & Nolan, 1992). Intermediate schools soon assumed the child-centred primary school culture with a philosophy of subject exploration (Beeby, 1938; Stewart & Nolan, 1992; Watson, 1964). Since 1932, therefore, schooling in NZ has had two tiers: primary and secondary, with the intermediate school capping the final years of primary schooling.

Enrollments in intermediate schools peaked in 1976, with 72% of Years 7-8 students. Intermediates were subjected to a period of sustained criticism from the public in the late 1970s and 1980s (Hinchco, 2004). The intermediate school lost its predominance (Neville-Tisdall, 2002) and by 2006 only accounted for 46% of Year 7-8 students (Durling, 2007). The decline in popularity of intermediates, along with a lack of a clear middle schooling philosophy, provided the conditions for renewed attention to alternative school structures, including the stand-alone middle school.

Origins of a Philosophy for Middle Schooling in New Zealand

In 1938 Beeby appraised the new intermediate school for the New Zealand Council for Educational Research (NZCER). Steeped in the progressive ideas of Dewey and Kandel, Beeby laid out a philosophy for middle schooling in NZ. Beeby (1938) acknowledged that, as in primary schooling, an important function of intermediate schooling should be exploration; thus he promulgated what he called a "multi-track 'try-out' curriculum" (p. 50)—also used in junior high schools in the United States at the time—where students could sample several subjects. Beeby favored expanding the 2-year intermediate into a 4-year middle school. Citing the developmental needs of young adolescents, he stated that "the four-year intermediate is advocated on both psychological and administrative grounds ... the group from (age 11-15) is relatively homogenous emotionally and socially" (pp. 179-180). Beeby, therefore, envisioned a three-tiered schooling structure for NZ education. In the 1930s a 4-year middle school would have limited secondary schooling to a span of 1 or 2 years which, as Beeby realized, would have resulted in an untenable 6-4-2 year structure for primary-middle-high schooling.

Nonetheless, Beeby wished to secure the general education of all young New Zealanders, especially those without academic aspirations (Alcorn, 1999). Conversant with developments in the United States, Beeby adopted the progressive idea of "general education." Founded on Dewey's (1916) democratic education, the 1930s concept of general education was based on the notion of "common learnings ... essential for all mature citizens in a democratic society" (Vars, 2000, p. 71). Beeby realized that middle schooling had a crucial role to play in general education. Refining his position on the function of the intermediate, he stated that "the chief function of the intermediate school (is) to provide ... a period of expansive, realistic, and socially integrative education that will give all future citizens a common basis of experience and knowledge" (1938, p. 210). Beeby's position of national leadership enabled him to infuse other school types then extant—the Native (Maori) Schools, District High Schools, and Maori District High Schools—with the progressive spirit of the American junior high school. In particular, the integrated curriculum designs utilized in Maori schooling in the 1930s and 1940s were inspired by practice in the United States (Dowden & Nolan, 2007).

The Thomas Report on the secondary school curriculum (Department of Education, 1943) echoed Beeby's thinking. The Report featured an innovative common core curriculum designed to develop democratic citizenship in Years 9-11. In particular, the Thomas Report stated that it was "strongly in favor" of classroom approaches that would take "full account ... of the interests, experiences and relative immaturity" of young adolescents (p. 25).

OUTCOMES OF THE SCHOOLING OF YOUNG ADOLESCENTS

Educational Performance of Young Adolescents

Measures of educational performance of young adolescents in NZ paint a complex picture: at first glance it appears to be rosy but closer inspection reveals various problems and issues related to the two-tiered nature of NZ schooling.

Academic Measures of Achievement

On the surface, academic achievement of young adolescents in NZ appears to be steady and positive. NZ students perform well in international surveys of the OECD countries. In 2006, the Programme for International Student Assessment (PISA) ranked NZ 15-year-olds third in scientific literacy, fourth in reading literacy, and fifth in mathematical literacy. Similarly in the Trends in International Mathematics and Science Study (TIMSS), Year 9 students have been achieving at above the 46 country average since 2000 (Chamberlain, 2007). NZ educators and policy makers regularly collect data on student achievement and competencies. Within NZ, data from the National Education Monitoring Project (NEMP), which assesses Year 8 students in all their subjects on a rotating basis, and from the Assessment Tools for Teaching and Learning (asTTLe) which provides teachers with student, class, and school-specific data on literacy and numeracy, shows that "student achievement increases in all subject areas from primary to middle schooling (and) some of the largest gains in reading, writing, and mathematics achievement occur during the middle school years" (Durling, 2007, p. 4). In addition, Cox and Kennedy's (2008) research on student transitions into secondary schools showed that students' asTTLe test results revealed sound or good achievement gains in the middle years.

While the data on academic achievement offer largely good news, they do not provide for clear differentiation between Years 7-8 and Years 9-10 and may obscure a complete view of student outcomes in the middle years. Indeed, the middle years are no exception to the very wide spread of achievement between NZ's top and bottom students. The large gap between the low achievers and the rest, combined with the relatively large number of low achievers, causes this group to be referred to as "the long tail" (Education and Science Committee, 2008, p. 5). The long tail phenomenon is related to the disparity in achievement between Pakeha and Maori students. On a positive note, although Maori achievement in literacy and numeracy in English medium schools is still below average (Education Review Office, 2007), disparities between Maori and Pakeha students declined between 2002 and 2006. And recent achievement of Year 8 Maori students, in particular, has shown substantial improvement (Ministry of Education, 2007a).

Affective Measures

The current New Zealand Curriculum (NZC) states that schools have a key role helping students "develop the values, knowledge and competencies that will enable them to live full and satisfying lives" (Ministry of Education, 2007b, p. 8). Three of the NZC's five "key competencies" relate directly to socioemotional development: managing self; relating to others; and participating and contributing. The key competencies align with and support the NZAIMS advocacy for developmentally responsive schooling. Many NZAIMS member schools address students' socioemotional development directly; for example, they give equal emphasis to pastoral care and academic achievement. This emphasis fits with NZAIMS' strategic plan that teacher-student relationships are "not pre-empted by academic demands divorced from the students' social and emotional needs" (NZAIMS, 2006, p. 2). The plan invites schools to address explicitly "the needs and known challenges of students' growth and social development while in the middle years of schooling" (p. 9).

Although a majority of young adolescent learners achieve well in NZ schools, the degree to which all students feel engaged, empowered, and supported tells a different story. NZ attitudinal and engagement data from several sources (including NEMP, asTTLe, TIMSS, PISA, Youth2000, and NZCER Engagement Survey) show that many students' views of schooling turn negative in the middle years; and that a sizable minority become dissatisfied with school in Years 7-8 (Cox & Kennedy, 2008; Crooks, 2008; Durling, 2007). NEMP data show that, with the exceptions of technology and physical education, "between Year 4 and Year 8 quite a lot of students change from a very positive to a moderately positive view of school subjects, and a significant percentage move from moderately positive to moderately negative" (Crooks, p. 8).

Teachers of Years 7-8 students in NZ traditionally have believed that student engagement is linked to the quality of teacher-student relationships (Watson, 1964), yet contemporary research shows that student-teacher relationships in Years 7-10 often deteriorate substantially (Durling, 2007). Fewer young adolescents report that teachers help them to do their best, treat them fairly, praise them and listen to them. Students' perspectives on school work become equally negative, as they are unable to link their schooling with their futures. In addition, absenteeism, suspension, and exclusion from school are most common in Years 7-10, when behavioral and social problems often escalate. Similarly, the rapid increase of suspension rates starting at age 11 indicates loss of engagement (Durling).

The trends for Years 9-10 particularly are of interest because, here, the greatest decrease occurs in the proportion of students who report liking school a lot, trying to do their best, and getting on well with their teachers (Adolescent Health Research Group, 2003); accompanied by decline in positive attitudes toward mathematics, reading and writing (Cox & Kennedy, 2008). Young Maori adolescents display the lowest levels of engagement, with the decrease more apparent in Years 9-10 than in Years 7-8. Stand-down, suspension, exclusion, and expulsion rates for Maori students are triple those of Pakeha (Ministry of Education, 2007a). Indeed, the general data for Maori, especially boys in Years 9-10, indicate the extent of disengagement with high truancy and 20% leaving school before age 16 (Education and Science Committee, 2008).

CURRENT ISSUES RELATED TO THE
SCHOOLING OF YOUNG ADOLESCENTS

Indictments

The two-tiered structure of the education system has the effect that Years 7-10 is split awkwardly between primary and secondary schooling. In the transition between the two, many young adolescents traditionally have "fallen through the crack" between primary and secondary school (Neville-Tisdall, 2002, p. 45). Attention to school types and teacher qualifications has not been effective.

School Type

For over a century the question of where to educate NZ's 10- to 15-year-olds has been laden with tension, philosophical difference, and political rivalry (Hinchco, 2004). Some educationalists assert that the two-year intermediate school is too short and seriously limits the potential for developmentally responsive schooling (Stewart & Nolan, 1992). Others claim that secondary schooling for young adolescents is unsuitable. Notably the strong emphasis in Years 9-10 on preparation for national qualifications tends to result in learning environments poorly suited for increasing personal efficacy; and the pedagogies used, which focus on coverage before active inquiry, generally are unresponsive to the developmental needs of young adolescents and result in lower motivation and engagement (Eccles et al., 1993). Attempts to link school type with achievement have been complex and uncertain at best (e.g. Weiss & Kipnes, 2006). An outcome of note in NZ is to focus less on the structure of the schooling system and more on what happens inside the classroom (Maharey, 2006).

Teacher Qualifications

If quality teaching is the most influential point of leverage on student outcomes (Alton-Lee, 2003), then teacher education is a crucial arena in which to effect change in schools by changing teacher registration: that is, change the current system that prepares teachers to be either primary or secondary teachers (Nolan, Kane, & Lind, 2003). This idea appears timely since school principals and teacher educators have rightly questioned the appropriateness of the current system for teacher preparation for the middle years. This may prove difficult since in NZ, 27 tertiary providers offer a total of 85 different qualifications through 131 teacher education programs (Kane, 2005). Yet no program offers a middle-years specialization (P. Bishop, 2008).

Inadequate Preparation for Teaching: Years 7-10

On the one hand, primary teacher education programs in NZ have been criticized for too little focus on subject knowledge; and the self-contained classroom model typical in full primary and intermediate schools requires teachers to be generalists able to teach most, if not all, subject areas. Some argue that it is unrealistic for Years 7-8 teachers to prepare the full range of subject content at this level, given the increasing cognitive abilities of their students. For instance, Dinham and Rowe (2007) suggested introducing a degree of subject specialization at the primary level to address teachers' concerns about feeling underprepared to teach mathematics and science, in particular.

On the other hand, the focus of secondary teacher education programs content knowledge and curriculum coverage seems no less appropriate. When interviewed, Crooks said the prime aim of middle school teaching, and by implication teacher preparation, should be "to maintain engagement, to (keep young people) interested and excited and not worry too much about what gets covered" (P. Bishop, 2008, p. 71). Crooks (2008) added that Year 10 is the "low point in school enthusiasm and academic commitment for many students" and speculated that this might be due to "limited subject choice that students have in the middle school years, and the extensive use of whole class teaching methods" (p. 7). According to the Education Review Office (2003), this is because secondary school teachers are not sufficiently aware of the needs of young adolescents in Years 9-10 and because "the focus of many secondary schools and of government policies for these schools is the education of senior students" (p. 51). By implication, both are arguing that in NZ it is time to change the way teachers are prepared to teach young people; the focus should be on meaningful and positive relationships and teachers assisting students to connect schooling with their everyday experiences (Stevenson, 2002).

The challenge for teacher preparation for Years 7-10 in NZ is to find a middle course between primary programs perceived as lacking in subject area content; and secondary programs, seen as lacking in practical classroom pedagogy and educational philosophy. Nolan, Kane, and Lind (2003) suggested that the way ahead could be a judicious balance between subject area generalization and specialization, the study of young adolescence, specialized classroom pedagogy, design of assessment and curriculum, and a sound understanding of middle schooling philosophy.

REFORM INITIATIVES AND NATIONAL POLICIES

Three reform efforts in NZ education over the last 20 years reflect the growing commitment to improving educational outcomes for young adolescents. In the mid-1980s, the Freyberg Integrated Studies Project implemented a student-centred curriculum design in Years 9-11. Rationalizations of schooling in the 1990s led to innovative reconfigurations and the appearance of a handful of schools with a Years 7-10 structure. In 2007, the New Zealand Curriculum recognized Years 7-10 as a distinct developmental stage requiring its own "learning pathway" (Ministry of Education, 2007b, p. 41).

The Freyberg Integrated Studies Project

The "Integrated Studies Project" at Freyberg High School in Palmerston North (1986-1991) provided evidence that middle level schooling in NZ—especially Years 9-10—was in need of reform. Responding to widespread criticism of middle level schooling at the time (Department of Education, 1984), the project implemented an "integrated studies" curriculum in an information and communication technologies (ICT) environment to develop collaborative learning communities in several Years 9-11 classrooms (Nolan & McKinnon, 1991). Over its 5-year term the project's research reported student achievement outcomes demonstrably superior to those achieved by non-Project students via the traditional single-subject approach. Specifically, the project research demonstrated achievement effects of one standard deviation above the norm in students' national Year 11 examination results for English, mathematics and science (Nolan & McKinnon, 2003). Although the project design relied on British theory and practice (Bernstein, 1971; Pring, 1976; Stenhouse, 1968), it paralleled American middle level developments of the period; for instance, Lounsbury and Vars' (1978) student-centered curriculum design. Initially the researchers were optimistic that the "right" conditions might have arrived for the systemic implementation of student-centered integrative curriculum designs in Years 9-10. Longer term, however, the Project encountered persistent resistance from secondary teachers who rejected the student-centred design in favor of traditional subject-centered pedagogy. Nonetheless, the project clearly showed that an integrative curriculum design responds to the educational and developmental needs of young adolescents and that it is a feasible curriculum model for middle level schooling in NZ. The long-run outcome of the project suggested that schooling in Years 7-8—involving primary trained teachers—might be more fruitful for integrative curriculum. Indeed, later trials of integrative curriculum designs in full primary and intermediate schools confirmed the project findings that student-centered approaches are especially effective in Years 7-10 (Harwood & Nolan, 1999).

The Re-Emergence of Middle Schools in New Zealand

In the early 1990s, a small minority of school leaders—mainly innovative intermediate school principals—challenged the hegemony of the two-tiered primary-secondary education system in NZ (Hinchco, 2004). In particular they questioned the capacity and capability of the system to adequately address and meet the distinctive development and educational needs of young adolescents and help young adolescents achieve outcomes commensurate with their diverse and rapidly emerging abilities, interests, and capacities (Stewart & Nolan, 1992).

Eight middle schools (Years 7-9 or Year 7-10) were formed in NZ during the 1990s (Hinchco, 2004). In 1995 the Ministry of Education granted permission to three communities to form middle schools: Raumanga Middle School in Whangarei (Years 7-9), St. Andrews Intermediate School in Hamilton (Years 7-10), and Clover Park Middle School in South Auckland (Years 7-10). In each case the outcome followed rationalizations of local schooling, thus favorable decisions may have been driven as much by economic imperatives concerning the distribution of resources, as the intention to improve educational outcomes at the middle level. Later in the 1990s, and following further rationalizations of local schooling, five more schools (all Years 7-10) were formed.

The formation of middle schools—and by extension, the wider philosophy and practice of middle schooling—was strongly resisted by the Post Primary Teachers Association (PPTA), who were intent on preserving union membership and repelling any attempt to divert Year 9 students from secondary schools (Neville-Tisdall, 2002). Nonetheless, PPTA President Martin Cooney (1996, cited in Hinchco, 2004) commented that "it has been accepted for some time" that young people go through two "reasonably clear stages of educational development … [age] 11-14 and [age] 15 and over. This provides [the] logic for treating the needs of [Years 7-10] somewhat differently from [Years 11-13] students" (p. 96). Thus the PPTA was, apparently, unwilling to endorse stand-alone middle schools, yet it recognized that young adolescents have distinct developmental needs.

Following changes in the political wind no more middle schools were formed until 2005 when Albany Junior High School (Years 7-10) in northern Auckland was opened by Prime Minister Helen Clark. She commented that the new school was a 'model' for future middle level schooling in NZ. The opening of Albany Junior High seemed to signal a new direction in government policy. Unlike the middle schools formed in the 1990s, this school was brand new and not born from a calculated rationalization of resources. Soon after, Minister of Education Steve Maharey (2006) stated that effective middle level schools need to be able to respond to "the specific needs" of young adolescents and that appropriate curriculum design should be a "key element" of middle schooling practice (p. 7).

The 2007 New Zealand Curriculum

For advocates of middle schooling, the NZC (Ministry of Education, 2007b) is perhaps the most important official document in NZ education, since the 1930s. The NZC effectively puts the middle years of schooling on the educational map of NZ; and presages reconstruction of the NZ educational landscape to acknowledge *three* distinct stages of development within the years of compulsory schooling. In particular, the NZC's three "learning pathways"—Years 1-6, Years 7-10 and Years 11-13 (p. 41)—redefine the traditional primary-secondary split of Years 1-8 and Years 9-13 accepted since the inception of state schooling in 1877. If school communities accept and move to enact the NZC statement, they arguably could alter substantially young adolescents' educational experiences and outcomes and make them radically different from the traditional experiences of primary and secondary schooling in NZ.

The learning pathways reflect the findings of ERO (2000, 2003) that caused the Ministry of Education and the wider NZ research community to redirect their gaze towards middle schooling. It was here that government policy for the curriculum, and thus schooling itself, started to change; not too surprisingly since in NZ, the Education Review Office is most closely in touch with how schooling is affecting students and producing—or failing to produce—satisfactory learning outcomes. The Education Review Office's (2000, 2003) message that Years 7-10 were "the forgotten years" appears to have struck a responsive chord with successive Ministers of Education. Following the Stewart and Nolan (1992) report, NZAIMS exercised due diligence, constantly putting the case to restructure schooling and the national curriculum, which they envisaged as the key to achieving a better outcome for students: a new kind of schooling for Years 7-10 that is more responsive to, respectful of, and effective for young adolescents. NZAIMS persistently argued (e.g. NZAIMS, 2006) that student outcomes in the middle years should be defined broadly so that wider considerations pivotal to young adolescents' developmental needs, not just subject areas, shape the curriculum.

The NZC provides school communities with an official mandate to change their ways. As intermediate school principal John McAleese (2007) remarked, the NZC represents a "quantum leap ... now [teachers] can put students first and not teach driven by achievement objectives" (2007, p. 13). The NZC ushers in a new era and may achieve the outcome that advocates have long articulated for young adolescents in NZ: a broad, inclusive, and integrative curriculum; with exploratory, relevant, and meaningful pedagogies linked to community; and subject areas taught by specialists sparingly and only as needed (Beeby, 1938; Stewart & Nolan, 1992; Watson 1964).

RESEARCH

Despite the two-tiered schooling structure in NZ, a growing research base contributes to the country's developing understanding of what constitutes effective teaching and learning during the middle years. These studies employ a variety of methodologies and have occurred primarily in the field of education. The research falls generally into the following categories: reviews of middle schooling, curriculum integration, transitions into secondary schooling, and young adolescents' experience of schooling.

Reviews of Middle Schooling

Each of the major reviews of middle schooling in NZ relied heavily on the use of qualitative methodology, ranging from archival document and literature review to observation and interview. Watson (1964) completed the first review of NZ middle schooling since Beeby's 1938 appraisal of the then fledgling intermediate school. Examining the intermediate's history, structure, and pedagogy, Watson's work culminated in 21 recommendations that largely endorsed Beeby's work. These included a call to continue, strengthen, and extend intermediate schools; to situate them as stand-alone schools; and to staff them with teachers who understand young adolescents and are specialists in at least one subject area. In particular Watson argued that a robust teacher-student relationship was prerequisite to establishing a positive classroom climate for young adolescents.

Thirty years later, the Stewart and Nolan (1992) report, *The Middle School: Essential Education for Emerging Adolescents,* investigated the educational and developmental needs of young adolescents. Their work deliberately built on Watson's (1964) work by reviewing the middle schooling literature and summarizing the research to inform the debate about the future of intermediate schooling. In a nutshell, Stewart and Nolan recommended: (1) the adoption of 3- or 4-year middle schools; (2) the addition of counseling in the middle years; and (3) employing primary and secondary teachers who understand young adolescent development, have specialist subject expertise, and are skilled in teaching core subjects.

Hinchco (2004) examined the emergence of 3- and 4-year middle schools in NZ in the 1990s. He employed a qualitative research methodology and a blended theoretical approach to analyze the tension between political and pedagogical considerations on the middle schools in the 1990s and the extent to which their presence proved to be problematic. Hinchco concluded that political pressures, most notably from the PPTA, constrained the development of stand-alone middle schools.

Integrative Curriculum at the Middle Level

The Freyberg Integrated Studies Project of the mid-1980s (Nolan & McKinnon, 1991) along with James Beane's work (1990, 1997)—who, echoing the reciprocal visits by educational leaders in the USA and NZ that had been so influential in the 1920s and 1930s, visited NZ and collaborated with Nolan—inspired continuing research on curriculum design for young adolescents in NZ (see Harwood & Nolan, 1999) along with a recent doctoral study.

Dowden (2007a) investigated the concept of curriculum integration with respect to the educational and developmental needs of young adolescents in NZ. Drawing extensively from Dewey's work and more recent American progressives including Lounsbury, Vars, and Beane; he provided historical, theoretical and ethical evidence to support his argument that any kind of integrated curriculum design for middle schooling worthy of trial in NZ should be based on Beane's (1990, 1997) student-centered integrative model of curriculum integration; as opposed to the subject-centred multidisciplinary model (Jacobs, 1989) that has been widely implemented in middle schools in the United States. Although NZ teachers have traditionally interpreted integrated curriculum in the multidisciplinary sense (Fraser, 2000), the NZC (Ministry of Education, 2007) offers strong support for implementing integrative designs in Years 7-10. Dowden (2007b) concluded that student-centered pedagogies and schooling for young adolescents should be aligned with student-centered curriculum designs.

Young Adolescents' Experiences of Schooling

Outside the field of education, the Adolescent Health Research Group (2003) conducted a self-reported, anonymous survey of a random sample of almost 10,000 middle years and secondary students from 114 schools.

The findings suggested helpful insights into young adolescents' perspectives on culture and ethnicity, home and family, school, health, and community. The research noted a significant decrease between Year 9 and Year 10 in the proportion of students who like school a lot, the proportion of students who report trying hard to do their best, and the proportion of students who get along well with their teachers.

Nelson's (2006) research also included a focus on students' experience of schooling. Combining image-based methods with the genres of voice research and participatory research, she invited 38 young adolescents across three participating schools to partake in auto-photography and photo elicitation interviews. Participants explored their perceptions of school and learning, their identity as young persons and learners, and the world in which they live. The findings revealed students' sound understandings of their educational and personal needs and provided a framework for teachers to reflect on their development as distinctly middle level practitioners.

Maori Learners

Related to this study of students' schooling experiences, "Te Kotahitanga" is an ongoing project working to improve student outcomes in "mainstream" (English-medium) secondary schools. As most Years 9-10 students in NZ attend secondary schools, this work is particularly relevant to young adolescent schooling. The study examined Years 9-10 Maori students' experiences in mainstream classrooms and identified the quality of interactions between the teachers and Maori students as a key factor to improving student achievement. The project then provided extensive, embedded professional development as a school-wide intervention. Mixed methods, including several measures of academic achievement, linked teacher participation in the project with improved student outcomes. The findings also revealed a decrease in truancy and suspensions (Bishop, Berryman, Powell, & Teddy, 2007).

Transitions to Secondary School

Students' movement from one school to another has been the focus of concern in NZ for many years, as—at least until very recently—school structure has taken prominence in the middle level debate. One longitudinal study of 500 students revealed that the transition to secondary school demonstrated the most marked shifts in engagement of any year span from early childhood to secondary school (Wylie, Hodgen, & Ferral, 2006). Researchers identified reduced engagement for those who were previously engaged and no increase in engagement for those who had shown signs of disengagement at age 12. There was no evidence that the transition to secondary school negatively affected students' academic performance; prior academic achievement and school engagement had a greater influence on early secondary school performance than the transition itself. However, taking longer to settle into a new school over the transition period negatively affected students' confidence and attitudinal scores (Wylie et al.).

Cox and Kennedy's (2008) mixed methods research on transitions studied a diverse group of approximately 100 students for 18 months as they moved from primary to secondary schooling. The purpose of their research was to identify factors that affect a smooth transition in terms of achievement, social adjustment, and learning attitudes. Participants were interviewed and tested in mathematics, reading and writing at each of four phases of the study. The majority of students quickly adapted to the move to secondary school both socially and academically. However, a significant minority of students found the Year 8 to Year 9 transition particularly challenging, either academically and socially; the difficulty being exacerbated in some cases by emotional issues or home circumstances. Cox and Kennedy identified the second half of Year 9 as the biggest 'danger period' for students to become more negative about schooling.

FUTURE DIRECTIONS

For over a century the educational experience for young adolescents in NZ has been conceptualized, resourced and practiced as either primary or secondary schooling. Although international comparisons and national monitoring indicate that the majority of young adolescents in NZ successfully navigate their way through primary and secondary school, qualitative data from a range of sources demonstrate that a significant minority of young people struggle in the middle years. Young Maori boys are especially prone to failure during the transition from primary school to high school. Despite promising beginnings and a sound philosophy, middle schooling has not been established at the systemic level in NZ.

CONCLUDING DISCUSSION

In conclusion, the inability, thus far, of NZ policymakers to implement a satisfactory type of schooling for young adolescents represented by a full cross-section of New Zealand society has been as much for political reasons as educational reasons. Recently, however, the signs are that momentum is gathering for the introduction of a third tier of schooling in the education system that will genuinely respond to the educational and developmental needs of young adolescents in NZ. In 2005, Albany Junior High School was opened as the first new stand-alone middle school within the state system since 1932. In 2006, the NZAIMS' (2006) "Strategic Plan" and, then Minister of Education, Steve Maharey (2006) stressed the need for pedagogical reform in the middle years regardless of school type. In 2007, the NZC "Learning Pathways" explicitly recognized that young adolescents have particular developmental and learning needs (Ministry of Education, 2007, p. 41). In 2008, the Ministry of Education (2008) formed the "Middle Schooling Steering Group" to develop a coherent evidence base for informing future middle schooling policy.

The time is ripe to reform middle level education in NZ by:

1. Restructuring teacher training to include preparation for middle schooling;
2. Encouraging schools to adopt, develop and implement middle schooling philosophy, concepts and strategies;
3. Restructuring or reorganizing existing sites so that:

    (a) Schools in the same locality form communities of practice (full primaries and secondaries; intermediates and secondaries) to ensure coherency and consistency of program design and delivery across Years 7-10, and
    (b) Schools with Years 7-13 or Years 1-13 structure develop autonomous Years 7-10 schools within their larger school;

4. Building new Years 7-10 middle schools in areas of rapid population growth and linking them to Years 11-13 senior colleges; and
5. On an ongoing basis the Ministry of Education should:

    (a) Work with schools to develop the particular design, curriculum, pedagogy and assessment needed for Years 7-10,
    (b) Run communications campaigns to develop awareness and understanding in both the community and the teaching profession, and
    (c) Fund case study survey research to document existing (and developing) exemplary practice across school types.

REFERENCES

Adolescent Health Research Group. (2003). *New Zealand youth: A profile of their health and well-being.* Retrieved March 3, 2008, from http://www.youth2000.ac.nz/

Alcorn, N. (1999). *To the fullest extent of his powers: C.E. Beeby's life in education.* Wellington, New Zealand: Victoria University Press.

Alton-Lee, A. (2003). *Quality teaching for diverse students in schooling: Best evidence synthesis*. Wellington, New Zealand: Ministry of Education.

Beane, J. A. (1990). *A middle school curriculum: From rhetoric to reality*. Columbus, OH: National Middle School Association.

Beane, J. A. (1997). *Curriculum integration: Designing the core of democratic education*. New York: Teachers College Press.

Beeby, C. E. (1938). *The intermediate schools of New Zealand: A survey*. Wellington, New Zealand: Whitcombe & Tombs.

Bernstein, B. (1971). On the classification and framing of educational knowledge. In M. F. D. Young (Ed.), *Knowledge and control* (pp. 47-69). London: McMillan.

Bishop, P. (2008). *Middle years teacher credentialing in Aotearoa/New Zealand* (Policy Report to Fulbright Board of Trustees and NZ Ministry of Education). Wellington, New Zealand: Ministry of Education.

Bishop, R., Berryman, M., Powell, A., & Teddy, L. (2007). *Te Kotahitanga: Improving the educational achievement of Maori students in mainstream education (Phase 2)*. Wellington, New Zealand: Ministry of Education.

Chamberlain, M. (2007). *Mathematics and science achievement in New Zealand: Summing up New Zealand's participation in three cycles of TIMSS at Year 9*. Retrieved June 22, 2008, from http://www.educationcounts.govt.nz/publications/series/2571/timss_200203/15581

Cox, S., & Kennedy, S. (2008). *The impact of the year 8 to year 9 transition on students' achievement*. Wellington, New Zealand: Ministry of Education.

Crooks, T. (2008, April). Goals for middle schooling. *Secondary Principals Association of New Zealand Journal*, 7-9.

Department of Education. (1943). *The post-primary curriculum: Report of the committee appointed by the Minister of Education in November, 1942*. Wellington, New Zealand: Government Printer.

Department of Education. (1984). *A review of the core curriculum for schools*. Wellington, New Zealand: Government Printer.

Dewey, J. (1916). *Democracy and education*. New York: MacMillan.

Dinham, S., & Rowe, K. (2007). *Teaching and learning in middle schooling: A review of the literature*. A report of the NZ Ministry of Education. Wellington, New Zealand: Australian Council for Educational Research.

Dowden, T. (2007a). *Curriculum integration for early adolescent schooling in Aotearoa New Zealand: worthy of serious trial*. Unpublished doctoral thesis, Massey University, New Zealand.

Dowden, T. (2007b). Relevant, challenging, integrative and exploratory curriculum design: Perspectives from theory and practice for middle schooling in Australia. *Australian Educational Researcher, 34*(2), 51-71.

Dowden, T., & Nolan, C. J. P. (2007). Curriculum integration in historical perspective: key innovations in Aotearoa/New Zealand in the 1930s and 1940s. *Proceedings of 2007 NZARE National Conference*. Christchurch, New Zealand: NZARE.

Durling, N. (2007). *Teaching and learning in middle schooling: A statistical snapshot*. Wellington, New Zealand: Ministry of Education.

Eccles, J. S., Midgley, C., Wigfield, A., Buchanan, C. M., Reuman, D., Flanagan, C., & Mac Iver, D. (1993). Development during adolescence: The impact of stage-environment fit on young adolescents' experiences in schools and in families. *American Psychologist, 48*(2), 90-101.

Education and Science Committee. (2008, February). *Inquiry into making the schooling system work for every child*. Report of the Education and Science Committee, Forty-Eighth Parliament. Retrieved May 25, 2008, from http://www .parliament.nz/NR/rdonlyres/6BCFBA0F-EF08-43EC-BD52-2B774716Ef/ 73434/DBSCH_SCR_3979_58291.pdf

Education Review Office. (2000). *Students in years 7 and 8*. Wellington, New Zealand: National Evaluation Reports.

Education Review Office. (2003). *Students in years 9 and 10*. Wellington, New Zealand: Author. Retrieved March 3, 2008, from http://www.ero.govt.nz/ero/publishing.nsf/

Education Review Office. (2007). *The achievement of Maori Students*. Wellington, New Zealand: Author.

Fraser, D. (2000). Curriculum integration: What it is and what it is not. *SET, 3*, 34-37.

Harwood, C., & Nolan, C. J. P. (1999). *Integration insights: Journeys from theory to practice* (Report for Institute for Professional Development and Educational Research). Massey University, New Zealand.

Hinchco, B. J. (2004). *Politics or pedagogy? The development of the New Zealand Middle School*. Unpublished doctoral thesis, Waikato University, New Zealand.

Jacobs, H. H. (Ed.). (1989). *Interdisciplinary curriculum: Design and implementation*. Alexandria, VA: Association for Supervision and Curriculum Development.

Kane, R. (2005). *Initial teacher education policy and practice*. Wellington: Ministry of Education and New Zealand Teachers Council.

King, M. (2003). *The Penguin history of New Zealand*. Auckland: Penguin.

Lounsbury, J. H., & Vars, G. F. (1978). *A curriculum for the middle school years*. New York: Harper.

McAleese, J. (2007). Welcoming the draft. *Middle Schooling Review, 3*, 10-15. Hamilton, NZ: NZAIMS.

Maharey, S. (2006). The middle years of schooling. *New Zealand Middle Schooling Review, 1*, 6-7.

Ministry of Education. (2007a). *Nga Haeata Matauranga/Annual report on Maori education*. Wellington, New Zealand: Author.

Ministry of Education. (2007b). *New Zealand curriculum framework*. Wellington, New Zealand: Learning Media.

Ministry of Education. (2008). *Middle schooling steering group: Terms of reference*. Wellington, NZ: Author.

Nelson, E. (2006). *Co-constructing early adolescent education through image-based research*. Unpublished masters thesis, Massey University, New Zealand.

Neville-Tisdall, M. (2002). Pedagogy and politics in New Zealand's middle schools. *Middle School Journal, 33*(4), 45-51.

New Zealand Association for Intermediate and Middle Schooling. (2006). *NZAIMS strategic plan*. Hamilton, New Zealand: Author.

Nolan, C. J. P., & Brown, M. A. (2002). The fight for middle school education in New Zealand. *Middle School Journal, 33*(4), 34-44.

Nolan, C. J. P., Kane, R., & Lind, P. (2003). Approaching and avoiding the middle: Teacher preparation in New Zealand. In G. A. Andrews & V. A. Anfara, Jr. (Eds.), *Leaders for a movement: Professional preparation and development of middle level teachers and administrators.* Greenwich, CT: Information Age.

Nolan, C. J. P., & McKinnon, D. (1991). Case study of curriculum innovation in New Zealand: The Freyberg Integrated Studies Project. *Curriculum Perspectives, 11*(4), 1-10.

Nolan, C. J. P., & McKinnon, D. (2003). Enhancing the middle in a New Zealand secondary school: integration, experiential learning and computer use. *International Journal of Educational Reform, 12*(3), 230-243.

Organization for Economic Cooperation and Development. (2008). *Country statistical profiles (New Zealand).* Retrieved July 10, 2008, from http://stats.oecd.org/wbos/viewhtml.aspx?queryname=475&querytype=view&lang=en

Pring, R. (1976). *Knowledge and schooling.* London: Open Books.

Stenhouse, L. (1968). The humanities curriculum project. *Journal of Curriculum Studies, 1*(1), 26-33.

Stevenson, C. (2002). *Teaching ten to fourteen year olds* (3rd ed.). Boston: Allyn & Bacon.

Stewart, D., & Nolan, C. J. P. (1992). *The middle school: Essential education for emerging adolescents.* Palmerston North, New Zealand: Massey University Educational Research and Development Centre.

Vars, G. F. (2000). Common learnings: A 50 year quest. *Journal of Curriculum and Supervision, 16*(1), 70-89.

Watson, J. E. (1964). *Intermediate schooling in New Zealand.* Wellington, New Zealand: NZCER.

Weiss, C. C., & Kipnes, L. (2006). Re-examining middle school effects: A comparison of middle grades students in middle schools and K-8 schools. *American Journal of Education, 112*(2), 239-272.

Wylie, C., Hodgen, E., & Ferral, H. (2006). *Completely different or a bigger version? Experiences and effects of the transition to secondary school. Evidence from the Competent Children Competent Learners project.* Retrieved April 30, 2008, from http://www.nzcer.org.nz/default.php?cpath=139_133&products_id=1675

CHAPTER 8

EDUCATING YOUNG ADOLESCENTS IN AUSTRALIA

Martin Dowson

The purpose of this chapter is to provide a coherent overview of the education of young adolescents in Australia. In order to achieve this purpose, this chapter outlines the contextual, sociological, historical, and educational antecedents of the current system of educating young adolescents in Australia. The chapter notes that the academic performance of Australian adolescents is high by international comparison and explains features of the current education system that may be contributing to this performance. The chapter also outlines perceived difficulties and problems with current education structures and processes and how these difficulties and problems may be limiting the effectiveness of education for young Australian adolescents. In particular, continuing concerns about the developmental appropriateness of schooling for young adolescents, and the fragmentation of education delivery throughout Australia due to the influence of multiple state and territory jurisdictions is noted. Major reforms that seek to address these issues, specifically the emergence of middle schools and moves toward a national curriculum are explained in some detail.

The education of young adolescents in Australia remains a fragmented and hotly debated, yet also vibrant and innovative, area of educational

An International Look at Educating Young Adolescents
pp. 157–177
Copyright © 2009 by Information Age Publishing
All rights of reproduction in any form reserved.

development and reform. This chapter outlines significant antecedents of, influences on, and possible future directions concerning the education young adolescents in Australia. The distinctives of the Australian experience are highlighted and explained throughout.

CONTEXTUAL NARRATIVE

Population and Demography

Australia's population is currently about 21 million, distributed across a landmass that is roughly the size of the United States, excluding Alaska. As a result, population density is extremely low at 6.9 persons per square mile, which was the fourth lowest population density in the world in 2007. Nevertheless, Australia is one of the most urbanized countries in the world, with less than 15% of the population living in rural areas. Infant mortality per 1,000 live births is approximately 4.7.[1]

Nearly two out of every seven Australians are foreign-born. Caucasians represent 92% of the population of Australia. Asians make up 6%, and aboriginal peoples account for 2%. At the end of 2003, 89,437 permanent settlers arrived in Australia, and the country hosted approximately 22,800 refugees. That same year, 48,148 persons departed Australia permanently.

English is the official language. However, according to the 2001 national census, 2.8 million people (16% of the population at the time) spoke a language other than English at home. The most commonly used languages after English are Italian, Greek, Cantonese, Arabic (including Lebanese), Mandarin, and Spanish. In addition, more than 50,000 Australians speak an indigenous language. In the 2001 Census, Roman Catholics represented 27% of the population, Anglicans 21%, other Christian denominations 20%, and non-Christian faiths 5%. Australians claiming no religious affiliation represented 16% of the population.

Education and Literacy

In 2003, Australia had 9,607 primary (elementary) and secondary (high) schools (72% of which were government schools). These schools educated 3.3 million students (2.3 million in government schools), and employed 229,576 full-time or full-time equivalent teachers (67% in government schools). Australia also has approximately 40 institutions of higher education. In 2003, 929,952 students attended institutions of higher education (including about 500,000 women), and institutions of higher learning employed 35,867 faculty (about 60% male) and 48,568 nonacademic staff (about 60% female). As of 2005, the nation's literacy rate was 85%.

The Australian Federation is comprised of six states and two territories. These states and territories are individually responsible for education within their borders. Hence, as might be expected, curriculum, instruction, and assessment practices for young adolescents vary considerably across the nation. Education is compulsory from 6 to 16 years of age in the states of South Australia and Tasmania and to 15 years of age elsewhere in Australia. The final 2 years of secondary school generally take place after the compulsory stage, and 75% of students attended the final 2 years of schooling in 2003. Curricula vary from state to state, however moves are currently underway to nationalize core curriculum areas and the age of commencement of students. These changes are intended to provide students access to 13 years of schooling on a comparable basis anywhere in Australia.

Health and Welfare

Australia enjoys one of the highest life expectancies in the world at 80.6 years, which was the fifth highest life expectancy in the world in 2007. In 2002-2003, total spending on health care (government, private health insurance, and individual outlays) as a proportion of gross domestic product was 9.5%. The leading causes of death in Australia in 2002 were cancer (28%) and cardiovascular disease (20%). In 2003, an estimated 14,000 Australians were living with human immunodeficiency virus/acquired immune deficiency syndrome (HIV/AIDS), representing 0.1% of the population. Fewer than 200 Australians died from HIV/AIDS during 2003.

Australia has an extensive social welfare system designed to address the educational, health care, housing, and income needs of its citizens. More than 4 million Australians are direct beneficiaries of income support payments including family assistance, youth and student support, child-care support, labor-market assistance, housing assistance (both rental and home ownership), and support for people with disabilities.

HISTORY AND ORGANIZATION OF SCHOOLING FOR YOUNG ADOLESCENTS

The first schools in Australia were established early in the nineteenth century by private individuals and churches. By the 1840s, however, governments began to express significant interest in the provision of education.

From 1848, a dual system of schools operated under which church or denominational schools were supported by government funding while at the same time a system of government controlled "national" schools was created. Between 1872 and 1895 all Australian "colonies" (i.e., the Australian "states" prior to federation) had passed public education laws which established a system of government primary schools administered by a Department of Education (or equivalent).

Secondary education, however, remained largely private until the early twentieth century and developed much more slowly than primary education. Nevertheless, by 1939 schooling was compulsory in most states between the ages of 6 and 15 (thus incorporating the first 3 years of secondary schooling), and by the 1950s government schools had become the main providers of secondary education. During the 1960s and 1970s public secondary education continued to grow rapidly. Moreover, an increasing number of students remained at high-school beyond the minimum school leaving age. Today, public secondary schools outnumber private secondary schools two to one, and most students (approximately 70%) attend public secondary schools. The recent emergence of nondenominational, low-fee paying private Christian schools has, however, impacted this balance somewhat.

Curriculum, Instruction, and Assessment Practices

Curriculum, instruction, and assessment practices for young adolescents vary considerably across the nation. However, curricula for young adolescents generally attempt to:

- specify a range of outcomes for students to achieve;
- provide an educational framework for programs that challenge students to achieve these outcomes;
- recognize diversity amongst students in terms of gender, language, culture, learning capacity, socioeconomic background and geographic location; and
- accommodate diversity by valuing the differing student knowledge and experiences, and by empowering schools and teachers to respond to local needs, concerns and contexts.

Core subjects usually include English, mathematics, science, society and environment, languages other than English (LOTE), technological and applied studies, creative arts, and personal development, health and physical education (PDHPE). Some subjects are offered at several levels of depth and complexity, and "streaming" of students according to ability is commonplace.

Instructional practices for young adolescents reflect a desire among educators to cater for the particular needs of students as they face the developmental and social challenges associated with young adolescence. These practices are typically designed to be:

- Outcomes based: Progress and achievement are recorded against explicit statements of competency.

- Learner centered: Curriculum is focused on the identified needs, interests and concerns of students in the middle-years, and emphasizes "active," self-directed learning.

- Vocationally relevant: Wherever possible learning in directed toward the development of understandings, skills, and attitudes that are relevant in vocational and occupational settings.

- Flexibly delivered: Actual curriculum arrangements are designed to be responsive to local needs and circumstances, while making best use of time, space, and other resources.

- Community oriented: Parents and representatives from the community beyond the school are encouraged to be involved in teaching-learning partnerships.

School-based assessment. Student achievement and progress is assessed by classroom/subject-area teacher(s). Assessment of the academic performance of young adolescents occurs across three levels: school-based assessment, state-based assessments, and national assessments.

Teachers use a variety of means to assess students including observations, assignments, and a variety of formal and informal tests. Teachers typically assess student progress throughout the year. In most states, teachers are also required to make twice-yearly judgements of each student's achievement compared with expectations described in syllabus documents for each Key Learning Areas (KLA) (e.g., mathematics, English, science). These judgements are often made on a scale of some description (e.g., using word descriptors such as *basic, limited, sound, high,* and *outstanding*).

State-based assessment. Most states award a "school certificate" (or equivalent) upon successful completion of Years 9 and 10. Assessment for the school certificate is partly school based and includes measures of academic performance, attendance, and conduct. However, students are also required to take statewide external tests in English/literacy, mathematics, science, Australian history, geography, and other subject areas, in order for the school certificate to be awarded. All students successfully completing Year 10 are eligible to continue to senior secondary school (Years 11 and 12).

National assessment. In 2008, The National Assessment Program: Literacy and Numeracy (NAPLAN) was introduced for all students in Years 3, 5, 7, and 9. The purpose of the NAPLAN is to assess the literacy and numeracy learning of students in all Australian schools, thus providing consistent information on student performance across the nation. In some States, the NAPLAN tests have replaced similar state-based tests such as the Basic Skills Tests (BST), English Language and Literacy Assessment (ELLA), and Secondary Numeracy Assessment Program (SNAP).

Organization and Structure

Three or 4 years of junior secondary schooling are compulsory in Australia. The first 1 or 2 years of junior secondary school (Year 7 and 8) are usually organized as a general program of instruction undertaken by all students. In the later years (Years 9 and 10), students take a core group of subjects and electives. Schooling for young adolescents generally involves a midway transition from a primary school to a separate secondary school. Nevertheless, many dedicated middle schools now exist in the private (non-government) sector, with an increasing number in the public (government) sector, which do not require a transition from one school to another. These dedicated middle schools usually exist as a school within the larger kindergarten (the first year of formal schooling) to Year 12 "colleges."

Instruction is organized on the Western classroom model—with young adolescents moving between classes that are taught by subject area specialist teachers. In many schools, however, a "home room" teacher (or equivalent) takes students in Years 7 and 8 (and sometimes Years 9 and 10) for at least one period per day. The school day is typically divided into "periods" (40 to 80 minute blocks of instruction). However, a wide variety of timetabling practices are utilized across the nation.

OUTCOMES OF THE SCHOOLING OF YOUNG ADOLESCENTS

Academic Performance Outcomes

While generalizations are somewhat problematic, certain "generic" (i.e., nonsubject specific) academic performance outcomes are generally promoted. These outcomes broadly aim to ensure that students become lifelong learners, achieve their fullest potential, and play an active part in civic and economic life. These outcomes include the student's ability to:

- use language to understand, develop, and communicate ideas and information, and to interact productively with others;
- select, integrate, and apply numerical and spatial concepts and techniques;
- locate and obtain relevant information from a range of sources—evaluating, applying and sharing this information with others;
- select, apply, and adapt technologies related to information and communication;
- describe and analyze patterns, structures and relationships in order to justify opinions, actions, and decisions;
- participate in creative activity while appreciating and engaging with the artistic, cultural, and intellectual work of others;
- test ideas, think laterally, visualize consequences, and recognize emerging opportunity and potential; and
- display a positive attitude toward continuing personal and academic development, resulting in an ongoing disposition toward life-long and life-wide learning.

In addition to the generic academic outcomes listed above, several nonacademic outcomes are also considered critical. These include the student's ability to:

- display an awareness of their cultural, geographic, and historical contexts, while interacting respectfully with people and cultures other than their own;
- value and promote civic participation in Australia and the global community;
- implement practices that promote personal heath, growth, and well-being;
- work individually or collaboratively as required, based on a strong sense of autonomy, personal confidence, and self-motivation; and
- recognize and embrace their rights and responsibilities to receive and provide care, compassion, and support appropriate to their needs, capacities, and contexts.

Despite the acknowledged importance of these academic and other outcomes, few targeted research studies have been conducted in Australia which demonstrate the extent to which these outcomes are being achieved.

Research Supporting Academic Performance and Other Outcomes

In the current context, perhaps the most helpful indicator of the academic performance outcomes of Australian young adolescents is student results from the Programme for International Student Assessment (PISA). PISA is a triennial world-wide test of 15-year-old students' scholastic performance, coordinated by the Organisation for Economic Cooperation and Development (OECD). The aim of the PISA study is to test and compare students' performance across the world, with a view to facilitating global improvements in educational methods and outcomes. The 2006, the Australian PISA sample included 358 schools and over 14,000 students. As with the 2003 Australian PISA sample, Indigenous students and students from regional areas were oversampled, so that reliable results would be available for these groups. Of the 57 countries participating in the 2006 PISA study, Australia was ranked 13th in mathematics, eighth in science, and seventh in reading. (By way of comparison, the United States was not ranked in the first 20 countries with respect to any of the PISA subject areas assessed.) These results suggest that Australian middle school students perform very well in comparison with students from other countries—including most developed nations in the Western world.

Solid, direct evidence for the achievement of nonacademic outcomes is virtually nonexistent and, hence, estimations of the level of young adolescents' nonacademic performance display wide variation. On the one hand, some point to the generally smooth transition of young adolescents to employment, to further education and to a variety of community roles as indirect evidence of the achievement of at least some of the nonacademic outcomes listed above. On the other hand, rising rates of metal ill-health (including teenage suicide), and continued problems with school alienation and dropout (noticeably in rural, regional, and low socioeconomic status urban areas) point in the other direction. In the absence of "hard" data, it is difficult to weigh opposing viewpoints. However, a balanced view might suggest that most young Australian young adolescents are, and will be, productively engaged in a variety of meaningful and satisfying activities (both educational and non-educational), with a significant minority experiencing difficulties at, and upon leaving, school.

CURRENT ISSUES RELATED TO THE
SCHOOLING OF YOUNG ADOLESCENTS

Concerns About the Current Educational System

Concerns relating the current education system for young adolescents in Australia are typical of those in many Western countries and include:

- the perceived inadequacy of funding and infrastructure support for education and perceived inequities in the distribution of that funding and support;
- the vocational relevance and effectiveness of the curriculum;
- the narrowing of the curriculum especially with respect to decreasing exposure to the humanities and the arts;
- the ability (or inability) of schools and governments to respond to emerging global trends, such as the (so called) digital revolution and the emergence of China and India as key world economies and key trading partners with Australia.
- standards in education, reflected in moves toward standardized testing and the generation of hard data to support the effectiveness (or otherwise) of schooling;
- the quality of teaching and, hence, concerns about initial teacher education programs, and the quality and availability of ongoing professional development for teachers;
- educational leadership at the local (school) and state (bureaucratic) levels; and
- the social climate of schools, particularly with respect to student discipline and alienation, respect for teachers, and other aspects of student attitudes and behavior in the school and the community.

More generally, there has been a growing concern amongst educators, researchers, parents and policymakers that current curriculum and teaching practices may not be adequate to address the intellectual development of young adolescents. Moreover, in the light of some highly concerning adolescent mental health statistics (e.g., Kosky, Eshkevari, & Kneebone, 1997) there is also a growing recognition of the need for schools to provide greater social and emotional support to young adolescents. As a result, educators have renewed efforts to develop curricula and instructional strategies that challenge students academically, to ensure that teachers receive appropriate training to meet the needs of young adolescents, to create more nurturing and supportive learning environments, and to reconsider schooling structures and processes as these relate to the progress and development of young adolescents.

Benefits of the Current Educational System

The quality of Australia's current education system for young adolescents is generally considered to be very high by world standards (as reflected, for example, in the PISA results cited previously). Australian young adolescents are almost exclusively taught by university qualified teachers and are provided (not always at the same level of quality in all locations) with extensive, government-funded educational facilities. These teachers and facilities are embedded in a harmonious, culturally diverse, and technologically advanced society that supports (and often demands) significant funding for education at all levels. As a result, all young adolescents in Australia have access to free public schooling to the completion of high school (Year 12) or, alternatively, to an increasing array of fee-paying private education choices. Australian high schools have increasingly sought to developing skills and knowledge required for contemporary workplaces, yet most (i.e., 75% nationally) high school students compete high schooling to Year 12, and more than half of all high-school graduates move to some form of postschool education in either the vocational or higher education sectors.

REFORM INITIATIVES AND NATIONAL POLICY

Perhaps the most significant reform of young adolescent education in Australia in recent years has been the emergence of middle schools and middle schooling as distinct area of teaching endeavor. The development of middle schooling has occurred mainly over the last 15 years. The impetus toward middle schooling in Australia can be traced to similar developments in the United States and, in particular, to a publication of middle schooling undertaken by the influential Carnegie Council on Adolescent Development in 1989, *Turning Points: Preparing American Youth for the 21st Century*. The findings of the Carnegie Council were mirrored in the findings of a number of subsequent Australian studies undertaken during the 1990s. These studies included:

- *The Report of the Junior Secondary Review* (Eyers, 1992);
- *In the Middle* (Schools Council, National Board of Employment, Education and Training, 1993);
- *From Alienation to Engagement* (Australian Curriculum Studies Association, 1996); and
- *A Report of the National Middle Schooling Project* (Barratt, 1998).

Each of these reports identified significant needs of Australian young adolescents, many of which are common to young adolescents in Western nations more generally, including the needs to:

- adjust to profound physical, intellectual, social and emotional changes;
- develop a positive self concept;
- experience, and grow toward independence;
- develop a sense of identify and of personal and shared social values;
- experience social acceptance, affiliation, and affection among peers of the same and opposite sex;
- increase their awareness of, ability to cope with, and capacity to respond constructively to the world around them; and
- establish relationships with particular adults that support these developmental needs.

In order to address the needs identified above, middle school reform in Australia has broadly been guided by the following principles.

- Student engagement in learning: Wherever possible, learning should be connected to things that matter in the worlds of students, and student satisfaction should be derived from sustained engagement in interesting learning activities. This principle has led to a renewed emphasis on learning activities that engage and develop students' social and intellectual capacities and skills.
- Catering for diversity in young adolescent needs and capacities: The national young adolescent student body has significantly diversified in the last 30 years reflecting changes, driven by migration, in Australia's social, cultural, and economic fabric. Thus, individualization and the identification of special requirements for some learners is now expected practice.
- Integration of curriculum, pedagogy, and assessment: To sustain reform in schools, there is a need to thoroughly and systematically integrate curriculum, pedagogy, and assessment. Reducing curriculum "overload" (an overly full curriculum), providing opportunities for transdisciplinary studies, and competency-based assessments have emerged as key strategies to promote educational integration.
- Enhanced intellectual outcomes: Sustained improvement in intellectual outcomes through greater intellectual challenge is a national priority, but implies the need for teachers to develop and utilize an expanded range of pedagogical skills and practices supplemented by improvements in the intra- and interschool systems by which pedagogical knowledge and skills are shared and developed.

- Innovative leadership and organization: Sponsorship of school-based reform initiatives by key educational leaders, especially the principal, is widely recognized as being critical to initiating, legitimating, and sustaining reform. However, innovative organizational structures are also required to establishing the conditions for ongoing, sustained reform.

- Currently, there is very little evidence attesting to the extent to which these guiding principles are driving and sustaining specific reform in schools—especially on a national level. Moreover, hard data on specific outcomes from middle schooling in Australia that may be linked to these principles are still scant and unreliable.

National Policy

The Commonwealth Government works with state and territory governments to improve the quality of schooling nationally. This cooperative work is coordinated through the Ministerial Council on Education, Employment, Training and Youth Affairs (MCEETYA). Membership of this council comprises state, territory, and commonwealth Ministers with responsibility for portfolios covering education, employment, training, and youth affairs. In 1999, MCEETYA adopted the *National Goals for Schooling in the 21st Century* (MCEETYA, 1999). The goals provide broad direction to schools and education authorities, a framework for national reporting on student achievement, and a agreed basis for enhancing public accountability by schools and other education authorities.

The goals recognize that the world of the twenty-first century is, and will continue to be, characterized by a variety of factors that profoundly influence the shape and direction of schooling. These factors include advances in information and communication technologies, increasing population diversity arising from international mobility and migration, and the emergence of a range of complex environmental and related challenges that could profoundly affect global and national social cohesion and economic stability. In seeking to address these factors, the National Goals acknowledge:

- the capacity of all young people to learn;
- the central role of parents and teachers in developing that capacity;
- the responsibility of schools to provide:
    o a foundation for young Australians' intellectual, physical, social, moral, spiritual, and aesthetic development,

o a supportive and nurturing environment that contributes to the
       development of students' sense of self-worth, enthusiasm for
       learning, and optimism for the future.
* the responsibility of governments to establish public policies that
   foster the pursuit of excellence, safeguard the entitlement of all
   young people to high quality schooling, recognize and support a
   diverse range of educational choices and aspirations, promote the
   efficient and effective use of public resources, and uphold the contribution of schooling to a socially cohesive and culturally rich society.

MCEETYA also recognized that the achievement of the National Goals
implied a commitment to:

* strengthening schools as learning communities that work in partnership with business, industry, and the wider community;
* enhancing the status and quality of the teaching profession;
* continuing to promote educational quality by developing curriculum and appropriate systems of assessment, accreditation, and credentialing; and
* increasing public confidence in school education through explicit
   and defensible standards that guide improvement in students' levels of educational achievement.

It is hoped that efforts toward the achievement of the National Goals
will assist young people to develop a disposition toward learning throughout their lives so that they can contribute to Australia's social, cultural,
economic and civic development in local, national and global contexts.

RESEARCH

Current Research Topics

There is no national coordination of research involving the education
of young adolescents in Australia. However, for example, the New South
Wales Department of Education and Training has established priority
research areas for school-based research, and specific topics relating to
these areas. Representative topics from each priority area (listed alphabet-
ically) that directly relate to young adolescent education are outlined in
Table 8.1. These areas and topics fairly reflect current research concerns
across the nation.

Table 8.1.   Priority Research Areas and Representative Topics

Priority Research Area	Topics of Interest
Aboriginal education and training	• Quality teaching of aboriginal students • Linking aboriginal culture to pedagogical strategies and practices • Supporting higher English language literacy in aboriginal communities • Recruitment and retention strategies for aboriginal staff, particularly aspiring educational leaders
Assessment, reporting and accountability	• Assessment for learning, assessment of learning, assessment as learning • Industry confidence in assessment • Relationships between accountability measures and the performance of education providers • Teachers' use of assessment data and its effect on teaching practice
Cooperation and competition within and between schools	• Cooperation at faculty and school levels to improve student achievement • Cooperation with other schools to achieve greater efficiency in the use of resources and to provide a broader choice in curriculum offerings • Partnerships between regular and special schools • Professional exchanges for teachers and the impacts of those exchanges on pedagogy, culture, and practice
Curriculum issues	• Teaching basic skills • Engaging students in reading and writing • Integrating information and communication technologies into teaching and learning • Evidence to support "best practice" programs in education
Environmental sustainability	• Environmentally sustainable systems and schools • Effective approaches to environmental education • The essential scope of environmental education in terms of disciplines, content, values, and skills • Effective sequence/s for environmental education
Information and communication technologies (ICTs)	• The impact of ICT on student learning and engagement • The impact o ICT in teacher learning and professional development • High-impact uses of ICT • Technological factors and strategies that facilitate connected and distributed learning
Quality teaching in schools	• Teacher, student, and parent perceptions of the characteristics of quality teaching • Promoting and rewarding quality teaching • Factors relating to the adoption of new and innovative teaching practices • School structures and organizational patterns facilitating quality teaching

(Table continues on next page)

Table 8.1.   (Continued)

Priority Research Area	Topics of Interest
Resourcing	• Funding models for effective schools • Estimating the costs of high quality education provision • Harnessing community and industry resources for education and training • Balancing efficiency and effectiveness in resource allocation
Respect and responsibility in schools	• Approaches to teaching values and ethics • Characteristics of effective antiracism, multicultural and community relations policies, programs, and procedures • Characteristics of effective school welfare and discipline policies, programs, and procedures • Connections between student well-being and academic achievement
Socially just schooling	• Reducing achievement gaps between various groups • Multicultural education in and for a culturally, linguistically, and religiously diverse and harmonious society • Building leadership capacity in schools, especially those that experience a high turnover of staff • Developing community capacity through effective home, school and community partnerships
Student engagement in schools	• Making schooling and learning more enjoyable for students without decreasing achievement levels • Arresting the decline in student engagement in the middle years of schooling • Strategies for addressing student engagement through transition phases • Curriculum adjustment to cater for students with special education needs
Workforce development and capability building	• Talent management of teachers, leaders, and executives • Factors motivating prospective teachers to choose a career in teaching • Best practice teacher recruitment and retention strategies and procedures • Models for evaluating the effectiveness of professional development strategies

Methodologies

Numerous papers on schooling for young adolescents have been published in Australia over the last decade. However, few of these papers are based on objective research findings, defensible methodologies, and scholarly critique. There has also been a significant growth in official reports into adolescent education, but again little empirical research evidence underpins these reports (Luke et al., 2003). Moreover, Chadbourne

(2001, 2003) noted that where actual research studies investigating schooling/education for young adolescents have been conducted, they tend to rely on "soft" data (e.g., single cases, anecdotal qualitative data, and statistically untested self-report type evidence). Thus, few studies have produced credible data on academic or other outcomes.

In addition, focusing particularly on middle schools, Hill, Mackay, Russell, and Zbar (2001) found that most middle schools have yet to generate any convincing evidence of improved learning in terms of educational outcomes. Claims concerning the effectiveness of middle schools, especially with respect to improvements in literacy and numeracy, have regularly been made by schools. However, these claims have been made on the basis of ad hoc anecdotal evidence rather than systematic empirical evidence. In contrast to the hard empirical data required to demonstrate middle-schooling effectiveness, almost all of the research evidence on middle schooling in Australia is related to student and teacher attitudes towards middle schooling. The studies (see Hill et al., 2001; Pendergast, Kapitzke, & Luke, 2002) generally show that teachers believe that the introduction of middle schooling practices has improved student engagement and attitudes to learning. Other studies (e.g., Centre for Applied Educational Research 2002; Culican, Emmitt, & Oakley, 2001; Siemon, Virgona & Corneille, 2001) similarly indicated that middle school programs may make a difference to students' attitudes, and to teachers' perceptions about their capacity to make a difference to student learning—without actually tracking these attitudinal and perceptual changes to specific student outcomes.

Important Research Findings

Despite the limitations of current studies, the Australian Council for Educational Research (ACER—an internationally recognized nongovernmental educational research organization) has collated some important research finding relating to young adolescents. These findings include:

(a) Higher achievers in literacy and numeracy in Year 9 are more likely to stay at school until Year 12, have a higher tertiary entrance performance, or be employed and earning more when they leave school (Penman, 2004).

(b) Young adolescent achievement varies across students with different characteristics, and is associated with a variety of social and demographic factors such as sex, socioeconomic status (SES), family background, teacher characteristics and school setting. Not surprisingly, students from higher SES backgrounds outperform students from lower SES backgrounds (Thomson, Cresswell & DeBortoli, 2004). Research also shows that, in general, boys are not achieving as well as girls across a range of educational and social measures. Boys are also more likely to drop out of school early and are less likely to go on to university than girls (Cuttance et al., 2007).

(c) Despite (b), recent research on school subject selection, and subsequent study and work participation in Australia, has found that males are still much more likely than females to be taking advanced mathematics and science at senior secondary school and are much more likely to move into mathematics and science-related courses in higher education (Thomson, Cresswell & DeBortoli, 2004).

(d) Students attending schools in rural and remote areas experience educational disadvantage in a variety of ways, with some major issues including recruiting and retaining teachers, accessing educational services and support systems, and dealing with higher-than-urban usage costs of information and communications technologies and other education resources (Department of Education, Science and Training, 2003a).

(e) Indigenous students and students from non-English speaking backgrounds, consistently underperform relative to other students in Australia, and in many other international comparisons (Department of Education, Science and Training, 2003b; OECD, 2004).

FUTURE DIRECTIONS

Several key directions can be identified in young adolescent education in Australia. These directions include:

- expanding transition programs from primary to secondary schools;
- encouraging a focus on teacher/student relationships;
- raising the confidence and motivation of students;
- improving literacy and numeracy levels;
- addressing perceived superficiality and fragmentation in the secondary curriculum; and
- providing targeted professional development support to teachers, including the need to support middle years teachers to deliver programs that cross more than one key learning or subject area.

There is also an emerging recognition that policy and strategy at government and bureaucratic levels needs to become more coherent and coordinated in order to assist schools to deliver the best possible support to students throughout the middle years. Government and bureaucracy also have a role to play in supporting and publicizing successful current practices in young adolescent education. Finally, while there are divergent views on the merits of establishing separate middle schools, there does appear to be sufficient professional (if not research-based) support to further investigate the value of such structures so that the benefits or otherwise of dedicated middle schools can be properly evaluated.

Toward a National Curriculum

Collaboration between the States, Territories, and the Commonwealth over the last decade has resulted in a number of agreements that provide a framework for the development of a national curriculum. These agreements include:

The Adelaide Declaration which outlined agreement on eight common areas of learning, a socially just approach to schooling, and a focus on student learning outcomes. Curricula in all States and Territories up to the start of Year 11 broadly comply with the Adelaide Declaration.

National Statements of Learning in English, mathematics, science, civics and citizenship, and ICT have been endorsed by all governments. These Statements outline what every student should have the opportunity to learn in Australian schools. School authorities have agreed to align their curriculum with these Statements by 2008.

Structurally, there also appears to be opportunity to develop a national curriculum. For example, a recent report (Matters & Masters, 2007) highlighted similarities across jurisdictions in core curriculum areas. Moreover, despite some continuing disagreements, there also appears to be a relatively strong national consensus around what students should study across curriculum areas. For example, there is little debate over the centrality of literacy, numeracy, information technology, and a range of other core skills.

An agreed national core curriculum could promote equity for all students. However, it is currently agreed that a national curriculum should provide some flexibility for States/Territories and schools to innovate and adapt curricula to suit local and regional contexts and conditions. Thus, a level of autonomy for individual schools and teachers to make professional decisions about curriculum is seen as critical for maximizing student learning outcomes. Moreover, it is also seen as important to allow schools flexibility in catering for different groups of students thus allowing different groups to achieve national curriculum outcomes standards in different ways. Politically, the capacity to contextualize any national curriculum is also a more-or-less essential prerequisite for the adoption of a national curriculum i.e., despite the fact that a country of only 20 million people has eight separate educational jurisdictions, State/Territory parochialism (not just with respect to education) remains strong.

CONCLUDING DISCUSSION

The emergence of middle schools, national assessment, and a national curriculum have, and will continue to have, substantial effects on the education of young adolescents in Australia. Hopefully, these reforms will continue to promote innovative patterns of teaching, curriculum design and school organization that better engage and motivate young adolescents—thereby improving student outcomes. The real test of these reforms, however, will be their capacity to deliver demonstrable improvements in educational and social outcomes. At this stage, there is little sound research evidence supporting the case that these improvements are extant. However, such evidence may emerge as reforms become more widespread and entrenched, and as researchers and policymakers engage substantively in investigations of these reforms.

In order to maximize the potential that current reforms will actually result in improved student outcomes, state, territory and federal (Commonwealth) governments must continue to collaborate in core areas where national convergence will enhance student results, while at the same time not stifling local and regional experimentation, innovation, and contextualization. A balanced approach of this type should assist reforms to provide young Australian young adolescents with a realistic chance of meeting the national goals for schooling and, hence, to progress to productive and satisfying lives as fully engaged citizens of Australia.

NOTE

1.   Statistics in this section were compiled from data from the National Office of Overseas Skills Recognition (2000), and from recent statistics available through the Organisation of Economic Cooperation and Development and the Australian Bureau of Statistics.

REFERENCES

Australian Curriculum Studies Association. (1996). *From alienation to engagement: Opportunities for reform in the middle years of schooling*. Belconnen, Australian Capital Territory: Australian Curriculum Studies Association.

Barratt, R. (1998). *Shaping the middle years of schooling: A report of the National Middle Schooling Project*. Belconnen, Australian Capital Territory: Australian Curriculum Studies Association.

Carnegie Council on Adolescent Development. (1989). *Turning points: Preparing American youth for the 21st century*. Washington, DC: Carnegie Corporation of New York.

Centre for Applied Educational Research. (2002). *Middle Years Research and Development (MYRAD) Project*. Melbourne: University of Melbourne.

Chadbourne, R. (2001, October). *Middle schooling for the middle years*. Paper prepared for the Australian Education Union. Retrieved June 26, 2008, from http://www.aeufederal.org.au/Publications/ index2.html#PAP

Chadbourne, R. (2003). Middle schooling and academic rigor. *International Journal of Learning, 10*, 540-550.

Culican, S. J., Emmitt, M., & Oakley, C. (2001). *Literacy and learning in the middle years. Major report on the middle years' literacy project*. Canberra, Australia: Deakin University.

Cuttance, P., Imms, W., Godhino, S., Hartnell-Young, E., Thompson, J., McGuinness, K., & Neal, G. (2007). *Boys' education lighthouse schools: Stage two final report 2006*. Canberra, Australia: Department of Education Science and Training.

Department of Education, Science and Training. (2003a). *National evaluation of the Country Areas Program, 2002-03*. Canberra, Australia: Author.

Department of Education, Science and Training. (2003b). *Final report on the National Evaluation of National Indigenous English Literacy and Numeracy Strategy*. Canberra, Australia: Author.

Eyers, V. (1992). *Report of the junior secondary review*. Adelaide: Education Department of South Australia.

Hill, P., Mackay, A., Russell, V., & Zbar, V. (2001). The middle years. In P. Cuttance, M. Angus, F. Crowther & P. Hill (Eds.), *School innovation: Pathway to the knowledge society*. Canberra: Department of Education, Training and Youth Affairs. Retrieved August 29, 2008, from http://www.dest.gov.au/sectors/school_education/publications_resources/school_innovation/chapter_1.htm

Kosky, R., Eshkevari, H. S., Kneebone, G. (1997). *Breaking out: Challenges in adolescent mental health in Australia*. Canberra: Australian Government Printing Service.

Luke, A., Elkins, J., Weir, K., Land, R., Carrington, V., Dole, S., et al. (2003). *Beyond the middle: A report about literacy and numeracy development of a target group students in the middle years of schooling, Volume 1*. Canberra, Australia: Commonwealth Department of Education, Science and Training.

Matters, G., & Masters, G. (2007). *Curriculum content and achievement standards*. Canberra, Australia: Department of Education, Science and Training.

Ministerial Council on Education, Employment, Training and Youth Affairs. (1999). *The National Goals for schooling in the twenty-first century*. Canberra, Australia: MCEETYA.

National Office of Overseas Skills Recognition. (2000). *Country education profile: Australia. The Australian education system*: Canberra, Australia: Author.

Organisation for Economic Cooperation and Development. (2004). *Learning for tomorrow's world; First results from PISA 2003*. Paris: Author.

Pendergast, D., Kapitzke, C., & Luke, A. (2002). *Directions for middle years of schooling*. Brisbane, Australia: Catholic Education, Archdiocese of Brisbane.

Penman, R. (2004). *An easy reference guide to Longitudinal Surveys of Australian Youth research reports, 1996-2003*. Camberwell, Victoria: Australian Council for Educational Research.

Schools Council, National Board of Employment, Education and Training. (1993). *In the middle: Schooling for young adolescents*. Canberra: Australian Government Publishing Service.

Siemon, D., Virgona, J., & Corneille, K. (2001). *The middle years numeracy project: Final report*. Melbourne, Australia: Royal Melbourne Institute of Technology.

Thomson, S., Cresswell, J., & DeBortoli, L. (2004). *Facing the future: A focus on mathematical literacy among Australian 15 year old students in PISA 2003*. Camberwell, Victoria: Australian Council for Educational Research.

CHAPTER 9

RWANDA'S AUDACITY

A Story of Hope at the Middle Level

Kathleen F. Malu

This chapter reports on the education of young adolescents in the central African country of Rwanda, a country most immediately identified with the horrific genocide of 1994. Although the needs of this country continue to be great, the people of this small nation have made great strides to improve their lives, including the education of their middle level children. This chapter reveals the challenges this nation faces after the slaughter of the majority of their teachers and the destruction of most of their schools. With nearly 85% of primary-age children enrolled in the nation's elementary schools, the realities at the middle level are less positive. Current national strategies and international efforts for increasing enrollment at this level, as well as, curriculum development and research are presented.

CONTEXTUAL NARRATIVE

The Republic of Rwanda is a small, landlocked country in central Africa, 10,169 square miles in size and slightly larger than Vermont. It is most immediately associated with the horrific genocide of 1994 in which more

An International Look at Educating Young Adolescents
pp. 179–195
Copyright © 2009 by Information Age Publishing
All rights of reproduction in any form reserved.

than 1 million people were brutally murdered in a systematic, state-sponsored, 100-day long wave of violence. An additional 2 million fled to neighboring countries, and 1 million were displaced internally (Government of the Republic of Rwanda, 2008). This chapter reports on the heroic efforts that this nation is making as it strives to heal, rebuild and advance the education and development of their young adolescents. The Rwandans deserve our special attention, focus, understanding, and support for their efforts.

Rwanda is often called *le pays des milles collines*. These thousand hills have significantly influenced the culture and educational opportunities of this densely populated country of an estimated 10,180,000 (U.S. Department of State, 2008). Their predicted growth is more than 2.8% per year (U.S. Department of State). The median age of the total population is 17.4 years (United Nations Development Programme, 2007a). Rwanda is located in the "heart of Africa," south of Uganda, east of La République Démocratique du Congo, north of Burundi, and west of Tanzania. There are 23 lakes including the beautiful Lake Kivu, several rivers, some of which contribute to the source of the Nile River, and six volcanoes including the Sabyingo which last erupted in 1959 (Charbonneau, 1973). These volcanoes are part of the mountain chain in the northwest that is also located in the Congo. Within this mountainous region is Le Parc National de Volcans, home to the mountain gorilla, made famous by the researcher, Dian Fossey whose work in Rwanda was featured in the movie, *Gorillas in the Mist*. In addition to the *mille collines*, Rwanda is also *le pays du printemps éternel* because its climate is generally spring-like except for March and April, the rainiest months of the year.

It is helpful to contextualize the 1994 genocide within the broader history of this country and region. Rwandan history dates back many more centuries than "simply" its "discovery" by Western explorers. Archeological evidence reveals a region that was ruled by benevolent kings who encouraged their people to form communes based upon the network of hills on which extended families lived. Unlike other Africans who lived in the tropical climate regions, these people, called Hutu, were farmers who grew temperate climate vegetables, including corn, potatoes, and beans. Eventually, the Tutsi, nomadic, herding peoples from eastern Africa including current day Kenya and Tanzania began to appear, bringing with them cattle and goats. For many, many years these two groups lived in relative harmony. At the end of the nineteenth century, this land and its people were invaded by the Germans and later the Belgians.

Belgian rulers controlled by pitting one group of people, in the case of Rwanda the nomadic Tutsi herders, against the Hutu farmers. Belgian colonial actions, documented with great detail, make it clear that these colonizers used atrocities to dominate and control the Africans (Hochschild, 1998). Belgian domination tactics are at the root of present-day politics in Rwanda and the surrounding region (Hochschild). Perpetrators of the 1994 genocide and numerous previous ones including those in 1973 and 1979 mimicked the ghastly Belgian atrocities of earlier times: victims slashed with machetes, heads decapitated, hands cut off, women raped and mutilated, witnessed by would be orphaned children. It may be unfair and inaccurate to hold the West entirely responsible for current events; however, this short historical outline makes it clear that the developments in this region can not be accurately explained as simply a conflict between two different ethnic groups (Dallaire, 2003) as was and continues to be so frequently and dismissively reported by the Western press.

Geography and history play important roles in Rwandan cultural norms. The "hills" are a useful way to identify family ties. The family support structure is extended and includes aunts, uncles, nieces, nephews, grandparents, and other extended family members, as well as the proverbial African *mon cousin*, who lives *dans les communes* on the family hill and surrounding hills. Family compounds are grouped into communes that often take their names from the hills on which the families live. Since Rwandan independence, July 1, 1962, these communes have been used by the various global aid agencies to promote the concept of cooperatives, farming communities that support each other and share farming tools and grain storage spaces. Family members generally have responsibility for each other and are wary of strangers and anyone not connected to the family commune and/or hill in some way (Gourevitch, 1998). The classic African proverb, "*It takes a village to raise a child*" might be modified in Rwanda to "*It takes a hill …*" Despite their recent contentious history, the extended Rwandan family is generally collaborative and cooperative (Rusesabagina, 2006).

In addition to the general hesitancy to befriend neighbors who are not "family," there is a general feeling of caution and fear, particularly since 1994. This fear is held by the entire population. The current government hopes that with indictments from the United Nations War Crimes Tribunal in Arusha, Tanzania and the traditional community *Gacaca* court pronouncements that have begun to occur, the country will begin to heal.

Rwanda's social issues are evident in several noteworthy statistics. On the human development index, Rwanda ranks near the bottom, at 158 out of 177 countries listed on this index (United Nations Development Programme, 2007a). Sixty percent of the population lives below the poverty line, earning less than one U.S. dollar per day. Literacy rates are inequitable: More than 58% of the male population is literate compared to 48% of females. Life expectancy is 43 years and out of every 100,000 births, 1,400 mothers die in child birth.

The role of women in this society is important and difficult. Rwandans are extremely proud that they have the world's highest rate of female parliamentarians: More than 48% of the seats are held by women (Government of the Republic of Rwanda, 2008). Rwandans have surpassed gender equality in primary school enrollment and they rank 119 out of 177 on the gender development index (United Nations Development Programme, 2007b). Considering the physical constraints of the hills, however, women must make physical contributions that are extremely difficult. The labor-intensive work of carrying water up the hills for family consumption (26% of the population does not have access to improved drinking water sources) is a basic, daily chore. Typically, girls fetch the water and sometimes must travel great distances for it, up and down the hills. They are at risk of gender-based violence and by consequence HIV infection. Further effects of the 1994 genocide fall heavily on women. Females head 35% of all households and 56% of these females are widows (United Nations Development Programme, 2007b). More than 33% of Rwandan women report having experienced physical, sexual and/or emotional violence (United Nations Development Programme, 2007b). Across all levels of poverty from poor to extremely poor more women were consistently poorer than men. In urban centers, for example, there were two poor women for every poor man, a difference of 100% (United Nations Development Programme, 2007b).

Children comprise more than 44% of the total population (United Nations Development Programme, 2007b). Infant mortality for children under five years old is more than 203 of every 1,000 live births. More than 22% of children under the age of five are moderately or severely underweight. Education at the primary level is compulsory, free, and gender-equitable with equal numbers of boys and girls attending primary schools. Enrollment in primary schools has risen consistently through the 21st century. The most current data reveal that more than 85% of children are currently attending primary school (United Nations Development Programme, 2007b). With this increase, however, has come the challenge of finding enough qualified teachers. At the primary level, the pupil/qualified teacher ratio is at 74:1 (United Nations Development Programme, 2007b). The gender drop-out rates are unequal. Although close to 8% of boys drop out by the end of primary school, more than 15% of girls leave school (United Nations Development Programme, 2007b).

As a former Belgian colony, Rwanda was descended upon by Catholic and Protestant missionaries. Most Rwandans practice one of these religions today. More than 93% are Christian (U.S. Department of State, 2008). The Muslim population is approximately 4% of the population (U.S. Department of State). Muslims, who reside in Rwanda, typically immigrated decades earlier from West Africa, the eastern coast of Africa, and the Arabian coast.

HISTORY AND ORGANIZATION OF SCHOOLING FOR YOUNG ADOLESCENTS

Historical Background

The history of schooling for young adolescents in Rwanda has its roots in the Belgian colonial rule and Rwandan history after independence in 1962. During the Belgian colonial period, the Belgian rulers took a very paternalistic approach to their colony and decided to first provide a primary school education to the entire population. Once there was a complete system of primary schools in place and the entire population completed their primary education, the Belgians proposed to build secondary schools nationwide. When the secondary school network was complete and all Rwandans had attended secondary school, a tertiary level was to be considered.

Independence came much too soon for this massive, cumbersome education plan to be fully implemented. By 1962, there were an adequate number of primary schools available and many Rwandans were in attendance. The construction of secondary schools had only just begun and there were very few qualified individuals to serve as school administrators and teachers at the secondary level.

In addition to these government sponsored schools, missionary schools were set up by the various Catholic and Protestant missionaries who came to convert the Rwandans to Catholicism or Protestantism. *L'école belge* was the only primary school established by and for the children of Belgian officials. Mission schools that were near Kigali, the capital, served the children from affluent Rwandan families whose Rwandan parents worked in prestigious jobs. *L'école belge* enrolled children of ex-patriot Belgians working in Rwanda on various Belgian projects and children of other international parents who worked for the Belgian government, non-profit aid agencies, or international businesses. These schools offered the first eight years of schooling. For high school, European families sent their children to various boarding schools in Europe. The Rwandan children had nowhere to go to continue their education, except to the few secondary schools.

After independence, each Rwandan Minister of Education favored his region with extra classroom seats for the children from his particular commune. After the coup d'état in 1976, President Habyarimana and his family took control of the education system. They built the nation's major secondary school network in the president's region, to the north and west of Kigali, and most of the students who attended secondary school were from that region. Because of this, the parents in the other regions, particularly those living in southern Rwanda, created their own system of private schools (Rwanda Development Gateway, 2003-2005).

Curriculum, Instruction, and Assessment Practices

The curriculum for young adolescents is similar to the traditional Belgian curriculum. At this level students continue their academic preparation. The curriculum includes academic courses (mathematics; history; science; French; English; and Kinyrwanda, the native African language of Rwanda; civics; physical education; and geography). These academic courses are taught in the *Tronc Commun*, the first 3 years of the secondary level. The content becomes increasingly more difficult over time. Students have no choice in the courses they take. Everyone follows the same curriculum. These courses are designed to prepare children to advance into the second phase of secondary school, *Le Second Cycle* where they make professional career choices or attend vocational schools, such as the Youth Training Centers where they are prepared for a trade such as electricity/electronics, general mechanics or public works for boys and for girls, secretarial skills, or nursing.

Curriculum content is determined by the National Curriculum Development Centre (NCDC), the General Inspectorate (GI) and the National Examinations Council (NEC), all part of the Ministry of Education (African Development Fund, 2006; Republic of Rwanda, n.d.). *Les inspecteurs/inspectrices* of the GI are content specialists, responsible for curriculum development in their specialty area. If possible, they identify and purchase appropriate curricular materials from international and local textbook publishers; however, due to the cost of such materials, *les inspecteurs/inspectrices* develop national curriculum materials. These materials frame the content in ways that Rwandan students can understand from a cultural perspective. For example, curriculum materials developed for the teaching of English use Rwandan cultural and geographic references and Rwandan names in dialogues and stories. Because these materials allow students to access prior knowledge that they are familiar with such in-country published materials are more educationally appropriate and cost-effective. If English language texts were purchased from an American publisher, for example, names, places and cultural references would have no relevance for Rwandan students.

Instruction is determined by classroom conditions, availability of books, copying machines, electricity, and technology. Typically, teachers work in schools that have blackboards, chalk, student and teacher desks, rulers, paper, pens, pencils and paper. An international aid grant was used to purchase 4,000 computers which were distributed to 400 schools. In addition, from other international assistance, some of the schools in the urban centers have state-of-the-art computer labs but these are only available to students who attend schools in the major cities such as Kigali and Butare.

A typical day for students in *Le Tronc Commun* is the same as a day for students at all levels of schooling. Students wake with the sun, around 6:00 A.M. Because Rwanda is close to the equator, the sun rises and sets, on average, close to a 12-hour cycle. By 6:30 students are finished with breakfast, typically bread, margarine, milk with tea and maybe a bit of fruit, mango or pineapple. Those from families with a bit more money may also have a slice of meat and/or cheese. Then they walk to school. Depending on the location of the school and whether the families live in a rural or urban setting, this walk can be as little as 10 minutes or as long as an hour. School begins at 7:30 A.M. In the government subsidized schools students have an assembly that includes a salute to the flag and singing of the national anthem. In the religiously supported schools, the assembly includes prayers. Then, students go to their respective classrooms for four morning classes. Typically, at *Le Tronc Commun* there are 50 students per classroom (personal communication). The students remain in their class-rooms. The teachers circulate at the end of each period. At noon, students return home for lunch and rest. For lunch they usually have whatever the family can afford. This may be rice and beans or potatoes. There may or may not be a bit of meat (beef, pork, chicken, or goat) and other vegetables such as greens or string beans. Students return for three afternoon classes that begin at 1:30 P.M. School ends at 4:30 P.M.

Students who live in urban areas and have access to electricity are expected to complete homework assignments such as memorizing the day's lecture or responding to short fact-based questions. Those who live in rural areas are less likely to have electricity and are not assigned home-work because they have family chores to do after school, such as carrying water or searching for firewood before sunset.

Typically, teachers teach the way they were taught. They lecture and write up their notes on the blackboard for the students to copy into con-tent designated copy books, similar to American black and white compo-sition books. Teacher lectures are developed from the curriculum materials provided to them from the NCDC. If textbooks are available, there are generally enough for half the class to share. This sharing is effective because students also share a desk, which is wide enough to accommodate two students.

Each class period is 60 minutes. Periodically during the lecture, the teacher asks students questions to ensure that they understand the material presented. Students are expected to raise their hands and wait to be called upon. When the teacher acknowledges a student, he or she is expected to stand and recite the answer. Teachers end their lectures in time for the students to copy the lecture notes from the board into their copy books. Teachers frequently circulate around the room to ensure that students copy accurately and clearly. Students are expected to keep an assignment book at the top of their desks where they must record the homework assignments. Teachers are expected to monitor these to ensure their accuracy and neatness. This instructional style matches the American "chalk-and-talk" delivery of information.

School administrators and teachers are expected to maintain all records, including assignment books, copy books, lesson plans, grades, and other student work such as tests and quizzes, in order at all times. One of the important roles of *les inspecteurs/inspectrices* is to make unannounced visits to schools. During a visit *les inspecteurs/inspectrices* review all documents and records to be sure they are in order. They observe teachers and expect to see their lesson plan for the day and the children engaged in listening, responding to questions, and diligently copying down the lecture information. At the end of the observation, *l'inspecteur/ inspectrice* may question and discuss the lesson with the teacher. A visit lasts anywhere between a half day to a complete day. Within a few weeks after the visit, *les inspecteurs/inspectrices* complete their report and mail it or hand deliver it to the school administrator and teacher. If infractions are noted, teachers are expected to make corrections in their teaching and/or record keeping immediately because it is certain that a second unannounced visit will occur within the next few months. If this second visit results in continued infractions, the school administrator and *l'inspecteur/ inspectrice* plan a course of action to help the teacher improve. In extreme cases, teachers may be removed from the school and/or have their teaching license revoked.

There are two types of assessments. Teacher-made assessments are short answer quizzes that teachers give to their students to ensure that they have mastered the material presented. The frequency of such tests is determined by the teacher. Mid-year exams are also developed and administered by the teachers. Teachers use these exams to determine how well students have mastered the lecture information. If students are successful on these exams then teachers present new material. If student scores are lower than expected teachers may review the information before advancing further in the curriculum.

The second form of assessment is *les examens nationaux*. Little has changed over the years in the power and influence these exams hold over the lives of Rwandan students. Students can only enter secondary school, if they pass the primary level state exams. State exams are written by *les inspecteurs/inspectrices* and are closely guarded during their development, distribution, administration, and scoring. All students who wish to continue their education must receive a passing score on the state exams. Each exam is evaluated holistically by two educators, usually the classroom teacher and *l'inspecteur/inspectrice* responsible for the curriculum content or their designate. If the two scores given by the two educators do not match, a third educator is asked to evaluate the exam and the scores that more closely match are used. Once all exams are graded, the educators identify the cut-off passing score. This score varies every year. A passing score permits students to continue on to secondary school. Students who do not attain this score generally return to their families to help with the family chores, farming the land and/or contributing to the family business to raise money to support the family. Students who pass their state exams can go on to the last three years of secondary school.

Organization and Structure

Currently, the educational system in Rwanda is organized into two levels. The primary level for ages 7-12 includes six grades. After completing the sixth grade in primary school and successfully passing *les examens nationaux,* students begin *l'école secondaire,* which includes six years of education. The first three years in the *Tronc Commun* are roughly the equivalent of the American middle school years and include students aged 13-15. *Le Second Cycle,* the final three years, is similar to the American high school.

OUTCOMES OF THE SCHOOLING OF YOUNG ADOLESCENTS

Academic Performance Outcomes

Information regarding academic performance outcomes in *Le Tronc Commun* can be more easily understood by first considering a few significant statistics for primary education. Although universal primary education is available and the net enrollment in primary school by 2005 was 86% with gender parity, for every 100 children who begin primary school, 64 graduate (United Nations Development Programme, 2007b). Only 50% of those who graduate from primary school continue onto secondary school. Only 16% of girls finish primary school (United Nations Development Programme, 2007b).

Secondary school enrollment is at barely 10% net enrollment nationally with less than 8% enrollment in rural areas (United National Development Programme, 2007b). Gender parity is no longer evident at this level with less than .89 girls per every boy (United National Development Programme, 2007b). For each level of *Le Tronc Commun*, there is close to a 10% drop-out rate and repeater rate per year (Rwanda Ministry of Education, n.d.-b). Approximately 50% of the students who enroll for the first year in *Le Tronc Commun* enroll in *Le Second Cycle* (African Development Fund, 2006). See "Concerns" for explanations of these statistics.

Other Important Outcomes

While there are other important outcomes that need to be studied, there are no data available that examine such outcomes. For example, it would be helpful to understand how children use the education they receive if they attend school beyond *Le Tronc Commun* and/or drop out before completing these grades. Further understandings of the role that these three years of schooling plays in their lives can be used to re-design the curriculum in ways that can help children who may not be in a position to advance to *Le Second Cycle*.

Research Supporting Academic Performance and Other Outcomes

The research that supports academic performance and other outcomes is available through the Rwanda Ministry of Education, the National University of Rwanda, the United Nations and its branches, including the UNDP, UNICEF and UNESCO. The Ministry of Education recognizes that such data are very important; however, they have many pressing research priorities such as the influence of poverty and health, malaria, HIV/AIDS, and other living conditions on school attendance, for girls in particular.

CURRENT ISSUES RELATED TO THE
SCHOOLING OF YOUNG ADOLESCENTS

Concerns about the Current Educational System

Reasons why children do not enroll in *Le Tron Commun* include malnutrition, the continued trauma from the genocide, failure to pass the state examinations, need to assist the family with chores and income, lack of money to pay for school items, and no secondary school within a reasonable walking/commuting distance. Gender equity at the beginning of *Le Tronc Commun* is quite close; 47% of the students are girls; however, the rate of girls who enter *Le Second Cycle* is alarming. Only 10% of the girls who complete *Le Tronc Commun* continue onto this final level (UNICEF, n.d.-a).

The student-to-qualified teacher ratio of 74:1 is a concern at the primary level but 88% of primary teachers are certified to teach according to the national standards (United Nations Development Programme, 2007b). At the secondary level the student-to-qualified teacher ratio is 55:1 and only 51% of teachers are certified to teach (United Nations Development Programme, 2007b). The quality of teachers is clearly a concern at the secondary level of education.

Another major concern regarding the current educational system is the need to educate children who were horrifically impacted by the genocide of 1994. Many children between the ages of 9-14 never attended school because their local schools were destroyed and their teachers assassinated. More than 810,000 children are orphans and 100,000 are heads of households (UNICEF, n.d.-a). The current educational system is not designed to help children who face such obstacles.

Although school fees at the primary level were abolished and secondary level fees will soon be, there are other costs for attending school. School supplies and copy books can easily cost $5.10 and school uniforms, $6.20. These are impossible sums of money for families who earn less than one dollar (U.S. equivalent). UNICEF supported the fee-free schooling and continues to call for the elimination of school uniforms (UNICEF, n.d.-d).

Another concern with the current educational system is the need to maintain and improve the quality of educational services given the rapid increase in the number of students who will be able to enter the secondary level. With universal fee-free primary education that reaches more than 85% of the population, the need for more seats in secondary schools will increase and the current system can not adequately respond to this increase. More schools will have to be built and more individuals trained to be qualified teachers.

Another concern is the question: How and what to teach about the genocide? (Kron, 2007; UNICEF, n.d.-b). To date, few individuals have attempted to discuss or plan for instruction of this painful and complex piece of Rwandan history. There may not yet be a safe space where educational leaders can explore this problem. One idea is to teach students about genocides committed in other countries so that the shame and pain for Rwandans may be placed in a global context (Kron, 2007).

Benefits of the Current Educational System

Educational leaders accepted the suggestion of UNICEF that those children who never attended school and/or stopped attending when the genocide began need to be educated. Classes were created to help children "catch up" (UNICEF, n.d.-d). These classes help children, regardless of their ages and education, catch up to the appropriate levels of literacy for their age.

Another innovative educational opportunity provided to some Rwandan children is Saturday activities (UNICEF, n.d.-c). Every Saturday the Amani Africa Organization (*amani*, from the Swahili word for peace) provides play and cultural activities for children in a few locations throughout the country. This nontraditional learning environment offers children an opportunity to learn, grow and heal from the traumas of the genocide and lack of education.

The fact that the Rwandan educational leadership responds to the needs of the children by designing these creative educational opportunities is extremely important. Given the tremendous challenges that continue to exist in this country, the flexibility and creativity that these leaders exhibit is extremely important and will undoubtedly benefit the nation's young citizens.

REFORM INITIATIVES AND NATIONAL POLICIES

The government of Rwanda states that their goal is to "reduce poverty and … improve the well-being of its population … the aim of education is to combat ignorance and illiteracy and to provide human resources useful for the socio-economic development of Rwanda" (Rwanda Ministry of Education, n.d.-a). The Rwandan Ministry of Education has identified several strategic priorities. They are for all levels of education, including *Le Tronc Commun*.

By 2020, the target date for the United Nations Millennium Goal Project, the Ministry of Education expects to offer fee-free education at the primary and secondary levels to all of its young citizens. The second priority is the education of girls. Given the significant disparity between boys and girls in secondary education, the nation has set this as an important priority. Trilingualism is another national initiative and it is based upon the national policy that there are three official languages: Kinyarwanda, French, and English. As a former Francophone country, the inclusion of English as an official language is significant and creates tremendous challenges for those teachers who only speak one of these two international languages. However, Rwanda views the need for the inclusion of English as justified economically, socially, and politically. English language learning begins at the fourth grade of primary school and resources and opportunities for qualified Kenyan teachers to work in Rwanda are available.

HIV/AIDS education is a priority that links with the Ministry of Health's goal to reduce the number of incidents within the population. Another priority is to develop secondary level classes in science, technology and information and communication technology (ICT). This priority is also targeted to encourage more girls to enter these fields. There is a tremendous disparity between the number of girls and boys who enter secondary schools and study these fields. This priority will be very difficult to meet because of the lack of access to electrical power in many regions of the country, qualified teachers, and equipment. Special education is another priority of this nation and the ministry is hopeful it will be able to begin programs that will bring this segment of the population into specially designed learning environments.

RESEARCH

Current Research Topics

The majority of research currently available addresses numerous areas at the primary level of schooling. Additional research topics include needs assessments of physical institutions, public expenditure tracking surveys, gender and poverty issues, special education, science and technology, and HIV/AIDS education. These research topics are critical at all levels of education, including *Le Tronc Commun.* Most of the research topics are designed to assist with the nation's application for international funds and grants.

These research topics emerge from the various proposals and offers for support that a wide variety of organizations offer to Rwanda. Various international organizations include those connected with the United Nations, the International Monetary Fund, and members of the European Union. Individual national donors include the United States and Canada and various African nations such as Kenya and Uganda. One significant funding source that celebrated its withdrawal from Rwanda was *Les Médecins Sans Frontières.* After 16 years in Rwanda to help with the aftermath of the genocide, this organization decided that Rwanda was on the road to recovery and their expertise was no longer necessary.

Methodologies

The research methodology used in all of the sources examined is quantitative in design with the outcomes reported in terms of statistical findings. The use of this type of methodology is critically important. Rwanda must be able to respond to various international aid and grant applications. Such applications typically require statistical information so it is clear that this quantitative methodology will continue to be critically important in the long term.

Important Research Findings

Important statistical research findings include the figures presented throughout this report. Of critical importance are enrollment, repeater and drop-out rates at all levels of education. Findings regarding gender parity and health and literacy are equally important findings. At a secondary level are the qualitative understandings that can play a critically important role in the interpretation of the statistics. For example, understanding that women are a major part of the workforce is more useful when placed within the context of the roles they play as heads of households. Statistics that reveal gender disparities are more meaningful when we know that girls are required to perform the majority of domestic chores such as the transport of water and the search for firewood.

FUTURE DIRECTIONS

For a variety of reasons, including the dropout rates after the *Tronc Commun,* the common-core syllabus, and the need to increase access to basic education for the maximum number of children, the Ministry of Education is in the process of reconfiguring the educational structure and proposes to extend primary education to include the three years of the *Tronc Commun* (African Development Fund, 2006).

The nation is addressing the issue of unqualified teachers. Because most of the nation's teachers were either slaughtered during the genocide or went into exile (Gribbin, 2005), there are few experienced, seasoned Rwandan teachers. Visiting teacher programs with neighboring countries, including Uganda, Kenya and Tanzania, are one way that Rwandan educational leaders have been able to temporarily address this shortage. At the time of this writing, the United States Peace Corps program was beginning its first year of reentry into Rwanda.

Given the continued need in Rwanda for outside assistance, it is important that the Rwandan government improve the coordination between the various donors in the country, particularly those who support education. A substantial research agenda for *Le Tronc Commun* should be developed so that administrators and teachers have a better understanding of the educational needs of their students, particularly given the fact that female drop-out rates are high.

There is a need to conduct long-term qualitative studies and case studies so that further understandings can be gained about dropouts and gender inequity, including the domestic responsibilities and dangers that girls face in and outside of school. Today, more than 86% of women in Rwandan society perform agricultural work. They have responsibility for the majority of financial decisions in the family. Using this information to re-design curriculum as it relates to girls should be a high priority.

CONCLUDING DISCUSSION

Rwanda has made great strides in some areas and rightly deserves to be proud of these accomplishments. The depth and complexity of her problems must continue to draw attention, help, support, and encouragement from the world community to ensure that the horrors faced by this nation, and the surrounding region, never happen again. Changes in the education of young adolescents will only be possible as fundamental life-style changes are made throughout the country, however. Food, shelter and health need to be adequate for children to learn and grow. Dallaire (2003), the highest ranking UN commander in Rwanda during the spring of 1994, "shook hands with the devil." Today, he calls us all to action. *Peux ce que veux. Allons-y!* Where there is a will, there is a way. Let's go!

ACKNOWLEDGMENTS

I wish to acknowledge the help and encouragement I received from the following people: Robert Gribbin, former U.S. ambassador to Rwanda; Patricia and Kevin Lowther, friends and former Africare representatives and William Noble, regional representative for Africare. The following individuals shared their expertise about current local conditions in Rwanda and I am very grateful for their time in responding to my questions: Orbu Willis, Africare country representative and Théophile Mudenge, Africare project coordinator for Africare's community orphan project. Although there were missed meetings and phone calls, I recognize the efforts of Moses Rugema, second consul at the Rwandan mission to the United Nations. I offer a "très grand merci" to Jean-Gratien Uwisavye who encouraged me to reclaim my Francophone "voice" and love of Rwanda and her people. Additional details for this chapter come from my professional and personal experiences working and living in Rwanda from 1980-1981 for the *Bureau Pédagogique* in the Ministry of

Education. Any errors in this chapter are my own and in no way reflect the contributions of the above mentioned individuals.

REFERENCES

African Development Fund. (2006). *Republic of Rwanda: Program in support of the education sector, Strategic plan (ESSP) 2006-2010 Appraisal Report.* Retrieved July 15, 2008, from http://www.mineduc.gov.rw/IMG/pdf/RWANDA_20EDUCATION_202006_20ENGL.pdf

Charbonneau, R. (1973). *L'Afrique Noire et L'Océan Indien Francophones Aujourd'Hui.* Paris: Editions Jeune Afrique.

Dallaire, R. (2003). Shake *hands with the devil: The failure of humanity in Rwanda.* New York: Carroll & Graf.

Gourevitch, P. (1998). We *wish to inform you that tomorrow we will be killed with our families: Stories from Rwanda.* New York: Farrar, Straus and Giroux

Government of the Republic of Rwanda. (2008). *Official website of the Republic of Rwanda.* Retrieved June 22, 2008, from http://www.gov.rw/

Gribbin, R. E. (2005). *In the aftermath of genocide: The U.S. role in Rwanda.* Lincoln, NE: iUniverse.

Hochschild, A. (1998). *King Leopold's ghost: A story of greed, terror, and heroism in colonial Africa.* Boston: Houghton Mifflin.

Kron, J. (2007). Rwandans need to know about other atrocities. *The New Times, Kigali.* Retrieved July 15, 2008, from http://www.africafiles.org/article.asp?ID=15874

Republic of Rwanda. (n.d.). *Ministry of Education, Science, Technology and Scientific Research: MINEDUC textbook policy.* Retrieved July 10, 2008, from http://www.mineduc.gov.rw/IMG/pdf/Mineduc_textbook_policy-_CNDC.pdf

Rusesabagina, P. (2006). *An ordinary man: An autobiography.* New York: Viking.

Rwanda Development Gateway. (2003-2005). *L'Éducation au Rwanda de 1960 au 1994.* Retrieved July 15, 2008, from http://www.rwandagateway.org/education/article.php3?id_article=4

Rwanda Ministry of Education. (n.d.-a). *Rwanda: Ministry of Education, mission statement.* Retrieved June 20, 2008, from http://www.mineduc.gov.rw/

Rwanda Ministry of Education. (n.d.-b). *Rwanda: Ministry of Education, secondary education statistics.* Retrieved July 15, 2008, from http://www.mineduc.gov.rw/IMG/xls/2005_secondaire_Rwanda.xls

UNICEF. (n.d.-a). *Information by country: Rwanda—background.* Retrieved June 24, 2008, from http://www.unicef.org/infobycountry/rwanda_1717.html

UNICEF. (n.d.-b). *Information by country: Rwanda. Beyond school books: A podcast series on education in emergencies: Segment #7.* Retrieved June 24, 2008, from http://www.unicef.org/infobycountry/rwanda_newsline.html

UNICEF. (n.d.-c). *Information by country: Rwanda. Rwandan children learn and play to celebrate the day of the African child.* Retrieved June 24, 2008, from http://www.unicef.org/infobycountry/rwanda_44514.html

UNICEF. (n.d.-d). *Rwanda's most vulnerable children get a second chance to learn.* Retrieved June 24, 2008, from http://www.unicef.org/infobycountry/rwanda_16162.html

United Nations Development Programme. (2007a). *Millennium Development Goals monitor: Tracking the Millennium Development Goals.* Retrieved June 19, 2008, from http://www.mdgmonitor.org/factsheets_00.cfm?c=RWA&cd=646

United Nations Development Programme. (2007b). *Turning Vision 2020 into reality: From recovery to sustainable human development, National Human Development Report, Rwanda, 2007.* Kigali, Rwanda: Author. Retrieved June 19, 2008, from http://www.undp.org.rw/NHDR2007_main_report.pdf

U.S. Department of State. (2008). *Bureau of African Affairs: Background note: Rwanda.* Retrieved June 25, 2008, from http://www.state.gov/r/pa/ei/bgn/2861.htm

CHAPTER 10

AN INTERNATIONAL LOOK AT EDUCATING YOUNG ADOLESCENTS IN SOUTH AFRICA

Paul Webb

While history and politics always play a crucial role in education, there are few countries in the world where they have more explicitly shaped the process than in South Africa over the past 6 decades. The major shaping forces have been the effects of apartheid legislation, the philosophy of fundamental pedagogics and the emancipatory vision of the postapartheid government. Currently it appears that South Africa has not 1, but 2 (unofficial) education systems. One caters to the elite and the White and Black middle classes, the other to the majority of South African working class and poor children. These 2 systems do not produce equitable academic achievements, with children learning within the second system achieving at unacceptably low levels. Issues that play a role in these inequities are poverty, health, nutrition, dysfunctional schools and educational systems, and a disjuncture between home language and the language of teaching and learning in schools.

An International Look at Educating Young Adolescents
pp. 197–221

CONTEXTUAL NARRATIVE

Fleisch (2008) wrote that South Africa has not one, but two (unofficial) education systems. The first is well resourced, consists mainly of former White and Indian schools, and enrolls children of the elite and White and Black middle classes. This system provides an education system comparable to those of middle class children anywhere in the world and produces the majority of university entrants and graduates. The second system enrolls the majority of South African working class and poor children, and provides a much more restricted set of knowledge and skills in institutions which are mostly less than adequate (Fleisch).

Disaggregation of the results of national systemic evaluations of students' abilities show a clear bimodal distribution of achievement between the children catered for in each of the systems (Department of Education, 2003; Western Cape Department of Education, 2005, 2006). This chapter focuses mainly on the schooling of children who are taught within Fleisch's second system as they form the vast majority (over 80%) of the South African school going population and provide clear examples of the effects of history, politics, poverty, language, and sub-standard teaching on educating young adolescents.

HISTORY AND ORGANIZATION OF SCHOOLING OF YOUNG ADOLESCENTS

While history and politics always play a crucial role in education, there are few countries in the world where they have more explicitly shaped the process than in South Africa over the past 6 decades. After the installation of the Nationalist government in 1948 (and consequent adoption of *Apartheid* as national policy), a system of "Bantu Education" was introduced for Black South Africans (Samuel, 1990) where education for 80% of the population was to be largely based in the Bantustans or homelands where "the natives" would be prepared for a life in reserves, that is, living in a designated tribal area which is characterized by limited infrastructure and work opportunities, and by the fact that there are very little or no amenities available (Davies, 1986).

Historical Background

In this chapter issues related to young adolescents are considered. In South Africa almost everything has to be considered within the context of Apartheid and Bantu Education, and issues such as the examination-driven curriculum that was offered and the teacher centered practices that were promoted. These issues become insignificant against the back-drop of resistance to Bantu Education by learners and defiance by teach-ers of governmental edicts. Decades of "liberation before education" produced what is now called the "lost generations" and have impacted not only on the schooling of young adolescents in the past, but still have an impact today (Christie, Butler, & Potterton, 2007).

In 1953 the Prime Minister, Hendrik Verwoed, explicitly outlined the aims of Bantu Education in speeches to parliament as being the stabiliza-tion of the proletariat, production of a semi-skilled workforce and the prevention of juvenile delinquency and political militancy among work-ing class youth (Cross & Chisholm, 1990). In terms of teacher education, the Nationalist government took over all missionary colleges of educa-tion, closed urban colleges and opened new ones in the homelands, replaced English speaking staff with Afrikaans speaking staff, and intro-duced different and inferior curricula—usually with no science or mathe-matics offerings (Hartshorne, 1992).

A turning point in the history of Black education in South Africa came in 1976 when African pupils collectively rejected Bantu Education, caus-ing a total collapse of schooling in their communities (Cross & Chisholm, 1990). Schools became sites of struggle. The upsurge of student power was linked to community consciousness and workers' organizations, and was accompanied by a wave of guerrilla incursions, which began to seri-ously threaten the system of apartheid (Kallaway, 1984).

The state responded by increasing expenditure on Black education, mainly for building more classrooms and for maintenance of schools (Samuel, 1990). The Education and Training Act of 1980 replaced the Bantu Education Act of 1953 and the Bantu Education Special Act of 1964 (Samuel). Subsequently, the De Lange Commission (1981) was appointed to investigate the education system of South Africa and specific references to science and mathematics education were made for the first time in the government's White Paper of 1983, namely that there were serious problems related to teaching and learning in these subjects in terms of learner achievement at all levels and teachers' poor subject knowledge and teaching ability.

The disintegration of Black education continued into the late 1980s, worsening with the increasing politicization of teachers, formation of mil-itant teacher organizations, and the rejection of educational authorities (Morphet, Schaffer, & Millar, 1986; Reeves, 1994). This resulted in, amongst others, the cessation of school inspections as teachers threatened anyone who tried to evaluate their performance (World Bank, 1995). This culture of no accountability to education authorities in Black schools con-

tinued even after the election of a new government in 1994 and has resid-
ual effect to the present (Taylor & Vinjevold, 1999; World Bank, 1995).

Curriculum, Instruction, and Assessment Practices

Fundamental pedagogics, which is an indigenous South African product drawing on Dutch phenomenological philosophy that claimed to have
developed a science of education, held sway in South Africa during the
apartheid years (Hartshorne, 1992). Fundamental pedagogics was particularly associated with the education faculty at the University of South
Africa (UNISA), which operated via distance education and was by far the
largest provider of pre- and in-service education for teachers in the country. Fundamental Pedagogics was also dominant discourse at a number of
Afrikaans and 'homeland' universities (staffed mainly by White Afrikan-
ers). This philosophy is based on premises that can be interpreted as
being authoritarian (e.g., the teacher, as knowing adult, leads the child to
maturity), but what is more important is the way in which it was taught,
viz. through a series of propositions that brooked no analysis or critique.

A number of researchers and organizational reports (African National
Congress [ANC], 1994; Chisholm, 1993; Enslin, 1990; Hartshorne, 1992;
NEPI, 1992) suggested that the ideology of Fundamental Pedagogics has
had wide ranging detrimental effects on teachers' thinking and practice,
and it is from this perspective and legacy that the latest attempts by government to find national solutions to the historical problems of education
in South Africa are framed, that is, the propagation of a liberatory ideology and the encouragement of teachers to follow learner-centred classroom practices. It is the above premises which underpin the new national
curriculum in South Africa, which is discussed in more detail in this chapter (Department of Education, 2002).

Organization and Structure

Teachers, pupils, and parents have had considerable influence on the
language policies that operate in schools in South Africa. This has
occurred from the mid-nineteenth century to the present postapartheid
dispensation, often in the form of resistance to government language policies in the form of boycotts and riots, and on an ongoing de facto level of
quiet disregard for official policy (Taylor & Vinjevold, 1999).

As has often been the case in South Africa, different policies have
applied to different race groups. The language policy in previously White,
colored and Indian schools has remained fairly constant since union in

1910 when English and Dutch (and later Afrikaans) were declared the official languages of the Union of South Africa (Hartshorne, 1992). The medium of instruction in these schools was either English or Afrikaans (with the other language a compulsory subject).

At the time of union, English was the dominant language in the limited number of Black schools that existed. After the National Party came to power in 1948, Black schools were removed from provincial administrations and were placed under the jurisdiction of the Department of Bantu Education (Hartshorne, 1992; Taylor & Vinjevold 1999). The Bantu Education Act of 1953 changed the language policy of these schools in order to extend the use of mother tongue and Afrikaans. By 1959 all 8 years of primary education was done in mother tongue and secondary education was to use English and Afrikaans for instruction in a ratio of 50:50. In order to implement this new policy all teachers in Black schools were given 5 years to become competent in Afrikaans via the intensive in-service Afrikaans language courses that were offered by the government (Hartshorne).

Teachers, parents and pupils never became reconciled to either mother-tongue primary education or the dual-medium policy for secondary schools (Hartshorne, 1992). The Soweto uprising of 1976 is the best-known manifestation of resistance to the Nationalist government's language policy (there had been ongoing resistance since its inception in 1953). In the Cape Province many Black teachers resigned or were dismissed because they would not implement the new language policy. In the Eastern Cape and on the Witwatersrand parents boycotted Bantu Education schools and attempted to set up schools in which English was the medium of instruction. School boards and the African Teachers' Association of South Africa (ATASA) drafted petitions and organized deputations against the language policy on educational grounds. However, the Department of Bantu Education remained inflexible in the face of resistance (Hartshorne).

Ironically, the government's rigid and unpopular language policy was undermined by its own policy of separate development. From the 1960s the homelands and self-governing territories opted for mother-tongue instruction in the first 4 years of schooling only and English thereafter. As such there was a divide in policy between Black schools in the homelands and those under the Department of Bantu Education. This prompted an investigation into the medium of instruction in Black schools by the Bantu Education Advisory Education. The findings of this investigation strongly rejected the 50:50 medium of instruction as contrary to good education principles, and recommended mother-tongue instruction up to Grade 6 and thereafter instruction in either English or Afrikaans. The secretary of the Department of Bantu Education accepted the recommendation for mother-tongue instruction up to Grade 6 but rejected the recommendation that either English or Afrikaans be used as the medium of instruction thereafter for a number of reasons, not least because of pressure from the Ministry to protect the position of Afrikaans (Hartshorne, 1992; Taylor & Vinjevold 1999).

This decision came at the same time as the government's decision to bring the number of years of schooling for Black South Africans into line with those of other race groups. This meant that primary schooling was reduced from eight to seven years. As such, the school-leaving certificate was now written in English or Afrikaans at the end of Grade 7, after pupils had received only one year of instruction in these languages (Hartshorne 1992).

Hartshorne (1992) wrote that, in the light of the above, it is not surprising that in 1976 resistance to the language policy came from the junior secondary and senior primary schools, institutions which provide education for 13-15 year old and 9-12 year old children, respectively. This resistance grew into violent confrontations between pupils and the police, first in Soweto and then in other parts of the country. By July of 1976 the Minister of Bantu Education reluctantly agreed to change the dual medium policy to a single medium of instruction decided on by the school. Although this only became official policy in 1979, the overwhelming majority of Black secondary schools adopted English as the medium of instruction immediately in mid-1976 (Hartshorne).

The Education and Training Act of 1979 stated that the medium of instruction should be mother-tongue at primary school but that the wishes of parents should be considered after Grade 4. The mother-tongue requirement was opposed by many Black parents and the de Lange (1981) commission included an investigation into language of instruction and recommended three options: (a) English instruction from the first grade, (b) a sudden transfer from mother tongue to a second language medium, and (c) a gradual transfer from mother tongue to a second language medium

An amendment to Act 20 of 1979 gave parents the right to choose from these options at each school. There has been no systematic survey of the options chosen by parent bodies in the 1990s, but anecdotal evidence suggests that many schools adopted English as the language of learning from Grade 1 (Taylor & Vinjevold, 1999).

Currently, one of the requirements of the South African Schools Act is that governing bodies develop formal language policies that describe the strategies that will be employed to encourage multilingualism. However, research has indicated that in general, most schools have not done this (Taylor & Vinjevold, 1999). The de facto policies and practices of schools are influenced by the perceptions of the value of English of socioeconomic power and mobility. Setati (1998) reported that most schools have adopted English as the language of instruction and her study confirms a widely reported drift towards the use of English "the earlier the better" in the Western Cape Province of South Africa.

OUTCOMES OF THE SCHOOLING OF YOUNG ADOLESCENTS

Academic performance outcomes

There have been several systemic evaluations of student performance by the South African government. The first systemic evaluation was for the Foundation Phase (Grades 1 to 3), the findings of which were released in 2003 (Fleisch, 2008). The results of the Grade 6 systemic evaluation, based on an analysis of the academic performance of a sample of 34,015 learners in three subjects, revealed an average of 35% for language, 27% for mathematics and 41% for science, that is, the mean scores for 11-year-old children was less than 50 out of a possible score of 100 for standardized tests in these subjects (Department of Education, 2005). As noted earlier, when disaggregated by type of school and poverty quintile, the results revealed an unacceptable achievement gap and the fact that the achievement levels of the majority of children were extraordinarily low—not only were few passing, but the majority had not mastered the basics of reading and mathematics (Fleisch, 2008). These data suggest the need for targeted interventions in these schools, particularly in the areas of language and mathematics.

The international Monitoring Learning Achievement (MLA) initiative was one of the first large cross-national studies in which South Africa participated. The South African sample included 10 fourth grade students in 400 schools in all nine of the country's provinces (Strauss & Berger, 2000). Of the 12 participating countries, South Africa had the worst score in numeracy at 30.2%, scored slightly better than Botswana, Malawi, Niger and Zambia in literacy at 48.1% and only better than Senegal and Niger in life skills at 47.1%. These figures should be read in the context of South Africa budgeting more than any other African country for education per capita and suggest that there is a need to consider issues other than financial ones when attempting to improve schooling for young South Africans.

Similarly, the first time South Africa participated in the TIMSS (Third International Mathematics and Science Study) testing in 1999 the outcome was a matter of national concern as South Africa came last in the rankings (Howie, 2005). Reddy (2005) notes that in the most recent TIMSS (Trends in Mathematics and Science Study) report that tests for eighth grade students revealed similar results, with South Africa appearing at the bottom of the list with the lowest average scores in both mathematics and science.

In 1991 the International Institute for Educational Planning (IIEP) established an international project for monitoring and evaluating the quality of basic education. The project was referred to as the Southern and East Africa Consortium for Monitoring Educational Quality (SACMEQ) and included 15 countries. There are two assessment tasks at the core of the SAQMEC studies, which eventually covered 2,300 schools, 42,000 learners in 14 countries. These two assessments covered reading and mathematics for representative samples of sixth grade students (Moloi & Strauss, 2005). The results showed that of these 34,596 randomly selected children in sixth grade in South Africa, just over half were not able to demonstrate the ability to read and make meaning of a simple comprehension task (Moloi & Strauss). More than half of the children had not even reached what is considered to be a basic numeracy level, that is, a two-step addition or subtraction operation involving carrying.

The Progress in International Reading Literacy Study (PIRLS, 2006) (Martin, Mullis, & Kennedy, 2007), which included the testing of over 30 000 children in Grades 4 and 5 in 2006, allowed the students to choose to take the test in any of the 11 South African languages. The data suggest that the reading levels differed very little between the students who chose to write the test in their mother tongue or in the language of instruction at school—usually English (Fleisch, 2008).

Other Important Outcomes

Other important outcomes of the political changes in South Africa for young adolescents can be considered in curricular terms. A committee was appointed by the Minister of Education in 2000 to review the structure and design of Curriculum 2005, teacher orientation, training and development, learning support materials, provincial support to teachers in schools, and implementation time-frames. The review committee recommended that the curriculum needed to be strengthened by streamlining its design features, simplifying its language, and aligning curriculum and assessment. The committee also recommended improving teacher orientation and training, learner support materials, and provincial support.

The revised curriculum builds on the vision and values of the Constitution of South Africa. These principles include social justice, a healthy environment, human rights and inclusivity, which reflect the principles and practices of social justice and respect for the environment and human rights, as defined in the Constitution. In particular, the curriculum attempts to be sensitive to issues of poverty, inequality, race, gender, age, disability and such challenges as HIV/AIDS. The philosophy of outcomes-based education is the foundation of the curriculum and there are high expectations of what South African learners can achieve and aims at the development of a high level of knowledge and skills for all. Social justice requires that those sections of the population previously disempowered by the lack of knowledge and skills should now be empowered (Department of Education, 2002).

Research Supporting Academic Performance and Other Outcomes

It was in the light of the widespread reform agenda post-1994 that the President's Education Initiative (PEI) Research project of Nelson Mandela was commissioned by the Teacher Development Centre on behalf of the South African Department of Education. The research report of this nationwide project funded by the Danish funding agency DANIDA and which included 35 separate studies was complied by Taylor and Vinjevold (1999) under the title "Getting Learning Right." The PEI was launched in 1997 with President Mandela's personal appeal to several foreign heads of government for assistance in developing teacher skills in South Africa. The research component of the initiative included (a) establishing best practices in the teaching of mathematics, science and English with particular reference to Curriculum 2005, (b) identifying difficulties in the teaching of large classes, multigrade classes or multilingual classes, and investigating ways of overcoming these, (c) investigating appropriate ways of implementing whole-school development (institutional development), and (d) investigating the availability and use of learning materials in primary school classrooms. A second publication expanding on the themes of the research findings emanated from these authors titled *Getting Schools Working: Research and Systematic School Reform in South Africa* (Taylor, Muller & Vinjevold, 2003).

The most definite point of convergence across the PEI studies was that teachers' poor conceptual knowledge of the subjects they teach is a fundamental constraint on the quality of teaching and learning activities. In the area of curriculum development, it was noted that the teachers observed did not have the knowledge base either to interpret the new curricula or to implement the intention of the policies. Many teachers, across the spectrum of schooling in South Africa, modelled surface forms of learner-centered activities without understanding the underpinning philosophies and it was found that what students know and can do is dismal (Taylor & Vinjevold, 1999).

Explanations for teacher-centered classroom practices in South African schools ranged from the influence of the ideology of Fundamental Pedagogics to more prosaic ones that focus on language and knowledge. For instance, Macdonald (1990, 1991) found that Black children spent most of their time in class listening to their teachers and that the dominant pattern of classroom interaction was oral input by the teacher with the children occasionally chanting in response. Teachers did ask questions, but these were aimed at data recall or checking whether the children were listening to the lesson rather than eliciting more challenging responses. Classroom tasks in general were aimed at the gaining of information rather than higher cognitive tasks.

Macdonald (1990, 1991) noted that teachers appeared unable to communicate attitudes of curiosity, respect for evidence, and critical reflection necessary for the development of higher-order cognitive skills. She also noted that in the early years of schooling pupils' listening, speaking, reading and writing skills were poorly developed in both their first language and in English. As further progress at school depends on these four skills, Black children, who generally came from disadvantaged homes, were further handicapped by the practices prevalent in their classrooms.

Furthermore, Macdonald (1990, 1991) found that rote learning appeared to have built up a self-sustaining momentum. Teachers explained that drilling was an effective way of teaching since children had difficulty reading. Furthermore, her diagnosis was that teachers' own lack of conceptual knowledge and reading skills were the foundations on which these practices rested. Notions that teachers' lack conceptual understanding are supported by other researchers (Taylor & Vinjevold, 1999) as well as the belief that this lack of understanding results in teachers remaining within their own very confined comfort zone and resorting to pedagogies that enable them to strictly control what their students learn. Teachers, unsure of their own knowledge base, and either unable or unwilling to expand it, manage their teaching—consciously or subconsciously—in a manner which prevents pupils from venturing beyond the confines they set. This prevents any learning opportunity for pupils that may threaten the shaky foundations of their teacher's knowledge and skills (Taylor & Vinjevold), a product of the inferior education offered at South African Teacher's Training Colleges, the major source of training for educators of Black children in their middle school years (ages 10-15).

Langham (1993) confirmed these findings. He found that pupils level of language competence in Black schools was so poor that they were unable to read the learning material provided for them, and that the tasks and exercises were conceptually too difficult and beyond their competence. This led to a heavy reliance on rote learning and made the learners dependent on the teachers for everything they learned.

Taylor (2006) suggested five major factors that might optimize learning in the short and medium term, and which could be used to improve the results of young adolescent's if applied more broadly. These include:

- *Home level factors, including language:* When schools teach in the language of the home, especially in early years, learning is improved. Learning is also improved when children read at home and do homework.
- *Time management:* Many teaching hours are lost through absenteeism, lack of punctuality, and the scheduling of activities such as choir and sports competitions. Increasing teaching hours where applicable would bring notable improvements.
- *Curriculum leadership*: This entails the principal or heads of departments ensuring that the curriculum is covered, monitoring student assessment and undertaking quality assurance measures, and managing books and stationery. Sound curriculum leadership should improve school functioning.
- *The teaching of reading:* In many cases, confusion over curriculum requirements meant that teachers do not actually teach basic reading and writing.
- *Teacher knowledge:* Teachers need stronger content knowledge and also knowledge of how to teach particular subjects.

CURRENT ISSUES RELATED TO THE SCHOOLING OF YOUNG ADOLESCENTS

Concerns About the Current Educational System

There are a myriad of indictments of the South African education system that can be expressed within the spheres of poverty and inequity, and which are exacerbated by dysfunctionality within schools and the broader education system (Fleisch, 2008; Taylor, 2006), and all affect young adolescents in the majority of South African schools to a greater or lesser degree. Less than six years ago it was reported that more than 5 million children regularly go to school hungry in South Africa (Institute for Democracy in South Africa, 2002), that at school there are few textbooks (Taylor & Vinjevold, 1999), poor sanitation (Ota & Robinson, 1999), and that their teachers are typically untrained and demotivated (Garson,

1994). There is broad consensus that teaching and learning in the majority of South African schools leaves much to be desired and that the problems can be generally described in terms of teacher-centeredness, pupil passivity, and rote learning (Taylor & Vinjevold, 1999). Currently, learner achievement is very poor in general, and there is a large number of underqualified primary and secondary school teachers who do not have the knowledge and skills to teach their subjects competently (Adler & Reed, 2002; Asmal, 2000; Taylor & Vinjevold). The above factors are further exacerbated by the fact that teaching and learning in nearly 80% of South African schools most often takes place in a second language and in under-resourced classrooms (Taylor & Vinjevold).

Health issues. The physical conditions under which teaching and learning take place in South Africa are often unsatisfactory. For example, in rural schools in the Eastern Cape (one of the poorer South African provinces) the teacher pupil ratio was (and generally still remains at) 1:54 (Edusource, 1994; Ota & Robinson, 1999). Ten years ago, of the 5,958 schools in the province, 80% did not have electricity, 2,578 needed repair, and 823 were "falling to pieces" (Bishop, 1997). Ten percent of children had no school to attend (Institute for Democracy in South Africa, 2002) despite the fact that schooling from Grade 1 to 9 is supposedly universal and compulsory. Generally, there is a shortage of classrooms with the result that teachers often share venues and large classes are the rule (Bishop, 1997). Retention and learning are hampered when children attend class in overcrowded and dilapidated schools, in noisy or unsafe environments, or in classrooms that are poorly supplied, lit and ventilated (Watkins, 2000). Girls and boys alike need access to clean water and latrines (U.S. Fund for UNICEF, 2007). Although there have been some recent improvements, the situation remains largely unchanged to date.

Children who are not properly fed are likely to have problems concentrating at school and studies in the United States and Mexico have shown the negative effects on learning of children who skip breakfast (Sibanda-Mulder, 2003). The Nelson Mandela Children's Fund study on rural education found that 14% of all children they surveyed reported that they had either tea or nothing for breakfast, and 75% reported having only tea and bread or porridge (Fleisch, 2008). There are school feeding schemes funded by the government, but these are often maladministered and periodically collapse leaving the children without support. Also there are a number of problems associated with these schemes including high costs, unsustainable benefits (during vacation time), administrative complexities and little direct impact on micronutrient deficiencies (Kloka, 2003). Ironically, while large numbers of children do not get enough to eat (to the extent that it directly affects their school performance), South African society as a whole is in the process of nutritional transformation, with obesity following urbanization (Bourne, Lambert, & Steyn, 2002).

Malaria, parasitic worms, hearing loss from ear infections, asthma, fetal alcohol syndrome and HIV/AIDS all play major roles in the lives and learning of South African young adolescents (Fleisch, 2008). HIV/AIDS is a major factor in the lives of a large number of South Africans; there is a high prevalence of HIV among educators (12.7%) (Education Labour Relations Council, 2005), rising incidence of orphans (1.2 million in 2005), and an increasing number of children who are living with HIV—240,000 in 2005 (Kates & Martin, 2006). Currently, schools are facing issues such as teacher absenteeism due to illness related to HIV infection and increased stress levels of educators as they struggle to compensate for the absence of their colleagues. Other issues include traumatized children due to the prevalence of death and sickness, poverty as a result of caregivers becoming ill or dying, and children not able to continue with their education for financial and other reasons (Carr-Hill, 2002; UNAIDS IATT, 2006).

Resource support. The Department of Education (DoE) in South Africa regards adequate learning materials as essential to the effective running of an education system and asserts that these materials are an integral part of curriculum development and a means of promoting good teaching and learning (Department of Education, 1996). Despite ambitious public commitment to the provision of high quality and progressive learning materials, many (if not most) South African schools do not receive the materials they need (Taylor & Vinjevold, 1999). In fact, government spending on books and stationery in the Eastern Cape fell from R48 per learner in primary schools in the 1995/96 financial year to R25 per learner in 1996/97. In secondary schools this figure fell from R167 per learner in 95/96 to R46 per learner in 96/97 (Crouch & Mabogoane, 1997). Spending figures have improved, but are still not noticeably higher ten years later.

Problems with the procurement and distribution of learning materials have been manifestly made public by the South African media, with schools often receiving their textbooks and stationery (if they receive any at all) in the last quarter of the year. After considerable media attention on the inadequate provision of textbooks in 1998, President Mandela promised that all children would receive textbooks within the first seven days of schools' opening in 1999 (Taylor & Vinjevold, 1999). This did not happen and every year since then the newspapers have reported on the nondelivery of learning materials and teachers' dissatisfaction on this issue. In 2007 South African newspapers were still reporting the nondelivery of textbooks to schools.

International research on learning materials has focused on the role and use of learning materials in improving the quality of education in schools. This literature suggests that one of the most important predictors or precursors of cognitive development is the access of pupils to learning materials such as books and stationery (Crouch & Mabogoane, 1997). No large scale studies on the effect of textbooks and other learning materials on student learning has been conducted in South Africa, apart from evaluations of the READ Trust (Read, Educate and Develop—a national South African nongovernmental organization that targets literacy in young children and adolescents) which examine the impact of that organization's reading programs (including the provision of books) on primary school pupils' reading and writing skills (Taylor & Vinjevold, 1999). Le Roux and Schollar (1996) found that in 49 READ schools across six of the country's nine provinces there were very significant differences between READ and control schools in terms of pupil's reading and writing skills, which emphasizes the need for the provision of reading material for young adolescents.

In 1996 Vinjevold conducted an investigation into the provision of cross-curricular workbooks to Grade 4, 5, and 6 pupils in the Northern Cape. The first part of the impact study examined the extent and nature of the use of the workbook provided. The following pupil activities and habits were reported, that is, increased individual work, increased group work, increase in educational activity at home, work which was both voluntary and eager, use of the book for a wide variety of subjects, a particular interest in the puzzles, crosswords and games, and less interest in extended pieces of reading and writing.

Vinjevold's (1996) study also found that pupils in the more disadvantaged schools benefited most from the intervention. Also, the degree to which the materials were used affected the results in the posttest. The more the workbook was used, the greater was the improvement in posttest scores. Vinjevold's report concluded that learning-material based interventions have the potential to contribute to greater equity in the school system: pupils in disadvantaged schools benefit most, especially if there is a high incidence of usage of the materials provided.

Taylor (2006) judged that at most 20% of South Africa's schools were functioning adequately. The other 80% of schools—mostly schools serving poor African communities—were essentially dysfunctional. This led him to conclude that South Africa faced a serious problem because of "the inability of most schools to provide young people with the attitudes and intellectual skills required to build a modern state" (p. 2). There is established South African literature to guide educators on what to expect in studying schools that work (Taylor, 2006; Taylor, Muller, & Vinjevold, 2003). This literature relates school performance to social context and highlights features that set effective schools apart from their ineffective counterparts. It provides insights into the exceptional schools that perform under difficult circumstances and it shows that good classroom practice depends upon teachers and their knowledge and assumptions, school organizational capacity, including leadership. This level of change cannot be mandated, since it depends on both capacity and will, particularly on the part of teachers and school leadership. Though the primary task of schooling may be clear, it is not necessarily simple to achieve, particularly when "psychopolitics" takes over. However, Christie et al. (2007) noted that there are examples of schools that do meet their mandates to deliver quality teaching and learning, and that the challenge is how to have more of these.

Benefits of the Current Educational System

While the benefits of the current educational system in South Africa appear to be far below what can be reasonably expected, there are schools that succeed, even within what is considered the disadvantaged sector of the country's society, that is, schools in poor, racially segregated Black communities. A ministerial committee to investigate "Schools that Work" was tasked with carrying out a pilot study on a sample of schools in middle economic quintiles (i.e., those not designated to the poorest or richest 20% of schools—in terms of parental income—by the South African Department of Education) that succeeded in achieving good Senior Certificate (Grade 12) results, while others in similar circumstances did not. The question that was asked was 'What were the dynamics of these exceptional schools that enabled their achievements within a system that is not characterized by equity and quality?' The study showed that it is possible for poor schools in the mainstream of South Africa's education system to perform at outstanding levels, through extraordinary commitment, competence and accountability (Christie, Butler & Potterton, 2007).

Sailors, Hoffman, and Mathee's (2007) interpretive study of six high-performing schools that served low-income South African students revealed that the schools were safe, orderly, and had positive learning environments. The schools were guided by strong leaders and staffed by excellent teachers who had a shared sense of competence, pride and purpose that included high levels of school and community involvement. In spite of their contextual struggles, these schools demonstrated determination, resilience and purpose (Sailors et al., 2007). These studies suggest that the dysfunctionality of the system can be overcome and that there is hope for schools that fall into Fleisch's (2008) second tier of education in South Africa.

REFORM INITIATIVES AND NATIONAL POLICIES

With the institution of the first fully democratically elected government in 1994 a vigorous effort was mounted to reform South African schooling (Taylor, Diphofa, Waghmarae, Vinjevold, & Sedibe, 1999). This new government embraced the vision of the international progressive agenda for systematic change and established a number of key policy instruments in terms of constitutional rights, qualifications, school governance, school funding, language, teacher management and alignment of qualifications, curriculum, assessment and gender. Together these documents represented an impressively coherent vision for the fundamental transformation of the South African schooling system (Taylor et al.).

Possibly one of the most important reforms to take in terms of its immediate impact on the education of young adolescents was the introduction of a new curriculum. Epistemologically the progressive consensus chosen is constructivist: learning must start in life experiences of students and classroom activities must be learner-centered and equip children for applying knowledge to real world problems. However, the implications of a constructivist approach for teaching and learning soon became one of the most controversial and difficult issues in South Africa education (Taylor et al., 1999).

Initially the curriculum reform was called "Curriculum 2005" (the date by which it was to be fully implemented). After this it earned the moniker the "Revised National Curriculum Statement" (RNCS), and finally simply the National Curriculum Statement (Christie, Butler, & Potterton, 2007; Department of Education, 2002). To date the implementation process is still underway and there have been a number of reactions to both its form and substance.

Tshoane (2001) noted that while postapartheid South Africa has seen major policy shifts and developments in education and while committees and commissions were set up and white papers and documents were produced with the aim of providing policy and implementation solutions, hopes have been raised, crushed and raised again. Some policies were made without proper consideration of the context in which they would be implemented and a number of policies were introduced and implemented in schools without support and monitoring procedures in place at the school level, while educators searched for a path in a complex terrain of ongoing changes.

Morrow (2007) noted that while it is sometimes claimed that in post-1994 South Africa we have developed a bold and imaginative (a "magnificent") set of education policies, admired across the world, the problem lies with lack of implementation. He asks the question "Why do we have this problem? Who is to blame?" and his answer is first that South Africa still has some educational institutions (at all levels of the system) that remain stuck in apartheid traditions and mindsets and have not yet embraced "transformation." Second, he noted that there are thousands of deficient schoolteachers, teachers who do not have the competences, or perhaps the willingness, to implement new policies capably. Educational change depends on what teachers do and think and Morrow (2007) felt that a high proportion of South African teachers have not yet accomplished the "paradigm shift" they need to, if they are going to be competent implementers of fine policies.

Elmore (1996) offered many different insights on education policy and change. One of these is his insight that it is "the core" of education practice that is the hardest part to change. He defined this core to include teachers' views of knowledge, their assumptions about how students learn, and their assumptions about how these should come together in classroom practice. Christie et al. (2007) demonstrated that politicians often favor high profile changes such as governance, but these have little effect on the core of classroom practice. Reform attempts worldwide have often lacked a clear theory of change, with the result that they have not reached the core of education, or if they have (like the Progressive Movement in the United States), they have not been sustainable (Elmore). Suggestions have been made to the effect that incentive structures be modified to encourage teachers to de-privatize and change their practice, that exemplars of good practice be made available for teachers to learn from (Elmore) and that teacher overload be considered in order to allow them time and energy to engage in activities which might improve their teaching (Chisholm, 2005).

RESEARCH

Policy issues are, in the first instance, determined by political rather than research considerations. For example, in the South African context, new curricula for schools are based on the principles of providing equal opportunities for all children to develop the knowledge best suited for building a peaceful and prosperous society (Taylor et al., 1999). However, important practical questions arise, for example whether the curricula adopted serve their purpose of achieving these aims in the majority of South African schools. It is at this point that research opens the space to delineate the conditions and contingencies which policy vehicles must overcome to achieve these aims.

Current Research Topics

As part of its recent strategic plan the South African National Research Foundation (2007) established seven research focus areas, two of which are applicable to education: "Education and the Challenges for Change" and "Indigenous Knowledge Systems." These national research focus areas include investigation of issues of teaching and learning pertaining to young adolescents. The organization has also encouraged higher education institutions to identify their own research niche areas within these focus areas. A great deal of educational research has been undertaken in South Africa, but the fact that the South African National Research Foundation (NRF) has commissioned a research project titled *An Audit and Interpretative Analysis of Education Research in South Africa: What have we Learned?* suggests that there is no clear consensus in terms of how educational research in general has developed in this country in the past few decades (NRF, 2007). This research audit was established as part of the NRF's commitment to advance education in South Africa whereby the first phase is an audit and interpretative analysis of research undertaken over the last ten years followed by meta-analyses of groupings as suggested by the data generated. Phase two is aimed at developing a research agenda through the identification of current research gaps and priorities and brainstorming on future research needs and priorities for the next decade. Expected deliverables of the project are an inventory database, an interpretive analysis with conclusions, lessons learned and recommendations, and possible identified areas of inquiry for further meta-analyses. The audit is expected to be complete before the end of 2008 and, hopefully, will provide both a much-needed resource in terms of educational research trends in this country and set the scene for South African research in education in the twenty-first century.

Methodologies

As noted before, there is no clear consensus as to how educational research has developed in South Africa. However, it is fairly apparent that for the past three decades there has been a preponderance of qualitative research in science education, with few attempts made using large-scale quantitative techniques (Laugksch, 2003). These findings are most likely mirrored in other fields of educational research, but this can only be confirmed or dismissed when the data generated by the Audit and Interpretative Analysis of Education Research in South Africa are made public.

Important Research Findings

Arguably, the findings of the President's Education Initiative (Taylor & Vinjevold, 1999) and the reports by Chisholm (Chisholm, 1993) and

Christie (Christie et al., 2007), which have been discussed earlier in this chapter, have had the greatest impact on educational policy which affects young adolescents in South Africa. Similarly, research on language issues by Langham (1993), MacDonald (1990, 1991), and Le Roux and Schollar (1996) have impacted on policy, as should the recent work of Morrow (2007) and Fleisch (2008). Generalized Department of Education studies (2003, 2005), and comparative and interpretive studies such as those by Reddy (2005) and Strauss and Berger (2000), are helping shape policy, as are more focused studies on language and mathematics by Adler (Adler & Reed, 2002), Setati (1998) and Howie (2005).

FUTURE DIRECTIONS

The discussions above suggest that there are a myriad of future directions that South African education should consider in terms of young adolescents. However the situation is not unique to this particular geographical context. Most African countries are struggling to produce transformative and culturally relevant education systems that incorporate adequate teaching techniques, culturally sensitive curriculum content and an appropriate medium of instruction (Alidou, Boly, Brock-Utne, Diallo, Heugh & Wolff, 2006). Alidou et al. (2006) reported that classroom observation studies conducted in several countries in Africa (Benin, Burkina Faso, Guinea-Bissau, Mali, Mozambique, Niger, South Africa, Togo, Tanzania, Ethiopia, Ghana, and Botswana) reveal that the use of an unfamiliar language such as English often results in traditional and teacher-centered teaching methods, such as, chorus teaching, repetition, memorization and recall. Teachers do most of the talking while children remain silent and passive.

As such, perhaps one aspect that might take precedence for consideration in a country with 11 official language and numerous other unofficial languages and dialects is that of a common medium of instruction. South African researchers who participated in the Presidential Education Initiative (PEI) research project instigated by Nelson Mandela noted two main features of classroom language, (a) the decrease in mother tongue instruction in the lower grades and consequent increase in the use of English as the medium of instruction, and, (b) the mismatch between the languages spoken by the teachers and their pupils (Taylor & Vinjevold, 1999).

Rodseth (1995) pointed to a number of African examples to counter the argument that it is only European and American research that supports mother-tongue teaching and learning, that is:

- An experiment in south Nigeria where better results were produced in schools where mother tongue instruction was continued until secondary school than in schools which adopted early-exit bilingualism
- Studies in Zambia that have shown that too early an emphasis on learning through English impairs children's subsequent learning
- A survey of African countries quoted by NEPI (1992), which reports "no success on the entire continent for submersion programs."

CONCLUDING DISCUSSION

The scrapping of Apartheid legislation saw the introduction of a learner-centered curriculum based on emancipatory ideology and rapid diversification of previously linguistically homogenous schools. Linguistic diversification is especially true of urban and peri-urban schools in the townships and squatter camps near big towns and cities. As such, Brown (1998) concluded that because of rapidly changing demographics a significant proportion of South Africa's learners will face a situation where their home language is not offered or utilized at the schools that they attend.

As noted earlier, since the 1950s Black African parents have opposed mother tongue instruction as it was seen as a strategy by the government to prevent African upward mobility and thereby ensure a perpetual reservoir of cheap labour (NEPI, 1992). However, other influences such as the low status of African languages and the obvious social and economic benefits of being fluent in English also played a role in choice of language of instruction in schools, with parents seeing English not only as a language, but as a resource and, to many of them, to delay acquisition to this resource is incomprehensible (Taylor & Vinjevold, 1999).

Setati's (1998) study suggested that it is not only parents, but also the teachers who perceive English as the language of power and socioeconomic advancement in South Africa. Therefore, in their view, using English as the language of learning is in the best interests of their pupils. As a result, the notion of mother tongue instruction in South Africa appears to be an increasingly difficult ideal to achieve.

The rapid changes in the linguistic profiles of schools have not been accompanied by changes in language policies of schools or by changes in teaching staff. This means that in many classes the teachers do not speak the language of a majority, or significant minority, of their pupils. Research in both primary and secondary schools has shown that discipline and control problems arise from the communications breakdown that occurs because of the mismatch of languages between teachers and pupils, with concomitant negative effects on teaching and learning (Taylor & Vinjevold, 1999).

Taylor and Vinjevold (1999) argued that under the prevailing circumstances the South African government is faced with one of two alternatives, allocating substantial resources to promoting added bilingualism, or, accepting the growing use of English as language of instruction at all levels of the schooling system and promoting the conditions requisite for effective teaching and learning in English. Taylor and Vinjevold noted that modernization in South Africa, and inexorable urbanization in particular, is undermining the possibilities for the first alternative and that the more realistic option is a 'straight for English' approach, except in linguistically homogenous classes where there is little exposure to English outside of the classroom, or where parents expressly request an alternative. However, if this course of action is adopted, the conditions that are most frequently quoted in international literature as important for instruction in a second language must be taken into account. These conditions are that teachers' must be proficient in the target language, they must have an understanding of the problems of learning in a second language as well as knowing how to overcome these problems, pupils' must be exposed to the target language outside of the classroom and that graded language textbooks, especially in the content subjects in the early phases of learning, must be provided (Duncan, 1993). However, the debate is currently far from settled with arguments strongly being placed for mother tongue education of young adolescents (Prah, 2008) and those arguing the practicalities and difficulties which arise within a heterogeneous language context (Mgqwashu, 2008).

REFERENCES

Adler, J., & Reed, Y. (2002). *Challenges of teacher development: An investigation of uptake in South Africa*. Pretoria, South Africa: Van Schaik.

Alidou, H., Boly, A., Brock-Utne, B., Diallo, Y., Heugh, K., & Wolff, H. (2006). *Optimizing learning and education in Africa—The language factor. A stock-taking research on mother tongue and bilingual education in Sub-Saharan Africa*. Libreville, Gabon: UNESCO Institute for Education.

African National Congress. (ANC). (1994). *A policy framework for education and training*. Johannesburg, South Africa: Author.

Asmal, K. (2000). *Report by Minister of Education, National Department of Education*. Retrieved January 23, 2003, from http://education.pwv.gov.za/Policies_Reports/Reports_2000/Report_President.htm

Bishop, C. (1997, September 5). The worst school in the country. *Mail and Guardian*, p. 3.

Bourne, T., Lambert, E., & Steyn, K. (2002). Where does the Black population of South Africa stand on the nutrition transition? *Public Health Nutrition, 5*(1a), 157-162.

Brown, D. (1998). *Educational policy and the choice of language in linguistically complex South African schools*. Durban, South Africa: Education Policy Unit, University of Natal.

Carr-Hill, R. (2002). Practical and theoretical problems in training teachers to confront HIV & AIDS. In E. Thomas (Ed.), *World yearbook of education 2002: Teacher education, dilemmas and prospects* (pp. 193-204). London: Taylor & Francis.

Chisholm, L. (1993, February). *Education policy in South Africa*. Speech presented to South African Society of Education, Soweto.

Chisholm, L. (2005). The state of South Africa's schools. In J. Daniel, R. Southall, & J. Lutchman (Eds.), *State of the nation: South Africa 2004/2005* (pp. 201-226). Cape Town, South Africa: HSRC Press.

Christie, P., Butler, D., & Potterton, M. (2007). *Report of the Ministerial Committee Department of Education South Africa*. Retrieved March 5, 2008, from www.isasa.org/component/ option,com_docman/task,doc_download/gid,531

Cross, M., & Chisholm, L. (1990). Roots of segregated schooling in 20th century South Africa. *Pedagogy of domination*. Trenton, NJ: Africa World Press.

Crouch, L., & Mabogoane, T. (1997). *Key numerical indicators 1991-1996*. Johannesburg, South Africa: Centre for Education Policy Development, Evaluation and Management.

Davies, J. (1986). *Crisis, education and Restructuring in South Africa. Capitalist crisis and schooling*. Melbourne, Australia: MacMillan.

De Lange Commission. (1981). *Teaching of natural science and mathematics*. Pretoria, South Africa: Human Sciences Research Council.

Department of Education. (1996). *White paper on the organisation, governance and funding of education. Notice 130 of 1996*. Pretoria, South Africa: Government Printer.

Department of Education. (2002). *Revised national curriculum statement grades R-9 (schools) policy*. Pretoria, South Africa: Government Printer.

Department of Education. (2003). *Systemic evaluation foundation phase mainstream national report*. Pretoria, South Africa: Author.

Department of Education. (2005). *Provincial expenditure on education: Comparison of new MTEF* (Budget Monitoring and Support). Pretoria, South Africa: Author.

Duncan, K. (1993). *Notes on mother tongue versus second language literacy*. Johannesburg, South Africa: Molteno Project.

Education Labour Relations Council. (2005). *The health of our educators: A focus on HIV & AIDS in South African public schools, 2004/5 survey*. Cape Town, South Africa: HSRC.

Edusource. (1994). A brief overview on education. *Data News, 5*. Johannesburg, South Africa: The Education Foundation.

Elmore, R. (1996). *School reform from the inside out*. Cambridge, MA: Harvard University Press.

Enslin, P. (1990). Science and doctrine: Theoretical discourse in South African teacher education. In. M. Nkomo (Ed.), *Pedagogy of domination: Towards a democratic education in South Africa* (pp. 77-92). Trenton, NJ: African World Press.

Fleisch, B. (2008). *Primary education in crisis: Why South African children underachieve in reading and mathematics*. Cape Town, South Africa: Juta.

Garson, P. (1994, June 4). Teachers fail curriculum 2005. *Mail and Guardian*, p. 7.

Hartshorne, K. (1992). *Crisis and challenge: Black education 1910-1990*. Cape Town, South Africa: Oxford University Press.

Howie, S. (2005). System-level evaluation: Language and other background factors affecting mathematics achievement. *Prospects, 35*(2) 184-185.

Institute for Democracy in South Africa. (2002). *Memo on child poverty rates.* Retrieved February 15, 2008, from www.idasa.org.za/gbOutputFiles.asp?WriteContent=Y&RID=588

Kallaway, P. (1984). An introduction to the study of education for Blacks in South Africa. *Apartheid and Education*. Johannesburg, Hofmeyr: Ravan Press.

Kates, J., & Martin, A. (2006). *HIV & AIDS policy fact sheet*. Kaiser Family Foundation. Retrieved October 12, 2006, from www.kkf.org

Kloka, D. (2003). *Nutrition of school-aged children*. Paper presented at the Colloquium on Improving the Health of School-Aged Children in an Era of HIV/AIDS—Linking Policies, Programmes and Strategies for the 21st Century, Pretoria.

Langham, D. P. (1993). *The textbook as a source of difficulty in teaching and learning: E.D.-21*. Pretoria, South Africa: HSRC.

Laugksch, R. C. (2003). *South African science education research. An indexed bibliography, 1930-2000*. Cape Town, South Africa: HSRC.

Le Roux, N., & Schollar, E. (1996). *A survey report on the reading and writing skills of pupils participating in READ programmes*. Braamfontein, South Africa: READ Educational Trust.

Macdonald, C. A. (1990). *School-based Learning Experience*. Pretoria: Human Sciences Research Council.

Macdonald, C. A. (1991). *Eager to talk, learn and think: Bilingual primary education in South Africa*. Cape Town, South Africa: Maskew Miller Longman.

Mgqwashu, E. (2008). *The South African language policy-in-education: realistic or an ideological import?* University of KwaZulu-Natal, Edgewood Campus, Language Education Programme. Retrieved March 16, 2008, from http://www.uwc.ac.za/arts/auetsa/emmanuelMmgqwashu.htm

Moloi, M., & Strauss, J. (2005). *The SACMEQ II project in South Africa: A study of the conditions of schooling and the quality of education*. Retrieved March 18, 2008, from http//:www.sacmeq.ord/links.htm

Morphet, A. R., Schaffer, A. J., & Millar, C. J. (1986). *An evaluation of science education in South Africa. Innovative policy study in education*. Cape Town, South Africa: University of Cape Town, Department of Adult Education and Extramural Studies.

Morrow, W. (2007). *What is teachers' work? Learning to teach in South Africa*. Cape Town, South Africa: HSRC Press.

Martin, M, Mullis, I., & Kennedy, A. (2007). *PIRLS 2006 technical report*. Chestnut Hill, MA: TIMSS & PIRLS International Study Center, Boston College.

National Research Foundation. (2007). *Call for proposals*. Retrieved November 24, 2007, from https://rita.nrf.gov.sg/IDM/default.aspx

National Education Policy Investigation. (1992). *Teacher education*. Cape Town, South Africa: NECC/Oxford University Press.

Ota, C. C., & Robinson, R. C. (1999). *Situation analysis of primary education in the northern region of the Eastern Cape Province*. Pretoria, South Africa: RTI.

Prah, K. (2008). *Going native: Language of instruction for education, development and African emancipation*. Cape Town, South Africa: The Centre for Advanced Studies of African Society. Retrieved March 5, 2008, from http://www.casas.co.za/papers_native.htm

Reddy, V. (2005). Cross national achievement study: Learning from South Africa's participation in the Trends in International Mathematics and Science Study (TIMSS). *Compare, 35*(1), 63-77.

Reeves, C. (1994). *The struggle to teach*. Johannesburg, South Africa: Maskew Miller Longman.

Rodseth, V. (1995). *Bilingualism and multilingualism in education*. Johannesburg, South Africa: Centre for Continuing Development.

Sailors, M., Hoffman, J., & Matthee, B. (2007). South African schools that promote literacy learning with students from low-income communities. *Reading Research Quarterly, 42*(3), 364-387.

Samuel, J. (1990). *The state of education in South Africa: Education from poverty to liberty*. Cape Town, South Africa: David Philip.

Setati, M. (1998). Code switching in a senior primary class of second language learners. *For the Learning of Mathematics, 18*(1), 34-40.

Sibanda-Mulder, C. (2003, September). Nutrition and school performance. *Annual ECOWAS Nutrition Forum*, 13-5.

Strauss, J., & Berger, M. (2000). *Monitoring Learner Achievement Project MLP South Africa*. Bloemfontein, South Africa: University of the Orange Free State, Research Institute for Education Planning.

Taylor N., Diphofa, M., Waghmarae, H., Vinjevold, P., & Sedibe, K. (1999). Systemic and institutional contexts of teaching and learning. In N. Taylor & P. Vinjevold (Eds.), *Getting learning right* (pp. 13-36) Johannesburg, South Africa: The Joint Education Trust.

Taylor, N., & Vinjevold, P. (1999). *Getting learning right* (Report of the President's Education Initiative Research Project). Johannesburg, South Africa: Joint Education Trust.

Taylor, N. (2006). Schools, skills and citizenship. *JET Bulletin, 15, Focus on Challenges across the Education Spectrum*. Johannesburg, South Africa: The Joint Education Trust.

Taylor, N., Muller, J., & Vinjevold P. (2003). *Getting schools working: Research and systematic school reform in South Africa*. Cape Town, South Africa: Pearson Education and Maskew Miller Longman.

Tshoane, M. (2001). *Strangers in their own territory: Searching for a path in a complex terrain*. Johannesburg, South Africa: Education Policy Unit, University of the Witwatersrand.

UNAIDS Inter-Agency Task Team on Education. (2006). *HIV & AIDS treatment education: A critical component of efforts to ensure universal access to prevention, treatment, and care.* Paris: UNESCO. Retrieved on April 18, 2006, from http://www.unesco.org/AIDS/iatt

U.S. Fund for UNICEF. (2007). *UNICEF's low-cost, high impact water and sanitation programs save lives.* New York: Author.

Vinjevold, P. (1996). *Evaluation report of the Northern Cape Primary School Workbook Pilot Project.* Johannesburg, South Africa: Joint Education Trust.

Watkins, K. (2000). *The Oxfam education report.* London: Oxfam.

Western Cape Department of Education. (2005). *Grade six learner assessment study. Final report.* Cape Town, South Africa: Author.

Western Cape Department of Education. (2006). *Grade three learner assessment study. Final report.* Cape Town, South Africa: Author.

World Bank. (1995). *Reshaping the future: Education and post-conflict reconstruction.* Washington, DC: Author.

CHAPTER 11

EDUCATING THE RUSSIAN YOUNG ADOLESCENT

Adopting the "Best from the West" While Maintaining the "Strengths of the Past"

Inna Gorlova and David Anderson

Over the past 2 decades, Russia has been going through the process of transitioning its education from the old Soviet model to one that resembles the standards of Western education while trying to retain the best features of its previous systems. Tremendous changes in the Russian education system are occurring because of shifting economics, emerging technologies, demographics changes, and the migration of people as responses to global forces. Educational reform at the middle school level is changing toward standardized tests, curriculum, instruction, and assessment. Russian higher education, impacted by Western education and the global market, pulls the lower educational levels toward internationalization and standardization of the educational system as a whole. In this chapter, the authors discuss the major issues of schooling young adolescents beginning with historical analysis and continuing through to an examination of the current political and social issues. The discussion covers an assessment of academic performance on the international, national, and local level, the curriculum in Russian middle schools, shifting teacher-student roles, and the span of contemporary Russian educational research.

Inspiring Student Writers: Strategies and Examples for Teachers
pp. 223–253
Copyright © 2009 by Information Age Publishing

CONTEXTUAL NARRATIVE

Russia is the largest transcontinental country in the world, with about 40% of its territory in Europe to the west, the Arctic Ocean to the north, the Pacific Ocean to the east, and the rest of its lands to the south in the northern part of Asia. Russia spans a total of 11 time zones which incorporate many very diverse landforms with a wealth of natural resources including oil and natural gas. The population of Russia has been in a continual decline since the collapse of the Soviet Union. According to information from the Federal Service on State Statistics (Federal State Statistics Service, n.d.-a), in 1996 the population was 148.3 million people and it has dropped down to 142 million people at the beginning of 2008.

Throughout many centuries, Russia has been a strict totalitarian country under the government of the Russian monarchy. Russian Tsar Peter the Great ruled the monarchy in the eighteenth century and was one of the most significant reformers of Russia. His purpose was to build a newly advanced economy which was based on the western European model and applied obligatory vocational training for the offspring of the upper class. Education was male oriented with only a very limited category of girls having access to educational training.

Russia is a very diverse country with more than 100 nationalities of which Russians represent approximately 85% of the entire population (Country Studies, n.d.). The larger ethnic minority groups have been assigned autonomous territories that are subjects of the Russian Federation. In the Soviet time, the educational system was uniform in terms of instruction, language, content, and school culture. Ethnic diversity was not recognized as strength of the society. Modern Russia, which inherited many of its nationality problems from the Soviet Union, is attempting to develop tolerance and a better understanding of diversity in the light of democratic changes in the country.

The role of women in Russian society remains quite traditional although official documents claim that men and women have equal rights and access to education, employment, promotions, and participation in social, cultural, as well as political activities (The Constitution of the Russian Federation, n.d.). Despite the fact that women, on average, are better educated than men, they remain the minority in senior management positions. Russian husbands, generally, have less family responsibilities and participate little in raising children which means that the women must often bear the double load of work and family.

Russia adopted Christianity in the tenth century and the Russian Christian Orthodox Church has served as the dominant religious institution in Russia. The Russian Orthodox Church is respected by both believers and nonbelievers as a symbol of Russian heritage and culture. Other traditional religions of different ethnic groups include Islam, Buddhism, and Judaism. It was prohibited for most citizens to attend church during the Soviet time and a large number of churches were destroyed or used for nonreligious purposes. Orthodox churches are now developing their power and influence on the masses, and the number of believers who regularly attend church was estimated, in 2005, to be as high as 8.5% of population (*V Rossii*, 2006).

The Soviet government launched a countrywide literacy program in the 1920s for the masses. Elementary education became obligatory in 1934; secondary education became obligatory in 1949 and free for all children aged from 6 years old through 18 years old. Soviet education was highly centralized with strong ideological communist organizations for children and youth being a crucial part of the school system. Students were raised and trained based on the belief that active citizens of a just society must put the needs of the collective, the school, and the country above their own individual needs. Educational programs were subject to strict censorship with limits on free and critical thinking. Soviet citizens were only allowed to receive information from outside the country from Soviet-controlled sources.

According to the data from the Federal Service of State Statistics (Federal State Statistics Service, n.d-b), migration to Russia has decreased from 597,651 people in 1997 to 286,956 people in 2007, and the number of refugees from former Soviet countries has declined from 271,977 people in 1995 to 85,404 in 2008. Unfortunately, the number of immigrants cannot be estimated accurately because many of the new arrivals settle with friends or relatives without official registration. Research shows that the migrant flows have a significant impact on education, mostly at the secondary school levels, particularly in those parts of Russia which have been traditionally been ethnically homogeneous. Given the continuously decreasing Russian population, experts suggest that Russia should become more open to immigrants because of the lack of Russia's own internal human resources (Ediev, 2005).

HISTORY AND ORGANIZATION OF
SCHOOLING FOR YOUNG ADOLESCENTS

Historical Background

The pre-Soviet history of Russian education includes three main periods of development (Latyshina, 2005). The first period, which lasted from the tenth century to the eighteenth century, was religious by its content where church organizations had the most prominent role in formal education. The second period lasted from the eighteenth century to the second half of the nineteenth century. This age of education was characterized by governmental involvement as it attempted to prepare employees for governmental service. The third period of Russia's educational history began during the second half of the nineteenth century and came to an end due to the Socialist Revolution in 1917. This period of time has been referred to as the rise of "public" education because of the large influence on educational systems from different social organizations, groups, and individuals.

Period 1: Tenth Century to Eighteenth Century

The religious age of education began when the Russian tsars adopted Christianity in the tenth century for the purpose of building a strong, united nation with common beliefs, values, and culture. Children were trained at churches, monasteries, and at home. Books such as an ABC-book (*Az Buka*), a collection of daily prayers and rituals (*Chasoslov*), and a collection of religious songs (*Psaltyr'*) were all handwritten during this period. Fairy tails about Russian giants and tsars told children the importance of being literate, intelligent, and knowledgeable. The first teachers, called "masters of literacy" (*mastera gramoty*), were laypersons affiliated with the church. These masters of literacy trained children individually or in groups of three to five students. Education was delivered in the Church Slavonic language which was very close to the spoken language of the Russian people at that time.

The main notion of religious education was to raise children in "God's fear" and masters of literacy trained children in the basic skills of reading and writing so they would be able to read religious books and understand the Christian orthodox services. Physical punishment was very common and applied to all of the children regardless of their age, gender, or social status. During the sixteenth century, one of the first books to be printed, "Domostroy," appeared in church-based schools. "Domostroy" was devoted to such issues as to how a family should be established and how children were to be raised. The name of the chapter about children was titled "How to raise your own children with punishment and God's fear" (Kako detey svoikh vospitati vo vsyakom nakazanii i strakhe bozhiy).

During the fourteenth century, Russia faced tension between the Russian Orthodox Church and Western Catholic Church that greatly impacted Russian culture, beliefs, and education. The Russians united into regional brotherhoods in order to oppose Western influence and created the so called *brothers'* schools. "Brothers" supported schools, established rules, and continuously monitored them. These schools were the first "public" schools by their nature. Attendance at brothers' schools was very strict with students who were "on duty" in charge of discipline, heating, lighting, and order. Students were divided into three groups, from beginners to advanced, based on their level of study and achievements. Each student was required to tell a teacher a lesson from the previous day, and on Saturdays students repeated what they had learned during a week. Poor students were not only accepted and studied for free but they were also accommodated with a room in the monastery.

Schools attached to churches (*tserkovnoe utchilische*) in the sixteenth century taught children from the early morning until the church bells rang for evening services. Similar to *brothers'* schools, the students at church schools were in charge of school maintenance. The elder students helped the teachers with the control of discipline and order. Children were trained in the strict morals of showing respect to others, of being polite, and of following the rules.

Yan Komenskiy developed the class-lesson system (*klassno-urochnaya sistema*) during the seventeenth century in which classes were formed by students of similar ages. This system, which established a clear design of the lesson and its components, spread out to many schools. The model of each lesson included checking the homework of each student, lectures, practicing exercises, control, and homework assignments. This class-lesson system generally remained the same for a period of well over 300 years in Russian schools.

Period 2: Eighteenth Century to Mid-Nineteenth Century

Education in the second half of the seventeenth century had been largely influenced by the Catholic Church and European countries so, during this time, Russian schools offered education in Latin and Greek languages. The curriculum included grammar, rhetoric, and mathematics. In the eighteenth century, the nature of education began to change. Michael Lomonosov (1711-1765), a founder of Moscow University, graduated from a seventeenth century type of school. Lomonosov became one of the greatest reformers in education. He wrote a few textbooks on different subjects, including his famous "Russian Grammar" (*Rossiyskaya gramatika*), published in 1755. Lomonosov also developed curriculum and instructional methods for schools and the university. The book printing as well as the growing number of educated people at the end of the eighteenth century brought on the emergence of a variety of textbooks and school supplies. Textbooks contained information on geography, history, nature and animals, social events, and life of people in other countries.

Peter the Great (1672-1725), who "opened a window to Europe" for the social, economic, political, and military development of Russia, was another significant reformer of the educational system. He brought thousands of professionals from European countries to Russia in order to build industry, ships for the navy, and the city of St. Petersburg. Professional vocational schools, which offered secular rather than religious education for young adolescents, were opened with an emphasis on mathematics, navigation, military, medicine, and engineering. Curriculum included algebra, geometry, trigonometry, astronomy, geography, and a number of specific subjects to prepare young people for their future professions. Education reforms, like other changes in Russia in the era of Peter the Great, were implemented forcefully and often violently. Children of the nobility, between 6 and 7 years old, were taken from their parents to study in closed schools for next 12-15 years and were prohibited to see their parents during these years of study. Adolescent males were trained for different professional fields and taught how to manage their estates while girls were taught household, arts, music, foreign languages, and dancing.

Wealthy parents hired nursemaids and tutors to teach their children different sciences, arts, and foreign languages. Most of these tutors were foreigners from France, Germany, and other European countries. It often happened in many provinces that unaware parents hired tutors who lacked any formal training, and it was found that some of them were former peasants, artisans, or even those who had run away from their country of origin's jurisdiction.

During the era of Peter the Great in the eighteenth century, schools were subordinated under the tsar government. Education was reproductive and certain schools were specifically designed for particular social classes. Forcible and violent enrollment, severe conditions at schools, as well as low value of education throughout the Russian society led to a high resistance by parents who hid their children from schooling and many of the young adolescents would often run away from the schools. The data from the so called *"tsifirnaya"* schools in 1727 showed that 2,000 students between the ages of 10-15 were enrolled in these schools. During the study program, 572 students left schools because their parents were given the permission to take their children home, 322 students ran away or did not come back to school after their break, 233 students were expelled because they were recognized as illiterate or unable to learn, 302 students completed their study, 93 students left the school before graduation because they were accepted for jobs, and 500 students continued to study at the schools (Kapterev, 2004).

The teaching approach based on physical punishment was criticized by Ivan Betskoy who, in the 1760s, along with Empress Ekaterina the Second, created a closed system of schools for children from all social stratum, excluding serf peasants. In the general plan for the Moscow Educational Home for Orphans (*Moskovskiy vospitatel'nyi dom dlya sirot*), Betskoy required the school administration to pass a policy to "never beat children" (Dautova, 2004). Betskoy wanted schools to create a warm family atmosphere with the educators being more like parents to the children.

Children were divided into three separate age groups: ages 2 through 7 years old, ages 7 through 11 years old, and ages 11 through 14 years old. Educational programs were designed in regards to the age, gender, and learning abilities of the students. Young adolescent males were taught gardening and a variety of handicrafts while the girls were trained to cook, sew, embroider, and iron. From the age of 7 through 11, children were taught reading, writing, and counting. Elder adolescents learned arithmetic, geography, history, drawing, and other basic subjects. The better students were taught advanced programs and, after graduation, they were sent to Moscow University or to the Arts Academy for further education. Those who performed well in vocational fields became artisans while the poorly achieved students were given a lot of work which required labor and, upon finishing school, they were sent to work as maids and servants for noble and merchant classes.

The governmental educational system was organized during the nineteenth century by different levels of educational organizations which were related to each other: 1-year elementary schools attached to churches (*prichodskoye utchilische*), 2-year advanced elementary schools in towns (*uezdnoye utchilische*), 4-year preuniversity schools in capital cities (*gubernskaya gimnaziya*), and 3-year universities. Russia was divided into six educational regions in which each region had a university. The government partly funded schools in towns and fully funded preuniversity schools. Church schools that were accessible to the masses of ordinary people were not supported financially from the state budget. It was suggested to the nobility that they open schools for children of peasants. The idea of educating the masses, however, was not a priority for the tsar government.

Cadet schools were another type of educational organization. Male children of nobility from the ages of 6 through 21 years old studied at cadet schools during a period of 12-15 years while being separated from their families without any contact. The educational programs were divided into five age groups: (1) ages 6-8-years-old, (2) ages 9-12, (3) ages 12 through 15, (4) ages 15 through 18, and (5) ages 18 through 21. The adolescents of the third and fourth age groups studied accounting, architecture, military service, engineering, French, and the Bible. At the end of their study, the fifth age group of cadets repeated their studies in order to strengthen their knowledge and skills. Isolation from the real world during these 12-15 years of study at cadet schools caused young people to feel very frustrated and unprepared for real life after their graduation. Near the end of the nineteenth century, cadet schools had three types of examinations—an entry exam, a transitional exam from one grade level to the next grade level, and graduation exam. Physical punishment was common at cadet schools with the suggestion to apply it according to the age, personality, and degree of guilt of each individual cadet (Korovin & Sviridov, 2007).

Overall, the pedagogy during this second period served the interests of the tsar government which demanded a very large number of literate employees for the state and bureaucratic system. Schools were opened in major towns throughout the country with a professional bias toward engineering, medicine, military, clerical work, architecture, and the like. Education became oriented around "social class" and reproduced existing social inequities. It was mandatory for the children of the nobilities as well as merchants; it was voluntary for the petty bourgeoisie, and the children of the peasantry were not educated whatsoever. Not surprisingly, the male dominated country developed this educational system for male adolescents only. For those children that qualified to receive an education, the school age was set between the ages of 7 to 20 years old. Parents were required to provide a basic literacy education at home for children from 7 through 12 years of age. Children that reached the age of 12 were examined by the governmental educational committee in order to see if they qualified to be transferred to the next level of education. Parents of wealth, those that owned more than 100 peasants, could hire tutors to continue the education of their children at home. Poorer parents were required to send their children to governmental schools. Upon reaching the age of 16, all adolescents who received an education were given an additional governmental exam for furthering their education on professional level. If a student failed the examination, he could be sent to the Army or the Navy as punishment.

The first school for girls from the aristocrat class (*Smol'nyi Institut Blagorodnykh Devits*) was opened in the city of St. Petersburg in 1764. Female adolescents studied there for a period of 12 years beginning at the age of 6 and graduating when they were 18 years old. Shortly thereafter, similar schools for adolescent female education appeared in different Russian towns. This period of time was quite remarkable with the appearance of elite schools such as classical gymnasiums and lyceums which prepared adolescents for higher education. One of the best examples of an elite school was the Tsarskosel'skiy Lyceum where the great Russian poet, Alexander Puskin, graduated from in 1817 when he was 18 years old.

Period 3: Mid-Nineteenth Century to 1917

The third period of pre-Soviet education history was characterized by a significant impact on education by different social and scientific organizations and groups. Wealthy educated people opened schools where they attempted to develop, examine, and implement different pedagogical approaches. It was during this historical stage that Konstantin Ushinskiy (1824-1871), a founder of Russian scholar pedagogy, discussed ideas of democratic education for ordinary people. Leo Tolstoy (1828-1910), the world-known Russian writer and philosopher, experimented with the school he created in the village, Yasnaya Polyana (1859-1862), where he promoted the idea of getting students interested and engaged without the use of discipline methods. Peter Kapterev (1849-1922), a famous Russian educator and author of the book *History of Russian Pedagogy* (1909), and other Russian thinkers and activists initiated a number of changes in education by attempting to make it accessible to ordinary people. They also sought better ways to train the younger generation. The discourse about education for the masses of people increased after 1861 when the serfdom was repealed and peasants received freedom from their owners. A legislative proposal in 1907 for accessible elementary education for all children from age 8 through 11 years old had been discussed in the Russian Parliament (*Gosudarstvennaya Duma*), but was declined.

Due to the pressure of the educated public on the government in the 1860s, the first public libraries, reading rooms, and pedagogical museums were opened for the ordinary people, peasants, and artisans. Pedagogical museums collected books, textbooks, and other educational supplements and delivered public lectures and organized courses for local residents. Philanthropic public organizations and educational committees appeared because of local leaders initiatives in many towns across the country. These organizations developed school systems and educational services for people in their locations.

Period 4: The Soviet Era

The Soviet government under Vladimir Lenin initiated a program in 1917 of illiteracy elimination (*Likvidatsiya Bezgramotnosti*) that aimed, through literacy basic training for the masses, to bring the Soviet country up to a new level of economic, political, and cultural development. Every citizen between the ages of 8 and 50 years old was obligated to attend literacy classes at schools, community clubs, or at work places. Young adolescents studied at numerous newly created schools, orphanages, and juvenile recreation centers. Ethnic nationals living on Russian territory were given written languages based on Cyrillic and written Russian. It is estimated that approximately 40 million people of all ages went through literacy trainings by the end of the 1930s and, according to the communist politicians of that time, "socialism won" and the problem of mass illiteracy was generally solved.

The education authority of the Soviet government in 1918 developed a decree about general principles of the common "working school" (*trudovaya shkola*) where the word "working" referred to a new type of active citizens of the nation of "workers and peasants" (Piskunov, 2003). It was proclaimed that new "working schools" were opened to the world and relationships between students and teachers should be based on respect, joy of common activities, and friendship. Violence and compulsion were strictly prohibited at schools and the students were supposed to develop their knowledge, abilities and skills through free creative work, art, drama, handicraft, singing, as well as other pleasant activities according to student personal needs and interests. Schools were required to diverge far from the typical boring classrooms and programs. Music, drama improvisations, and short concerts were inserted into the regular school day to increase the enthusiasm and positive mood of students and teachers. Different professionals such as artists, actors, and qualified workers were involved in the educational process to develop the linkage between school and real life as well as help students prepare for adulthood as active citizens. Homework, grades, and punishments became prohibited at these new soviet schools as the schools became clubs of interests and creativities.

The club approach was greatly appreciated by students because in the 1920s, after the socialist revolution and during the civil war, schools struggled with the lack of textbooks, boring activities, and student disinterest toward learning. Schools needed ideas that would spark students and teachers for common work and active learning. Flexibilities of the learning programs fully met the needs of young adolescents. Students participated in different *circles* (*kruzhok*). They held discussions in *political circles* on events throughout the country as well as events that had taken place abroad and teacher supervision strengthened student ideological foundation as patriots and loyal fighters for communist ideas. *Scientific circles* promoted antireligious notions. Students learned about nature, the earth and human creation, and conducted open public discussions involving their parents and neighbors. Specialized *circles* with focuses on agriculture, mechanics, environment, first aid medicine, drama, music, rhetoric, and literature played a very significant role in the life and future career of young adolescents.

The Soviet government ended the school-club approach in the 1930s and moved toward a strict authoritarian system. Education changed its direction to better serve the national goals of preparing future professionals and qualified workers who would build the economy and support the communist party. The social and educational systems became highly ideologized and the role of a teacher became authoritarian. Punishment by giving lower grades, notes to parents, and visits to the principal's office became common in daily school practices. The content of programs was bounded by selected information with the top educational authority deciding what students needed to learn, discuss, and what was not allowed and even prohibited. Instructional methods became teacher-centered. Homework, structured lessons, and after-school activities were directed to make students learn what they were supposed to know. This ideologized authoritarian approach served for decades during the Soviet times and was named a traditional education.

By 1934, the Soviet government made elementary education across the country obligatory and free of charge. Children and adolescents between the ages of 7 through 17 years old were required to attend public schools regardless of their social background, ethnicity, sex, and family income. The next step in the development of the Soviet education system was during the period of 1933-1937 when a 7-year secondary education became available for all adolescents. Later, in 1949, it became mandatory.

The communist party was playing a very important role in educating the younger generation of Soviet citizens in order to prepare them to serve their country and communist ideals. All students were assigned to be members of different levels of communist organizations which were created to deal with certain age groups of people. Children in the elementary school level aged from 7 years old through 9 years old were called *"oktyabryata"* which was named after the October Socialist Revolution in 1917. Adolescents, aged from 9 years old through 14 years old, were affiliated with the Pioneer organization. The elder students, aged from 14 years old through 16-17 years old, were accepted into Komsomol, the communist youth organization. All of these ideological communist organizations had very well designed structure, norms, rules, requirements, and methods of stimulating or punishing children. The worse punishment for students and their parents was expulsion of a student from the school communist organization but this happened very seldom because classmates, teachers, parents, and other community members acted jointly to help each child be a well behaved person and a good member of the communist organization. Communist school organizations acted at every school in every class and were managed by the school administration which, in turn, was supervised by the higher level of the local communist party division.

The general educational system during 1930-1980s was represented by the following structure: 4-year kindergarten (3-7 years old), 1-year preschool (7-8 years old), 4-year elementary school (8-12 years old), 3-year not-complete secondary school (*nepolnaya srednyaya shkola*) (12-15 years old), 3-year complete secondary school (*polnaya srednyaya shkola*) (15-18 years old), postsecondary vocational and higher education.

Compulsory education included two educational levels—elementary and not-complete secondary schools. The length of the obligatory education was increased from 7 years of study to 8 in 1958 and later in 1984 to 9 years.

The number of 7-year schools increased tremendously across the Soviet country in very short period of time. A variety of school structures were created to serve all categories of adolescents from all income classes throughout the entire country and, in order for them to complete their compulsory 7-year secondary education, evening schools served those adolescents who worked during the day. The program of education development was interrupted by the Great Patriotic War (1941-1945) that significantly destroyed the country. During and after the war, the government opened a large number of boarding schools and orphanages for millions of children whose parents had lost their lives defending their country.

A lot of efforts and resources for schools, educators, and local authorities were used to meet the demand of the Soviet government. All of this effort is reflected in the slogan "To catch up and leave America behind!" (*Dognat' i peregnat' Ameriku!*). The political and educational systems were very much focused on the higher achievements which brought the country to the level of discovering nuclear weapons and the ability to successfully go into space during the 1950s and 1960s.

Overall during Soviet times, starting in the 1930s until the end of 1980s, the curriculum was designed based on a strict communist ideology. All of the textbooks and selected literature for students were published under very careful censorship. All school subjects were examined for their appropriateness in terms of how they promoted communist ideas and beliefs. Any information that could lead to doubts and questions about the validity of the communist ideology was removed from the textbooks and the authors were severely punished.

The priority of the Soviet education was aimed toward governmental goals. Personal educational needs and intentions had to be adjusted to Soviet policies. This country of "workers and peasants" needed masses of qualified workers in order to successfully develop the Soviet economy. Education accompanied with labor was the main approach for secondary schools. In the 1950s, handicraft lessons were applied at all grades and a large number of adolescents received certificates in the primary level of vocational professions along with the graduation certificate (*attestat zrelosti*). Adolescent females could work as cooks, seamstresses, sellers, secretaries, and assistants in industrial organizations after graduating from the eighth grade. Males received qualifications which enabled them to work as car and tractor drivers, auto mechanics, electricians, computer technicians, and in many other types of employment. Taking internships at places of industry allowed the students to gain skills in dealing with metals, wood, and electricity for which they were ordered to produce simple parts or items for local organizations.

The communist party's order "To catch up and leave America behind" was implemented by secondary schools through programs in mathematics, physics, and chemistry when adolescents started to learn fundamental disciplines in the sciences in the fifth grade. Elite schools located in populated cities prepared graduates for the universities and higher education military institutions where more advance programs were offered. After-school learning activities engaged adolescents in a number of contests and competitions which were organized by higher educational institutions.

Implementation of the Soviet Union Cabinet of Ministers' Decree, *About Improvement of the Study of Foreign Languages*, was passed in 1961 and led to the opening of approximately 700 new schools in major Soviet cities. Teachers in these schools began to teach some of their subjects in a foreign language. As of 1963, foreign language study was set up so that 50% of the students would learn English, 20% of the students—French, 20% of the students—German, and 10% of the students—Spanish and other foreign languages.

The assessment practices in Russian schools changed a number of times and continue to be a subject of debate. At the beginning of the era of formal education, one of the ways to recognize student performance was to observe students distribution in the classroom: better students were seated in front desks closer to the teacher and the students that performed at a lower level sat in the back seats. The students performing at the lowest levels, however, were often on the floor, sitting on their knees in various corners of the classroom.

Michael Lomonosov developed an assessment system and suggested that schools should apply this on a daily basis. His system contained 10 grades for which each had an abbreviation such as "WS—was sick" (BB—*byl bolen*) or "ED—everything is done" (VI—*vse ispolnil*) (Kostylev, 2000).

The Russian assessment system moved from commendational word grades to numerical scores when the five-score scale was accepted by the Russian Ministry of Education in 1837. The numerical grading scale was criticized over decades by different scholars and educators who found that this grading system did not stimulate students to learn but only to get better grades. Scholars found that any grading system contributed to cheating, dishonesty, and lack of student motivation.

The Soviet government abolished the five-score grading system in 1918 but did not offer any alternative grading methods to educators. Therefore a testimonial (*kharakteristika*) became the main assessment document that described students. In 1935, the Soviet government returned back to a five-word grade scale: "excellent," "good," "satisfactory," "poor," and "very poor." The numerical grading system was reinstituted in 1944 this time using numbers ranging from five to one, with five being the highest grade that a student could achieve.

Socialist competition in all spheres of life in the USSR impacted the education system influencing schools to compete against each other for better performance. Higher grades were intentionally given to students even though they performed at lower grade levels and poor achievements were purposely hidden. The competition between schools for better performance was officially cancelled in 1944 because it was recognized as being harmful to education and not effective for students. Student grades, however, continued to be a problem for teachers who were trying to avoid criticism and authoritarian punishment. Thus, they attempted to look better by not giving the lowest grade "1," which eventually disappeared from the assessment documents.

Period 5: The Post-Soviet Era

New types of secondary schools, called gymnasiums and lyceums, appeared after the collapse of the Soviet Union at the beginning of the 1990s when schools, in their attempts to survive, sought ways to get more funds from the federal and municipal budgets, to get parents that were more solvent, and getting better students. The programs at these elite schools focus on the earlier educational and professional specializations of children. Gymnasiums provide training in a wide field of humanitarian and scientific knowledge, and they work with students from the elementary and middle school levels. Lyceums offer preprofessional specializations for elder adolescents of the middle and high school levels.

Elite schools collaborate with higher education institutions that are interested in the preparation of their future students to meet their particular expectations. Through early involvement in activities, future university students become better prepared to qualify for enrollment and understand the values and the culture of the university. Universities organize different types of contests, competitions, corresponding schools, and long-distance learning certificate programs for students in the tenth and eleventh grades. The younger adolescents who study at the middle school level in gymnasiums and lyceums are more aware of their possibilities regarding further study than their non-elite counterparts, that allows them to take the easier path to higher education.

Elite secondary education is in high demand in Russia. According to data provided by the Ministry of Education in the Russian Federation (Federal Agency on Education, n.d.-a), referring to schools throughout the country, the total number of non-elite secondary schools decreased from 12,808 in 1999-2000 to 11,213 in 2005-2006 while the number of gymnasiums and lyceums increased from 1,726 to 2,167 in the corresponding years. In 2007, the President of the Russian Federation, Vladimir Putin, signed a law requiring that compulsory full secondary education last for a period of 11 years of study at the secondary school level.

OUTCOMES OF THE SCHOOLING OF YOUNG ADOLESCENTS

Academic Performance Outcomes

It was stated in the international assessment report (National Training Foundation, 2004a) regarding Russian young adolescent academic performance that Russia participated in TIMSS (Trends in International Mathematics and Science Study) in 1995, 1999, and 2003. The results showed that Russian young adolescents between the ages of 14-15 years progressively decreased their academic achievements through the years of this study. In 1995, eighth grade Russian students took 14th place in mathematics and the sciences among the 45 participating countries. In the study conducted in 2003, Russian eighth grade students in mathematics dropped from a score of 524 in 1995 to a score of 508 in 2003, and the mean score fell from 523 in 1995 to 514 in the sciences.

In 2003, the Russian Federation also lost the title of being the "most literate country." Russians, former Soviets, "got accustomed to being proud of the Soviet education system and level of education. It is sad to see how we are being passed up" (Kuz'minov, 2002). Russian 15-year-old students performed poorly in reading, analyzing, and understanding texts. Of the 41 countries that participated in the Programme for International Student Assessment (PISA) (National Training Foundation, 2004b), Russia took 27th place in reading, 22nd place in mathematics, and 26th place in the sciences. At the beginning of the 1990s, Russia was on top of the international assessment list, however, at the beginning of 2000, Russia moved to the bottom.

Discussions regarding the findings of PISA were held in Moscow in 2005 where Russian officials shared concerns about the quality of Russian secondary education and how academic programs correlate with European educational standards. Some of the authorities criticized the methods and content of the tasks that were used by PISA for student testing (Ivanova-Gladil'schikova, 2005).

The results of the international tests are difficult to interpret objectively because of existing differences between the educational systems and their educational traditions relating to teaching, learning, and assessment practices. The international tests are relatively new in Russian education which had previously focused on face-to-face examinations of fundamental knowledge but now moved toward the competencies related to the application of knowledge to practice.

Academic achievements of young adolescents in Russia can also be assessed based on the results of the national standardized test (*Edinyi Gosudarstvenniy Ekzamen*—EGE). The laws of 2007 (titled, "About changes in the Law of Russian Federation," and "About higher and post-higher professional education") require all schools to implement a graduation exam and for all universities to accept EGE results for student enrollment starting in 2009. The data on EGE-2007 (www.centeroko.ru) show that more than 80% of secondary school graduates have taken the national test. The report (Ershov et al., 2007) indicated that Russian schools gradually become more accustomed to utilizing standardized tests. Being unfamiliar with the standardized test approach in the past, Russian students experience difficulties in understanding the test format and requirements. One of the main problems for test-takers is the lack of skills in dealing with different sources of information such as text, diagram, and tables.

Hypothetically, the national standardized test increases the opportunities for non-elite school students to be accepted by the higher educational institutions. Different levels of preparation, however, have shown that graduates of different types of secondary schools perform differently. Graduates from gymnasiums and lyceums have had the best results and students from regular secondary schools perform better than those who have studied at evening schools or primary vocational schools (*nachal'noe professional'noe uchilische*). Graduates from larger towns achieved better results when compared to their peers from rural schools.

Competition among school graduates for enrollment in university "budget places," where tuition is paid by the federal government, forces young adolescents and their parents to think many years ahead of time about higher education. The number of students who enter higher education institutions as well as the reputation of those universities are a very important indicator of the quality of every secondary school's education. Elite schools, gymnasiums and lyceums, conduct a very tough selection process of their students at the elementary level or middle school level (fifth grade).

Increasing academic mobility of secondary school students as well as college/university students and the growing opportunities for furthering post-secondary education abroad motivates Russian adolescents to develop skills in applying their school subject knowledge on national and international tests. Tourism outside Russia also contributes to the motivation of young people to study foreign languages to better understand other cultures and to be able communicate with people in and from other countries.

Adolescents are becoming more familiar with international tests although these tests require years of preparation. A large number of adolescents receive foreign language training at private schools and international education centers after their regular school hours in order to become better prepared for tests such as TOEFL (Test of English as a Foreign Language), IELTS (International English Language Testing System),

GRE (Graduate Record Examination), GMAT (Graduate Management Admission Test), and other tests which are required to enter American and European higher education institutions.

Academic achievement on the school level is based on the traditional "5-2" grading system which is applied by every teacher. During their study at secondary schools, adolescents receive certificates, grants, and other awards for their academic achievements in addition to grades in the record books. They compete for prizes and places of honor at school, as well as in towns, regions, and country contests and competitions, and many of the students also participate in different international contests. Gold and silver medals are the highest awards for secondary school graduates. Parents, focusing on their child's achievement of a gold or silver medal, put a lot of effort into keeping their kids motivated, encouraged, and supported from first grade at the elementary school to the day of graduation.

Other Important Outcomes

In order to support and recognize the achievements of children and young adolescents' in sports and other fields, the federal program "Children of Russia" was launched in 2007. The program joined with three existing subprograms: "Healthy Generation" (*Zdorovoe pokolenie*), "Gifted Children" (*Odarennye deti*), and "Children and Family" (*Deti i sem'ya*).

From 2001 through 2003, 450 gifted young adolescents were recognized for their high achievements by the federal government and awarded with money, gifts, and certificates. Groups of adolescents from different regions were sent to Moscow to meet with the President of the Russian Federation, Vladimir Putin, at the Kremlin. Among the rewarded children were winners of the academic national competitions, young musicians, inventors, programmers, designers, ecologists, researchers, writers, artists, and athletes.

During the first decades of the Soviet time, the government created so called "*additional education*" system of organizations that offered after-school activities for children aged 6 through 18. This additional education united the schools of sports, music, art, Children's and Youth's Palaces, summer camps, and other types of organizations for children and youth. In 2005, about 50% of school age children and youth were involved in activities provided by the system of additional education (Federal Agency on Education, n.d.-b). Most athletes and international competition winners have been trained at children-youth sports schools and most of the famous musicians as well as artists have graduated from the system of additional education.

Research Supporting Academic
Performance and Other Outcomes

Russian researchers continuously reflect on the problems in educating young adolescents which are related to their physiological, mental, and social development, as well as their social interactions and behavior. Existing research investigates a number of issues in the transition of students from one school level to another, in the socialization of adolescents, their health, social engagement, and academic achievement.

Transition from the elementary school level to the middle school level often results in decreased academic performance. Training in a traditional Russian school at the elementary level is provided by one main teacher who deals with one group of students and is with these students throughout most of their school day. In the middle level of schooling, however, different subjects are taught by different teachers, and teachers that are assigned to be class mentors (*klassnyi rukovoditel*) do not have enough time to give their complete attention to each and every student in their classes. Children experience psychological difficulties as they try to relate to many different teachers and their teaching styles, and adjust their attitude toward the many new teachers, peers, and new classmates. Those students with extroverted personalities adapt to the new conditions in a short time whereas those who are introverts experience stress and anxiety for a number of years (Kukushin, 2002).

Research on gifted children (Schelanova, 2003) explored cognitive abilities, personal qualities, and social factors as components of the phenomenon of giftedness. The researcher attempted to apply worldwide developed theories on giftedness to the issues of educating gifted students in Russian schools, such as how to recognize giftedness, how to analyze the factors that have an influence on the development of giftedness, and what kind of programs must be designed to support students during the entire school period. In discussing the reasons of poor achievement, Schelanova pointed out that lower performance can be linked to earlier developmental conditions. Poor socioeconomic conditions and cultural discouragement in the family negatively impacts the blossoming of the inborn abilities of students. Traditional school culture very often fails to deal with the extra abilities of those who are not like others. Research on giftedness is very important for Russia's education which, during decades of the Soviet time, was teacher-centered and ignored the features of those students who did not meet the expectations of the homogenized ideological Soviet system.

Research on so called *pedagogical valeoogy* is a relatively recent approach in Russian pedagogy. It appeared at the beginning of the1980s reflecting health problems of Russian students. Researcher (Tatarnikova, 1995) found that academic overloads, poor social and environmental conditions, lack of physical movement, and misbalanced nutrition increased predisposition to the sickness of students. The results of the examined cohort of fifth grade students show that only 16% were estimated as being healthy, 48% had one health problem, 25% had two health problems, and 11% of the students had three or more health problems. In an examination of students attending specialized schools with advanced programs, the rate of unhealthy children is two and a half times higher. New courses for middle school and high school students on health-saving technologies have been taught by teachers that have not received any special preparation because the educational system has not engaged health-related specialists. One doctor and one nurse at a school of over 1,000 students can not solve the problems of students who are in poor health. Scholars suggested that schools should create *pedagogical valeology* centers within the school structure in order to develop the awareness of teachers, students, and parents on health-related issues. The researcher pointed out a contradiction in Russia's education system between the priorities of the educational needs of individuals and the priorities of social demands and conditions for individuals to achieve.

Research on the quality of secondary education was also conducted by the Center OKO (*Otsenka Kachestva Obrazovaniya*) (www.centeroko.ru) which was founded by the Russian Academy of Education (*Rossiyskaya Academiya Obrazovaniya*) in 1994. The goals of the center are to develop methods of assessment on the quality of education, to conduct studies measuring the indicators on the quality of education, and to conduct comparative studies of student academic achievements between Russia and other countries. The findings of these studies are applied at educational organizations and schools for the improvement of education. Center OKO collaborates with international assessment organizations on projects such as TIMSS, PISA, IAEP, LES, and others. Within Russia, Center OKO collects and analyzes the data on the national standardized test.

An experimental study with practical application was conducted on separating different levels of schooling (Bashev & Sergomanov, 2006). Traditionally, the majority of Russian schools contain a few or all secondary levels of education from the elementary school level through the high school level. Schools in rural areas, because of the small number of students, usually contain elementary and middle school levels. During the decades of the Soviet time, the approach to have substructured schools within one organization had been considered as a strength which allowed increased efficiency based on a single administration, targeted allocation of resources, and continuity between the different levels of schooling. The study investigated the advantages of splitting schools by levels as separate organizations and Bashev and Sergomanov pointed out the benefits for students at an age-oriented school which allows for more effectively meeting the needs of students and helping them succeed. Humanization of education and the continuous changes in the content of education have required educators to seek and implement new pedagogical approaches, technologies, and educational models that will help students achieve academically, to successfully become adapted and socialized in this very quickly changing world, to enter adulthood well prepared, educated, and mentally as well as physically healthy.

CURRENT ISSUES RELATED TO THE SCHOOLING OF YOUNG ADOLESCENTS

Concerns about the Current Educational System

The many concerns of educators and politicians about losing the strength of the Russian education system are gradually transforming to notions on how to adjust the fundamental theoretical school approach. A country that moves from being a closed society toward being an open, democratic society, cannot avoid the painful changes within its entire system, the resistance from the conservative part of society, and the mistakes in applying democratic ideas to a recently totalitarian environment. Resistance from the conservative generation of educators toward the reforms that are very much needed in the education system is becoming weaker but still remains to be one of the main obstacles on all levels of education.

Newly introduced standardized examinations continue to be the hot topic of public debates. Teachers often feel frustrated and overloaded by the large number of requirements that they need to accomplish in order to complete their many tasks throughout the workday. To achieve better results as they work, teachers have to meet the educational and personal needs of their students, implement programs according to the existing educational standards, and train students in how to properly prepare themselves for taking tests. The task of training students on test taking has just recently appeared and it is quite different from the other two tasks because of the impact it has on school graduates furthering their educational path. The standardized test is a new phenomenon in Russian educational system, and it is quite evident that teachers lack the knowledge in proper testing techniques and that the quality of the test content is poor. Teachers have a very limited time to prepare their students to take a test and, with this additional work load, the amount of stress on both the student and teacher has increased.

Another concern in education relates to the appropriateness of compulsory secondary school education that became obligatory in September 2007. Conflicting opinions have arisen between politicians who want to return to Russia the image of a well-educated country and practitioners, who deal with the school settings on a daily basis. The law regarding compulsory complete (11th grade) education is applied to a category of adolescents who normally do not perform well academically. In the past, those students who were willing to obtain their complete secondary education would usually continue their studies at the high school level whereas some students with lower academic achievements would go to work or enroll in a vocational school upon completion of the ninth grade. Under the current situation, young adolescents are required by law to graduate from the secondary school and, because of that, unmotivated students must stay in school for 2 additional years as they struggle with a lack of interest in study as well as with various disciplinary problems.

Demographic shifts have decreased the number of secondary school students from 20 million in 2000 to 14 million people in 2007. Secondary schools receive federal and municipal funds on a "per-student" basis. A lot of rural schools have been closed because of the lack of students. Schools in populated cities enroll one-third less students than their capacity. Reduced funding negatively affects school improvement, maintenance, equipment, supplies, and teachers' salary. Schools have been forced to increase the cost of lunches for students and to collect more money from parents through various fundraising strategies.

Benefits of the Current Educational System

The current Russian educational system is usually considered as a transitional system, spanning the close of the totalitarian system of the Soviet Union to the open democratic one characterized by changes toward homogenization, internationalization, and globalization. Increasing decentralization of the educational system, global academic mobility, flow of information, and differentiation and flexibility in the content of curriculum not only bring difficulties within the system, but also a number of benefits which were not possible 15-20 years ago. Decentralization gives schools the opportunity to change their status (for instance, from a regular secondary school to a gymnasium or a lyceum, depending on their resources and local needs) and to select their students (if the school status is different from a regular secondary school). It also affords the establishment of partnerships with educational organizations, agencies, and businesses on the local, regional, national, or international level (during the Soviet time, a "partnership" (*shefstvo*) was assigned by the local authorities), and the initiation, design, and implementation of different educational programs for students, teachers, parents, and their community (authoritarian approval is no longer required in order to launch a new course).

Differentiation (*variativnost'*) is one of the strengths of the current education system. Federal education standards for secondary schools address federal, regional, and local/school components. The federal component establishes the minimum level of knowledge, skills, and competencies for each level of school and each single grade level. Schools must adhere to these standards to guarantee each student the same minimal level of education for a particular number of years of study. The regional component deals with decisions about what students should be taught and what features of the region must be reflected in the school curriculum. The regional component usually includes local lore study, local ethnic group languages, or religious courses. The local component is developed by teachers and the school administration and is, therefore, subject to changes depending on school resources, student educational needs, as well as the expectations of parents and local community. The school component for adolescents consists of numerous preprofessional subjects that help students learn professions and assist them in finding a field for their future specialization at the high school level and/or the vocational/higher education level. Thus, due to the school component, many students now have the opportunity to learn about the world of professions during their study at the middle school level.

Increasing student mobility across other countries is a very significant feature of the current educational system. Under the Bologna process, Russian education is now involved in many programs which are developing a student and professor movement in higher education. The United States Agency for International Development and numerous nonprofit American organizations provide funds and support for Russian elder adolescents to study at secondary schools in the United States. Many young people have the opportunity to see another country, to live in a diverse society, to study in a foreign school, and to develop tolerance and other values that are necessary for successful work and life in a rapidly developing global community.

REFORM INITIATIVES AND NATIONAL POLICIES

The Bologna process (n.d.), which is aimed toward creating a European Higher Education Area by 2010, is the main outside force for educational reforms in Russia. The major changes, which are being implemented on the levels of Russia's higher education and high school systems, relate to correlating educational programs with the European system, homogenizing the content of programs, applying the Western credit/hour system, and developing assessment tools in higher education. The movement toward the European higher education system also impacts the lower educational levels. In order to prepare school students to study at higher education institutions, professional training courses (*profil'noe obuchenie*) have been developing at the high school level, and preprofession oriented courses (*preprofil'noe obuchenie*) at the eighth and ninth grade levels of the middle schools. Another impact of the Bologna process on the secondary school is humanization of the content of education: students have more classes in languages, culture, society development, contemporary environmental issues, as well as other courses which help students better understand this rapidly changing world and develop their adaptation skills to succeed professionally and personally in the future.

New federal policies and laws have been enacted in the attempt to adjust the structure and content of the Russian educational system toward the European standards. The Federal Component of State Standard of Secondary Complete Education (*Federalnyi Komponent Gosudarstvennogo Standarta Obschego Obrazovaniya*) (Federal Agency on Education, n.d.-c), which is devoted in part to middle school (young adolescent) education, has set three main benchmarks for students to achieve: developing an integrated understanding of the world based on knowledge, skills, and ways of acting; gaining the experience of different actions (individual and collective) to learn about the world and about oneself; and preparing to choose an individual educational or professional path. Middle schools are required to meet federal education standards and provide professional and pre-professional training, to provide a differentiation in elective courses, to develop their assessment system and instructional techniques, as well as to initiate and experiment with innovations in order to find the best practices for their students.

Federal policies also demand that educational organizations seek ways to involve public institutions with educational administrative offices for creating trustworthy boards of education for the schools, developing public-professional mechanisms for program accreditation, and developing a nationwide system of evaluation on the quality of education. According to the federal decrees, the modernization of the financial and economic mechanisms in education includes funding schools on a "per-student" basis, increasing the funding for education from the federal budget, raising the prestige of the teaching profession, developing paid educational services, and developing the economic sustainability of the schools.

The educational reforms, which are in the process of being implemented, are based on the Constitution of the Russian Federation, Law of the Russian Federation "About Education," Concept of Modernization of Russian Education by 2010, Concept of Profession Oriented Education

(*Kontseptsiya profil'nogo obucheniya*), Federal Component of State Standard of Secondary Education of 2004, Federal Basis Teaching Plan (*Federal'nyi bazisnyi uchebnyi plan*) (2004), the Federal list of textbooks and instructional methodological supplements, and the Letters and Orders of the Ministry of Education and Science of Russian Federation.

RESEARCH

Current Research Topics

Most educational studies published in Russian scholarly journals, pedagogical books, and online sources are more didactic and normative in nature than in the United States. In general, Russian educational scholars write articles with little reference to methods of data collection and analysis. Most of the papers contain problem descriptions, suggested solutions, and general discussions; however, these discussions tend to be more emotionally biased and subjective than equivalent research in the United States. Researchers, for the most part, rely more on passion than empirical evidence to persuade the readers to accept their theoretical assertions. Thus, it is quite difficult to evaluate the validity and usefulness of most research projects. However, we can provide an overview of the types of research currently being done.

At the request of the Ministry of Education and Science of the Russian Federation, The Russian Academy of Education, one the main national research organizations which includes 23 research institutions and four regional branches, has been conducting nationwide studies on its own research programs. According to the academy's 2007 annual report, research topics on Russia's middle school level of education have been focused on two major issues: "The axiological, theoretical and legislative foundation of the content theory of secondary education," and "The development of secondary education as a factor of the competitive capacity of Russia on the world arena" (Russian Academy of Education, n.d.-a).

Research projects were conducted on the following topics:

- modernization of the content of education at the middle school level;
- national educational standards;
- the development of a monitoring system;
- methods of information and communication technologies in middle schools;

- the modernization of materials and technical maintenance of the schools;
- social-pedagogical preventative measures for controlling violence at schools;
- aesthetic education of middle school students in the "additional" education system (after-school educational programs);
- physiology of adolescence development;
- problems of education at rural schools;
- spiritual development of adolescents and healthy life style;
- education in this era of the internet;
- "competence" approaches in middle schools;
- migration and polycultural education;
- transitioning educational systems in the countries of the former Soviet Union;
- teaching for gifted students;
- health-saving learning environments for middle school students;
- academic load and physical training for adolescents;
- nutrition and health of students; and
- preprofessional training for adolescents with disabilities.

Additional research projects addressing the development of middle schools have included the following federal programs: "Russian Language (2006-2010)," "Social Village Development by 2010" (*Sotsial'noe razvitie sela*), "Children of Russia (2007-2010)," "Prevention of drug misuse and illegal drug circulation (2005-2009)" (*Kompleksnye mery protivodeystviya zloupotrebleniyu narkotikami i nezakonnomu oborotu*), "Electronic Russia (2002-2010)," "Development of physical culture and sports in the Russian Federation (2006-2015)," and "Increasing the safety of roads (2006-2012)."

Pedagogical comprehensive universities and pedagogical departments at the classic universities have their own research programs, priorities, and interests. Herzen State Pedagogical University (Herzen University, n.d.), for example, investigated children and youth nonprofit organizations and the partnerships of local organizations in preventing negative social occurrences among adolescents. The Department of Pedagogy and Psychology at Voronezh State University investigated the effectiveness of pedagogical social worker activities at middle schools in Voronezh with the purpose developing a relatively new educational program for social workers at the classic university during 2006 (Berezhnaya, 2006).

Methodologies

Research studies have been conducted using many different units of analysis and include studies on the international, national, regional, and local levels. Most of the studies have mixed qualitative and quantitative methods. However, the research methods in Russian education are changing rapidly based upon influence from Western research practices. Most Russian research projects focus more attention on normative rather than explanatory approaches, consistent with a history of didactic approaches to educational practice.

Quantitative research is commonly used for exploring student performances. Data, such as grades and test scores of middle school students, have been collected and analyzed on all levels of education including school grade, cohort, school, schools in a district, districts, city, region, country, and schools in other countries. Schools and research institutions lack modern statistical tools as well as the knowledge of how to accurately summarize data and analyze statistics. Thus, descriptive statistical analysis is much more common than inferential statistical analysis.

Important Research Findings

The Russian Academy of Education conducted a study (Russian Academy of Education, n.d.-b) on the impact of academic loads on the physical conditions of elder adolescents, using data from a total of 4678 middle school students from five regions of Russia. Personal data on the health conditions of every student, aged from 10-11 years old to 16-17 years old, were collected and analyzed in order to accurately follow the changes in health of each of the participants throughout their years of study at secondary school. The results of the research indicated that approximately 20% of the students involved in the study were at risk because of deteriorating health conditions and indicators also revealed that the health of female students was at a higher risk than that of male students. Specifically, irregular nutrition, lack of physical activity, smoking, and alcohol have a more negative impact on females than males. It was also found that the physical and emotional environments at most secondary schools do not support the normal healthy growth and development of adolescents. Despite the fact that elite schools, gymnasiums and lyceums possess better physical conditions, the study shows that these schools also have a lot of problems which have a negative effect on student health. High academic load was found to be the top factor negatively affecting adolescent health. Health problems are considered to be one of the existing problems in the Russian Federation which can be resolved with the improved allocation of material, technical, and human resources at all levels of the educational system.

FUTURE DIRECTIONS

Within the near future, the Ministry of Education and Science of the Russian Federation (www.mon.gov.ru) is planning to implement the national project "Education." The goals of this project include: (1) providing access to high-quality education for students of all social classes as a foundation for improved social mobility and decreased socioeconomic differentiation in the society; (2) meeting the demands of current and future needs of the economy and society by providing properly trained professionals; (3) creating conditions for lifelong learning; (4) creating conditions for the involvement of children and youth in the economic, social, political, and cultural life of the country; (5) developing the scientific and technical potential of the country; and (6) supporting innovative activities in education.

The national project Education includes 15 subprojects of which nine relate to secondary education. Middle school students will benefit from the installation of Internet access within every school throughout the country, free hot lunches by 2010, school buses for rural areas, improved school learning conditions based on academic and nonacademic competitions, and improved school atmosphere through monetary support as well as official recognition for higher achieving students, administrators, and teachers. Middle school students will continue to be prepared for taking national standardized tests as well as being more involved in academic and non-academic competitions.

According to the "Concept of Modernization of Russian Education by 2010" (Elementy, n.d.), Russian young adolescents regardless of gender, age, social status, and place of residence must have equal access to high-quality education, social support, benefits, health care and conditions for a healthy life, and physical as well as emotional development. Secondary school students will also receive more attention and much needed support from the different institutions involved in secondary school education.

CONCLUDING DISCUSSION

The Russian Academy of Education, the major research institution in Russia, designs its own research programs in accordance with the Federal laws, decrees, and orders. The academy's goal is to be the main nationwide provider of textbooks, supplementary materials for school subjects, and to establish the majority of the research goals in order to develop "a scientific foundation" (*nauchnoe obosnovanie*) for existing state programs and directions. The president of the Russian Academy of Education, N. D. Nikandrov, regrets the fact that the academy has lost its influence on private schools which are now developing and implementing their own educational programs. In a statement, Nikandrov is quoted as saying, "It is a pity that different private groups and individuals have co-opted an initiative from the Academy to be scientific 'curators' for these schools, and providers of textbooks and other methodical materials for them" (Russian Academy of Education, n.d.-c).

In this centralized authoritarian system, where the government priorities are driven by existing research programs, the needs of the students have not always been addressed. For many Russian educators, transitioning the education system toward Western democratic models has mostly been interpreted as being a movement toward standardization and homogenization with the European educational system. Thus, there are many areas which require further research. No research projects have focused on the impact of globalization on young adolescents. There is very little research addressing the social and emotional development of young adolescents. These represent serious deficiencies in Russian educational research, given the challenges confronting young adolescents.

In spite of this perception, Russian educators have been trying to adopt the best features of Western middle school education while maintaining the strengths of its previous middle school systems. Specifically, this means that Russians want to draw upon Western organizational and instructional strategies that address the social and emotional development of young adolescents as well as the impact of globalization on young adolescents, while at the same time retaining the rigor and relevance of a traditional Russian educational system that has traditionally held students to high standards and produced some of the world's greatest writers, artists, and scholars.

Today's Russian adolescents aged from 10 years old through 17 years old represent a generation that was born shortly after the collapse of the Soviet Union during the 1990s. These youth came into life in a nation going through major transitions where the rate of births have dropped remarkably and the rate of deaths has increased tremendously (DaVanzo & Adamson, 1997). Within the next decade or two, an aging population will put a tremendous amount of pressure on the shoulders of this new generation. What do we know about today's Russian adolescents? How are we going to raise them and how are we going to prepare them for their future? They lack the experience of the Soviet system and only learn about their country's transitional stage of moving from communism toward democracy from the media and from the elder generation. They are more likely to have negative perceptions about communism, and they tend to associate democracy with Internet access, elevated standards of living, and American music and movies.

The uniqueness of the today's generation of Russian adolescents is that they have numerous opportunities to contribute to tomorrow's global society because they are coming from a country with a very rich history, high levels of achievement, and a wealth of resources. It is important to provide today's adolescents with a deep awareness of their national history in order to understand the current economic and political processes that occur within and outside of Russia. Ultimately, Russian middle schools must provide young adolescents with the appropriate knowledge, skills, and dispositions, so that the next generation of Russian citizens can engage in social, political, economical, environmental activities in rapidly changing world.

REFERENCES

Bashev, V. V., & Sergomanov, P. A. (2006). *Model' organizatsii obrazovaniya v shkolakh stupeney obucheniya: Vozrostnoy podkhod v obrazovanii* [Model of schools with the different levels of education: Age oriented approach in education]. Krasnoyarsk, Russia: Univers.

Berezhnaya, I. F. (2006). *Vliyanie vospitatel'noy sredy na formirovanie social'nykh orientatsiy studentov* [Influence of the university learning environment on social development of students]. In I. F. Berezhnaya & L. R. Surinova (Ed.) *Vospitatel'naya sreda vuza kak factor professional'nogo stanovleniya spetsialista* [University learning environment as a key factor for developing the future professionals] (pp. 24-31). Voronezh, , Russia: Voronezh State University.

Bologna process. (n.d.). Retrieved September 3, 2008, from http://www.ond.vlaanderen.be/hogeronderwijs/bologna/

The Constitution of the Russian Federation. (n.d.). *Chapter 2. Rights and freedoms of man and citizen. Article 19.* Retrieved September 3, 2008, from http://www.constitution.ru/en/10003000-03.htm

Country Studies. (n.d.). *Ethnic composition.* Retrieved September 3, 2008, from http://countrystudies.us/russia/32.htm

Dautova, O. B. (2004). *Zhizn' i pedagogicheskaya deyatel'nost' I. I. Betskogo* [Life and work of I. I. Betskoy]. Retrieved July 3, 2008, from http://ideashistory.org.ru/pdfs/51dautova.pdf

DaVanzo, J., & Adamson, D. (1997, July). *Russia's demographic "crisis": How real is it?* Washington, DC: RAND Issue Paper—Center for Russian and Eurasian Studies Labor and Population Program.

Ediev, D. M. (2005). *About impact of demographic crisis in Russia on problems in education and science.* Retrieved July 3, 2008, from http://rosmu.ru/activity/statements/5.html#top

Elementy. (n.d.). *Kontseptsiya modernizatsii rossiyskogo obrazovaniya na period do 2010* [Concept of modernization of Russian education by 2010]. Retrieved September 3, 2008, from http://elementy.ru/Library9/pr393.htm

Ershov, A. G., Kovaleva, G. S, Denischeva, L. J., Krasnyanskaya, K. A., Mel'nikova, N. B, Ryazanovskiy, A. R., et al. (2007, May-June). *Resul'taty edinogo gosudarstvennogo ekzamena* [Results of the National Standardized Test]. Retrieved September 3, 2008, from http://www.centeroko.ru/public.htm

Federal Agency on Education. (n.d.-a). *Osnovnye pokazateli. Dnevnye gosudarstvennye obrazovatel'nye uschrezhdeniya* [Main indicators. State educational organizations]. Retrieved September 3, 2008, from http://www.ed.gov.ru/uprav/stat/1849/

Federal Agency on Education. (n.d.-b). *Vospitanie i dopolnitel'noye obrazovanie detey* [Nurturing and additional education of children]. Retrieved September 3, 2008, from http://www.ed.gov.ru/junior/new_version/vospit_dop_obraz_det/

Federal Agency on Education. (n.d.-c). *Federalnyi Komponent Gosudarstvennogo Standarta Obschego Obrazovaniya* [The federal component of state standardards of secondary complete education]. Retrieved September 3, 2008, from http://www.ed.gov.ru/ob-edu/noc/rub/standart/

Federal State Statistics Service. (n.d.-a). *Resident population*. Retrieved September 3, 2008, from http://www.gks.ru/bgd/regl/b08_12/IssWWW.exe/stg/d01/05-01.htm

Federal State Statistics Service. (n.d.-b). *International migration*. Retrieved September 3, 2008, from http://www.gks.ru/bgd/regl/b08_12/IssWWW.exe/stg/d01/05-09.htm

Herzen University. (n.d.). *Science and research*. Retrieved September 3, 2008, from http://www.herzen.spb.ru/en/Science_and_Research/

Ivanova-Gladil'schikova, N. (2005). *Gryadyot generation PISA* [Generation PISA is coming]. Retrieved July 4, 2008, from http://www.inauka.ru/education/article53598.html

Kapterev, P. F. (2004). *History of Russian pedagogy*. St. Petersburg, Russia: Aleteya

Korovin, V. M., & Sviridov, V. A. (2007). Pedagogicheskaya deyatel'nost' Glavnogo upravleniya voenno-uchebnymi zavedeniyami Rossii vo vtoroy polovine XIX-nachale XX veka. In *Aktual'nye problemy obucheniya i vospitaniya shkol'nikov i studentov v obrazovatel'nom uchrezhdenii* [Pedagogical work of the governmental military education institutions of Russia in the second half of the 19th-beginning of the 20th century]. In I. F. Berezhnaya (Ed) *Contemporary problems in education of students at the education institution* (pp. 27-33). Voronezh, Russia: Voronezhskiy Gosudarstvennyi Universitet.

Kostylev, F. V. (2000). *Uchit' po-novomu: Nuzhny li otsenki-bally? Kniga dlya uchitelya* [Teaching in new way: Do we need scores/grades? Book for a teacher]. Moscow, Russia: Gumanitarnyi izdatel'skiy tsentr VLADOS.

Kukushin, V. S. (2002). *Teoriya i metodika vospitatel'noy raboty* [Theory and methods of education]. Rostov-on-Don, Russia: MarT.

Kuz'minov, Y. (2002). Obrazovanie i reforma [Education and reform]. *Otechestvennye zapiski*, *2*(3). Retrieved July 3, 2008, from http://www.strana-oz.ru/?numid=3&article=165

Latyshina, D. I. (2005). *Istoria pedagogiki: Istoria obrazovaniya i pedagogicheskoy mysli.* [History of pedagogy: History of education and pedagogical conceptions]. Moscow, Russia: Gardariki.

National Training Foundation. (2004a). *Osnovnye resul'taty mezhdunarodnogo issledovaniya kachesva matematicheskogo i estestvennonauchnogo obrazovaniya TIMSS-2003* [Main outcomes of the study in mathematics and science education TIMSS-2003]. Retrieved September 3, 2008, from http://www.centeroko.ru/public.htm

National Training Foundation. (2004b). *Osnovnye resul'taty mezhdunarodnogo issledovaniya obrazovatel'nykh dostizheniy uchaschikhsya PISA-2003* [Main outcomes of the study of academic student achievements PISA-2003]. Retrieved September 3, 2008, from http://www.centeroko.ru/public.htm

Piskunov, A. I. (Ed.). (2003). *Istoria pedagogiki i obrazovaniya* [History of the pedagogy and education]. Moscow, Russia: Sfera.

Russian Academy of Education. (n.d.a). *Otchet o rabote Rossiyskoy Akademii Obrazovaniya za 2007 god* [Annual report of the Russian Academy of Education-2007]. Retrieved September 3, 2008, from http://raop.ru/pages.php?folder=7

Russian Academy of Education. (n.d.b). *Otchet o rabote otdeleniya psikhologii i vozrastnoy fiziologii za 2007 god* [Annual report of the Psychology and Age Physiology Division-2007]. Retrieved September 3, 2008, from http://raop.ru/pages.php?folder=7

Russian Academy of Education. (n.d.c). Kratkiy ocherk istorii—sovremennost'—blizhayshee buduschee [Brief review of the history—present—nearest future]. Retrieved September 3, 2008, from http://raop.ru/pages.php?page=485

Schelanova, E. I. (2003). Trudnosti v uchenii odarennykh shkol'nikov [Challenges in educating gifted students]. *Voprosy Psikhologii, [Issues in Psychology]*, *3*, 132-145.

Tatarnikova, L. G. (1995). *Pedagogicheskaya valeologiya: Genezis. Tendentsii razvitiya* [Pedagogical valeology: Genesis. Tends for development]. St. Petersburg, Russia: Petrogradskiy i K⁰.

V Rossii veruyuschikh stanovitsya vse bol'she, a ateistov—men'she. Krugly stol "Religiya v sovremennom obschestve" [In Russia, the number of believers increases but the number of atheists decreases. Round table "Religion in modern society"]. (2006, November 9) Retrieved September 3, 2008, from http://www.pravmir.ru/article_1446.html

CHAPTER 12

MIDDLE SCHOOL EDUCATION IN GERMANY

Sigrid Blömeke, Johannes König, and Anja Felbrich

Germany's middle school system is characterized through a tripartite stratification. These 3 kinds of school were founded during the eighteenth and
nineteenth centuries according to an earlier tripartite idea of abilities: manual, technical, and intellectual. Sorting into *"Hauptschule," "Realschule,"* and
"Gymnasium" takes place at the end of the fourth grade and is based on
teachers' recommendations. Comparisons of these recommendations with
student achievement measured in standardized tests and inquiries of students' socioeconomic background show a strong social bias. Teacher education for middle school mainly happens as part of a shorter and less subject-
matter focused elementary program or as part of a longer and more subject-
matter focused secondary program. Programs specialized on middle school
education are rare. After important progress in research on the achievement
of middle school students, the focus of research has recently changed
towards teacher education for middle school. Professional competencies of
middle school teachers heavily depend on the kind of teacher education
they receive.

An International Look at Educating Young Adolescents
pp. 255–286
Copyright © 2009 by Information Age Publishing
All rights of reproduction in any form reserved.

CONTEXTUAL NARRATIVE

Germany is a federal republic comprised of 16 states that have a high degree of autonomy when it comes to educational decisions. According to the Freedom House Index (2008), which measures the level of political rights and civil liberties in 193 countries and 15 related and disputed territories, the German democracy is ranked among the highest developed political systems in the world. With 82 million inhabitants, the country has the largest population of all member states of the European Union. Ten million inhabitants (i.e., about 12% of the population) are immigrants, mainly from Turkey and the former Soviet Union (Statistische Ämter des Bundes und der Länder, 2008). Germany is located in Central Europe and surrounded by Poland and the Czech Republic in the east, by Austria and Switzerland in the south, by France, Belgium and the Netherlands in the west, and by the Atlantic Ocean, Denmark and the Baltic Sea in the north.

Germany's gross domestic product (GDP) of 3 trillion U.S. dollars is the third largest in the world (International Monetary Fund, 2008). Only the United States and Japan have a larger GDP. The country's relatively high developmental status is also shown in United Nation's ranking of human development. The Human Development Index (HDI) summarizes several indices of health conditions, educational features, and economic status in one measure. Within a range from 0.336 (Sierra Leone) to 0.968 (Norway), Germany is placed at the upper end with an HDI of 0.935 (United Nations, 2008).

Individual freedom and economic competition in a liberal market system can be regarded as main cultural values (Inglehart 1997; Landes 1999). These values are mirrored on Hofstede's (2001) and Triandis' (1995) individualism-collectivism scales on which Germans show a very high level of individual beliefs. From a religious point of view, three groups exist. In Southern and Western Germany, Catholics have the majority; overall they represent about 30% of the German inhabitants (Religionswissenschaftlicher Medien- und Informationsdienst, 2008). In Northern and Eastern Germany, Protestants have the majority; overall they represent 30% of the inhabitants as well. Another 30% of Germans are not members of a church; this applies especially to Eastern Germany and big cities. Four percent of the inhabitants belong to the Islam.

HISTORY AND ORGANIZATION OF
SCHOOLING FOR YOUNG ADOLSCENTS

Historical Background

Due to federalism, as early as the nineteenth century, there were regional differences in the development of the educational system. Moving into the twentieth century, the authority of the federal states regarding educational issues has been untouched. Between 1933 and 1945 the political influence of the Nazi state on the educational system was strong (Dithmar, 2001; Keim, 1995). After an examination of these dynamics, one of the most important societal agreements after 1945 was to never again allow dictatorial influence on educational questions. For Western Germany, this implied—among other changes—the formation of a Federal Republic (FRG) in which the rights of each federal state are extensive, especially regarding educational policy, to prevent strong central power. Thus, legislation for education devolves to the 16 federal states. In 1948, the *Ständige Konferenz der Kultusminister der Länder* (KMK, Conference of Ministers for Education and Cultural Affairs) was established to coordinate educational issues between the federal states. Since then, the KMK has served as a forum of permanent cooperation. Its resolutions only have the status of recommendations until they are enacted by the parliaments of each of the federal states.

The basic structure of the present German school system evolved between the 15th and the eighteenth century although first schools on German territorium had been founded as early as 100 A.D. as part of the Roman Empire (Blömeke, Herzig & Tulodziecki, 2007). As part of christianization, schools had been founded starting in the eighth century, but they mainly served the religious purpose of training of priests. The language of instruction in these early schools was Latin. The economic development during the late Middle Ages showed a need for well-trained workers for craft and trade professions, especially in the cities. So, during the fifteenth century for the first time a large number of schools were founded. These focused on preparation for vocation and served mainly commercial purposes; their language of instruction was German. Two centuries later, the building of German nations with combined political and religious leadership required an education of the respective state populations according to the leaders' values. A comprehensive school system with schools not only in cities but also in rural areas was founded, followed by compulsory education starting in the eighteenth century.

For young adolescents, stratification is the most important feature of this school system. On the middle school level, from the eighteenth century forward two kinds of schools (*Volksschule*/lower school system and *Gymnasium*/higher school system) have existed. From the end of the nineteenth century forward, three kinds of schools (*Volksschule*, *Realschule*, and *Gymnasium*) have been existing. This stratification follows a "theory" according to which different kinds of natural talent exist (i.e., manual, technical and intellectual) that must be developed in different kinds of schools (Deutscher Ausschuss für das Erziehungs- und Bildungswesen, 1966; Spranger, 1974). The stratified school system was meant to result in

**Table 12.1.   Characteristics of the
Stratified School System in Germany in Mid-Nineteenth Century**

	"Volksschule"/ *Lower School System*	*"Gymnasium"/* *Higher School System*
Structure	6 years elementary school	3 years primary school, followed by 9 years *Gymnasium*
Funding	Local authorities, no school fees (except for teaching materials)	Churches, state; school fees; payment for teaching materials and housing
Curriculum	Religion, basic cultural techniques (reading, writing, mathematics)	Subject matter, preparation for university
Teachers	Low-paid staff, hired by local authorities, generalists	Subject specialists, senior civil servants
Teacher training	Secondary level (after elementary school)	University based (tertiary level)
Graduation	None (school is left with only a report card, without the right to continue)	After Grade 10 military service reduced to 1 year, start as an officer candidate; after Grade 12 high school exit exam with the right to continue at university

Source: Diederich and Tenorth (1997)

separate levels within society (i.e., working class, middle class and upper class). Table 12.1 shows details of the stratification as it was in place in the mid nineteenth century.

Politically, the stratification of the German school system has been subject of highly controversial clashes with ideological connotations throughout the nineteenth and the twentieth century. However, the forces of persistence have been strong enough to maintain this structure even after it was faced with empirical findings disproving the basic theory of talent during the twentieth century (Roth, 1969). After the Second World War, attempts were made to give up the stratified school system. In Western Germany, the fundamental characteristics of the educational systems in the federal states as they had been in place during the 1920s were reinstalled, including the tripartite system on the middle school level (Führ, 1998). One reason for this was that stratification was considered a response to the installment of a comprehensive school model from grades 1 through 9 in Eastern Germany. Since the two German countries represented the frontline countries of the Western bloc and the Eastern bloc, any decision in Western Germany was highly political and its repercussion upon the Western bloc was always the subject of critical discussion.

Against this background, it has been almost impossible to reform the education system for a long time because any proposal was compared either to Nazism or to the politics in the German Democratic Republic (GDR).

The development of the school system was closely linked to the development of teacher education. Until 1800 teacher education did not have an organized structure. In the first decade of the nineteenth century, the structural core characteristics of the present teacher education system developed under the influence of Wilhelm von Humboldt. Since then, German federal states have demanded that teachers for the *Gymnasium* undergo a university-based teacher education program leading to a state examination. For Germany, this policy marks the starting point of the teaching profession as a special career (for more details see Blömeke, 2002). In the last decade of the nineteenth century, a 1-year, on-the-job training was introduced as a second phase of teacher education for the "Gymnasium."

Starting in the 1820s, teachers for the lower school system received their preparation at teacher training institutions which built on the *Volksschule*. Over the nineteenth century, these teacher training institutions and their courses were continually expanded (Sandfuchs, 2004), and examinations at the end of the training were introduced. However, teachers at the *Gymnasium* and teachers for the lower schools system were considered to be two totally different professions. This differentiation can still be observed today.

Organization and Structure of Today's German School System

Today's German school system is characterized by a strong selection after the elementary years. The selection process is expected to happen by ability. In reality, a strong socioeconomic and ethnic bias has to be noticed (Bos et al., 2007). During the first 4 years (in three federal states during the first 6 years), all students attend elementary school, except children with severe handicaps or learning disorders who attend special needs schools. After fourth or sixth grade, selection into three different kinds of middle schools representing different kinds of ability takes place. Therefore each student receives a recommendation by his or her class teacher for a certain school type according to the prospective kind of ability. Nonetheless, parents may try to ignore or override this recommendation by enrolling their child in the school type of their preference. It is up to the school principals to decide about this kind of request (see Table 12.2).

Table 12.2.   Structure of the German School System

Grade	Regular School System				Special Needs School
13	Several kinds of vocational schools				Sonderschule (several kinds of special-needs schools, attendance depends on the kind of handicap)
12					
11				Gesamtschule (comprehensive school)	
10		Realschule (secondary modern school)	Gymnasium (high school)		
9	Hauptschule (practical abilities)				
8					
7					
6					
5					
4	"Grundschule" (Elementary school) [in 3 federal states lasting for six years]				
3					
2					
1					

Source: Blömeke, Herzig, and Tulodziecki (2007).

The *Hauptschule*, which represents the lowest track of secondary schools, is attended by students whose abilities are considered more practical and less academic in nature. Education in this type of school ends in most federal states after ninth grade and the teaching is mainly practice-oriented. Students are supposed to become blue-collar workers. The *Realschule* (intermediate track in British Educational system) ends after 10th grade and prepares students for middle-level careers—mainly white-collar workers—in trade and the industry. Only the Gymnasium (highest track) offers the final high-school exit examination ("Abitur") at the end of the 12th or 13th grade, depending on the state, qualifying students for studies at the university or equivalent institutions. The exam takes place in at least four school subjects; in more and more federal states it is a centralized exam with anonymous review procedures.

Grades 5 and 6 at middle school are considered an orientation phase, wherein students in principle are allowed to change between the three kinds of schools if their ability does not fit the chosen track. In reality most of these changes are in the downward direction, very few in the opposite. Moreover, in the course of middle schooling the change of an individual student from one school type to another one is clearly an exception rather than a regular procedure (Cortina, 2003). Because of this, the sorting at the end of primary schooling has far reaching consequences for the individual student's school career.

Aside from these traditional kinds of middle school, more recently comprehensive schools have been introduced. These comprehensive schools were founded in the last 30 years and vary in type, either having two or three of the prior mentioned middle schools (*Haupt-, Realschule*, and *Gymnasium*) under one roof while keeping the former school differences or integrating these schools but offering a streaming of students by individual subjects. Both kinds of comprehensive middle schools should open the doors of higher education for students from families with little education. Social inequality promoted by the tripartite system was supposed to decrease and flexibility of students changing from one school career to another (*Durchlässigkeit*) was supposed to increase. However, it has not been completely possible to put these ideas into practice, which is partly due to the fact that comprehensive schools have not been able to replace the tripartite system. Instead, comprehensive schools are regarded as an additional or "fourth school type" (Köller, 2003).

In this context, it has become problematic that in each grade comprehensive schooling requires the whole student body in order to successfully set up heterogeneous learning groups. Since the Gymnasium is the more attractive school type for students who have good grades at the end of primary schooling, the upper end of the student body does not normally attend comprehensive schools, a phenomenon which is denoted as "creaming" (Köller, 2003). Therefore, upper secondary students of the Gymnasium end up significantly better than students from comprehensive schools on standardized tests (Köller, Baumert, & Schnabel, 1999). By contrast, in some federal states comprehensive schooling actually has led to a structural loosening of school type and to a school certificate which enables students with a lower socioeconomic background to pursue upper secondary schooling as well as to get the general school leaving certificate, and thus the opportunity to study at the university level. However, it seems as if the Gymnasium is still the better-regarded learning environment to prepare students for tertiary education.

The prevalence of comprehensive schools differs widely between federal states (see Figure 12.1). In four out of the five Eastern federal states the majority of students—roughly between 50 and 60% of an age cohort—attends this kind of middle school. Hamburg is the only Western federal state with a significant proportion of students in comprehensive schools. Remarkable differences in the student populations at the other kinds of middle school can be observed, too (see Figure 12.1). For instance, the *Hauptschule* in the state of Berlin represents a "leftover school" with only the bottom 5% of the ability distribution of students attending this school. In contrast, in Bavaria approximately 40% of students attend the *Hauptschule*. It is obvious that the *Hauptschule* has not been able to offer a specific career program in the Eastern federal states,

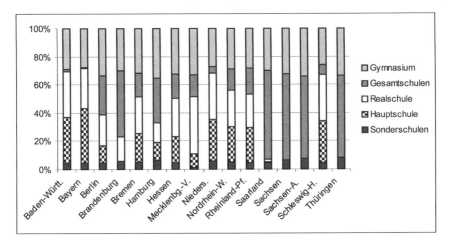

Figure 12.1.   Distribution of students in eighth grade in Germany's 16 federal states (KMK [*Ständige Konferenz der Kultusminister der Länder*], 2002a).

whereas the Gymnasium has clearly turned out to be the successful school type in all federal states (Baumert, Roeder, & Waterman, 2003). That is also why the proportion of students attending the highest track, the *Gymnasium* is roughly the same in all 16 federal states: between 25 and 35% of an age cohort.

Middle school is followed by an upper-secondary level with a a dual system of schools: *Gymnasium* and comprehensive schools with an orientation toward general academic education on the one side and vocational schools on the other side. Both types afford two or three years of schooling. About 5% of the student body attends private school (KMK, 2002a). Private schools differ widely in their specific profiles but they all have to follow the state curriculum. The only type of private school that represents a significant proportion includes "Waldorf schools" which have a special pedagogical profile following Rudolf Steiner's ideas.

Since education is a matter of the federal states, they provide the majority of the funding (more than 80%; see Figure 12.2). Local authorities provide only one-eighth of the funding, and only 5% of the funding comes from the national level. Schools are funded according to the number of students. Federal states set up a teacher-student ratio based on class sizes and allocate a corresponding number of teaching positions to every school. Elementary school classes have on average 22.1 students while middle school classes have on average 24.7 students. Each size is slightly above the OECD average (OECD, 2007a).

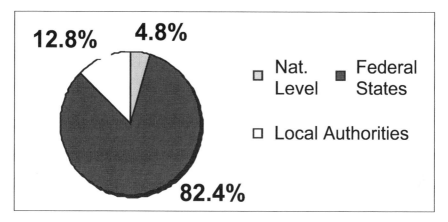

Figure 12.2.   Funding of the German school system (KMK [*Ständige Konferenz der Kultusminister der Länder*], 2002a).

Fully qualified teachers can apply for permanent employment (KMK, 2004a; OECD, 2005). The employment procedures vary across federal states. Teachers apply either at the ministry of education or at the local education authority (*Schulaufsichtsbehörde*). In more and more federal states, the schools themselves play a major role in the selection of teachers. Selection is firstly based on the teachers' subjects and secondly on their grades on the first and the second state examinations. In most federal states, teachers are employed as civil servants. However, there are teachers with salaried employee status, employed on a contractual basis. In federal states that belonged to the former GDR, teachers with salaried employee status represent the majority.

The state expenditures per student per year are very different regarding school levels (see Figure 12.3). They increase slightly from elementary level to middle school level. On both level they are below the OECD average. The expenses increase drastically when it comes to the upper-secondary level, and in this case they are also much higher as the OECD average. The difference is mainly due to teacher salaries. Elementary and middle school teachers are only junior civil servants whereas teachers at the *Gymnasium* are senior civil servants. Another reason for the higher expenses is a lower teacher-student-ratio on upper-secondary level compared to elementary and middle school.

Teachers for the highly stratified middle-school level are trained in different teacher-education programs, usually either as part of an elementary school program or as part of a secondary school program. There are only very few programs specifically designed for middle school. Three

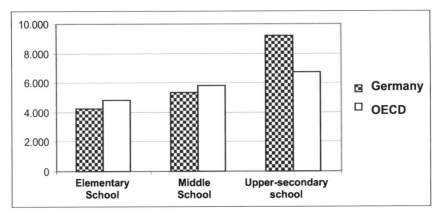

Figure 12.3.   State funding per student per year in Germany compared to the OECD average (2004, in U.S. Dollars; OECD, 2004).

levels of regulation exist (i.e., national level, federal states, and teacher education institutions), each giving rise to considerable variation in the requirements for study of future middle school teachers between federal states as well as between institutions of teacher education.

On the national level, teacher education is under the regulation of the *Kultusministerkonferenz* (KMK), which is a committee of the 16 federal states' ministers of education. Here basic guidelines for the arrangement of teacher education programs are negotiated in order to ensure comparability of licensure across all federal states (KMK, 1999, 2002b). This agreement is based on general regulations dealing with the structure and the intended length of the teacher education programs. These basic guidelines include the definition of several types of teacher licences (differentiated by school type and grade level), minimum study duration, licensing process, content areas of study, number and kind of practice elements of the curriculum, and the duration of practical experiences.

On this general level of description, it has to be pointed out that German teacher education is divided into two phases (KMK, 2006): the academic study at a university as the first phase and the practical preparatory service (*Vorbereitungsdienst*) as the second phase. The KMK requires at least three years of university study (and passing a first state examination as the exit exam) for all teaching certificates. A practical phase of at least 18 months in schools is also required along with teacher education seminars (leading to the second state examination). The high-school exit exam ("Abitur") is the minimal qualification required for entry into the first phase of all teacher education programs; in terms of international classification systems, it corresponds to the "International Standard Classification of Education (ISCED)" level 3 (OECD, 1999).

On this national level, two kinds of middle school teachers can be differentiated (Bellenberg & Thierack, 2003):

A. teachers with a teaching licence for either one or all kinds of middle school except the *Gymnasium* (i.e., *Hauptschule, Realschule*, and Grades 5 through 10 of comprehensive schools), in many states this licence also qualifies for teaching of the elementary grades;

B. teachers with a teaching licence for the *Gymnasium* and Grades 11 through 13 of comprehensive schools, but explicitly no teaching in primary grades.

The first phase of teacher education for the *Gymnasium* (licence B) includes the study of two major subjects including subject-related pedagogy, the study of general pedagogy and practical components related to the study of general pedagogy as well as related to the two subjects. Only those subjects can be chosen that are regularly taught at school. The first phase of teacher education for licence A includes the study of general pedagogy, the study of up to three subjects including subject-related pedagogy (beyond these at least one major subject), and practical components related to the study of general pedagogy as well as related to the subjects. As elementary school teachers have to teach all school subjects from Grade 1 to 4 or 6, the study of German and/or Mathematics is compulsory for licence A in those federal states which certify middle school teachers also for teaching in elementary grades. In most federal states the first phase lasts 3.5 (mainly for licence A) or 4.5 years (mainly for licence B) and the second phase lasts 1.5 (mainly for licence A) or 2 years (mainly for licence B). So, overall teacher education for middle schools in Germany lasts between 5 and 6.5 years.

Within these framing guidelines issued by the KMK considerable variance exists in the arrangement and requirements of programs among the 16 federal states. For instance, for licence A the prescribed number of study hours for subject-related pedagogy varies from 8 to 52 hours and variation in the number of study hours for general pedagogy ranges from 40 to 96 hours. The number of hours for the study of each subject varies from 70 to 120 hours for type A and 110 to 160 hours for type B. Every federal state has its own legislative framework for teacher education programs.

Again, within these prescriptions on the federal state level, the content and the quality of study varies across institutions of teacher education. The implemented curriculum of future teachers is usually quite variable for each individual as students have a great deal of freedom of choice with regard to courses selected. Especially in general pedagogy and also in subject-related pedagogy students are relatively free in their choice of courses and it is very common that no obligatory curriculum regarding the specific content or the sequencing of content and courses for future teachers exists. Freedom of choice is usually less pronounced in the subjects where a prescription of mandatory courses and their sequencing often exists, especially for the first 2 years of study.

Both phases end with a high-stakes exit exam. These exams are under the responsibility of the federal states and therefore called "state examinations". The first state examination takes place after the university step and consists of several written and oral examinations related to the subjects studied. A thesis on a particular subject is part of the examination as well. This first state examination corresponds to ISCED level 5A First Degree, on the elementary as well as secondary level (OECD, 1999). Passing this first examination is the entry requirement for the second phase of teacher education which takes place at specialized teacher training institutions (*Studienseminare*). These institutions are directly under the control of the federal states. The teacher education content of the second phase is determined by the subjects a future teacher has chosen at the beginning of the first phase. Future teachers have to work part-time at schools and attend teacher training courses in general pedagogy and subject-related pedagogy. The second state examination (*Zweites Staatsexamen*) is taken at the end of the second phase. Future teachers have to teach lessons that are observed and assessed by a board of examiners consisting of school staff, teacher educators, and state officials. Furthermore, an essay on a practical issue has to be written (*Zweite Staatsexamensarbeit*). The second state examination corresponds to the ISCED-Level 5A Second Degree (OECD, 1999).

Curriculum, Instruction, and Assessment Practices in German Middle School

Even if middle school is basically characterized by its stratification, the three kinds of middle schools share many cultural features. In all of them, classes remain widely the same from fifth through 10th grades. The students usually only separate for single lessons, such as, according to the choice of foreign languages or religious instruction. Most subjects are taught in the students' classroom while teachers move. Usually two students share one table which are in some schools arranged in semi-circles. German schools do not have school uniforms or shared dress codes. In contrast to English-speaking countries, school activities like sports teams, radio stations, or TV channels are of much less relevance. Some extracurricular activities are organized on the class level, such as, excursions or parents' meetings.

The school year starts after the summer break in August and it is divided up into two semesters. At their ends in January and July, report cards are issued. For every subject a grade between 1 as the top mark and 6 as the lowest mark is given. The report card in July decides whether a student can go on to the next grade or whether he or she has to repeat a grade. The latter takes place if a student has more than one "5" in a core subject or more than two "5s" in minor subjects. On the middle school level about 5% of the student body every year has to repeat 1 year (Statistisches Bundesamt Deutschland, 2006). Over the course of schooling this means that more than one quarter of the students has to repeat a class at some point. During the school year students have 12 weeks of holidays: 6 weeks during summer, 2 weeks in the fall, 2 weeks around Christmas and 2 weeks around Easter.

On the middle school level, students have only a few choices regarding their subjects. They have to take German and mathematics, a first foreign language (usually English, this is determined by the federal state and continues from Grade 1 or 3 depending on the state), two sciences (whether it is biology, chemistry or physics is determined by the respective federal state as well) and two social sciences (history, geography, politics again determined by the states) as well as sports, music or arts and religion every year. From sixth or seventh grade forward, they have to take a second foreign language. Here students have a choice (e.g., Latin or French). From eighth or ninth grade forward, students can decide to choose one more subject out of a broad range of subjects including a third foreign language or bilingual education.

A lesson lasts for 45 minutes. Half-day schooling is the regular schedule in all federal states (see Table 12.3). Three to four times each semester written tests have to be taken in core subjects like mathematics, German, and English. They last for one lesson and they are essay based. Multiple-choice tests are widely unknown in Germany. In minor subjects like biology, history or music two or three oral tests or smaller written exercises ("tests") are used to diagnose student achievement.

Curriculum, instruction, and assessment practices have a subject-specific profile. So, it is neither possible nor meaningful to make generic statements if one wants to capture curriculum, instruction, and assessment details. Therefore, mathematics, as one of the core subjects in middle school, is utilized as an example to demonstrate these details.

The leading ideas for mathematics instruction as pointed out by federal regulations ("*Richtlinien*" and "*Lehrpläne*") are concerned with the mastery of algorithms and concepts necessary for everyday life in society and other

**Table 12.3.   Exemplary Schedule of a
Middle-School Student at the *Gymnasium* in Eighth Grade**

	Monday	Tuesday	Wednesday	Thursday	Friday
07:40-08:25	English	Physics	Biology	—	French/Latin
08:30-09:15	French/Latin	Mathematics	German	Mathematics	French/Latin
09:15-09:25			Break		
09:25-10:10	Music	Sports	Cath./Prot. religion	German	Biology
10:15-11:00	Cath./Prot. religion	French/Latin	Mathematics	English	Social science
11:00-11:15			Break		
11:15-12:00	German	Arts	Social science	Information technology	Sports
12:05-12:50	History	Arts	—	Information technology	Music
12:50-13:00			Break		
13:00-13:45	Physics	English	—	History	—

subjects, with the solving and understanding of nonmathematical phenomena through competencies gained in mathematics, with critical thinking and insight into mathematics as a cultural creation, as a theoretical study and as a tool for solving problems (Heymann, 1996; Krauthausen & Scherer, 2003). Students should become acquainted with fundamental ideas in mathematics, with methods for getting insight, with various levels of argumentation and representation and with the history of mathematics. The correct use of the mathematical language and terms as well as the use of formal notations is considered very important and thus frequently reinforced. Units of teaching usually cover large areas of mathematical content, whereas an approach to teaching according to a spiral curriculum is seldom used.

The content of mathematics is about the same in the three kinds of schools. In fifth and sixth grades, the use of variables in simple equations, fundamental geometric concepts, elementary number theory and fractions are taught. In seventh and eighth grades, relations and functions, congruence transformations, angle measurement and associated theorems, linear equations, algebraic structures and integers and rational numbers are taught. Finally, in the last 2 years of middle schools, in ninth and 10th grades, real numbers, quadratic functions and equations, theorems on right triangles and circles, exponential functions and trigonometry are taught.

How these general features of mathematics instruction are translated into instruction and how much of the overall time of schooling is devoted to mathematics differs between grade levels, school types, single schools, and also between teachers. In the elementary grades mathematics is taught five lessons per week and constitutes approximately 20% of the overall instruction time in these grades. In middle school grades the percentage of mathematics lessons drops to 13% with nonetheless three to four lessons of mathematics per week. There is no grouping of students according to achievement within the three kinds of middle school.

Although there are no significant differences in the content of mathematics, there are major differences in the didactical approach between the three kinds of middle school (Baumert et al., 1997; Blum & Neubrand, 1998): At the *Hauptschule* teaching and learning of mathematics is orientated toward elementary rules and algorithms. Teachers use example-bound explanations and mainly real-world examples but do not require theoretical reflections and proofs. At the *Realschule* teaching is similar to that in the *Hauptschule* but more ambitious in the choice of problems and algorithms, and teachers require some theoretical reflection and reasoning of students. In contrast, in the *Gymnasium* the emphasis of instruction is on general education, and thus theorems and general rules of mathematics are the focus of instruction. Proofs and the acquisition of insight are regarded as important, but at the same time less real-world examples as in the *Haupt-* or *Realschule* are used.

Assessment in mathematics instruction is partly regulated by national prescriptions, i.e. regarding the number of tests during a term and the relation of written to oral tests (50:50 in early years and 70:30 in the later years), but at the same time very teacher-based. Teachers assess an individual student's achievement on the basis of this student's participation in classroom discussions, homework, and results on written tests.

Textbooks used for instruction require permission of the state authorities, whereas the teacher is relatively free in choosing or creating additional material for instruction, such as worksheets, computer simulations, and the like. Until recently there have been national examination standards only for the high-school exit exam "Abitur" specifying the necessary knowledge of students in general. After the PISA "shock" of 2001 when the results of the PISA study of 2000 were published in which Germany did very badly, nationwide standards for mathematics instruction for Grades 4, 9 and 10 were developed (KMK, 2004a, 2005).

OUTCOMES OF THE SCHOOLING OF YOUNG ADOLSCENTS

Academic Performance Outcomes

Western Germany, one of the former front countries during the Cold War, was deeply affected by the so-called "Sputnik shock" in the 1960s.

That the USSR—as the leading nation for the Eastern bloc—was the first to be able to send a satellite into the space raised doubts about the level of technical knowledge in the country, followed by inquiries on its educational system. In the following decades serious innovations were discussed with several reforms implemented. Nevertheless, in IEA's Third International Mathematics and Science Study (TIMSS) from 1995 Germany ended up significantly lower than the international average (Baumert et al., 1997). The study especially revealed deficits of German middle school students in their ability to model mathematically and to lead mathematical argumentations. The study also identified difficulties in the execution of complex operations and the independent solution of problems by students. Furthermore a larger amount of German students exhibited only rudimentary mathematical abilities compared to more successful countries as Sweden or Switzerland. Five, 8, and 11 years later, OECD's Program for International Student Assessment (PISA) confirmed the TIMSS-results by still showing Germany only in the middle of the field of the industrialized countries (Deutsches PISA-Konsortium, 2001, 2003, 2006; see Figure 12.4).

Other Important Outcomes

In general, the teaching of mathematics at secondary schools can be described as very poor regarding the variation of teaching methods (as identified by the TIMSS-Video Study; Baumert et al., 1997) with one prevailing teaching method, the guided-class discussion. Typically a mathematics lesson starts with the introduction of a complex problem, often representing a real-world example. But instead for students working on the problem with its full complexity in groups or individually, the problem is solved by a class discussion, with the teachers guiding the students to the correct solution in a stepwise manner. Thereby the original complexity of the problem is reduced, so that students only have to give simple answers involving the mere recall of definitions and facts or the execution of simple solution procedures. Since the teacher follows a previously planned questioning strategy, which results in the correct solution of the problem as the teacher conceives it, usually no alternative or student approaches to problem solving are discussed. At the end of the lesson the previously developed mathematical procedure or concept is practiced by students individually.

However, currently, in part as a response to these findings, a new orientation in mathematics education is demanded with attention shifting to mathematization and mathematical modeling in order for students to learn the usefulness of mathematics for other sciences and also real life (Blum et al., 2007; Maaß, 2004, 2007). Furthermore the cooperation

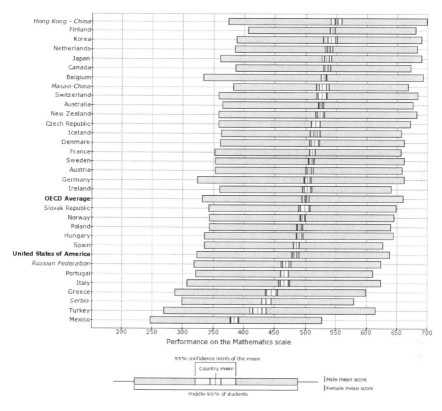

Figure 12.4.   PISA 2006, Student achievement in mathematics (OECD, 2007b).

between teachers of mathematics and other subjects is emphasized in order to create forms of integrated teaching and learning. Last but not least portraying mathematics in instruction as a history of core ideas is supposed to make students aware of the contribution of mathematics to German culture. The problem is that such fundamental changes in mentality and acting patterns are difficult to realize, especially in an institution like school. Even if all participants follow the same goals, such changes will need at least 10 or 15 years before being realized widely.

CURRENT ISSUES RELATED TO THE
SCHOOLING OF YOUNG ADOLESCENTS

Besides the less than desired performance of German students in international comparisons, the biggest concern is currently related to the associa-

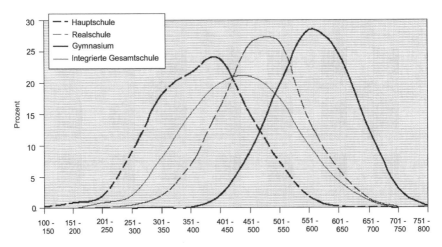

Figure 12.5.   Overlap in the achievement of students at the three kinds of German middle schools (Blömeke, Herzig, & Tulodziecki, 2007).

tion between family background and pupil achievement. Regarding this, Germany was the second highest in the world (OECD, 2001, 2004). Germany's press has given much attention to this result, leading to heated debates among policymakers, researchers, and lay people. Various reasons for the close relationship between background and achievement have been discussed. Discussions about the school structure emerged because of the distribution of student achievement in the three kinds of middle school (see Figure 12.5). There is a large overlap in the achievement of students at the *Hauptschule*, *Realschule*, and *Gymnasium*, but a student's economic and societal chances after school are very different. Only those students at the *Gymnasium* have a chance to get into a university and with this into the higher level of the labor market. The *Hauptschule* is generally regarded as a kind of "dead end."

Discussions are further enhanced by the selection bias at the end of elementary school. Comparisons of student achievement in PIRLS with teachers' recommendations and parents' preferences show that it is much easier for a child from an upper-middle class family to receive a teacher recommendation for the *Gymnasium* than for a child from a lower-middle or working class family (see Table 12.4). Parents with a lower middle or working class status are much more hesitant to opt for the *Gymnasium* for their children.

The consequence of this bias, which obviously has already been in place for a long time (Müller & Haun, 1994; Schimpl-Neimanns, 2000), is a skewed distribution of social class background in the three kinds of mid-

Table 12.4.   Points Needed to be Nominated for the Gymnasium

Socioeconomic Status	From Teachers	From Parents
Upper middle class	537	498
Lower middle class	569	559
Self-employed parents	580	556
Upper working class	592	583
Lower working class	614	606

Source: Bos et al. (2007).

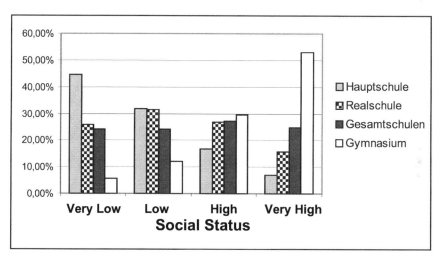

Figure 12.6.   Proportion of students at the different kinds of middle schools in relationship to their social status (Deutsches PISA-Konsortium, 2004).

dle school (see Figure 12.6). In a democratic society this kind of bias is not defendable.

REFORM INITIATIVES AND NATIONAL POLICIES

Even if policy discussions started about the structure of the German school system, most reform initiatives are currently focusing on higher education and especially on teacher education. Two important initiatives are the transition of university programs to bachelor/master-degrees (BA/MA) as we know them from English-speaking countries and the implementation of a European-wide credit-point system (ECTS = European Credit Transfer System). The main purpose of these changes is to make the achievement of students comparable across the European Union (Blömeke, 2001). The duration for bachelor degree programs is specified as ranging from three to a maximum of four years with study loads of 180 ECTS. A final thesis (6 ECTS) is required. Study duration for master programs is specified as ranging from one to a maximum of two years with study loads of 60 ECTS for one year and 120 ECTS for 2 year programs. Furthermore, entrance to a master program can be restricted and selection of students is based on their achievements in previous BA studies is possible. The curriculum of BA/MA programs has to be organized into modules, which can be finished by students within a semester or a year, ensuring a better "study-ability" of programs. In order to make new BA/MA licences comparable to traditional teacher education programs, the new programs have to incorporate the following criteria (KMK, 2005):

1. BA and MA programs for teachers have to include two subjects, general and subject-specific pedagogy as well as practical phases already during the BA program,

2. study duration should range from seven to nine semesters (without practical phases) and the programs are differentiated by the kind of middle school, and

3. the content of the MA exam has to be comparable to the former first state examination even if it is now a pure university responsibility.

A bachelor *and* a master's degree have to be acquired in order to become a teacher. While the requirements for BA/MA degrees are strongly oriented towards the old programs, the above mentioned distinction into licence A and B holds for these new programs. Most of the type A programs require study durations of three years for the BA phase and one year for the MA phase of education; for licence B, three and two years are required, respectively. Opposed to a demand made by the European Union regarding the polyvalence of bachelor degrees, most new programs require students to decide in the beginning of their bachelor studies, whether they would like to have the option of becoming a teacher. In this case, they have to attend specific courses and practica specific for future teacher students, which are not required for students not opting for the teaching profession.

As a measure of quality assurance, accreditation of the new BA/MA teacher education programs by an independent council is demanded. The council consists of representatives of the 16 federal states, teacher education institutions, and students. An issue that has not been resolved yet is whether students who have successfully completed a teaching program with a master's degree have a legal claim for entering the second phase of teacher education (as has been the case in the traditional programs upon successful completion of the first state examination).

Currently, two thirds of the federal states have implemented programs of teacher education to be finished with a BA/MA degree, at least as model programs at single universities; the other federal states are planning to follow (except Bavaria and Baden-Württemberg) (HRK, 2007).

RESEARCH

Current Research Topics

The 1990s saw a strong development in research on student achievement in Germany on the middle school level (Helsper & Böhme, 2004). This research was mostly connected to large international comparisons like PISA or TIMSS. It led to sophisticated methods of sampling as well as of data analyses, e.g. multilevel modeling of student achievement, scaling of data according to the Item Response Theory, and more appropriate approaches to dealing with missing data. Extensive empirical research exists also on classroom instruction—at least for those subjects targeted in PISA and TIMSS, i.e. mainly mathematics and science (Hiebert et al., 2003; Kaiser, 1999; Schmidt et al., 1997). In contrast, the current state of research on teacher education is lacking. Only recently has there been research on qualifications of employed mathematics teachers (Ball & Bass, 2003; Brunner et al., 2006). So, currently the focus of research is changing towards teacher education. To test professional competencies of future teachers and to grasp opportunities to learn in teacher education beyond distal indicators like certification or majors are two new approaches to inquire about the effectiveness of middle school teacher education. They require a careful, theory-driven definition of "professional competencies" as the core dependant variable and a model of how teacher education is expected to influence the acquisition of the future teachers' professional competencies.

The value added by doing teacher education research this way is to overcome the main deficits of the existing state of research: Teacher-education research lacks a common theoretical basis which prevents a convincing development of instruments and makes it difficult to connect the studies to each other. Recently, the 800-paged American Educational Research Association's volume, *Studying Teacher Education*, led to this conclusion (Cochran-Smith & Zeichner, 2005). There is a lack of research pertaining to specific fields. It makes a difference when one is studying English teachers or science teachers, mathematics teachers or history teachers (Shulman, 1985). The subject represents an increasingly important feature, may be even a bias, which is dangerous to neglect in order to avoid false conclusions about the efficacy of teacher education.

In many countries recent efforts to improve the education of future middle school teachers have been driven by the idea that increasing their subject matter knowledge will improve their practice yielding better-educated students (Darling-Hammond, 1996). However, until now convincing empirical analyses of teacher education that can support this or other hypotheses is virtually nonexistent, neither in Germany nor in other countries (Blömeke, 2004; Houston, 1990; Wilson, Floden & Ferrini-Mundy, 2001). The few studies actually carried out rely on indicators that can only insufficiently describe the kind of education a future teacher had experienced or his/her professional knowledge. Regardless how common it is to use majors, the number of courses taken or examination results as indicators (e.g., Akiba, LeTendre, & Scribner, 2007; Goldhaber & Brewer, 2000), this approach is risky in its potential to wash out any kind of relationship between opportunities to learn in teacher education and its outcomes. This methodological weakness results in a disturbing inconsistency of study results due to the huge differences in what it means to hold a "major" or a teaching licence. Differences between programs overlay differences between programs. On this basis almost any inference can be drawn: teacher education might or might not matter, personality might or might not matter (e.g., Abell Foundation 2001a, 2001b; Darling-Hammond, 2000).

Methodologies

As it was the case with research of student achievement, the recent focus on German teacher education was triggered by international comparisons. Germany was included in the six-country study titled *Mathematics Teaching for the 21st Century* (MT21) (Blömeke, Kaiser, & Lehmann, 2008; Schmidt et al., 2007) as well as in the larger IEA study, *Teacher Education and Development: Learning to Teach Mathematics* (TEDS-M) (Tatto et al., 2004). International comparisons give an implicit benchmark since some countries do better in studies like TIMSS or PISA than others. This suggests that their teacher education might consist of more reasonable features than those systems of countries that do relatively worse. So, if one carefully samples the countries participating in a cross-country study, the comparisons are quite meaningful. However, analyzing teacher education for international comparisons is a particular challenge, too. Differences in the structure of teacher education make acquiring comparable data complicated, and different meanings of the constructs inquired make the interpretation of the results complicated. Unfortunately, there is nothing in teacher education "that share a relatively common meaning across var-

Table 12.5.   Core Tasks of Middle School Teachers as Defined in *MT21*

Teacher tasks	Situations
Choice of themes, methods; sequencing of learning processes	1. Selecting and justifying content of instruction 2. Designing and evaluating of lessons
Assessment of student achievement; counselling of students /parents	1. Diagnosing student achievement, learning processes, misconceptions, preconditions 2. Assessing students 3. Counselling students and parents 4. Dealing with errors, giving feedback
Support of students' social, moral, emotional development	1. Establishing teacher-student relationship 2. Foster the development of morals and values 3. Dealing with student risks 4. Prevention of, coping with discipline problems
School development	1. Initiating, facilitating cooperation 2. Understanding of school evaluation
Professional ethics	1. Accepting the responsibility of a teacher

Source: Blömeke (2005, p. 4).

ious cultural contexts" (Akiba et al., 2007). On the other hand, it is precisely this phenomenon that represents one of the values added to nationally bounded research. The variety of manifestations makes hidden national characteristics visible. Like everyone else, researchers are embedded in their own culture so that they often are not able to recognize matters of culture (Blömeke & Paine, in press).

The central dependent variable of MT21 (Schmidt et al., 2007) and TEDS-M (Tatto et al., 2004) is based on the notion of "professional competencies." MT21 defines these in reference to Weinert (1999, 2001) as core professional tasks that teachers must be able to master (Bromme, 1992). Middle school teachers are expected to master tasks like instruction, assessment, and the nurturing of students' social and emotional development (see Table 12.5). To accomplish these tasks teachers need cognitive abilities and skills in terms of professional knowledge as well as professional convictions and conception of values in terms of beliefs. In MT21 as well as in TEDS-M data on these components are gathered on a large scale. In TEDS-M representative samples are used.

Demographics

A multifaceted approach was chosen in describing learning opportunities in teacher education. In the tradition of other studies, those of the International Association for the Evaluation of Educational Achievement

Macro level	Level III	Cultural context		
		Rationale of the society	Social status of the teaching profession	Social status of mathematics
	Level II	Education system		
		Rationale of the education system	Goals of schooling	Working conditions of teachers
	Level I	Teacher-education system				
		Goals of teacher education	Content structure	Institutional structure	Relationship of theory and	Selectivity

Meso level	Level II	Institutionally intended curriculum				
		Learning goals and content	Teaching methods	Accountability	Academic advising	Selectivity
	Level I	Teacher educators			Institutionally implemented curriculum		
		Knowledge	Beliefs	Demographics	Learning goals/ content	Teaching methods	Selectivity
		Intended learning goals		Intended teaching methods	Accountability	Academic advising	FTs com- position

Micro level	Level II	Individual FTs preconceptions		Individual FTs use of curriculum		
		Knowledge	Beliefs	Perception of learning goals and use of content	Experience of teaching methods	
		Personality	Demographics	Accountability	Academic advising	Selectivity
				Amount of learning time	Learning strategies	Emotions
	Level I	Individual FTs competencies			
		Knowledge	Beliefs	Personality	Demographics

Figure 12.7.   Model of teacher-education effectiveness in MT21.

(IEA) and MT21 distinguishes at the institutional level between intended and implemented characteristics of teacher education. These individual instruments are largely organized parallel to one another. The components include an expert survey about the formally designated requirements, a document analysis of a sample of course offerings, a survey of teacher educators as mediators of the educational offerings, and a survey of the future teachers. MT21 can provide differentiated empirical results for professional competencies of future mathematics teachers in middle schools as an outcome of teacher education. Figure 12.7 provides an overview of the model of relevant levels and factors in MT21 (Blömeke, Felbrich & Müller, 2008).

Important Research Findings

The *MT21* data lead to the following main conclusions about the effectiveness of teacher education for middle school (for more details see Schmidt et al., 2007):

- Significant differences were noted among the six countries participating in MT21 (Bulgaria, Germany, Mexico, South Korea, Taiwan and the United States) in terms of the mathematics, the mathematics pedagogy, and the general pedagogical knowledge of future teachers.

- Important differences were noted in the nature of the preparation future lower secondary teachers received across countries as well. This was true both in terms of the mathematics topics studied as well as the mathematics pedagogy and general pedagogy topics studied.

- Teacher education matters! Future teachers' knowledge and beliefs depend heavily on how they are trained. They gain knowledge in those fields emphasized in teacher education and their beliefs change in accordance with the curriculum taught at their institutions.

- Regarding mathematical knowledge, future middle school teachers trained as part of an elementary program are at a disadvantage compared to future middle school teachers trained as part of a secondary program.

- There are, however, noteworthy relative strengths and weaknesses associated with the respective routes. Again, these reflect the amount of emphasis in the corresponding teacher-education programs. Middle school teachers trained as part of an elementary program outperform middle school teachers trained as part of a secondary program as far as pedagogical knowledge is concerned. Taking into account that both mathematical knowledge and pedagogical knowledge are required to teach well, deficits may exist in both types of middle school teacher education.

- Multilevel analyses show that it makes a difference in which institution a candidate is trained. Future teachers with more extensive training in each of the three areas do better on the MT21 tests than teachers elsewhere.

FUTURE DIRECTIONS

One of the core challenges of future research is to connect research on student achievement, classroom instruction and teacher education. One research topic should be to externally validate the above mentioned findings (from MT21) about professional competencies of middle school teachers as a function of teacher education, such as by testing practicing teachers with the same instrument, observe their classroom performance, and assess the achievement of their students.

Another important direction would be to study middle school students and their teachers in a longitudinal design. Most data on both levels comes from cross-sectional designs meaning that the data are collected at the same time but interpreted in a causal way. Strictly speaking, it would have to be pointed out that causal conclusions are not possible based on cross-sectional data. It is hardly possible to control for the different influences and to decide about causes, conditions, and consequences.

Finally, there is a lack of in-depth qualitative studies. Most studies on middle schools triggered by TIMSS and PISA are based on large-scale assessments. These reveal important insights but they are strongly limited regarding the potential to inquire about educational processes in a more detailed way. One issue is, for example, how the social bias precisely works in teachers' recommendations after fourth grade. Another issue is the culture of middle school education. Students at the three different kinds of middle school differ very much in their thinking, in their values, and in their behaviour. What these differences are is widely unknown.

CONCLUDING DISCUSSION

Middle school in Germany is mainly characterized by its stratification into three different types of school which are supposed to support different kinds or levels of ability. This structure has been in place for more than 100 (three kinds of school) or 200 years now (two kinds of school). So, even if it has been criticized a lot, especially after Germany's bad performance in international comparisons like PISA and TIMSS, it is obviously very hard to change a system that has been in place for such a long time. We can identify at least two crucial issues preventing a fundamental reform of secondary school structure in Germany:

1. First, the tradition of the German *Gymnasium* as the classical institution for the academic preparation of young adolescents is very strongly supported by a corresponding group of advocates. Thus, it is virtually unbelievable that at some time in the future the *Gymnasium* will be abandoned in Germany.

2. Second, although there have been comprehensive schools in Germany for decades, it has never been able to put into practice the basic idea of integration at the middle school level as it exists on the primary level (and as it exists on the middle school level in other European countries such as Finland). As described above, this is partly due to the fact that comprehensive schooling on the

middle school level has to compete with the tripartite system for high ability students, and processes of "creaming" reduce the spectrum of high ability students from comprehensive schools resulting in a decrease of the average student achievement at comprehensive schools.

In contrast to these features supporting expectations of continuity, a minor reform movement of the secondary school structure can be observed in Germany. Since unification, the *Hauptschule* as the "left over" middle school has been merging together with the *Realschule* into one middle school type in several federal states (Hamburger & Heck, 1999; Holtappels & Rösner, 1996)—a process starting in Eastern Germany but now going on in Western Germany as well. This development will endure for probably one or two decades until only two major kinds of middle school—the *Gymnasium* and a less academic kind of middle schools—can be distinguished.

In parallel to this, single schools will be given more and more autonomy, e.g., to manage entry level standards for students or to finance and hire teaching staff. Achievement outcomes measured by standardized testing procedures will indicate the quality of single schools. If these reforms on school autonomy are seriously continued and turn out to be helpful, maybe the question whether Germany should have a stratified or a comprehensive school system will increasingly lose its relevance. In contrast to school structure, the importance of the quality of teachers and teacher education will definitely increase—as this chapter has outlined in detail.

REFERENCES

Abell Foundation. (2001a). *Teacher certification reconsidered. Stumbling for quality.* Retrieved August 30, 2003, from http://www.abell.org/pubsitems/ ed_cert_1101.pdf

Abell Foundation. (2001b). *Teacher certification reconsidered. Stumbling for quality—Appendix. Review of research teacher certification and effective teaching.* Retrieved August 30, 2003, from http://www.abell.org/pubsitems/ed_cert_appendix _1101.pdf

Akiba, M., LeTendre, G., & Scribner, J. P. (2007). Teacher quality, opportunity gap, and national achievement in 46 countries. *Educational Researcher, 36*(7), 369-387.

Ball, D. L.,& Bass, H. (2003). Toward a practice-based theory of mathematical knowledge for teaching. In B. Davis & E. Simmt (Eds.), *Proceedings of the 2002 annual meeting of the Canadian Mathematics Education Study Group* (pp. 3-14). Edmonton, Alberta, Canada: CMESG/GCEDM.

Baumert, J., Lehmann, R., Lehrke, M., Schmitz, B., Clausen, M., Hosenfeld, I. et al. (1997). *TIMSS—Mathematisch-naturwissenschaftlicher Unterricht im internationalen Vergleich. Deskriptive Befunde*. Opladen, Germany: Leske & Budrich.

Baumert, J., Roeder, P. M., & Watermann, R. (2003). Das Gymnasium—Kontinuität im Wandel. In K. S. Cortina, J. Baumert, A. Leschinsky, K. U. Mayer & L. Trommer (Eds.), *Das Bildungswesen in der Bundesrepublik Deutschland* (pp. 487-524). Hamburg, Germany: Rowohlt.

Bellenberg, G., & Thierack, A. (2003). *Ausbildung von Lehrerinnen und Lehrern in Deutschland. Bestandsaufnahme und Reformbestrebungen*. Opladen: Leske + Budrich.

Blömeke, S. (2001). B.A.- und M.A.-Abschlüsse in der Lehrerausbildung—Chancen und Probleme. In N. Seibert (Ed.), *Probleme der Lehrerbildung. Analysen, Positionen, Lösungsversuche* (pp. 163-183). Bad Heilbrunn: Klinkhardt.

Blömeke, S. (2002). *Universität und Lehrerausbildung*. Bad Heilbrunn/Obb.: Klinkhardt.

Blömeke, S. (2004). Empirische Befunde zur Wirksamkeit der Lehrerbildung. In S. Blömeke, P. Reinhold, G. Tulodziecki, J. Wildt (Eds.), *Handbuch Lehrerbildung. Bad Heilbrunn* (pp. 59-91). Braunschweig: Klinkhardt/ Westermann.

Blömeke, S., Felbrich, A., & Müller, C. (2008). Theoretischer Rahmen und Untersuchungsdesign von P-TEDS. In S. Blömeke, G. Kaiser, & R. Lehmann (Eds.), *Professionelle Kompetenz angehender Lehrerinnen und Lehrer. P-TEDS: Erste Ergebnisse zum Wissen, zu den Überzeugungen und zu Lerngelegenheiten deutscher Mathematik-Studierender und -Referendare im internationalen Vergleich* (pp. 15-48). Münster: Waxmann.

Blömeke, S., Herzig, B. & Tulodziecki, G. (2007). *Gestaltung von Schule. Eine Einführung in Schultheorie und Schulentwicklung*. Bad Heilbrunn/Obb.: Klinkhardt.

Blömeke, S., Kaiser, G., & Lehmann, R. (Eds.). (2008). *Professionelle Kompetenz angehender Lehrerinnen und Lehrer. Wissen, Überzeugungen und Lerngelegenheiten deutscher Mathematikstudierender und -referendare—Erste Ergebnisse zur Wirksamkeit der Lehrerausbildung*. Münster: Waxmann.

Blömeke, S., & Paine, L. (in press). Getting the fish out of the water: Considering benefits and problems of doing research on teacher education at an international level. *Teaching and Teacher Education*.

Blum, W., Galbraith, P., Henn, H. W., & Niss, M. (2007). *Modeling and applications in mathematics education*. New York: Springer.

Blum, W., & Neubrand, M. (Eds.). (1998). *TIMSS und der Mathematikunterricht. Informationen, Analysen, Konsequenzen*. Hannover: Schroedel.

Bos, W., Hornberg, S., Arnold, K. -H., Faust, G., Fried, L., Lankes, E. -M., et al. (Eds.). (2007). *IGLU 2006. Lesekompetenzen von Grundschulkindern in Deutschland im internationalen Vergleich*. Münster: Waxmann.

Bromme, R. (1992). *Der Lehrer als Experte. Zur Psychologie des professionellen Wissens*. Bern: Hans Huber.

Brunner, M., Kunter, M., Krauss, S., Baumert, J., Blum, W., Dubberke, T. et al. (2006). Welche Zusammenhänge bestehen zwischen dem fachspezifischen Professionswissen von Mathematiklehrkräften und ihrer Ausbildung sowie beruflichen Fortbildung? *Zeitschrift für Erziehungswissenschaft, 9*, 521–544.

Cochran-Smith, M., & Zeichner, K.M. (Eds.). (2005). *Studying teacher education. The report of the AERA Panel on Research and Teacher Education.* Mahwah, NJ: Erlbaum.

Cortina, K. S. (2003). Der Schulartwechsel in der Sekundarstufe I: Pädagogische Maßnahme oder Indikator eines falschen Systems? *Zeitschrift für Pädagogik, 49*(1), 128-142.

Darling-Hammond, L. (1996). The quiet revolution: Rethinking teacher development. *Educational Leadership, 53*(6), 4-10.

Darling-Hammond, L. (2000): Teacher quality and student achievement. A review of state policy evidence. *Education Policy Analysis Archives, 8*(1), Retrieved May 27, 2003, from http://epaa.asu.edu/epaa/v8n1/

Deutscher Ausschuss für das Erziehungs- und Bildungswesen. (1966). *Empfehlungen des Deutschen Ausschusses für das Erziehungs- und Bildungswesen 1953-1965.* Stuttgart: Klett.

Deutsches PISA-Konsortium. (Ed.). (2001). *PISA 2000: Basiskompetenzen von Schülerinnen und Schülern im internationalen Vergleich.* Opladen: Leske & Budrich.

Deutsches PISA-Konsortium. (Ed.). (2003). *PISA 2003: Der Bildungsstand der Jugendlichen in Deutschland—Ergebnisse des zweiten internationalen Vergleichs.* Münster: Waxmann.

Deutsches PISA-Konsortium. (Ed.). (2006). *PISA 2006: Die Ergebnisse der dritten internationalen Vergleichsstudie.* Münster: Waxmann.

Diederich, J., & Tenorth, H. -E. (1997). *Theorie der Schule. Ein Studienbuch zu Geschichte, Funktionen und Gestaltung.* Berlin, Germany: Cornelsen Scriptor.

Dithmar, R. (Ed.). (2001). *Schule und Unterricht im Dritten Reich.* Ludwigsfelde: Ludwigsfelder Verlagshaus.

Freedom House. (2008). *Combined average ratings. Independent countries.* Retrieved August 8, 2008, from http://www.freedomhouse.org/uploads/Chart116File163.pdf

Führ, C. (1998). Zur deutschen Bildungsgeschichte seit 1945. In C. Führ & C. L. Furck (Eds.), *Handbuch der deutschen Bildungsgeschichte. Bd. VI: 1945 bis zur Gegenwart Erster Teilband: Bundesrepublik Deutschland* (pp. 1-24). Munich, Germany: C. H. Beck.

Goldhaber, D. D., & Brewer, D. J. (2000). Does teacher certification matter? High school teacher certification status and student achievement. *Educational Evaluation and Policy Analysis, 22*(2), 129-145.

Hamburger, F., & Heck, G. (Eds.). (2004). *Neue Schulen für die Kids. Veränderungen in der Sekundarstufe I.* Opladen: Leske und Budrich.

Helsper, W., & Böhme, J. (Eds.). (2004). *Handbuch der Schulforschung.* Wiesbaden: Verlag für Sozialwissenschaften.

Heymann, H. W. (1996). *Allgemeinbildung und Mathematik.* Weinheim: Beltz.

Hiebert, J., Gallimore, R., Garnier, H., Givvin, K.B., Hollingsworth, H., Jacobs, J. et al. (2003). *Teaching mathematics in seven countries: Results from the TIMSS 1999 video study* (NCES 2003-013). Washington, DC: U.S. Department of Education.

Hofstede, G. (2001). *Culture's consequences: Comparing values, behaviors, institutions, and organizations across nations* (2nd ed.). Thousand Oaks, CA: SAGE.

Holtappels, H. G., & Rösner, E. (1996). Schulsystem und Bildungsreform in West-deutschland: historischer Rückblick und Situationsanalyse. In W. Melzer & U. Sandfuchs (Eds.), *Schulreform in der Mitte der 90er Jahre* (pp. 23-46). Opladen: Leske und Budrich.

Houston, R. W. (Ed.). (1990). *Handbook of research on teacher education: A project of the Association of Teacher Educators.* New York: Macmillan.

HRK (Ed.). (2007). *Von Bologna nach Quedlinburg. Die Reform des Lehramtsstudiums in Deutschland.* Bonn: HRK.

Inglehart, R. (1997). *Modernization and postmodernization. Cultural, economic, and political change in 43 societies.* Princeton, NJ: Princeton University Press.

International Monetary Fund. (2008). *World economic and financial surveys: World economic outlook databases, April 2008 edition.* Retrieved August 8, 2008, from http://www.imf.org/external/pubs/ft/weo/2008/01/weodata/index.aspx

Kaiser, G. (1999). *Unterrichtswirklichkeit in England und Deutschland. Vergleichende Untersuchungen am Beispiel des Mathematikunterrichts.* Weinheim: Deutscher Studien Verlag.

Keim, W. (1995). *Erziehung unter der Nazi-Diktatur. Vol. 1: Antidemokratische Potentiale, Machtantritt und Machtdurchsetzung.* Darmstadt: Wissenschaftliche Buchgesellschaft.

KMK—Sekretariat der Ständigen Konferenz der Kultusminister der Länder in der Bundesrepublik Deutschland. (Ed.). (1999). *Gegenseitige Anerkennung von Lehramtsprüfungen und Lehramtsbefähigungen. Beschluss von 1999.* Retrieved August 8, 2008, from http://www.kmk.org/doc/beschl/anerk_1.pdf

KMK—Sekretariat der Ständigen Konferenz der Kultusminister der Länder in der Bundesrepublik Deutschland. (Ed.). (2002a). *Schule in Deutschland. Zahlen, Fakten, Analysen.* Retrieved June 9, 2005, from http://www.kmk.org/statist/analyseband.pdf

KMK—Sekretariat der Ständigen Konferenz der Kultusminister der Länder in der Bundesrepublik Deutschland. (Ed.). (2002b). *Gegenseitige Anerkennung von Lehramtsprüfungen und Lehramtsbefähigungen.* Retrieved August 8, 2008, from http://www.kmk.org/doc/publ/anerklab.pdf

KMK—Sekretariat der Ständigen Konferenz der Kultusminister der Länder in der Bundesrepublik Deutschland. (Ed.). (2003). *Schüler, Klassen, Lehrer und Absolventen der Schulen 1993 bis 2002.* Bonn: KMK.

KMK. (2004a). *The Education System in the Federal Republic of Germany 2004. A description of the responsibilities, structures and developments in education policy for the exchange of information in Europe.* Retrieved August 8, 2008, from http://www.kmk.org/dossier/dossier_en_ebook.pdf

KMK. (2004b). *Standards für die Lehrerbildung: Bildungswissenschaften. Beschluss der Kultusministerkonferenz vom 16. 12. 2004.* Retrieved August 8, 2008, from http://www.kmk.org/doc/beschl/standards_lehrerbildung.pdf

KMK. (2005). *Eckpunkte für die gegenseitige Anerkennung von Bachelor- und Masterabschlüssen in Studiengängen, mit denen die Bildungsvoraussetzungen für ein Lehramtsstudium vermittelt werden.* Retrieved August 8, 2008, from http://www.kmk.org/doc/beschl/D38.pdf

KMK. (2006). *Lehrerprüfungen in den Ländern der Bundesrepublik Deutschland.* Retrieved August 8, 2008, from http://www.kmk.org/schul/Lehramtspruefung.pdf

Köller, O. (2003). Gesamtschule – Erweiterung statt Alternative. In K. S. Cortina, J. Baumert, A. Leschinsky, K. U. Mayer & L. Trommer (Eds.), *Das Bildungswesen in der Bundesrepublik Deutschland* (pp. 458-486). Hamburg: Rowohlt.

Köller, O., Baumert, J. & Schnabel, K. (1999). Wege zur Hochschulreife: Offenheit des Systems und Sicherung vergleichbarer Standards. *Zeitschrift für Erziehungswissenschaft, 2*(3), 385-422.

Krauthausen, G., & Scherer, P. (2003). *Einführung in die Mathematikdidaktik.* Heidelberg: Spektrum.

Landes, D. (1999). *Wohlstand und Armut der Nationen. Warum die einen reich und die anderen arm sind.* Berlin: Siedler.

Maaß, K. (2004). *Mathematisches Modellieren im Unterricht. Ergebnisse einer empirischen Studie.* Hildesheim: Franzbecker.

Maaß, K. (2007). *Mathematisches Modellieren. Aufgaben für die Sekundarstufe I.* Berlin: Cornelsen.

Müller, W., & Haun, D. (1994). Bildungsungleichheit im sozialen Wandel. *Kölner Zeitschrift für Soziologie und Sozialpsychologie, 46*(1), 1-42.

OECD. (1999). *Classifying educational Programmes. Manual for ISCED-97 implementation in OECD countries.* Paris: Centre for Educational Research and Innovation.

OECD. (2001). *Knowledge and skills for life. First results from the OECD Programme for International Student Assessment (PISA) 2000.* Paris: Author.

OECD. (Ed.). (2004). *Education at a glance. OECD indicators 2004.* Retrieved September 4, 2004, from http://thesius.sourceoecd.org/upload/9604081e.pdf

OECD. (2005). *Teachers matter. Attracting, developing and retaining effective teachers.* Paris: Author.

OECD. (2007a). *Education at a glance 2007. OECD indicators.* Paris: Author. Retrieved August 8, 2008, from http://www.oecd.org/document/30/0,3343,en_2649_39263238_39251550_1_1_1_1,00.html#data

OECD. (2007b). *PISA 2006 Science Competencies for Tomorrow's World. Volume 1: Analysis.* Paris: Author.

Religionswissenschaftlicher Medien- und Informationsdienst. (2008). *Religionen in Deutschland: Mitgliederzahlen.* Retrieved August 8, 2008, from http://www.remid.de/remid_info_zahlen.htm

Roth, H. (Ed.). (1969). *Begabung und Lernen. Ergebnisse und Folgerungen neuer Forschungen.* Stuttgart: Klett.

Sandfuchs, U. (2004). Geschichte der Lehrerbildung in Deutschland. In S. Blömeke, P. Reinhold, G. Tulodziecki & J. Wildt (Eds.), *Handbuch Lehrerbildung* (pp. 14-37). Bad Heilbrunn/Braunschweig: Klinkhardt/Westermann.

Schimpl-Neimanns, B. (2000). Soziale Herkunft und Bildungsbeteiligung. Empirische Analysen zu herkunftsspezifischen Bildungsungleichheiten zwischen 1950 und 1989. *Kölner Zeitschrift für Soziologie und Sozialpsychologie, 52*(4), 636-669.

Schmidt, W. H., Jorde, D., Cogan, L. S., Barrier, E., Gonzalo, I., Moser, U. et al. (1997). *Characterizing pedagogical flow: An investigation of mathematics and science teaching in six countries*. New York: Springer.

Schmidt, W. H., Tatto, M. T., Bankov, K., Blömeke, S., Cedillo, T., Cogan, L., et al. (2007). *The preparation gap: Teacher education for middle school mathematics in six countries—Mathematics teaching in the 21st century (MT21)*. East Lansing: Michigan State University.

Shulman, L. S. (1985). Paradigms and research programs in the study of teaching: A contemporary perspective. In M. C. Wittrock (Ed.), *Handbook of research on teaching* (3rd ed., pp. 3-36). New York: Macmillan.

Spranger, E. (1974). *Gesammelte Schriften. Bd. 4. Psychologie und Menschenbildung*. Tübingen: Niemeyer.

Statistische Ämter des Bundes und der Länder. (2008). *Gemeinsames Datenangebot der Statistischen Ämter des Bundes und der Länder*. Retrieved August 8, 2008, from http://www.statistik-portal.de/Statistik-Portal/

Statistisches Bundesamt Deutschland. (2006). *Eine viertel Million Wiederholer an allgemein bildenden Schulen*. Retrieved August 8, 2008, from http://www.destatis.de/jetspeed/portal/cms/

Tatto, M. T., Schwille, J., Senk, S., Schmidt, W. H., Ingvarson, L., Rowley, G., & Peck, R. (2004). *IEA teacher education study in mathematics (TEDS-M): Conceptual framework*. Unpublished manuscript.

Triandis, H. C. (1995). *Individualism and collectivism*. Oxford, England: Westview Press.

United Nations. (2008). *2007/2008 Human Development Index rankings*. Retrieved August 8, 2008, from http://hdr.undp.org/en/statistics/

Weinert, F. E. (1999). *Konzepte der Kompetenz. Gutachten zum OECD—Projekt Definition and Selection of Competencies: Theoretical and Conceptual Foundations (DeSeCo)*. Neuchatel, Schweiz, Switzerland: Bundesamt für Statistik.

Weinert, F. E. (2001). Concept of competence: A conceptual clarification. In D.S. Rychen & L. H. Salganik (Eds.), *Defining and selecting key competencies* (pp. 45–66). Göttingen, Germany: Hogrefe.

Wilson, S. M., Floden, R. E., & Ferrini-Mundy, J. (2001). *Teacher preparation research. Current knowledge, gaps, and recommendations*. Washington, DC: Center for the Study of Teaching and Policy. Retrieved September 30, 2003, from http://depts.washington.edu/ctpmail/PDFs/TeacherPrep-WFFM-02-2001.pdf

CHAPTER 13

EDUCATING YOUNG ADOLESCENTS IN THE REPUBLIC OF IRELAND

Toward a "New Young Ireland"

Aaron Thornburg and Hiller A. Spires

Having seen dramatic economic and social changes in the last 2 decades, many in the Republic of Ireland have embraced discourses in favor of the Celtic Tiger or a "New" Ireland. Central to the emergence of this new Ireland is a perceived interdependence between education, individualism, inclusiveness (with regard to both internal subaltern groups and non-national migrants), and the economic growth that policymakers in the republic support. This idea is fueling innovations in educational curricula in the country, which have targeted the Junior Cycle and Transition Year Programme of young adolescents. This chapter details the system for educating young adolescents as it has resulted from Ireland's past and been altered in recent times. In so doing, it shows how the ideals of "New" Ireland are being imparted to young adolescents through changes in the educational system while, simultaneously, highlighting historical legacies behind some of the (seemingly) modern aspects of these changes.

An International Look at Educating Young Adolescents
pp. 287–311

287

CONTEXTUAL NARRATIVE

The renowned Irish poet, William Butler Yeats, once claimed that "education is not the filling of a pail, but the lighting of a fire." Interestingly, the contrast that Yeats captures in his well-known quote describes the tension within the evolving educational system of the Republic of Ireland today, especially in terms of young adolescents. In the face of new economic developments, the Republic is demonstrating its ability to embrace current and widespread neoliberal social and economic imperatives while retaining a culture that is steeped in history and tradition. Perhaps nowhere is this more apparent than in the system for educating young adolescents.

At 68,890 square kilometers, the Republic of Ireland comprises approximately five sixths of the island of Ireland, which lies off the western coast of Great Britain in northwestern Europe (Central Intelligence Agency, 2006). The remaining 14,135 square kilometers constitute Northern Ireland (Turner, 2007), which is part of the United Kingdom as a result of Ireland's particular political history.

Due to its close proximity to Great Britain, Ireland was ruled by the English Crown for centuries. Pope Adrian IV granted Ireland to King Henry II of England as a fief by papal bull in the twelfth century. While lordship of Ireland by the English Crown was asserted from that time, control of areas of the island continued in the hands of local rulers off and on for centuries. An attempt to (re)consolidate control of Ireland was undertaken under Elizabeth I in the late sixteenth century (Canny, 1973). In 1801, the Act of Union united Great Britain and Ireland into the United Kingdom of Great Britain and Ireland (Bloy, 2002). This state of affairs was maintained until 1922, when Ireland gained its independence.

Shortly after passage of the Act of Union, dissent and struggle for its repeal began to rise. Out of this movement came a group that was called Young Ireland. This group was distinctive in their tying of repeal of the Act of Union and Irish independence to a revived notion of "Nationality," which would become a lasting characteristic of movements for Irish independence from that point forward. Also of note with regard to the Young Irelanders, however, was the almost unprecedented inclusiveness of their discourse pertaining to nationhood. A prospectus for a liberal journal entitled *The Nation*, which Young Irelanders would later establish and is considered the official organ of the group, suggests that nationality is the primary object of the founding members. But, it must be "a Nationality which may embrace Protestant, Catholic, and Dissenter—Milesian and Cromwellian—the Irishman of a hundred generations *and the stranger who is within our gates*" (quoted in Mulvey, 2003, p. 63, italics added). This statement reflects the novel inclusiveness inherent in the goals of the Young Irelanders.

Rising popularity of Irish nationalism and associated violent resistance/ rebellion throughout the nineteenth and into the twentieth centuries led to the 1921 Anglo-Irish Treaty. The terms of the treaty provided for the formation of the Irish Free State, which came into being in 1922. However, the provisions of the Treaty fell short of those envisioned by many Irish Republicans, and a short civil war ensued between those in favor and those against the formation of the Irish Free State under the terms of the Treaty. This civil war was quickly won by the Free State supporters and governance of the 26 counties that made up what would later become the Republic of Ireland continued under the Free State.

Under the Free State, the church played an undeniable role in politics. Any government in Ireland at this time had to acknowledge the place of the church in its (civil) affairs. For example, with regard to healthcare, orders of religious sisters had been responsible for the establishment of Catholic health care services and their maintenance for over 100 years prior to this time (Inglis, 1998). Likewise, the huge role of the Catholic Church and other religious institutions in education was unquestionable, as will be discussed in further detail below. In both this regard and in terms of the political influence that church officials had from the pulpit, the tenuous government of the Free State relied on the support of clergy in the early days of the civil unrest and war.

Over the course of the first decade of the Irish Free State, Republicans who had previously taken up arms against the Free State came to take seats in the Irish Parliament and participate in the political processes of the state. These Constitutional Republicans were led by the hugely popular former leader of the struggle for independence from the United Kingdom, Eamon de Valera, and were voted into power in 1932. Over the next number of years, aided by legislation in the United Kingdom that conceded greater independence to Canada and other dominions, this government successfully established a greater degree of independence from the United Kingdom. In 1937, a new constitution that was drafted primarily under the authorship of de Valera was narrowly accepted by referendum. This is the constitution that the Republic of Ireland has today, other than changes that have been passed by plebiscite in the intervening years. According to the interpretation of many, multiple articles in this constitution cemented the role of the Catholic Church in Irish civil/social life, perhaps particularly so in the field of education. As a result, in this constitution can be seen how the historical development of the Irish state has secured for the Catholic Church a continued role in Irish society that cannot be denied.

The effects that Ireland's legacy as a colonized territory has had on the development and present state of the Republic of Ireland is easily discernable in this mini-history of Irish politics. Ireland's particular political history has led Drudy and Lynch to suggest "Ireland's most distinctive historical feature is that it is a postcolonial state" (1993, p. 129). However, this statement came at the virtual beginning of Ireland's recent "Celtic Tiger" era, which has undoubtedly fostered a great number of changes in the small island country.[1]

The first several decades of the Republic saw the imposition and maintenance of protectionist economic and conservative social policies, largely under the leadership of de Valera, in an attempt to buffer the country's industries and citizens from the influence of Great Britain and the United States. By many, at least as reflected in much of the public sphere, this period is considered to have been stifling and wrong-headed, associated with a Church-supported social conservatism counter to individual liberty and an open, plural society (Pilkington, 2002).

The decisive shift away from this type of economic and social policies that eventually made room for the Irish economy of today is often considered to have had its origins in the late-1950s and early-1960s. Terence Brown (1985) suggested it is the 1958 White Paper on Economic Development and the First Programme for Economic Expansion that resulted from it that marks a decisive break with the prior economic policies of independent Ireland and initiated a period of growth beginning in the 1960s. At least, according to Brown, "most Irish people would still identify 1958-63 as the period when a new Ireland began to come to life" (p. 185). Ireland's 1961 application for membership in the European Economic Community (EEC), which would later become the European Union, is also attributed to changing the economic climate in Ireland as they went about opening their markets and making the other changes necessary to become members of the community (Pratschke, 2005). In particular, the Irish government began to woo foreign investment, enticing companies from outside of Ireland to set up manufacturing facilities in the Republic, for exclusive export of products, with favorable corporate tax rates/benefits.

This shift in economic policy is considered a major contributing factor to the strong economic growth that has been sustained in the Republic of Ireland since the early 1990s, which has led the Republic to be referred to as the "Celtic Tiger" since the mid-1990s. A number of significant sociocultural changes in Ireland have accompanied Celtic Tiger economic growth. Among the most pertinent is an increasing number of women entering the workforce. Beginning concurrent with the Republic of Ireland's 1973 admission into the EEC, women in the workforce increased by 34% throughout the 1970s and into the early 1980s (Kennedy, 2003). This trend only accelerated with the coming of the Celtic Tiger economy with 102,000 additional women entering the workforce between 1991 and 1996, and 128,000 more women entering the workforce between 1996 and 2000 (Kennedy). Immigrants to Ireland from outside of the European Economic Area (EEA) are another social group that are entering Irish society and labor market in recent times. A perceived potential labor shortage in the growing (Celtic Tiger) economy led to the increased issuing of work permits to non-EEA workers. "In 1993, 1,103 work permits were issued.... By the end of 2001 it stood at 36,431" (Loyal, 2003, p. 80). As can be expected, associated changes have been reflected in debates about and alterations in the Republic of Ireland's education system, in particular education for young adolescents.

HISTORY AND ORGANIZATION OF SCHOOLING FOR YOUNG ADOLESCENTS

Historical Background

As a result of historical influences, the church plays a dramatic role in the contemporary organizational structures of the Republic of Ireland's educational system, including secondary education, where the majority of young adolescent (i.e., ages 10-15) instruction takes place. (Note that students ages 12-15 are in secondary education and students who are ages 10-11 are most often in primary education based on Irish education organizational structures.)

The state of affairs in Irish education is a direct result of the country's colonial history. Under British rule, penal laws dating from the seventeenth century actively prohibited Catholic secondary schools, while some secondary schools were established by the state in an attempt to foster Protestant practice (Coolahan, 1981). Much education of Catholics in Ireland during this era was conducted in illegal and underground classes held by traveling tutors, called "hedge schools," which began to rapidly increase in numbers with the relaxation of the penal laws in the second half of the eighteenth century (McElligott, 1981).

During the period when the penal laws were relaxed, Catholic religious orders began founding secondary schools without the assistance of public funds (Coolahan, 1981). The denominational nature of these schools presented a particular problem with regard to state funding, as the religious patrons were unwilling to cede control of the schools they had founded and developed in exchange for state monies, and the state was reluctant to finance institutions that were largely seen as training grounds for future (Catholic) clergy. "A compromise was arrived at," according to Coolahan, "whereby the Intermediate Education Act of 1878 permitted the state to give indirect funding to denominational secondary schools by establishing an examination board which disbursed funds to school managers on the basis of success rates of their students at the public examinations" (1981, p. 53). While the system found in the Republic of Ireland today is much different than the one referred to here, the 1878 act established the basis of a model that is largely still reflected in Ireland's education system today. It is a collaboratory system in which the state controls curricula, assessment, regulations for management, staffing, organization, and facilities. At the same time, immediate management, a portion of school costs, the appointment of teachers, and implementation of policy at the school level is controlled by managing bodies. The majority of second-level schools is under the management of patron institutions. They receive funding from the state pursuant to their meeting of state-mandated regulations.

Despite the strong religious influence on schools historically, schools in Ireland have become more secular over the past few decades. The proportion of teachers from religious orders has shrunk from 57% in 1961-1962 to approximately 5% by the late 1990s and many schools have instituted "devolved" management structures that include nonclerical representatives on their boards of management (O'Flaherty, 1999). But, the overall management of the majority of second-level schools and, perhaps more importantly, the long historic legacy of control of education by clerical orders has had long-lasting effects on the shape of education in Ireland that is likely to persist. These effects can be seen both in the "Curriculum, Instruction, and Assessment Practices" and the "Organization and Structure" of Irish second-level education. Each of these will be covered in turn.

Curriculum, Instruction, and Assessment Practices

The traditional secondary school curriculum in Ireland, which includes students ages 12-17, can be characterized as particularly literary- and humanities-based (Coolahan, 1981). An explanation for this (traditional) characteristic of Irish second-level education may, at least in part, be found in the 1878 Intermediate Education Act and the system of payment-by-examination-results discussed above. Given a narrow view of what material was appropriate for these examinations that developed, this system set the mold for curricula in Ireland for some time and (to a degree) into the present day. The system, further, helped to set teaching practice in Ireland by disincentivising schools from teaching anything outside of materials to be on the examination(s). "Because departures from the syllabus prescribed for the examinations cost the school examination fees, teachers were not encouraged to adapt the curriculum to their classes' individual situations" (Akenson, 1975, p. 12).

The system of payment-by-exam-results is not currently utilized in the Republic of Ireland. It was disestablished after independence. In 1924, the Department of Education was created. In that same year, the previous examination system was replaced by a system of capitation grants, "a set amount being awarded for each child following an approved course" (Akenson, 1975, p. 12). And, two courses were set up dividing second-level education into a junior and senior course: the junior course lasting three years and culminating in an examination, the senior course lasting two additional years and culminating with a higher-level examination.

The drive to change the education system from one that perpetuated rote learning rather than personal development was not at all new in Ireland at this time. In an 1840 address to the Historical Society, Young Irelander Thomas Davis suggested, "the common fault of all education, public and private, is that memory, which requires less care, receives an exclusive attention. No crop is sought from the other faculties—reason, fancy, imagination; and accordingly the business of life finds too many unschooled in thinking, unprepared to act" (O'Donoghue, 1974, pp. 37-38). It was hoped that the removal of the payment-by-exam-results system would free up the teaching practice in schools by changing the education system from one that perpetuated rote learning to that of personal development. The changes that were made to the system at this time, however, "were more apparent than real" (Akenson, 1975, p. 74). While the monetary system had been modified, it was not abolished. Schools still had to provide courses of study that were tied to terminal certification exams in order to be eligible for capitation grants. More importantly, the subjects to be studied for the two certificate examinations were determined by the Department of Education. "Inevitably, the combination of state-determined syllabus and examinations with the social and economic advantages acruing to the student from acquiring one of the secondary school certificates, meant that the new system which had been intended to emancipate the Irish secondary school from slavish cramming, did no such thing" (Akenson, p. 74).

Junior Cycle. Students in the Republic of Ireland generally enter second-level schools, thus commencing the Junior Cycle, at age 11 or 12.[2] (See Table 13.1 for organizational structure of the educational system with usual ages of students in each year of primary and secondary education. Note that young adolescents, ages 10-15, must negotiate two different educational structures: Primary Education and then Junior Cycle and Transition Year within Secondary Education.) The Junior Cycle is comprised of a 3-year course of study culminating with a final Junior Certifi-

**Table 13.1. Organizational Structure for the
Republic of Ireland's Education System
in Relationship to Young Adolescents Ages 10-15**

Primary Education	
Years 1 - 8	Ages 4-11
Secondary Education	
Junior Cycle (Years 1-3)	Ages 12-14
Transition Year (Year 4)	Age 15
Senior Cycle (Years 5-6)	Ages 16-17
Tertiary Education	
Universities	
Institutes of Technologies	
Colleges of Education	
NUI Colleges	
Independent Colleges	

cate Examination. A new curriculum was instituted in 1989 with the first
Junior Certificate Examination administered in 1992. The intention of
this was "to provide a programme which will encompass those skills and
competencies to which all young people should have access as a right,
together with qualities of creativity, initiative and enterprise" (Hyland,
1999, p. 29). The stated objective of the Junior Cycle is for students to
complete a broad, balanced, and coherent course of study in a variety of
curricular areas that will allow them to achieve levels of competence that
will enable them to proceed on to complete further second-level education (Department of Education and Science, 2004). The curriculum
includes a number of compulsory courses including civic, social and political education (CSPE), English, Irish Gaelic (Gaeilge), mathematics, and
social, personal, and health education (SPHE) and a number of noncom-
pulsory subjects including art, business studies, classical studies, geography, home economics, languages (French, German, Latin, etc.), music,
religious education, science, technical graphics, and other subjects.

The Junior Certificate Examination is accredited by the State Examinations Commission of the Republic of Ireland and given in early June of
each year. Most of the subjects on the examination are available to be
taken at different levels: Higher and Ordinary. The required subjects of
English, Gaeilge, and Mathematics are available to be taken at Higher,
Ordinary, or Foundational levels. The required CSPE subject is only available at a "Common" level. On average, students test in nine subjects in

the Junior Certificate Examination (McNaboe & Condon, 2007). This system reflects the heritage of the examination system outlined previously.

In 1996, however, the Junior Certificate School Programme (JCSP) was launched in 32 schools as an alternative approach to the Junior Cycle. The number of schools participating had expanded to 174 by 2005 (Department of Education and Science, 2005b). The JCSP specifically targets potential dropouts and students having difficulty coping with the Junior Cycle curriculum with the objective of encouraging these students to stay in school at least until the Junior Certificate is attained (O'Gorman, 1998). It is the program's system of student profiling, providing students with a record of their achievements, that is at the core of the JCSP (Department of Education and Science, 2005b). Relatedly, the JCSP necessitates flexibility in teaching in order to help (individual) students set and reach short-term goals of achieving particular skills and knowledge. A press release from the Department of Education and Science suggested that a 2005 report on the JCSP "shows that the programme has encouraged teachers to engage with a wide range of teaching methodologies and approaches" (Department of Education and Science, 2006). And, a former Research and Development Officer of the JCSP, Elizabeth O'Gorman, suggested "the emphasis of the JCSP is on the whole process of learning rather than on a terminal examination. This involves developing all aspects of the individual's potential" (1998, p. 36). Such statements demonstrate the interconnection between emphasizing individualism and student-centered instruction within education and deemphasizing the one-size-fits-all, examination-based system that the Republic inherited as a result of its past.

Another relevant aspect of the Junior Cycle is the compulsory civic, social, and political education (CSPE) course taken throughout the three years of study and tested in the final examination. This course was introduced as a required subject in the Junior Certificate Curriculum in 1997. Among the stated aims of this course are to "make students aware of the civic, social and political dimension of their lives and the importance of active, participative citizens to the life of the state and all people," to "develop the autonomous potential of all students as socially literate, independent and self-confident young people," and to "encourage students to apply positive attitudes, imagination and empathy in learning about, and encountering, other people and cultures" (Department of Education and Science, 2005a, p. 2). Further, the course is broken down into a ladder of four constituent units—The Individual and Citizenship, The Community, The State-Ireland, and Ireland and the World—with recommendations to progress from the first to the fourth over the three-year course (Department of Education and Science, 2005a). Aspects of the course reflect the emphasis on both individualization and inclusiveness (with regard to nonnational people) that are prevalent in the Celtic Tiger initiatives ongoing in Ireland and neoliberal policies more generally.

Transition Year Programme. The emphasis on individualization evident in the adaptations to the Junior Cycle discussed above is perhaps even more evident in the relatively recent Transition Year Programme. The program was initiated as a direct response to concerns that the Junior Cycle/Senior Cycle format of the Irish education system was too rigid and failed to develop important aspects of Ireland's young adolescents. As indicated in a 1974 speech given by Minister of Education Richard Burke to the Dublin Education Council for Secondary Schools.

> Because of the growing pressures on students for high grades and competi-
> tive success, education systems are becoming, increasingly, academic tread-
> mills. Increasingly too, because of these pressures, the school is losing
> contact with life outside and the student has little or no opportunity "to
> stand and stare" to discover the kind of person he is, the kind of society he
> will be living in and, in due course, contributing to its shortcomings and
> good points. (Smyth, Byrne, & Hannan, 2004, pp. 1-2)

The program was initially introduced as early as 1974 in a pilot project including just three schools. Largely because of budgetary constraints the program was not significantly expanded until 1986, following the 1985 publication of a document suggesting the regularized extension of second-level education to six years (Humphreys, 1998). This "phase two" of program development saw more schools adding Transition Year as an option up to 1994. In 1994, the program was more formally integrated as part of the educational structure. This initiated another rise in the per-
centage of participating schools. "Presented in terms of the proportion of schools offering Transition Year, this represents a growth from less than 1% of second-level schools in the pilot phase to less than 20% in phase two to a remarkable 69% in phase three (by the 2002/03 school year)" (Smyth, Byrne, & Hannan, 2004, p. 5). At the writing of this chapter, approximately 75% of second-level schools in the Republic of Ireland offer Transition Year as an option for some or all of their young adolescent students (Transition Year, 2008).

As there are no prescribed syllabi for the Transition Year Programme, what the program actually entails varies from school to school. "Each school designs its own program according to a set of guidelines issued by the Department of Education and Science, the needs of the students, parents' views, resources available, possibilities offered by employers and other agencies in the local community" (Humphreys, 1998, p. 49). Stu-
dents in the Transition Year will commonly participate in work experience opportunities, community-work projects, field trips and travel, and extra-
curricular activities (hikes, biking trips, etc.) around classes on a wide

range of subjects, some of which overlap with courses taken during the Junior and Senior Cycles. When courses overlap with those in the other phases of second-level education, Transition Year provides teachers with an opportunity to be creative and flexible in both content and pedagogical methods that is unique in the Irish education system.

Assessment of students participating in the Transition Year is likewise flexible, usually done utilizing any of a number of recommended instruments. These recommended instruments of assessment include reports sent two or three times throughout the year to the students' homes, in which (in most schools) teachers rate the student on a scale of 1 to 5, and periodic and/or end-of-year assessment of student-work portfolios, both of which often include elements of student self-assessment (Humphreys, 1998).

Though the Transition Year Programme is generally characterized as an option for students, in many schools (and increasingly) participation in the Transition Year is compulsory. "Schools are found to differ in the way in which they make Transition Year available to students, that is, whether the program is compulsory for all students or optional for some or all students" (Smyth et al., 2004, p. 24).

As can be noted in this characterization of the program, the Transition Year Programme runs counter to the other examination-results-based phases of the education system in the Republic of Ireland. In so doing, it avoids some of the traditional curricular pitfalls inherent in the Irish educational system commented on previously and fosters the individualism that is very much in line with neoliberal reforms seemingly making increased headway in the Irish context.

The hidden curriculum. The focus on individuals as citizens and productive members of society is part of greater trend in education systems in western countries generally. As suggested by Madeleine Arnot, "Western European liberal democratic approaches to the education of the citizen have tended to focus [*sic*] the development of individual potential" (2003, p. 3). Such trends are in line with those accepted by and implicated in Celtic Tiger, neoliberal economic and social reforms ongoing in the Republic of Ireland. The dominant discourse about the changes leading to and continuing in the Celtic Tiger or "New" Ireland is that there is an interdependent relationship between the increasing economic growth, access (at least relatively) to equal education and resources, personal liberty, plurality, and inclusiveness. This idea is behind the recent changes to the educational curriculum for young adolescents in the Republic of Ireland, including but not entirely limited to innovations in the Junior Cycle and the Transition Year Programme. These ideals are being imparted to students educated in that changing system.

Organization and Structure

There are a number of notable different types of institutions for second-level education, which include young adolescents ages 10-15, in the Republic of Ireland.

> At second level ... [t]here are four distinct school types to be found in the second-level sector. These are (1) secondary schools, (2) vocational schools, (3) comprehensive schools, and (4) community schools. Secondary schools are in the 'voluntary' sector and are privately owned and managed; ownership is mainly in the hands of the churches and religious orders.... (and) Secondary schools form by far the greatest proportion of post primary schools. (Drudy & Lynch, 1993, p. 6)[3]

These different types of schools result from the evolution of second-level education in Ireland at different points in the island's past and vary somewhat in the courses that are offered and the management structure. However, the majority (all except for the vocational schools) can be considered denominational and, given the regularization of curriculum that came with the institution of the Junior Cycle in 1989, the differences between them are not significant for the purposes of this chapter.[4] Two aspects of Irish second-level schooling that should be commented on here are the propensity toward single-sex schools and perceived social inequalities that still persist in the form of fee-paying schools. These two aspects will be discussed, respectively, in the following subsections.

Coeducation and single-sex education. As in many other countries, education in Ireland was differentiated by gender from its beginnings. Like much in Irish education this characteristic largely results from the country's colonial legacy. Primary-level education that catered to the poor, majority Catholic, girls of Ireland was provided by congregations such as the Presentation Sisters, the Mercy Sisters, and the Irish Sisters of Charity following the relaxation of the penal laws in the eighteenth century (Fahey, 1987). In the second half of the nineteenth century, religious orders like the Ursulines, Dominicans, and the Loreto Order began providing second-level education for girls (Parkes, 2007). However, these institutions of education were commonly single-sex, catering exclusively to girls and providing a decidedly different curriculum from that provided for their male counterparts in separate classes.

Many Catholic clerical commentators maintained support for the separation of boys and girls in primary and second-level schooling well into the twentieth century. For example, in 1926 the Catholic Bishops of Ireland passed a resolution that "mixed education in public schools is very undesirable, especially among older children" (O'Flaherty, 1999, p. 54). The opinion of these clerical voices was codified in the 1937 constitution and maintained through a ban on married women working in the public service until that rule was abolished with Ireland's 1973 acceptance into the EEC (Hyland, 2007, p. xiv). It was at this same time in the 1970s that, facing increasing debate regarding the previously unquestioned control of education by religious institutions and parallel with the Celtic Tiger-influenced increase of entry of women into the workforce, clerical concern regarding the issue of coeducation often gave way to concern about maintaining overall control of educational institutions.

In 1980, 58% of second-level students attended single-sex schools (Department of Education and Science, 2007). According to the 2005/2006 *Statistical Report*, 38.6% of students attended single-sex schools in the Republic of Ireland in the 2005-06 school year (Department of Education and Science, 2008). So, it is clear that there is a trend toward mixed-sexed education in the Republic of Ireland. Despite this seemingly substantial reduction in the number of students attending single-sex schools, with a majority of European countries having virtually no single-sex education and those that do having a small minority of students attending single-sex schools, Ireland still maintains "by far the highest proportion of pupils in single-sex education in Europe" (Department of Education and Science, 2007, p. 31).

It is possible to see how the history of Ireland and its system of education has established a propensity toward single-sex education that is peculiar to the Republic of Ireland. Not that this trend is unalterable. Indeed, it is changing, if slowly relative to other industrialized countries. In light of a lack of overt attempts to alter the educational landscape in this regard, the path of least resistance in Ireland's secondary schools is the status quo separation of the sexes.

Fee-paying schools and Ireland's legacy of inequality in second-level education. Some have suggested that the issue of exclusion may be particularly acute among a particular class of Irish secondary schools. Reflecting this sentiment Hyland suggested:

> The exclusive origins of secondary education in Ireland continue to be manifest in the underpinning philosophy and organization of many of our schools. For example, a small number of secondary schools in Ireland continue to be fee-paying schools and, therefore, accessible only to a relatively small number of wealthy families. (1999, p. 33)

Adding to this critique of some secondary schools, O'Flaherty (1999) claims that there is evidence to suggest that the greater the religious involvement in second-level schools, the higher will be the participation rates of the middle to upper-middle classes in such schools. Few of the fee-paying schools that are filled to a greater extent by the sons and daughters of middle and upper-middle class parents have the devolved management structures mentioned above. They, further, enjoy a particular privilege in Ireland, as the State continues to pay a high proportion of the teachers' salaries (O'Flaherty). This added to the advantage of the significant income coming in from the fees paid by the parents of the students who attend these schools provides them with substantial resources. Meanwhile, lower-class parents send their children to the non-fee-paying schools, which have substantially fewer resources. As suggested by O'Flaherty, "in these instances the presence of religious can appear to reinforce social divisions" (p. 63).

OUTCOMES OF THE SCHOOLING OF YOUNG ADOLESCENTS

Academic Performance Outcomes

Junior Certificate Examination. The instrument of record to assess the academic performance outcomes for the majority of students in the Junior Cycle is the Junior Certificate Examination. A great deal of importance is placed on end-of-cycle examinations, both at Junior and Senior levels. Records of the results on this state board accredited exam are readily available and are mined for trends on a yearly basis. Grades on the Junior Certificate Examination in recent years continue within a normal distribution at a time when the proportion of students taking subject examinations at higher levels is increasing. Data supporting these claims are addressed in the *Junior Cycle academic performance outcomes research* subsection below.

Transition Year Programme. As outlined above, the Transition Year Programme is most notable in its blatant absence of end-of-grade/course testing. While students are assessed through a number of flexible methods, there remains an overt aversion to the examination regiment that characterizes most of the rest of the education system in the Republic of Ireland. This does not mean, however, that academic outcomes are not considered in assessing the potential benefits of Transition Year. Most often, in research pertaining to academic effectiveness of Transition Year, indicators are drawn from participating students' grades in the Senior Cycle/ Leaving Certificate Examination and/or whether they continue on to third-level education. Limited research findings indicate positive outcomes for young adolescent participation in Transition Year programs. This research is addressed in the *Transition Year Programme academic performance outcomes research* subsection below.

How do Irish young adolescents measure up compared to other countries? In the context of the Republic of Ireland, which is a member of the European Union, it is essential that indicators of the effectiveness of the country's education system be on par with those of other industrialized countries. Educationalists in Ireland demonstrate an ongoing concern with the academic ability level of Irish students compared to the students in other countries. As is detailed in the *comparative academic performance outcomes research* subsection below, research suggests the academic performance of Irish young adolescents compares favorably to that of other industrialized countries/regions.

Other Important Outcomes

An important outcome of education in the Republic of Ireland, as in all locales throughout the world, is to prepare young adolescent students for participation in society. This process includes imparting the knowledge of political structures necessary for participation in political processes, imparting the literacy skills necessary to receive and interpret information in society, imparting social values such as (in the case of Ireland and most western countries) individualism and the refusal of racist reaction to members of minority groups, and the like.

Research Supporting Academic Performance and Other Outcomes

Junior Cycle academic performance outcomes research. As suggested above, Junior Certificate Examination results are readily available.[5] Interpretations regarding the relative performance of young adolescents taking the exam are presented yearly in numerous reports. A recent publication that presented the findings based on results of the 2006 Junior Certificate Examination was *Monitoring Ireland's Skills Supply: Trends in Education and Training Outputs* (McNaboe & Condon, 2007). This publication reports that, with almost 58,000 students taking the examination in 2006, this year saw the first increase in numbers taking the Junior Certificate Examination since 2002. Though, over 2,200 fewer students took the examination in 2006 than did so in 2002. "This is largely a reflection of the declining numbers in the relevant age cohort and the consequent drop in the overall number taking the Junior Certificate Examination" (McNaboe & Condon, p. 21). More importantly, perhaps, is the reported increase in the proportion of students taking subject examinations at a higher level in six of the top ten subjects (McNaboe & Condon). These results might indicate a continued improvement of Junior Cycle students in examination preparation and learning.

Transition Year Programme academic performance outcomes research. The most thoroughgoing and recent research into multiple aspects of the Transition Year Programme is *The Transition Year Programme: An Assessment*, published by researchers of the Economic and Social Research Institute (Smyth et al., 2004). In introducing their work, Smyth and associates suggested that "to date, therefore, comparatively little research has been conducted on the nature of the Transition Year programme, the kinds of students who take part and their subsequent outcomes" (p. 8). They do cite a longitudinal study conducted for the Irish National Council for Curriculum and Assessment that concluded students who participated in a Transition Year program received higher Leaving Certificate Examination scores than those that did not, with students attending designated disadvantaged schools showing a greater performance gain (Millar & Kelly, 1999). "However," Smyth and associates suggested, "this study was unable to control for other prior differences (such as attitudes to school or educational aspirations) between participants and nonparticipants in assessing the impact of Transition Year on their exam outcomes" (p. 8). Smyth and associates utilize propensity score matching techniques to measure outcomes of Transition Year Programme participation while controlling for characteristics prior to entry into the program. This assessment concludes: "In sum, Transition Year participation appears to confer a performance advantage even when participants and non-participants are matched in terms of prior background, attitudes and performance" (Smyth et al., p. 218). In this regard, the Transition Year Programme is largely considered to be successful both in terms of overt academic outcomes and in terms of developing students' individualism and their motivation and ability to participate in the New Ireland.

Comparative academic performance outcomes research. When considering the overall academic performance of young adolescents, a frequently cited research project is the Programme for International Student Assessment (PISA) put out by the Organization for Economic Cooperation and Development (OECD). PISA is an international assessment of 15-year-olds implemented across OECD member states and partner countries. "It aims to provide internationally comparable indicators of the educational attainment of 15-year old students in the key areas of reading, mathematical and scientific literacy" (McNaboe & Condon, 2007, p. 24).

In the Republic of Ireland, 4,585 students participated in the 2006 study. Sixty-two percent of participating students were in the second or third year of Junior Cycle, 21% were in Transition Year, the remaining 17% were in second-level education beyond the Transition Year (Eivers, Shiel, & Cunningham, 2007). In the three categories tested, the mean score of Irish students place them equal to or above the average of other OECD members. Additionally, the students' mean scores put the Republic of Ireland's rankings high in the ranking of the 57 countries (or regions) participating in the research program.

> Irish students' best performance was on reading literacy, where the Irish mean score of 517.3 was well above the OECD mean of 491.8. This performance placed Ireland 5th among OECD countries.... Performance on science (the major domain) was also slightly, but significantly, above the OECD average (508.3, compared to the OECD mean of 500.0). Ireland ranks 14th of OECD countries on the science assessment. For mathematics, Ireland's mean score of 501.5 does not differ significantly from the OECD mean of 497.7, giving it a rank of 16th.... In sum, Ireland's students performed very well on the reading assessment, reasonably well on science, and about average on mathematics. (Eivers et al., p. 33)

These results are generally greeted favorably in the Republic of Ireland and held up as an example of the effectiveness of the Irish education system.

CURRENT ISSUES RELATED TO THE SCHOOLING OF YOUNG ADOLESCENTS

Concerns About the Current Educational System

The majority of recurring issues of concern about the current system of educating young adolescents in the Republic of Ireland seem to revolve around the questions of inclusiveness and disparities in performance or resources. Recent debates along these lines have focused on two major topics of concern: gender-based performance disparities and perceived inequities in enrollment policies of some schools. Each of these will be covered in turn.

Gender disparities in Irish education. As in many Western, industrialized countries, the Republic of Ireland has been experiencing increasing disparities in academic performance based on gender, with female students increasingly outperforming male students. As a result, research was commissioned by the Department of Education and Science and a report entitled *Sé Sí—Gender in Irish Education* (2007) was published. In summarizing the gender disparities covered in the report, Minister of Education and Science Mary Hanafin suggested:

> Boys are significantly more likely to leave school early and to demonstrate low levels of attainment in education. Although our gender differences in examination performance would appear to be moderate in an international context, these gender differences are substantial and they have increased

slowly but steadily over time. Females now outnumber males among students of higher education and this gap has increased steadily over the last decade. (Department of Education and Science, 2007, p. i)

Education researcher Mark Morgan has suggested that, in Ireland, this trend might be exacerbated by the relatively large number of students, including young adolescents, attending single-sex schools, as discussed above (Single-sex gets results blame, 2007). Research and debate on this topic continues.

Inequalities in enrollment policies. In September of 2007, the Department of Education and Science hurriedly organized the opening of primary school by Educate Together, a private organization that operates 56 "multidenominational" primary schools across the Republic, after it was realized that hundreds of students in a suburb north of Dublin, most of them the sons and daughters of immigrants of non-Irish ancestry, had failed to receive places in any of the denominational primary schools in the area, reportedly because of the church's policy to give first preference to Catholics and to siblings of current students (Sullivan, 2007). This controversial occurrence led the Department to initiate an audit of enrollment policies in primary and second-level schools throughout the country, the results of which were released in March 2008. The audit results suggest that, while the level of discrimination does not constitute a nationwide problem, some schools engage in "subtle practices" to avoid admitting some groups of students. The issue was a hot topic at the 2008 annual meeting of the Teachers Union of Ireland (TUI), where it was suggested that many of the schools engaging in such subtle practices were the fee-paying schools discussed above. This led the President of the TUI, Tim O'Meara, to call for a review of funding allocated to fee paying and non-fee paying schools to establish if public money was ensuring that all students were being treated equally irrespective of their economic and other statuses (Anderson, 2008).

Benefits of the Current Educational System

In spite of these recent controversies, few would suggest that the vast majority of young adolescents in the Republic of Ireland do not have educational opportunities to take advantage of if they wish. The disparities between various types of students, while at times glaring and are rightly questioned, are in line with those found in other industrialized countries. The PISA data outlined above indicate that Irish young adolescents compare favorably to those in other OECD countries. As a result, "the general public consensus is that the (Irish) education system is sound and the quality of its graduates compares well internationally" (Lalor, de Róiste, & Devlin, 2007, p. 157).

The Transition Year Programme in particular is increasingly heralded as a success that is perfectly suited to meet the needs of the Republic of Ireland's young adolescents. Limited research findings have indicated positive outcomes resulting from participation. As a result, the percentage of schools offering Transition Year programs has quickly increased and educators from outside of Ireland have shown interest in this approach to educating young adolescents. Further research on the Transitions Year Programme is warranted.

REFORM INITIATIVES AND NATIONAL POLICIES

In line with the issues raised above, recent reform initiatives relate to perceived equality of education for all young adolescents in the Republic of Ireland. The Department of Education and Science's recent audit of enrollment policies may be a first step in the reassessment of the relatively privileged place of fee-paying schools and a reevaluation of state school funding practices, as called for by the president of the teachers union. In addition, Educate Together has an application into the Department of Education and Science for permission to open second-level schools (Murray, 2008). If approved, this will bring the multidenominational model to a greater number of schools that serve young adolescents.

In addition to these calls for reforms toward greater equity in the education of young adolescents, significant resources have been put forward to emphasize technology in the Irish education system. In line with this, it is often suggested that educators must remain vigilant in fostering a system that appropriately prepares students to compete in the knowledge economies of today and the future. One of the major on-going efforts along these lines is represented in an attempt to provide computers and related technologies in schools and to give schools the support necessary to utilize these tools.

In 1998 the government implemented the Schools IT 2000 program in an attempt to get internet connected computers with appropriate software in every school in the Republic of Ireland and assure that pupils in those schools have the opportunity to achieve computer literacy within the following two years. The National Centre for Technology in Education (NCTE) was established in order to continue providing research and support in the process of keeping Ireland's schools up to international standards with regard to computers and related technologies. Despite these efforts, many have suggested a lack of diligence on the part of the government to make good on its intentions. As an example, in February of 2007 the management bodies for almost 500 Irish second-level schools, citing research suggesting that 20% of school computers were more than 6 years old, 89% of schools were without technical support and maintenance, and that the Republic ranked 20th in a list of 30 OECD countries on provision of computers for schools, called on the Irish government to provide the investment necessary "to pull Irish schools from the bottom of the league in the use of computers in classrooms" (Flynn, 2007, p. 3). Computers and related technologies in schools continue to be put forward as a priority by educational policymakers in the Republic.

RESEARCH

Current Research Topics

Current research topics that are being aggressively pursued related to educating young adolescents include streaming/banding/mixed ability classes and studies of young adolescent well-being. Each of these are covered in the following sections.

Methodologies

Current research methodologies being used in studies on young adolescent education include mixed methods with an emphasis on combining both quantitative and qualitative data. Mixed method studies attempt to bring together methods from different paradigms. In a mixed method study the researcher may conduct a series of interviews with students and also carry out a large-scale survey.

Important Research Findings

Streaming/banding/mixed ability classes. The public debate regarding whether it is desirable to "stream" classes according to the (perceived) ability/performance of students was reignited towards the end of 2007, with the publication of *Gearing Up for the Exam? The Experiences of Junior Certificate Students* (Smyth, Dunne, Darmody, & McCoy, 2007). This last installment of a three-part longitudinal research project following a cohort of Junior Cycle students definitively claims that the grouping of students based on attributed abilities was detrimental to those students that were placed in the lower-ability classes. Despite the opinions of these social researchers, or perhaps rather in spite of them, many commentators maintain that strict adherence to mixed-ability classes keeps high-achieving students from reaching their fullest potential (O'Hanlon, 2007).

Studies of well-being of young adolescents. Interest in the field of well-being in educational settings is growing around the world with the Universal Education Foundation providing leadership by defining well-being in different learning environments. Progress has been made by United Nations agencies to put forward the agenda of promoting health through schools and of creating school environments that are conducive and supportive to youth and learning. These models range from UNICEF's Child Friendly Schools (UNICEF, 2007) to the Health Promoting School Concept (Clift & Jensen, 2005) of the World Health Organization. All are supported by a broad base of mix-method research pertaining to the effectiveness of whole school approaches and interventions to benefit young adolescent health and academic performance.

Ireland was ranked in the top one-third on educational well-being of the 21 countries included in a recent UNICEF report (2007) that examined and classified rich countries according to six dimensions of well-being (material, health and safety, education, family and peer relationships, behaviors and risks, and subjective well-being). The definition of educational well-being was based on school achievement in reading, math, and science literacies. A specific example of the Irish education system creating structures that affect young adolescent well-being, and in particular, the constructs of individualism and inclusiveness is the Junior Cycle and the Transition Year. For example, in a survey of second-level school principals and teachers regarding CSPE, over 82% of CSPE teachers surveyed agreed with the statement that the course "helps students develop greater understanding and tolerance" (Redmond & Butler, 2003, p. 40), thus supporting claims that this element of Junior Cycle may encourage acceptance of non-Irish immigrants. Additionally, over 85% of the teachers surveyed agreed with the statement that the course "promotes the personal development of the student" (Redmond & Butler, 2003, p. 40), highlighting the individualization inherent in the curriculum. Overall, the survey report claims, "respondents are very positive toward the potential impact CSPE has on their students" (Redmond & Butler, p. 41). These research results seem to indicate satisfaction that the implementation of mandatory CSPE is having effects on students that support neoliberal ideals and policies.

FUTURE DIRECTIONS

At the writing of this chapter, the Republic of Ireland's Department of Education and Science is undergoing a change. Following the recent resignation of Bertie Ahern and naming of Brian Cowen as Taoiseach (prime minister), Batt O'Keeffe was named as minister for education and science in May of 2008, replacing Mary Hanafin who had held the post for the previous three and half years. These changes may precipitate some changes in policy emphases and direction. However, especially given that the change in Taoiseach was not accompanied by a change in the party coalition currently in power in the Irish Parliament, it can be expected that the general trend of governmental policies in line with the neoliberal economic ideas that have characterized Celtic Tiger policy reforms to date will continue unabated. This, it can be assumed, will mean that young adolescent education policies based on discourses of individualism, technological innovation, and inclusiveness will, likewise, continue to be developed and pursued.

In line with this, assuming that social conditions in line with Celtic Tiger Ireland continue, trends toward coeducational and multidenominational schools will likewise continue. Trends in the individualization of teaching, as exemplified in the Junior Certificate School and Transition Year programs, are also likely to continue and perhaps intensify. Initiatives of this type are at the heart of imparting neoliberal ideals to the Republic of Ireland's young adolescent population.

CONCLUDING DISCUSSION

Highlighted in the discussion above is the interconnection between history, educational structure, curricula, and educational outcome goals. Education, perhaps particularly in the Republic of Ireland, is not simply at the behest of current socio-politico-economic interests and imperatives. As a result of its particular historical legacy, change is necessarily slow. "New Ireland" cannot be built in a day. But, change can and does happen, change that furthers the neoliberal Celtic Tiger goals of education and other policymakers. At the same time, current calls for a more plural and inclusive social system that are so often taken as entirely novel to neoliberal and western democratic ideals of today can be heard in the voices of Young Irelanders of over 150 years ago, as can corresponding statements with regard to favored educational curriculum. In this reserved regard, the "project" of Celtic Tiger educational reform is an attempt at the belated fulfillment of nineteenth-century revolutionary goals. It is the attempt to establish a "New Young Ireland."

NOTES

1. A number of writers argue against the supposed dichotomy between "Old" (Traditional, Catholic, and Nationalist) Ireland and "New" (Modern, Cosmopolitan, and Plural) Ireland that may be implied in the minihistory pre-

sented here. While this is one theme running through our argument, a detailed discussion along these lines is beyond the scope of this chapter. For more on this see Kirby, Gibbons, and Cronin (2002).

2. The Department of Education and Science states that "for registration in a second level school, students must be aged 12 on 1 January in the first year of attendance" (2004, p. 6).

3. Of the 735 Department of Education and Science aided second-level schools operating in the Republic of Ireland during the 2005/2006 school-year, secondary schools accounted for 54% (398), vocational schools accounted for approximately 34% (247), and community and comprehensive schools together accounted for around 12% (90) of the total number (Department of Education and Science 2008).

4. The reader is referred to Drudy and Lynch (1993, pp. 6-14) for more on the differences between the four types of second-level education institutions.

5. The reader may access past Junior and Senior Certificate Examination results at the Irish State Examination Commission's statistics Web page, http://www.examinations.ie/index.php?l=en&mc=st&sc=r8.

REFERENCES

Akenson, D. H. (1975). *A mirror to Kathleen's face: Education in independent Ireland 1922–1960*. Montreal, Québec: McGill-Queen's University Press.

Anderson, P. (2008, March 26). Schools discriminating on enrollment—Hanafin. *The Irish Times*. Retrieved May 27, 2008, from http://www.ireland.com/newspaper/breaking/2008/0326/breaking52.htm

Arnot, M. (2003). *Gender, education and citizenship: Background paper prepared for all global monitoring report 2003/4. Gender and education for all: The leap to equality*. Paris: UNESCO.

Bloy, M. (2002). Britain and Ireland 1789–1801. *The Victorian web*. Retrieved May 7, 2008, from http://www.victorianweb.org/history/ireland1.html

Brown, T. (1985). *Ireland: A social and cultural history, 1922 to the present*. Ithaca, NY: Cornell University Press.

Canny, N. P. (1973). Ideology of English colonization: From Ireland to America. *The William and Mary Quarterly, 30*, 575–598.

Central Intelligence Agency. (2006). *The world factbook 2006*. Washington, DC: Central Intelligence Agency, Superintendent of Documents.

Clift, S., & Jensen, B. B. (Eds.). (2005). *The health promoting school: International advances in theory, evaluation and practice*. Copenhagen, Denmark: Danish University of Education Press.

Coolahan, J. (1981). *Irish education: Its history and structure*. Dublin, Ireland: Institute of Public Administration.

Department of Education and Science. (2004). *A brief description of the Irish educational system*. Dublin, Ireland: Author.

Department of Education and Science. (2005a). *Civic, social and political education junior certificate: Guidelines for teachers*. Dublin, Ireland: Stationary Office.

Department of Education and Science. (2005b). *The junior certificate school pro-gramme: Building on success.* Dublin, Ireland: Author.

Department of Education and Science. (2006, February 22). *Study shows improved attendance and motivation for students taking part in junior certificate school pro-gramme.* Retrieved May 27, 2008, from http://www.education.ie/robots/view.jsp?pcategory=10861&language=EN&ecate-gory=40280&link=link001&doc=30409

Department of Education and Science. (2007). *Sé sí—Gender in Irish education.* Dublin, Ireland: Author.

Department of Education and Science. (2008). *Statistical report/Tuarascáil staitistiúil 2005/2006.* Dublin, Ireland: Stationary Office.

Drudy, S., & Lynch, K. (1993). *Schools and society in Ireland.* Dublin, Ireland: Gill & Macmillan.

Eivers, E., Shiel, G., & Cunningham, R. (2007). *Ready for tomorrow's world? The com-petencies of Irish 15-year-olds in PISA 2006—Summary report.* Dublin, Ireland: Department of Education and Science.

Fahey, T. (1987). Nuns in the Catholic Church in Ireland in the nineteenth cen-tury. In M. Cullen (Ed.), *Girls don't do honours: Irish women in education in the 19th and 20th centuries* (pp. 7–30). Dublin, Ireland: Women's Education Bureau.

Flynn, S. (2007, March 1). Schools here 'miles behind' in providing IT support. *The Irish Times,* p. 3.

Humphreys, E. (1998). Transition year—An opportunity for creative assessment. In Á. Hyland (Ed.) *Innovations in assessment in Irish education* (pp. 49–63). Cork, Ireland: Multiple Intelligence, Curriculum and Assessment Project, Education Department, University College Cork.

Hyland, Á. (1999). Inclusiveness in education. In N. Ward & T. Dooney (Eds.), *Irish education for the 21st century* (pp. 25–34). Dublin, Ireland: Oak Tree Press.

Hyland, Á. (2007). Foreward. In D. Rafferty & S. M. Parkes (Eds.), *Female education in Ireland* (pp. xii-xv). Dublin, Ireland: Irish Academic Press.

Inglis, T. (1998). *Moral monopoly: The rise and fall of the Catholic Church in modern Ire-land.* Dublin: University College Dublin Press.

Kennedy, S. (2003). Irish women and the Celtic Tiger economy. In C. Coulter & S. Coleman (Eds.), *The end of Irish history? Critical reflections on the Celtic Tiger* (pp. 95–109). Manchester, United Kingdom: Manchester University Press.

Kirby, P., Gibbons, L., & Cronin, M. (Eds.). (2002). *Reinventing Ireland: Culture, society and the global economy.* London: Pluto Press.

Lalor, K., de Róiste, Á, & Devlin, M. (2007). *Young people in contemporary Ireland.* Dublin, Ireland: Gill & Macmillan.

Loyal, S. (2003). Welcome to the Celtic Tiger: Racism, immigration and the state. In C. Coulter & S. Coleman (Eds.), *The end of Irish history? Critical reflections on the Celtic Tiger* (pp. 74–94). Manchester, United Kingdom: Manchester Uni-versity Press.

McElligott, T. J. (1981). *Secondary education in Ireland 1870–1921.* Blackrock, Ire-land: Irish Academic Press.

McNaboe, J., & Condon, N. (2007). *Monitoring Ireland's skill supply: Trends in educa-tion/training outputs.* Dublin, Ireland: FÁS.

Millar, D., & Kelly, D. (1999). *From junior to leaving certificate: A longitudinal study of 1994 junior certificate candidates who took the leaving certificate examination in 1997.* Dublin, Ireland: National Council for Curriculum and Assessment.

Mulvey, H. F. (2003). *Thomas Davis and Ireland: A biographical study.* Washington, DC: Catholic University of America Press.

Murray, N. (2008, July 23). Parents seek second level educate together school. *Irish Examiner.*

O'Donoghue, D. J. (1974). *Essays of Thomas Davis: Centenary edition.* New York: Lemma.

O'Flaherty, L. (1999). Catholic church influence in the management of second-level schools. In N. Ward & T. Dooney (Eds.), *Irish education for the 21st century* (pp. 53–64). Dublin, Ireland: Oak Tree Press.

O'Gorman, E. (1998). Profiling in the junior certificate school programme. In Á. Hyland (Ed.) *Innovations in assessment in Irish education* (pp. 35–48). Cork, Ireland: Multiple Intelligence, Curriculum and Assessment Project, Education Department, University College Cork.

O'Hanlon, E. (2007, November 4). School report leaves our students bottom of class. *Irish Independent.*

Parkes, S. M. (2007). Intermediate education for girls. In D. Raftery & S. M. Parkes (Eds.), *Female education in Ireland 1700–1900* (pp. 69–104). Dublin, Ireland: Irish Academic Press.

Pilkington, L. (2002). Religion and the Celtic Tiger: The cultural legacies of anti-Catholicism in Ireland. In P. Kirby, L. Gibbons, & M. Cronin (Eds.), *Reinventing Ireland: Culture, society and the global economy* (pp. 124–139). London: Pluto Press.

Pratschke, B. M. (2005). A look at Irish-Ireland: Gael Linn's *Amharc Éireann* films, 1956–64. *New Hibernia Review, 9*(3), 17–38.

Redmond, D., & Butler, P. (2003). *Civic, social and political education: Report on survey to principals and teachers.* Dublin: Nexus Research Cooperative.

Single-sex gets results blame. (2007, September 3). *Irish Independent.*

Smyth, E., Byrne, D., & Hannan, C. (2004). *The transition year programme: An assessment.* Dublin, Ireland: Economic and Social Research Institute.

Smyth, E., Dunne, A., Darmody, M., & McCoy, S. (2007). *Gearing up for the exam? The experiences of junior certificate students.* Dublin, Ireland: Economic and Social Research Institute.

Sullivan, K. (2007, October 24). Hustling to find classrooms for all in a diverse Ireland: Shortage of space for immigrants' children reflects challenges of integrating newcomers. *Washington Post,* p. A12.

Transition Year. (2008). *Citizens information.* Retrieved May 27, 2008, from http://www.citizensinformation.ie/categories/education/primary-and-post-primary-education/going-to-post-primary-school/transition_year/?searchterm=transition%20year

Turner, B. (2007). *The statesman's yearbook: The politics, cultures and economies of the world: 2008.* Basingstoke, United Kingdom: Palgrave Macmillan.

UNICEF. (2007). *An overview of child well-being in rich countries* (Innocenti Report Card 7). Florence, Italy: UNICEF Innocenti Research Centre.

CHAPTER 14

EDUCATING YOUNG ADOLESCENTS IN BRAZIL

Evely Boruchovitch, José Aloyseo Bzuneck, and Marília Saldanha da Fonseca

This chapter describes the education of young adolescents in Brazil. History of Brazilian educational policy, reform initiatives, national policies, current educational system, instruction, and assessment for this age group and the structure and the organization of the curriculum are critically analyzed. Moreover, it provides data regarding young adolescents' academic performance and other important outcomes related to their formal education. Research on academic performance and other relevant issues of young adolescents' psychosocial development is reviewed. Educational implications and future directions for improving the schooling process of young Brazilian adolescents are also presented.

CONTEXTUAL NARRATIVE

Brazil is a country in South America and occupies the central-west part of the continent. It is considered to be the fifth largest country in the world in terms of its geographical area (8,511,996 km²). According to a study by the *Instituto Brasileiro de Geografia e Estatística* (IBGE, 2000)—[Brazilian

An International Look at Educating Young Adolescents
pp. 313–343
Copyright © 2009 by Information Age Publishing

Institute of Geography and Statistics]—the country has 189,335,187 inhabitants and a population density of 22 inhabitants/km². Portuguese is its official language. There is religious freedom in Brazil. The vast majority of the population is Catholic; however, other religions coexist harmoniously, such as Protestantism, Spiritism, Islam, and Judaism.

The Brazilian economy is the eighth largest in the world and the largest in South America. The country is part of the G-20, a group of countries with emerging economies. In 2005, its Human Development Index—HDI (Programa das Nações Unidas para o Desenvolvimento [PNUD], 2005) was 0.800, and thus became part of the group of countries with High Human Development.

The Brazilian population is distributed among five macroregions: north, north-east, center-west, south-east, and south. These regions are very different in relation to their geography; climate; soil; and occupational, historical and cultural characteristics; which, in turn, determine their economic, social, and political development.

Historically, the south-east region is the most industrially developed and it has a growing market. The poor living conditions of the people from the north-east make them the main migrant group looking to improve their lives by settling in the big metropolises. These cities also receive foreign immigrants of different nationalities who, together with the local migrants, establish communities in the deprived peripheries in precarious structural conditions. If on the one hand industrial wealth attracts those coming from outside, on the other, extreme social inequality and the centralization of power marginalizes this population more and more, giving rise to slums of different sizes. According to the Indicadores Sociais Educacionais Brasileiros (ISEB [Brazilian Social and Educational Indexes]), in 2004 30.27% of the Brazilian population was living in poverty and infant mortality was 22.58%.

In 1988, the Brazilian Constitution ensured women's political rights and established, for the first time, gender equality as a fundamental right. However, forms of inequality persist in labor relations. Women are less likely to be employed, despite the increase of female participation within the economically active population.

It could be said that Brazilian society is one of the most multi-racial in the world, since it comprises European descendants, indigenous people, and people from the African and Asian continents. The Portuguese have played the most significant part in the creation of Brazil. Other immigrants make up the Brazilian population; migratory waves came from Italy, Germany, Spain and Japan, and on a smaller scale, from Poland, Switzerland, Lithuania, and the Ukraine.

The indigenous population was estimated at 5 million in the sixteenth century. Relations between the Portuguese colonizers and natives were characterized by conflict involving direct attacks and extermination. For this reason, the surviving indigenous populations opted to migrate to inland areas of difficult access. Nowadays, there are approximately 500,000 indigenous people who represent 0.25% of the Brazilian population, according to data from the *Fundação Nacional do Índio (Funai)* (2008 [National Indian Foundation]). The indigenous people have profound knowledge of their environment and for this reason it is important to guarantee their means of physical and cultural survival, indigenous knowledge about biodiversity, and the preservation of Brazilian biological property.

Brazil has the largest population of African descendants outside Africa. According to the demographic census (IBGE, 2000; IPEA [Instituto de Pesquisas Econômicas Aplicada], 2007), Blacks and *pardos* (mixed-race) represent 50.5% of the Brazilian population. Brazilian Black history began with slavery. In captivity, Black people found ways to resist up to the time they attained their freedom. Currently, Black struggles are no longer based on slavery, but on racial inequalities and the social recognition of Black identity. In Brazil, the black movement brought about advances for Black men and women in terms of social mobility, personal development, professional qualification, as well as in the employment market. The main demands of the Black movement are affirmative action public policies, that is, policies adopted by the state to minimize racial inequalities and to promote equal opportunities.

Nonetheless, educational inequalities still exist despite advances in recent years. Brazil has 16 million illiterate people. The total illiteracy rate among 10- to 14-year-olds is 5.88%, 2.99% in the White population and 8.6% in the Black population. From the age of 15, the total illiteracy rate is 12.94%, 8.32% in the White population and 18.69% in the Black population (PNUD, 2003). Illiteracy is a perverse kind of social exclusion since it reproduces poverty and denies people their full citizenship rights, hindering future perspectives.

HISTORY AND ORGANIZATION OF SCHOOLING FOR YOUNG ADOLESCENTS

Historical Background

Throughout the past 5 centuries, the history of Brazilian education policy has been selective and discriminatory. Until the twentieth century, the population did not have access to education, which was for the benefit of the ruling classes. The period from 1920 to 1940 saw the establishment of a new educational ethos which emphasized the role of the state in education, the expansion of teaching and good quality public schools. However, education remained inaccessible to a large part of the poor population, mainly to the 11 to 15 age group. To meet the demands of these young adolescents, a parallel educational system was established with the purpose of producing a qualified work force. These were training schools funded by industry and commerce. In 1960, the movement set up in favor of democratic education achieved the promulgation of the first *Lei de Diretrizes e Bases da Educação Nacional*—LDB—Law n. 4.024/60 (Law of Directives and Foundations for National Education), which established free and compulsory education from the age of seven (Brasil, 1961). As a result, young adolescents graduated in the upper elementary in seven years. In 1971, Law n. 5.692 was sanctioned, which established directives and foundations for elementary and middle school teaching, thereby reaffirming the compulsory and free nature of education from the ages of seven to fourteen (Brasil, 1971). The educational policy behind this legislation was to meet the demands of the "regime of exception" established by the military dictatorship which was in power in the country at the time. In order to consolidate the economic development of the country, a professional education curriculum was established and implemented for 10 to 15 year old students. The reconstruction of the Brazilian democracy with the establishment of the 1988 Federal Constitution defined a new phase in education. In 1996, Law n. 9.394 (Brasil, 1996) was approved establishing further directives and foundations, signaling that education would be organized along democratic lines.

Curriculum, Instruction and Assessment

In Brazil, the *Parâmetros Curriculares Nacionais*—PCNs (National Curriculum Parameters) are quality benchmarks for basic education throughout Brazil (Ministério de Educação. Secretaria de Educação Fundamental [MEC/SEF], 1997). Their purpose is to guide and to guarantee coherence and equity in relation to the teaching and learning of scientific content and school subjects within the educational system, for each phase of elementary and middle school. PCNs include eight subject areas for young adolescent students attending the fifth to eighth grades, including Portuguese language, mathematics, natural sciences, geography, history, arts, physical education and a foreign language.

Apart from the traditional subjects, PCNs also recommend that transversal themes are addressed. Considered to be essential for the exercise of citizenship, these themes, which are approached in an interdisciplinary way, comprise a set of subjects which address present-day needs and current issues such as health, ethics, cultural plurality, the environment, sexual orientation, work and consumerism.

The School Census (INEP [Instituto Nacional De Estudos e Pesquisas Educacionais Anísio Teixeira], 2006) shows that there were 33,282,663 pupils enrolled at elementary school. Of this total, 27,127,536 are young adolescents, that is, 81.5% of pupils are between 10 and 15 years of age. The data obtained from this year's student population were as follows: 77.3% passed, 13.2% failed, while the dropout rate was 9.57%. Enrolled students over 14 years of age account for 15.78% (5,253,557) of the dropout population.

In 2003, 61 million people had not completed elementary school. Of these, only 10% were still in education (IBGE, 2007). The LDB (article 37) established *Educação de Jovens e Adultos*—EJA [Education for Young People and Adults] aimed at those who interrupted their schooling. It ensures that there are free educational opportunities available, appropriate to the characteristics, interests and life and work conditions of these students. There is a strong association between illiteracy and young adolescents who have exited the education system. The illiteracy rate among 10- to 15-year-olds is 4.2%.

Evasion and repetition in public schools are still important problems to be resolved. Despite the fact that education is structured in school years, it is important to view school life within a more flexible time frame. The PCNs adopt a differentiated conception of education based on cycles. Thus, the first cycle refers to the first and second grades; the second cycle to the third and fourth; and so on in relation to subsequent grades. Students aged between 10 and 14 are expected to be in the third and fourth cycles. Organization in cycles addresses the problem of the noninterruption of students' schooling throughout compulsory education. There is less evasion when students are not held back through repetition and they remain longer at school, ensuring the continuity of the educational process.

Another model of educational practice known as the system of continuous progression in learning could also be used to ensure the permanence of students in school. Continuous progression in cycles requires the school curriculum to be carefully planned. Recuperation classes during school holidays improve performance and increase the chances of success. This is essential to keep children in school, enabling evasion rates to fall.

The curriculum is at the center of education policy and therefore should be subjected to assessments. The 2005 Directive n.931 (MEC/INEP, 2005) instituted the *Sistema de Avaliação da Educação Básica*—SAEB (Basic Education Assessment System) made up of the *Avaliação Nacional da Educação Básica*—ANEB (National Assessment of Basic Education) and the *Avaliação Nacional de Rendimento Escolar*—ANRESC (National Assessment of School Achievement), for the purpose of assessing educational public systems. ANEB, also known as SAEB, is an assessment based on samples, in which students attending the fourth and eighth grades of elementary school and the third grade of middle school take part, from both public and private schools in urban and rural areas. Students do Portuguese and mathematics examinations with emphasis on reading and problem-solving, respectively. SAEB assesses the quality of Brazilian education in each state of the federation and focuses on educational management systems. The information produced substantiates the formulation, reformulation, and monitoring of public policies. ANRESC, known as "Prova Brasil," assesses students attending the fourth and eighth grades of elementary school within the urban public education system. Insofar as it is based on a universal set, this assessment is censual, thus providing results for each school unit in assessing the quality of teaching. Its aim is to improve the quality of education and reduce existing inequalities. These assessments are largely used for diagnostic purposes. They are developed by the *Instituto Nacional de Pesquisas Educacionais* (National Institute of Educational Research) and the Ministry of Education and Culture—INEP/MEC, and are based on standardized tests and socioeconomic questionnaires.

This new assessment prompted the creation of the *Índice de Desenvolvimento da Educação Básica*—IDEB (Basic Education Development Index), using a scale from 0 to 10 (INEP, 2007). IDEB is an indicator of educational quality which combines the performance of students in standardized tests at the end of educational stages (fourth and eighth grades of elementary school and the third grade of middle school) with information on school productivity (average pass rate during each educational stage).

Another diagnostic tool is the *Exame Nacional do Ensino Médio*—ENEM (National Secondary Education Examination), the main purpose of which is to assess the performance of pupils at the end of basic education. It is an individual examination of a voluntary nature and it is offered every year to students who have finished their secondary education in previous years. The average mark for 2007 was 51.276 on a scale of zero to 100.

Organization and Structure

The 1996 LDB Law n. 9.394 regulated the curriculum, the number of hours of instruction, compulsory attendance and the minimum requirements for passing the year, on a national basis. School education is divided into: I—basic education, and II—higher education. The purpose of basic education is to prepare students for the exercise of citizenship and to provide them with the means to progress in work and later studies.

It can be organized in yearly grades, six-monthly periods, or in cycles. It is divided into preschool education, elementary school, and middle school. The purpose of preschool education is the all-round development of the child to the age of six. Elementary education is compulsory and free in public schools. It lasts for nine years and starts at the age of 6. Students between the ages of 10 and 15 are expected to attend the fourth to eighth grade of elementary school and the first grade of middle school.

Middle school is the final stage of basic education, with a minimum duration of three years. Middle schools are planned taking into account the biopsychosocial characteristics of the young adolescent. The student who is enrolled or has graduated from elementary and middle school is able to have access to professional education, which is structured as follows: initial training for pupils from elementary school and professional technical teaching for middle school pupils. The purpose of professional education is to integrate different types of education with work, science, and technology, leading to the permanent development of skills for a productive life.

The 1996 Law n. 9.394, in Articles 9 and 87 respectively, states that the Federal Government is responsible for the elaboration of the *Plano Nacional de Educação*—PNE (National Education Plan), in conjunction with the states, the federal district and municipalities, and has instituted the *Década da Educação* (Education Decade). It also decreed that the federal government had to send the PNE to the national congress a year after the above-mentioned law was published, with directives and targets for the next ten years. The PNE—2001 Law n. 10.172—is the second most important steering document for Basic Education. The *Programa de Avaliação e Acompanhamento do PNE* (Program for the Assessment and Monitoring of the PNE) was created with the purpose of following up and assessing the results of the implementation of this Plan (Brasil, 2001).

OUTCOMES OF THE SCHOOLING OF YOUNG ADOLESCENTS

Academic Performance Outcomes

The relationship of young adolescents to schooling has been considered in Brazilian research and policy according to three criteria, namely, achievement, attendance, and flow. Therefore, problems in achievement for this age group are inseparable from all that occurs across the entire elementary and middle school system.

Access to elementary school has now been universalized, though completing it to the eighth grade has not. In addition, few students finish basic education with a level of achievement that could be considered adequate. Repetition and dropout rates in elementary schools have stopped falling in recent years, but they are increasing in middle schools (Brasil, 2007).

In SAEB evaluations (Brasil, 2007), the results of Brazilian students in Portuguese and mathematics have remained stable at relatively low levels since 1995. According to the 2003 evaluation in Portuguese, 55% of fourth graders, 45.6% of eighth graders and 38.6% of middle school third graders performed below the minimum level. In mathematics this minimum level was not achieved by 51.6%, 57.1%, and 79.1%, respectively. More recently, according to the 2005 published assessment, there was a small improvement among fourth graders but as a group they did not reach satisfactory levels. There was no improvement among eighth graders and a decrease among middle school third graders. SAEB led to the creation of the new Education Development Index—(IDEB), expressed on a scale from zero to 10. In 2005, IDEB average score was 3.8 at fourth grade, 3.5 at eighth grade and 3.4 at middle school third grade, compared with an average score of 6 found in more developed countries. Such outcomes are quite consistent with Brazil's position on international evaluations as the Program for International Student Assessment (PISA) (Organization for Economic Co-operation and Development, 2004). One can conclude that elementary and middle school systems in Brazil have much to improve. As a rule, there is educational failure when a student, or the whole school, does not reach a certain pre-established score in this examination, while a student or school is successful when this score is achieved.

However, official data produced by SAEB examinations (Brasil, 2007) also reveal appreciable disparities among students in the same school, different schools in the same system, and between private and public schools, and states and municipalities. Group average scores also show large standard deviations. That is, there are successful students and also successful schools where the educational level of young adolescents is absolutely adequate. Some examples of this in private schools are described in detail by Brandão, Mandelert, and De Paula (2005). In an extensive study among eighth graders in 230 public schools in Belo Horizonte-MG a difference of up to 60 points in mathematics performance was revealed, equivalent to a difference of two school grades (Soares, 2007).

Other Important Outcomes

It can be said that studies on young adolescents within the context of school have predominated within Brazilian research during recent years. That is, in this category there has been research on various topics, including: motivation (Ferreira et al., 2002; Gloria, 2003; Locatelli, Bzuneck & Guimarães, 2007), cognitive, emotional and social aspects of learning (Bandeira, Rocha, Magalhães, Del Prette, & Del Prette, 2006; Carneiro, Martinelli, & Sisto, 2003; Costa & Boruchovitch, 2004; Cruvinel & Boruchovitch, 2004 Gomes & Boruchovitch, 2005; Lelis, 2005; Loos, 2004; Oliveira, Boruchovitch, & Santos, 2007; Santos & Graminha, 2006), and teacher and student interaction (Carvalho, 2004; Viecili & Medeiros, 2002).

Overall designs of these studies varied in number of participants from 4 to 1,594. Age range was between 6 to18. In fact, the studies investigated very specific variables which made comparisons difficult to establish. Through data derived from some of the research on motivation it was possible to observe that students display motivational orientation and causal attributes compatible with high quality learning (Ferreira et al., 2002). However, other studies showed that young adolescents were not very committed to studying, and it was extrinsic factors, rather than intrinsic ones, that motivated them at the end of fundamental education (Lelis, 2005). Students who have experienced school failure did not have a good evaluation of educational measures of nonretention (continuous progression). Such measures were seen as ways of decreasing their interest and responsibility for their own learning, since they made them advance in their schooling with the awareness that they had not reached the optimal achievement level (Glória, 2003). Future perspectives were associated to more adaptive patterns of behavior within the school context such as more investment and the use of learning strategies (Locatelli et al., 2007).

Those who researched the relationship between emotional, cognitive, and social aspects of learning agree with regard to the importance and interference of nonintellective variables in school performance, which frequently, when associated to other variables, can act as risk or protection factors in relation to learning (Bandeira et al., 2006; Carneiro, Martinelli & Sisto, 2003; Costa & Boruchovitch, 2004; Cruvinel & Boruchovitch, 2004; Loos, 2004; Santos & Graminha, 2006).

Research Supporting Academic Performance Outcomes

Notwithstanding criticisms by some scholars of the philosophy, purposes and implementation of SAEB (Arelaro, 2005; Bonamino, Coscarelli, & Franco, 2002; Freitas, 2004; Souza, 2003), this periodical evaluation of school achievement outcomes led to apposite research and insightful observations. Angelucci, Kalmus, Paparelli, and Patto (2004) critically analyzed 71 theses and dissertations on educational failure produced at a large public university in the period 1991-2002. In short, four approaches were identified in these studies which addressed children and adolescents. For the first group, educational failure was mainly caused by the psychological problems of students, particularly emotional disturbances, with most responsibility falling on students themselves and parents. In the second group of studies, educational failure was attributed to poor teaching, with a cumulative effect year after year. Other researchers saw failure as an outcome of a Brazilian educational policy which submits public schools to the logic of capitalism. Finally, and in a similar vein, some authors interpreted educational failure among students from low socioeconomic backgrounds as an expression of class conflict inside the school, mirroring the struggle in society as a whole.

Angelucci et al. (2004), in seeking to explain failure in public education, discuss in depth methodological issues in the studies they have reviewed, pointing out limitations and internal contradictions of each approach in isolation. In particular they argued that for the most part research is still limited and therefore needs to be further developed both in conceptual and methodological terms.

Recently, Ireland et al. (2007) used quali-quantitative methodology to analyze data produced by SAEB in 2003. Through questionnaires, local observations, and interviews with students, parents, and teachers, the authors sought to identify processes and variables underlying low average scores in reading proficiency. Questionnaires were given to about 17,000 fourth graders (average age 10.4) from 225 public elementary schools in ten metropolitan regions. Students were asked, among other things, about their perceptions of school tasks, homework, help, and their understanding about what learning is and what it means to be a good or bad student.

In their study, Ireland et al. (2007) found the main factors, as pointed out by the participants, which would explain the poor school performance of this sample. Many parents criticized school conditions and failings or incompetence on the part of teachers, though many others recognize their effort, commitment, and teaching skills. On the other hand, teachers complain of lack of institutional support and very often attributed educational failure to unmotivated students and to deficiencies in the family. However, because it is a qualitative study, the research did not disclose the frequencies or quantity of positive or negative findings. While the authors emphasize the importance of raising students' self-esteem, they did not specify any way to achieve this.

Reading comprehension was the most researched basic skill (Gomes & Boruchovitch, 2005; Oliveira et al., 2007; Maia & Fonseca, 2002). Positive correlation was found between reading comprehension, use of learning strategies, educational progress, type of school (Gomes & Boruchovitch;

Oliveira et al.). No correlation was found between IQ and reading comprehension (Maia & Fonseca). Dias, Enumo, and Turini (2006) assessed, in a public school, second to sixth grader's performance in reading, writing, and mathematics, on two occasions with a one year interval. As expected, all children improved significantly when they reached the next grade, but their average scores in these subjects remained at low levels. Oliveira et al. investigated reading comprehension among seventh to eighth grade 14-year-olds in another public school. The scores were slightly above average levels.

According to Klein (2006), all evaluations have showed a positive relationship between better performance and higher socioeconomic status. Inversely, lower socioeconomic status is related to lower achievement, repetition, and dropout. In fact, low socioeconomic status does not directly influence students' achievement and motivation, but it is a condition that has at its core specific beliefs, concerns, and behaviors. In a survey (Datafolha, 2001) researchers found that for wealthier people with higher education, Brazil's current problems include health, education, violence, and unemployment. However, among those with a low income, only 3% considered education an important issue. Other concerns, related to satisfying basic living conditions are more prominent for this part of the population. Ireland et al. (2007) found that those students who were considerably behind their age-related grade at public schools were 1.6 times more likely of being pressured by their families to work, when compared with their peers who did not repeat years. It can be assumed that money-making activities, outside school, are closely related to retention. At the same time, when these researchers asked fourth graders about their disposition to go to school, 18.5% of the sample answered that they went unwillingly. However, students over 12 years old were overrepresented in this group. This suggests that previous educational failure seems to diminish their motivation to go to school. Worse still, and for the same reason, even with repetitions their performance remained low, as was demonstrated in the case of mathematics (Klein, 2006). Boruchovitch (2001) found that third to seventh grade retained students were less likely to use effective strategies for text comprehension. In the face of these results, some authors (Gomes, 2005; Klein, 2006) concluded that retaining low achieving students for one or more years was not an effective way to recover them. On the contrary, every repetition (i.e, retention of student) raises the probability of a new repetition. Consequently, the authors suggest eliminating grade repetitions.

On the other hand, it was shown that teachers sometimes exert an additional negative influence on their low achieving students. Viecili and Medeiros (2002) found that teachers behave discriminatively in their interaction with students depending on whether they have a history of

failure in school. With non-failing students, teachers use positive rein-
forcements more frequently, while with failing students, coercive and
more controlling methods prevail. Similarly, it is more common for teachers to assign low grades and enroll in remedial programs students that are
male, Black, and/or from low income families (Carvalho, 2004).

CURRENT ISSUES RELATED TO THE
SCHOOLING OF YOUNG ADOLESCENTS

Concerns About the Current Educational System

In their study on the educational failure identified by SAEB, Ireland et
al. (2007) stressed high rates of grade repetition and dropout in public
schools. In fact, 64.6% of 10-year-olds were in the grade compatible with
their chronological age, but this was the case for only 37.1% of 15-year-
olds due to previous repetitions. For the same reason, 16% of fourth graders were 13 or over, that is, 2 or more years behind the expected grade.
There is clear evidence of dropout among young adolescents, since only
86.7% of 15-year-olds attend school, as opposed to 98% of 10-year-olds.
However, according to more recent official data 97.6% of the population
aged between 7 and 14 now attend school. The impressive rise in school
attendance in recent years is noteworthy—in 1996 30.5% of seven to fourteen year olds were outside school, while this rate dropped to 2.4% in
2006. In the 15-17 year range (middle school), it fell from 22.5% to 16%
(Brasil, 2007) in the same period.

Both grade repetition and dropout, associated with inadequate learning, are characteristic of the traditional educational system in Brazil and
were historically considered a pressing problem. For this reason since the
1990s—as an alternative to the original structure of eight (now nine)
grades—several states and municipalities introduced a new system com-
prising cycles of 2 or more years. In a promising move retention was abolished, at least within each cycle: for example, in the first 2 or 4 years,
students progressed automatically to the next grade. In the São Paulo State
system retention was only possible at fourth and eighth grades. At the same
time, many different programs of acceleration were adopted with the
intention of overcoming age and grade distortions. Students in grades
incompatible with their ages were targeted to receive individualized support aimed at improving learning and recovering the cognitive skills they
needed to perform adequately in the subsequent grade. Underlying these
experiences was a concern for efficiency and costs reduction in education.

The outcomes of these initiatives have been continuously assessed and
discussed in the literature (Arelaro, 2005; Gomes, 2005; Mainardes, 2006;

Oliveira, 2002; Viégas & Souza, 2006). Gomes reviewed 62 studies with diverse theoretical and methodological approaches and concluded that such experiences have risks and disadvantages and only partially reached their desired educational goals. Retention dropped drastically over the past 15 years, in many cases achievement improved, but national average scores through official evaluations did not rise significantly. Researchers generally attribute these results to the shallow commitment of teachers and parents to programs. Teachers in particular have not been sufficiently involved by authorities in discussing alternatives and they have not been adequately prepared to deal with new teaching requirements and assessment systems. In short, it was acknowledged that it is not enough to reduce costs in education through the elimination of retention and the introduction of acceleration programs if there isn't similar concern about the quality of education in order to secure a positive effect on student flow and achievement. For this reason, improving teachers' resources and promoting their professional development should be an important part of the agenda for educational policies.

In addition, Klein (2006) in discussing recent SAEB results, argued that it is not enough to change labels—from cycles to grades. Most importantly, students' competencies should be more carefully assessed every year, with special attention given to motivational problems, since failing students are very often prone to low self esteem and to giving up.

School dropout and absenteeism in public schools, mostly related to lower socioeconomic levels, have been targeted by a large federal program since 2001, in which low income families receive through the municipality monthly financial assistance (Valente, 2003). In exchange parents have to be more involved with their (7-14-year-olds) children's school, and ensure their regular attendance. More recently, a similar program was extended to 15-year-olds or over. It can easily be assumed that it is difficult for municipalities to follow up on parents' obligations with regard to their children's education. On the other hand, it is reasonable to suppose that the current higher levels of school attendance among children and young adolescents are due, in a large part, to this policy. Nevertheless, there is no available research based on data about the relationship between school attendance and achievement, on the one hand, and the monetary support low income families receive from the government for this purpose, on the other.

Benefits of the Current Educational System

The current Brazilian education system offers benefits to the elementary and middle school population which includes young adolescents between the ages of 10 and 15. Programs and projects aim to provide services to these students, some directly and others indirectly (MEC). Benefits which relate directly to the student population include: Books about the importance of Black people in Brazil and the Program of Ethics and Citizenship, the Project of Health Care *and* Prevention in Schools, the Brazilian Open Technical School and Public Domain Site. In relation to the books about the importance of Black people for Brazil, publications are given to schools and are aimed at teachers and pupils of elementary school. The purpose of the Ethics and Citizenship Program is to build these values in society and in school. It states that schools have a duty to teach and act according to the principles of democracy, ethics, social responsibility, collective interest, national identity and the human condition itself. The Program is not part of the curriculum. It should take place in Education Forums of Ethics and Citizenship, spaces where children and young adolescents can learn to deal with present-day complexities. The Project of Health Care and Prevention in Schools has the following objectives: (a) to promote the sexual and reproductive health of young adolescents and young people, integrating the health and education departments; (b) to contribute to the reduction of HIV/STDs infection and levels of school dropout due to pregnancy during young adolescence in the 10-24 age group; (c) to encourage young people to participate in the formulation and implementation of STDs/AIDS prevention policies and in policies regarding the harmful use of drugs; (d) to support the different initiatives in the area of health care and prevention in schools; and (e) to establish a culture of health prevention in schools and their surroundings. The Brazilian Open Technical School Program offers technical courses at the middle school level, especially for those living in suburban metropolitan areas. The *Public Domain Site*, a virtual library with an archive consisting of texts, images, sounds and videos, aims to share knowledge in an equitable way with teachers, students, researchers and with the population in general.

In relation to indirect benefits to students, we can highlight the following: Information Packs, TV Escola [educational television] and WebEduc—the Ministry of Education's educational Web site. Information Packs are distributed to families throughout the country, explaining how they can assist their children in education, inviting families to become involved in the education of their children, and monitoring their attendance and performance at school. TV Escola is a program directed to the training of elementary education teachers and the updating and improvement of their skills, thus generally adding value to the teaching-learning process. WebEduc, the Ministry of Education's educational site has research material, learning objectives, and other free educational material.

REFORM INITIATIVES AND NATIONAL POLICIES

The Brazilian education system must promote equality of opportunities with regard to access and permanence in school without discrimination due to origin, ethnicity, race, gender and beliefs. However, equality of opportunities cannot be understood as the exercise of a homogenized set of policies. It means including while at the same time preserving difference and ensuring diversity in equality. Education policies for 2001-2010 aim to strengthen social inclusion in education and help to maximize educational actions and programs in relation to diversity.

The inclusion and diversity thematic axis is concerned with education in rural areas, education and Afro-descendance, indigenous education, and special needs education. The public policy priority is to invest in quality elementary and middle school education. Actions and programs must include the school curriculum, school management and teacher training, and also the production of educational materials.

In Brazilian rural areas, 60% of students who finish their eighth grade do not enroll at middle school and of those that do, 92% move to urban areas. In rural areas, the priority in education is to build schools closer to rural communities and settlements to provide for young adolescent students in the fifth to eighth grades of elementary school. The curriculum needs to contextualize regional diversity, essential for students to value their own culture and finish studies in their own regions. Furthermore, teachers must be trained in this area.

Afro-Brazilian topics are now compulsory within the curriculum of elementary and middle schools. Law n. 10.639/2003 (Brasil, 2003) added two articles to the law establishing the directives and foundations in education: 26-A and 79-B. The first article establishes the teaching of Afro-Brazilian culture and history and determines that priority should be given to the study of the history of Africa and Africans, the struggle of Black people in Brazil, Brazilian Black culture and the role of Black people in the formation of the national society. The same article also determines that these should be taught as part of the school curriculum, and in particular, within Brazilian Art, Literature, and History. Article 79-B established National Black Awareness Day in the school calendar, commemorated on November 20 of each year. However, the implementation of the law in all elementary and middle schools is only possible if there are enough trained teachers and appropriate educational material.

Indigenous School Education is based on an educational paradigm of respect for interculturality, multilingualism, and ethnicity. As teachers in their own communities, Indians themselves can formulate curricula; establish a spelling system for their mother tongues, produce teaching materials, and conduct anthropological research. Two universities in the country already offer graduation courses in indigenous teacher training (FUNAI). The School Census (INEP, 2006) showed that in indigenous schools there were 163,693 Indians enrolled at elementary school level. Of these students, 71.66% are between 10 and 15 years old.

The *Política Nacional de Educação Especial na Perspectiva Inclusiva* (National Policy for Special Education from an Inclusive Perspective) ensures the right to an education for Brazilian children and young adolescents with special educational needs (CNE/CEB, 2001). One of the aims of this new public policy is to guarantee regular schooling while at the same time providing out-of-school-hours specialized education. Educational guidelines for elementary school from first to eighth grades are found in *"Parâmetros Curriculares Nacionais: adaptações curriculares, estratégias para educação de alunos com necessidades especiais"* (National Curriculum Parameters: Curricular Adaptations, Strategies for the Education of Students With Special Needs) (MEC/SEESP, 2001).

RESEARCH

Current Research Topics

Current national research on young adolescence is being carried out in various fields of psychology. More precisely, major areas of investigation include educational, developmental, social, and health psychology. The main themes currently being investigated are practically the same as those studied between 1991 and 2002 (Arelaro, 2005). There has been, however, a greater concern with issues linked to young adolescent health, their family relations and with the development and validation of national instruments to measure cognitive, motivational, and socioemotional variables for this stage of development. It is also worth emphasizing the increase in theoretical studies and literature reviews in many of these fields.

Methodologies

More recently, regional and quantitative studies with large and more representative samples predominate in comparison with earlier research. There are a large number of studies based on convenience samples. There is a smaller amount of qualitative studies, as well as those based on mixed research designs. Likert-type scales, projective tests, open and closed questionnaires, open and semi-structured interviews, Cloze tests, WISC, WAIS, Rey figures, the discernment of fictitious propositions, games, natural observation, mathematical problems, and focus groups were the main tools used for gathering data in Brazilian research. Studies of descriptive-correlational design predominate, employing both descriptive and inferential statistical procedures.

One area which has recently grown in Brazil has been psychological assessment. Efforts have mainly focused on the construction of national assessment tools. More specifically, in relation to young adolescence, tools were produced and validated in various areas of psychology, above all in educational and clinical psychology. It could be said that all studies were based on regional samples with sizes appropriate to validation objectives. New tools are more sensitive to the national reality and demonstrate adequate psychometric properties. Indeed, they represent more reliable ways of assessing young adolescents which in turn contribute to advancements in the national body of knowledge about young adolescence. The following can be cited as examples of tools in the areas of school and educational psychology: learning motivation scales (Martinelli & Bartholomeu, 2007; Neves & Boruchovitch, 2007; Siqueira & Wechscher, 2006; Zenorini, 2007) and learning strategies scales (Boruchovitch et al., 2006; Joly, 2006; Oliveira, Santos & Boruchovitch, in press). Efforts are also being made to create tools to assess family relationships (Teixeira, Oliveira, & Wottrich, 2006) and professional guidance (Noronha, Santos, & Sisto, 2007).

Important Research Findings

There follows a general thematic synthesis of the main research results in relation to the most investigated psychosocial topics on young adolescence. The inclusion criteria adopted in the review included: studies had to encompass at least 1 year within the 10-15 age group; be published in one of the main national journals; be of significant scientific quality; and be in the areas of psychology and education during the 2002-2007 period. More precisely, results on studies about street kids, young adolescence and violence, young adolescence and drugs and sexuality are briefly discussed. It is worth noting that the main results with regard to young adolescence and school have already been described on heading three in this chapter.

Street kids. As described in Bzuneck and Boruchovitch (2003), street kids are a special phenomenon which has arisen in the past few decades in all larger Brazilian cities. These are children or adolescents who spend most of their time on the streets when they should be at school or at home. Scholars have identified two distinct categories: those who actually live in the streets, and those who just prefer to spend most of their time there, often engaged in begging or in informal jobs. Although many of these street kids are linked to gangs and are easily involved with drug traffic, many are not really full-fledged thieves or criminals. Most actually have a home and family, and those who spend their time begging or working contribute with what they get to the family budget.

There has been less research about street kids and it concentrates on the following subjects: the meaning young adolescents attach to institutions which care for them (Santana, Doninelli, Frosi, & Koller, 2005); resilience issues regarding the life of a street kid (Paludo & Koller, 2005); social representations of social educators of young adolescent offenders about young adolescence (Espindula & Santos, 2004); the judgment of possible offenses hypothetical situations (Menin, 2003); increasing knowledge about the different types of street children (Martins, 2002); and the impact of an action research to improve social interaction among young adolescents, and between young adolescents and educators of social institutions (Santos & Bastos, 2002).

Results from these studies reveal that young adolescents see institutions as being very valuable for their lives, for providing food, leisure, professionalizing activities and basic care as well as social and emotional support (Santana et al., 2005). Individual characteristics and a support network were the factors which partly explained the resilience found in case study of a street kid (Paludo & Koller, 2005). Social educators revealed both normal and deviant representations of young adolescence, associated to disrupted homes and the belief that changes are not possible in the lives of these young people (Espindula & Santos, 2004). Middle class boys gave higher scores to hypothetical life-threatening offenses, while girls from more disadvantaged backgrounds were more likely to rate all types of offences higher (Menin, 2003). The research-action methodology was useful to improve social interaction amongst young adolescents, and between young adolescents and institution educators (Santos & Bastos, 2002). The cluster analysis was valuable to gain a greater knowledge of the different types of street children in a city in the interior of Brazil (Martins, 2002).

Violence and young adolescence. Violence in school is another topic which—despite limited research—has awakened the interest of a growing number of researchers. According to a study by Sposito (2002), violence takes on three forms within the school environment: vandalism, theft, and physical aggression between students and of students against teachers. The results of research in this field revealed that, dealing with situations by resorting to violent behavior is more common among boys who drive without a driving license, whereas coping strategies are more frequently used by people who, in general, are looking to relax, are part of groups and/or go out in pairs (Câmara, Sarriera, & Carlotto, 2007). Low self-esteem and poor relationships with their colleagues and teachers make students more likely to be victims of violence (Mariel, Assis, Avanci, & Oliveira, 2006).

Regardless of the type of school, public or private, young adolescents considered that futile and silly things could be causes of violence. Both groups pointed to drugs and alcohol as major causal factors of violence and saw school more as a place to socialize than to study. Moreover, young adolescents from public schools also attributed violence to social inequality, money, power and the lack of activities for young people (Gomes et al., 2006).

Dramatization, moral dilemmas and group dynamics proved to be useful techniques in helping and empowering teachers to deal with and combat violent behaviors of young adolescents from deprived schools areas (Gonçalves, Piovesan, Link, Prestes & Lisboa 2005).

Young adolescence and the family. Forms of communication between parents and children and their association to psychosocial problems predominated among research that focused on the relationship of young adolescents with their families. Young adolescents considered good family communication to be essential. The mother is the person they most turned to for conversation and she was seen as the main caregiver (Wagner, Falckle, Silveira, & Mosmann 2002) and better at communicating and participating than fathers (Cia, Pamplim, & Del Prette, 2006). Good participation and communication in the family was positively associated with students´ social skills and negatively associated with externalizing behavior and with anti-social behavior (Cia et al., 2006; Gomide et al., 2003). Lack of family support was also associated to learning difficulties in a study by Ferreira and Marturano (2002). Lack of dialogue was identified as the main modality of family communication among female drug users (Pratta & Santos, 2007a).

Studies also evince that young adolescents had good communication skills to deal with their parents, being sensitive to their parents' moods and knowing when to choose the right moment to, for example, tell them about a low mark (Wagner, Carpenede, Melo & Silveira, 2005). Watching TV at meal times was the choice of many young adolescents and was found to be an impediment to communication between parents and children according to a study by Gomide, Bussadori, Sabbag, and Furtado (2003).

Literature in relation to young adolescence and the family seems to be conclusive with regard to the family characteristics which best promote the development of young adolescents. Parents who encourage their children to think carefully about their problems before making decisions, who encourage them to participate in family decisions, who offer to help their children when they need or when they show low achievement at school, who have leisure time to spend with their children and who encourage studying contribute toward the development of healthy young adolescents.

Young adolescence and drugs. There have been some important studies conducted in Brazil about the use of drugs amongst students. The *Centro Brasileiro de Informações sobre Drogas Psicotrópicas*—CEBRID (Brazilian Center for Information on Psychotropic Drugs) is a reference in this area. CEBRID conducted the 5th National Survey on the use of psychotropic drugs amongst public elementary and middle school students in the 27 Brazilian capitals. It included 48,155 students between the ages of 10 and 18 (Galduróz, Noto, Fonseca, & Carlini, 2004). Data obtained revealed that 22.6% of the participants said that they had used drugs at least once in their lives—"life use," and 2.3% declared "heavy use" (with the exception of alcohol and tobacco). It can be noted that 12.7% of young adolescents start using drugs between the ages of 10 and 12. The most widely used drugs were, in order: legal drugs—alcohol and tobacco; drugs legally available but used illicitly (solvents, anxiolytics, and amphetamines); and finally illegal drugs, such as marijuana and cocaine.

The results of the CEBRID study indicated that alcohol and tobacco started to be consumed at 12.5 years. Marijuana was the main illegal drug. "First use" occurs at 13.9 years. Referring specifically to the 10 to 15 age group, results found in the epidemiological study regarding consumption rates were as follows: alcohol—55.35%; tobacco—15.85%; solvents—13.4%; energetic drinks—8.55%; amphetamines—2.8%; anxiolytics—2.8%; anticholinergics—1.05%; marijuana—2.25%; cocaine—0.95%; crack—0.4% (Fonseca, 2006; Galduróz et al., 2004).

Some studies provided additional data to the understanding of drug misuse among students. Results showed that psychotropic drugs were obtained first of all through friends, followed by traffickers, pharmacies and family relations (Fonseca, 2002). Abramovay and Castro (2002) report that drug use and low school achievement are related. There is a discrepancy between school grade level and age amongst users who are more likely to be involved in school problems than are their non-user counterparts (Rigoni, Oliveira, Moraes, & Zambon, 2007). Differences in leisure activities between users and nonusers also emerged. While users were more prone to going to clubs and beaches, going out with friends and going to bars, non-users were more likely to go to church/religious services, practicing sports and going out with the family (Pratta & Santos, 2007b).

Young adolescence and sexuality. It can be said that research in this area is mainly focused on the study of representations about sexually transmitted diseases (STDs) and the detailing and assessment of programs aimed at promoting the development of a healthy sexual life among young adolescents (Camargo, Bárbara, & Bertoldo, 2007; Lira & Dimenstain, 2004; Maheirie, Urnau, Vavassori, Orlandini, & Baierle, 2005). Though less linked to education of young adolescents, some research efforts concentrated in the study of representations about motherhood, fatherhood and sexual violence, as well as in the implementation and evaluation of prenatal care programs (Dias & Lopes, 2003; Levandowski & Piccinini, 2002; Rodrigues, Brino, & Williams, 2006; Silva & Salomão, 2003; Siqueira, Mendes, Finkler, & Gonçalves, 2002; Trindade & Menandro, 2002). The literature was slim on more specific aspects associated to the sexual and reproductive life of young adolescents.

Disease, death, fear, suffering, prejudice, prevention and responsibility were elements present in social representations of AIDS by students attending public middle schools. Lack of adequate knowledge of AIDS was also found (Camargo, Bárbara, & Bertoldo, 2007). Overall, young adolescents usually evaluate positively special programs devoted to discussing sexual themes (Lira & Dimenstain, 2004). Group dynamics and dramatizations of real life situations proved to be useful strategies for increasing participants´ information and awareness of the importance of engaging in sexual preventive behaviors (Maheirie et al., 2005).

Young adolescence, health and leisure. Some studies focused on young adolescent mental and/or physical health. Psychological violence, disturbed family relationships, life satisfaction, sexuality, drug abuse, low self-esteem and school achievement were found to be factors which can affect the health of young adolescents (Brasil, Alves, Amparo, & Frajorge, 2006).

According to Santos (2006), the analysis of medical records of children and young adolescents seen by a public psychology service revealed that the main complaints were related to aggression, learning difficulties, low frustration tolerance and/or difficulties in controlling impulses, and a lack of interest in school. Young adolescents between 13 and 15 who were behind at school were more likely to look for psychological services in general; their main complaint being problems relating to school (Schoen-Ferreira, Silva, Farias, & Silvares, 2002).

Intervention strategies directed toward the development of life skills for young adolescents based on group dynamics and weekly meetings evinced potential benefits for the improvement of psychosocial skills in young adolescence, contributing for both health promotion and an increase in the life quality of this age group (Minto, Pedro, Netto, Bugliani, & Gorayeb, 2006).

Sarriera, Tatim, Coelho, and Busker (2007) found that, during their free time young adolescents tended to do nonstructured activities such as watching TV and going out. They also had difficulty in having access to leisure, cultural and sporting activities. Günther, Nepomuceno, Spehar, and Günther (2003) investigated the favorite places of young adolescent residents in Brasília, the capital of Brazil. Homes, followed by going to shopping centers, were the most cited places. Bars, nightclubs, and parties were less mentioned by participants.

FUTURE DIRECTIONS

There is still little research in relation to more specific topics, such as student-teacher interactions, motivational beliefs, school drop out and students' grade retention, school violence, teacher education, and professional development. There is also a need to overcome a number of limitations inherent to earlier studies. For this reason, new research should more precisely address at least the following issues.

First, within the school context, an important research proposal would be to investigate the following topics which are relevant to educational praxis: how do teachers react to, and what are their expectations in relation to repeating students, or to those with learning difficulties in their classes? How are educational professionals dealing with repeating students, and conversely, what type of help is given to those who have been upgraded by a staff decision-making process? How do self-efficacy beliefs of repeating students rate? How do these students perceive emotional and instructional support from teachers and colleagues in relation to their learning and recuperation? Research which focuses on these topics has become even more urgent in view of the fact that there has been a return to the practice of failing students at every grade, which has leading to multiple repetitions. Also, in certain cases, at the end of the school year, a Class Council decides that some low achieving children should be upgraded. It is not known what criteria are being used when upgrading takes place. We therefore cannot discard the possibility that, in many cases, there is a certain amount of leniency, thus students will continue to under perform, and as a result group averages remain low.

Likewise, there has been very little research on the background and components of motivation and de-motivation of Brazilian young adolescents (Bzuneck & Boruchovitch, 2003; Lelis, 2005). Studies are few and far between, with small samples, lacking in continuity and integration, and sometimes without theoretical foundation. It is therefore suggested that the relationship between classroom and school environmental aspects and the perceptions, beliefs and behavior of young adolescents are studied in a more systematic way. In particular, it is worth expanding studies on which learning strategies—superficial or deep—are preferred by students for different subjects, and in relation to their motivational goals. Thus, significant progress in relation to studies about young adolescent motivation will occur when they are based on theories, such as achievement goals theory, self-determination theory, causal attribution theory, and expectancy-value theory. In relation to methodology, the use of self-report surveys—which have specific advantages—should be complemented with observational studies in the classroom, aiming to identify, for example, teacher-pupil interaction, pair interaction, and communication of expectations and feedback.

Finally, with regard to the teachers of young adolescents, there is a need for research on the effects of the professional development programs. It is necessary to investigate how far they have been effective, what improvements they have produced, and what still needs to be done. At present, therefore, it is worth concentrating on these areas of research.

CONCLUDING DISCUSSION

Despite the various limitations of Brazilian research on young adolescents, it can nevertheless provide useful information for the drafting of national public policies. However, as a prerequisite, it is necessary to bridge the gap which exists between those who build knowledge about specific Brazilian situations and those who work on the design and implementation of national public policies. According to Arelaro (2005), it seems that public organizations seldom request research for the purpose of guiding education policy; conversely, research is solicited to show the appropriateness of the decisions already made, even if the data do not support such decisions.

It is hoped that a greater approximation between researchers and those who draft public policies can lead to new ways of building the national body of knowledge about Brazilian young adolescents and how best to educate them, assisting in the development of national theories which can be representative of the Brazilian reality (Bzuneck & Boruchovitch, 2003).

Studies also point to the fact that, when faced with learning difficulties, teachers should take into consideration behavioral problems which are usually associated with them (Santos & Graminha, 2006). As problematical behavior can lead to anti-social behavior, it is important to take preventive actions aiming to promote social skills from the beginning of a student's schooling. Special attention should be given to certain groups such as boys and those from a low socio-economic background, since research indicates that they are target risk groups (Bandeira et al., 2006). Likewise, we highlight the importance of future research for a better understanding of the effects of non-intellective variables since they could be powerful risk or protection factors in the learning-teaching process.

If on the one hand it is clear that school is an essential context for changing the current scenario, on the other hand, it is also clear that it is unable to deal with current demands and issues, and needs to be strengthened through solid national public policies which—despite having improved significantly in recent years—still leave Brazil trailing in various aspects. Thus, there is much discussion about the need to view schools as a privileged space for social transformation and school culture as a potent source for establishing more egalitarian social relations.

According to Lelis (2005), it is possible that school is being displaced as a social and identity forming arena. Nowadays, it is clear that the media impacts on the way in which students relate to their time in and out of school. According to the author, it is necessary to break with the paradigm of the republican school, singularly centered on school-based knowledge, authority, and discipline. There is a need, therefore, to analyze the learning opportunities which exist outside school life, developing and increasing knowledge about the relationship between curriculum and schooling outside the model of traditional pedagogy.

School has an important role in the socialization of children and young adolescents, and it should take on the challenge of making society less violent. Câmara, Sarriera, and Carlotto (2007) defended the urgent need for public policies to prevent violence in schools. Violence has become the norm. There has been a growing involvement of young people in gangs, drug trafficking, sexual violence, prostitution, crime, thefts, and physical aggression.

Mariel et al. (2006) argued that professionals have limited capacity within schools to create fairer and more democratic mechanisms for managing school life. The low social status of teachers makes them undervalued in school. Teachers are not well prepared to deal with the disruptive behavior of students. The teacher-pupil relationship has been marred either by excessive leniency or abuse of power. The authoritarian attitude of teachers makes young adolescents shun a trusting relationship. There is a need, therefore, to deconstruct the concept of the strong teacher and the weak student, and to question schools as places where teachers manage classes and students obey. We need to move toward the establishment of trust pacts and a renewed belief in young people. According to Mariel et al. (2006), there is a need to focus on strengthening the self-esteem of students and the self-effectiveness of teachers. An important challenge would be for teachers to improve their skills so as to make use of conflict situations and help students to experience them as constructive, ethical and non-violent social interactions. Hence, it is the responsibility of the teacher to create educational situations where constructive social norms can be internalized by students. As Gonçalves et al. (2005) claimed, it is essential to use conflict situations as learning opportunities.

Castro and Abramovay (2002) argued that there are many situations and social structures which produce vulnerability and determine violent behavior. Improving the working conditions of the population can contribute toward moving young people away from violent situations.

Leisure can be a positive factor against violence. In Brazil there is a lack of leisure and cultural facilities for the young population, in particular for those living in poverty. Seventy-five percent of municipalities do not have a performance theater and 83% have no cinemas. There is also a lack of sport centers. Young people, in particular the poor, have few opportunities to enjoy cultural activities. The importance of leisure, sports, art, cultural and educational opportunities for citizens is indisputable. Sarriera et al. (2007) claimed that knowledge about the ways young adolescents manage their free time is a useful source of information for developing psychosocial interventions and for promoting the health of this population.

More specifically, with regard to the health of young adolescents, Avanci et al. (2007) highlighted the need to develop public policies with the purpose of promoting young adolescent health. According to Santos (2006), there is a need to rethink mental health public policies, in view of the increase in aggression, depression and difficulties at school during this stage of development. Drug prevention strategies should take into account the family and the strengthening of young people's future objectives (Pratta & Santos, 2007).

Gomide et al. (2003) highlighted the need for substantial improvement in family communication. Multiple forms of dealing with the psychosocial problems of young adolescents must be developed at various levels—institutional, interpersonal, and individual (Mariel et al., 2006; Pratta & Santos, 2007a). There is a need to invest in values which encourage a culture of peace, health prevention and promotion, ethics in communal life, the building of dignity and self-esteem and the right of the young adolescent to participate (Câmara et al., 2007; Castro & Abramovay, 2002; Mariel et al., 2006; Santos, 2006). There is also a strong need to develop specific public policies for young people, particularly in the areas of health, education, and the social development of Brazilian young adolescents.

REFERENCES

Abramovay, M., & Castro, M. (2002). *Drogas nas escolas*. Brasília, Brazil: UNESCO, Coordenação DST/AIDS do Ministério da Saúde, Secretaria do Estado dos Direitos Humanos do Ministério da Justiça, CNPq, Instituto Ayrton Sena, UNAIDS, Banco Mundial, USAID, Fundação Ford, CONSED, UNDIME.

Angelucci, C. B., Kalmus, J., Paparelli, R., & Patto, M. H. S. (2004). O estado da arte da pesquisa sobre o fracasso escolar (1991-2002): Um estudo introdutório. *Educação e Pesquisa, 30,* 51-72.

Arelaro, L. R G. (2005). O ensino fundamental no Brasil: Avanços, perplexidades e tendências . *Educação e Sociedade, 26,* 1039-1066.

Bandeira, M., Rocha, S. S., Souza, T. M. P., Del Prette, Z. A. P., & Del Prette, A. (2006). Comportamentos problemáticos em estudantes do ensino fundamental: características da ocorrência e relação com habilidades sociais e dificuldades de aprendizagem. *Estudos de Psicologia (Natal), 11*(2), 199-208.

Bonamino, A., Coscarelli, C., & Franco, C. (2002). Avaliação e letramento: concepções de aluno letrado subjacentes ao SAEB e ao PISA. *Educação e Sociedade, 23,* 91-113.

Boruchovitch, E. (2001). Algumas estratégias de compreensão em leitura de alunos do ensino fundamental. *Psicologia Escolar e Educacional, 5,* 19-35.

Boruchovitch, E., Santos, A. A. A., Costa, E. R., Neves, E. R. C., Cruvinel, M., Primi, R., et al. (2006). Estudo preliminar para construção de uma escala de estratégias de aprendizagem infantil. *Psicologia Teoria e Pesquisa, 22*(3), 297-304.

Brandão, Z., Mandelert, D., & De Paula, L. (2005). A circularidade virtuosa: Investigação sobre duas escolas no Rio de Janeiro. *Cadernos de Pesquisa, 35,* 747-758.

Brasil. (1961). *Lei No.4.024, de 20 de Dezembro de 1961. Fixa as Diretrizes e Bases da Educação Nacional.* Retrieved April 5, 2008, from http://www.histedbr.fae.uni-camp.br/navegando/fontes_escritas/6_Nacional_Desenvolvimento/1db   lei no.4.024,de 20 de dezembro de 1961.htm

Brasil. (1971). Lei No. 5.592, de 11 de Agosto de 1971. *Fixa Diretrizes e Bases para o ensino de 1° e 2° graus, e dá outras providências.* Retrieved April 5, 2008, from http://www.planalto.gov.br/Ccivil_03/Leis/L5692.htm

Brasil. (1996). *Lei No. 9.394, de 20 de Dezembro de 1996. Estabelece as bases da educação nacional e dá outras providências.* Retrieved April 5, 2008, from http://www.planalto.gov.br/ccivil_03/LEIS/L9394.htm

Brasil. (2001). *Lei No. 10.172 de 9 de janeiro de 2001. Plano Nacional de Educação.* Retrieved April 9, 2008, from http://www.planalto.gov.br/ccivil/LEIS/LEIS_2001/L1072.htm

Brasil. (2003). *Lei No.10.639, de 9 de Janeiro de 2003. Altera a Lei No. 9.394, de 20 de dezembro de 1996, que estabelece as diretrizes e bases da educação nacional e dá para incluir no currículo oficial da Rede de Ensino a obrigatoriedade da temática "história e Cultura Afro-Brasileira" e dá outras providências* Retrieved April 5, 2008, from http://www.planalto.gov.br/ccivil_03/revista/Rev_44/Leis.htm

Brasil. (2007). Instituto Nacional de Estudos e Pesquisas Educacionais INEP. *SAEB 2005: Primeiros Resultados.*

Brasil, K. T., Alves, P. B., Amparo, D. M., & Frajorge, K. C. (2006). Fatores de risco na adolescência: discutindo dados do DF. *Paidéia, 16*(35), 377-384.

Bzuneck, J. A., & Boruchovitch, E. (2003). Adolescence and education: Contemporary trend in Brazilian research. In F. Pajares & T. Urdan (Eds.), *International perspectives on adolescence* (pp. 215-236). Greenwich, CT: Information Age.

Camargo, B. V., Bárbara, A., & Bertoldo, R. B. (2007). Concepção pragmática e cientifica dos adolescentes sobre a AIDS . *Psicologia em Estudo, 12*(2), 277-284.

Carneiro, G. R., Martinelli, S. C., & Sisto, F. F. (2003). Autoconceito e dificuldade de aprendizagem em escrita. *Psicologia Reflexão e Crítica,16*(3), 427-434.

Carvalho, M. P. (2004). Quem são os meninos que fracassam na escola. *Cadernos de Pesquisa, 34*(121), 11-40.

Câmara, S. G., Sarriera, J. C., & Carlotto, M. S. (2007). Fatores associados a condutas de enfrentamento violento entre adolescentes escolares. *Estudos de Psicologia (Natal), 12*(3), 213-219.

Castro, M. G., & Abramovay, M. (2002). Jovens em situação de pobreza, vulnerabilidades sociais e violências. *Cadernos de Pesquisa, 116*, 143-176.

Cia, F., Pamplin, R. C. O., & Del Prette, Z. A. P. (2006). Comunicação e participação pais-filhos: correlação com habilidades sociais e problemas de comportamento dos filhos. *Paidéia, 16*(35), 395-406.

Conselho Nacional de Educação. Câmara de Educação Básica. (2001). *Resolução CNE/CEB Nº 2, de 11 de Fevereiro de 2001.* Retrieved May 20, 2008, from http://portal.mec.gov.br/seesp/arquivos/txt/res2.txt

Costa, E. R., & Boruchovitch, E. (2004). Compreendendo as relações entre estratégias de aprendizagem e ansiedade de alunos do ensino fundamental de Campinas. *Revista Psicologia Reflexão e Crítica, 17*(1), 15-24.

Cruvinel, M., & Boruchovitch, E. (2004). Sintomas depressivos, estratégias de aprendizagem e rendimento escolar de alunos do ensino fundamental. *Psicologia em Estudo, 9*(3), 369-378.

Datafolha. (2001). *Pesquisa Datafolha mostra crescimento do temor com desemprego.* Folha de S. Paulo.

Dias, A. C. G., & Lopes, R. C. S. (2003). Representações de maternidade de mães jovens e suas mães. *Psicologia em Estudo, 8*, 63-73.

Dias, T. L., Enumo, S. R. F., & Turini, F. A. (2006). Avaliação do desempenho acadêmico de alunos do ensino fundamental em Vitória, ES. *Estudos de Psicologia,* Campinas, *23*, 381-390.

Espíndula, D. H. P., & Santos, M. F. S. (2004). Representações sobre a adolescência a partir da ótica dos educadores sociais de adolescentes em conflito com a lei. *Psicologia em Estudo, 9*(3), 357-367.

Ferreira, M. C., Assmar, E. M. L., Omar, A. G., Delgado, H. U., González, A. T., Silva, J. M. B., et al. (2002). Atribuição de causalidade ao sucesso e fracasso escolar: Um estudo transcultural Brasil-Argentina-México. *Psicologia: Reflexão e Crítica, 15*(3), 515-527.

Ferreira, M. C., & Marturano, E. M. (2002). Ambiente familiar e os problemas de comportamento apresentados por crianças de baixo desempenho. *Psicologia Reflexão e Crítica, 15*(1), 35-44.

Fonseca, M. F. (2002). Aquisição de Drogas: Um estudo entre estudantes brasileiros. *Psico-USF, 7*(3), 147-56.

Fonseca, M. F. (2006). *Prevenção ao abuso de drogas na prática pedagógica dos professores do Ensino Fundamental.* Campinas. Tese de doutorado não publicada Universidade Estadual de Campinas, Faculdade de Educação.

Freitas, D. N. T. (2004). Avaliação da educação básica e ação normativa federal. *Cadernos de Pesquisa, 34*, 663-689.

Fundação Nacional do Índio. *Índios no Brasil.* Retrieved April 19, 2008, from http://www.funai.gov.br/indios/terras/conteudo.htm.

Galduróz, J. C., Noto, A. R., Fonseca, A. M., & Carlini, E. L. A. (2004). *V Levantamento sobre o uso de drogas entre estudantes do ensino fundamental e médio 27 capitais brasileiras.* São Paulo, Brazil: Centro de Informações sobre Drogas Psicotrópicas—CEBRID, Departamento de Psicobiologia da Escola Paulista de Medicina.

Glória, D. M. A. (2003). A "escola dos que passam sem saber": A prática da não-retenção escolar na narrativa de alunos e familiares. *Revista Brasileira de Educação, 22,* 61-76.

Gomes, C. A. (2005). Desseriação escolar: Alternativa para o sucesso?. *Ensaio: Avaliação e Políticas Públicas em Educação, 13,* 11-38.

Gomes, C. A., Valenzuela, C., Silva, C. N. N., Portugal, E. A., Amorim, H. C. C., Paim, J., et al. (2006). A violência na ótica de alunos adolescentes do Distrito Federal. *Cadernos de Pesquisa, 36*(127), 11-34.

Gomes, M. A. M., & Boruchovitch, E. (2005). Desempenho no jogo, estratégias de aprendizagem e compreensão na leitura. *Psicologia Teoria e Pesquisa, 21*(3), 319-326.

Gomide P. I. C, Bussadori, D. J., Sabbag, G. M., & Furtado, M. S. (2003). A influência da TV e dos estilos parentais nos horários de refeição das famílias. *Psicol Argum, 21*(32), 27-35.

Gonçalves, M. A. S., Piovesan, O. M., Link, A., & Lisboa, J. G. (2005). Violência na escola, práticas educativas e formação do professor. *Cadernos de Pesquisa, 35*(126), 635-658.

Günther, I. A., Nepomuceno, G. M., Spehar, M. C., & Günther, H. (2003). Lugares favoritos de adolescentes no Distrito Federal. *Estudos de Psicologia (Natal), 8*(2), 299-308.

Indicadores Sociais Educacionais Brasileiros. (2007). Programa Melhoria da Educação no Município. Retrieved May 13, 2008, from Centro de Estudos e Pesquisas Em Educação, Cultura e Açã Comunitária at http://www.cenpec.org.br/modules/home/

Instituto Nacional de Estudos e Pesquisas Educacionais Anísio Teixeira. (2004). *Relatório Nacional SAEB 2003.* Retrieved May 13, 2008, from Instituto Nacional de Estudos e Pesquisas Educacionais Anísio Teixeira at http://www.inep.gov.br/

Instituto Nacional De Estudos e Pesquisas Educacionais Anísio Teixeira. (2006). *Censo Escolar.* Retrieved May 2, 2008, from http://www.inep.gov.br/basica/censo/default.asp

Instituto Nacional de Estudos e Pesquisas Educacionais Anísio Teixeira. (2007). *SAEB 2005: Primeiros Resultados.* Retrieved May 13, 2008, from Instituto Nacional de Estudos e Pesquisas Educacionais Anísio Teixeira at http://www.inep.gov.br/

Instituto Brasileiro de Geografia e Estatística. (2000). *Censo 2000.* Retrieved May 11, 2008, from http://www.ibge.gov.br/censo

Instituto Brasileiro de Geografia e Estatística. (2007). *Contagem da população.* Retrieved May 11, 2008, from http://www.ibge.gov.br/home/estatistica/populacao/contagem2007/default.shtm

Instituto de Pesquisas Econômicas Aplicadas. (2007, February). *Políticas sociais—Acompanhamento e análise* (pp. 99-199). Retrieved May 2, 2008, from http://ppe.ipea.gov.br/index.php/

Ireland, V., Charlot, B., Gomes, C., Gusso, D., Carvalho, L. C. R., Fernandes, et al. (2007). *Repensando a Escola.* Brasília: UNESCO, MEC/INEP.

Joly, M. C. R. A. (2006). Escala de estratégias de leitura para etapa inicial do ensino fundamental. *Estudos de Psicologia (Campinas), 23*(3), 271-278.

Klein, R. (2006). Como está a educação no Brasil? O que fazer? *Ensaio: Avaliação e Políticas Públicas em Educação, 14,* 139-172.

Lelis, I. (2005). O significado da experiência escolar para segmentos das camadas médias. *Cadernos de Pesquisa, 35*(125), 137-160.

Levandowski, D. C., & Piccinini, C. A. (2002). A interação pai-bebê entre pais adolescentes e adultos. *Psicologia: Reflexão e Crítica, 15*(2), 413-424.

Lira, J. B., & Dimenstain, M. (2004). Adolescentes avaliando um projeto social em uma unidade básica de saúde. *Psicologia em Estudo, 9*(1), 37-45.

Locatelli, A. C. D., Bzuneck, J. A., & Guimarães, S. E. R. (2007). A motivação de adolescentes em relação com a perspectiva de tempo futuro. *Psicologia: Reflexão e Crítica, 20*(2), 268-276.

Loos, H. (2004). Ansiedade e aprendizagem: Um estudo com díades resolvendo problemas algébricos. *Estudos de Psicologia (Natal), 9*(3), 563-573.

Maheirie, K., Urnau, L. C. Vavassori, M. B., Orlandi, R., & Baierle, R. E. (2005). Oficinas sobre sexualidade com adolescentes: Um relato de experiência. *Psicologia em Estudo, 10*(3), 537-542.

Maia, A. C. B., & Fonseca, M. L. (2002). Quociente de inteligência e aquisição de leitura: Um estudo correlacional. *Psicologia: Reflexão e Crítica, 15*(2), 261-270.

Mainardes, J. (2006). Organização da escolaridade em ciclos no Brasil: Revisão da literatura e perspectivas para a pesquisa. *Educação e Pesquisa, 32,* 11-30.

Martinelli, S. C., Bartholomeu, D. (2007). Escala de motivação acadêmica: uma medida de motivação extrínseca e intrínseca. *Avaliação Psicológica, 6*(1) 21-31.

Mariel, L. C., Assis, S. G., Avanci, J. Q., & Oliveira, R. V. C. (2006). Violência escolar e auto-estima de adolescentes. *Cadernos de Pesquisa, 36*(127), 35-50.

Martins, R. A. (2002). Uma tipologia de crianças e adolescentes em situação de rua baseada na análise de aglomerados (Cluster Analysis). *Psicologia: Reflexão e Crítica, 15*(2), 251-260.

Menin, M. S. S. (2003). Atitudes de adolescentes frente à delinqüência como representações sociais. *Psicologia: Reflexão e Crítica, 16*(1), 125-135.

Ministério de Educação, Secretaria de Educação Fundamental. (1997). *Parâmetros Curriculares Nacionais.* Brasília: Author.

Ministério de Educação. Instituto Nacional De Estudos e Pesquisas Educacionais Anísio Teixeira. (2005). *Portaria nº 931, de 21 de Março de 2005.* Retrieved June 10, 2008, from http://www.inep.gov.br/download/saeb/2005/portarias/ Portaria931_NovoSaeb.pdf

Minto, E. C., Pedro, C. P., Netto, J. R. C., Bugliani, M. A. P., & Gorayeb, R.(2006). Ensino de habilidades de vida na escola: Uma experiência com adolescentes. *Psicologia em Estudo, 11*(3), 561-568.

Neves, E. R. C., & Boruchovitch, E. (2007). Escala de avaliação da motivação para aprender de alunos do ensino fundamental. *Psicologia: Reflexão e Crítica, 20*(3), 406-413.

Noronha, A. P., Santos, A. A. A., & Sisto, F. F. (2007). *Escala de aconselhamento profissional.* São Paulo: Vetor.

Oliveira, J. B. A. (2002). Correção do fluxo escolar: Um balanço do programa Acelera Brasil (1997-2000). *Cadernos de Pesquisa, 116,* 177-215.

Oliveira, K. L., Boruchovitch, E., & Santos, A. A. A. (2007). Compreensão de leitura em alunos de sétima e oitava séries do ensino fundamental. *Psicologia Escolar e Educacional, 11*(1), 41-49.

Oliveira, K. L., Boruchovitch, E., & Santos, A. A. (in press). Estratégias de aprendizagem e desempenho acadêmico no ensino fundamental: evidências de validade. Manuscript submitted for publication to *Psicologia Teoria e Pesquisa.*

Organization for Economic Cooperation and Development. (2004). *Learning for tomorrow's world: First results from PISA 2003.* Paris: Author.

Paludo, S. S., & Koller, S. H. (2005). Resiliência na rua: Um estudo de caso. *Psicologia: Teoria e Pesquisa, 21*(2), 187-195.

Pratta, E. M. M., & Santos, M. A. (2007a). Opiniões dos adolescentes do ensino médio sobre o relacionamento familiar e seus planos para o futuro. *Paidéia, 17*(36), 103-114.

Pratta, E. M. M., & Santos, M. A. (2007b). Lazer e uso de substâncias psicoativas na adolescência: possíveis relações. *Psicologia: Teoria e Pesquisa, 23*(1), 43-52.

Programa das Nações Unidas Para o Desenvolvimento. (2003). *Atlas do Desenvolvimento Humano no Brasil—2003.* Retrieved May 4, 2008, from http://www.pnud.org.br/atlas

Programa das Nações Unidas para o Desenvolvimento—PNUD. (2005). *Índice de Desenvolvimento Humano.* Retrieved June 2, 2008, from http://www.pnud.org.br/idh/

Rigoni, M. S., Oliveira, M. S., Moraes, J. F. D., & Zambom, L. F. (2007). O consumo de maconha na adolescência e as conseqüências nas funções cognitivas. *Psicologia em Estudo, 12*(2), 267-275.

Rodrigues, J. L., Brino, R. F., & Williams, L. C. A. (2006). Concepções de sexualidade entre adolescentes com e sem histórico de violência sexual. *Paidéia, 16*(34), 229-240.

Santana, J. P., Doninelli, T. M., Frosi, R. V., & Koller, S. H. (2005). Os adolescentes em situação de rua e as instituições de atendimento: Utilizações e reconhecimento de objetivos. *Psicologia: Reflexão e Crítica, 18*(1), 134-142.

Santos, M. F., & Bastos, A. C. S. (2002). Padrões de interação entre adolescentes e educadores num espaço institucional: Resignificando trajetórias de risco. *Psicologia: Reflexão e Crítica, 15*(1), 45-52.

Santos, P. L. (2006). Problemas de saúde mental de crianças e adolescentes atendidos em um serviço público de psicologia infantil. *Psicologia em Estudo, 11*(2), 315-321.

Santos, P. L., & Graminha, S. S. V. (2006). Problemas emocionais e comportamentais associados ao baixo rendimento acadêmico. *Estudos de Psicologia (Natal), 11*(1), 101-109.

Sarriera, J. C., Tatim, D. C., Coelho, R. P. S., & Büsker, J. (2007). Uso do tempo livre por adolescentes de classe popular. *Psicologia: Reflexão e Crítica, 20*(3), 361-367.

Schoen-Ferreira, T. H., Silva, D. A., Farias, M. A., & Silvares, E. F. M. (2002). Perfil e principais queixas dos clientes encaminhados ao Centro de Atendimento e Apoio Psicológico ao Adolescente (CAAA)–UNIFESP/EPM. *Psicologia em Estudo, 7*(2), 73-82.

Silva, D. V., & Salomão, N. M. R. (2003). A maternidade na perspectiva de mães adolescentes e avós maternas dos bebês. *Estudos de Psicologia (Natal), 8*(1), 135-145.

Siqueira, L. G. G., & Wechsler, S. M. (2006). Motivação para a aprendizagem escolar: Possibilidade de medida. *Avaliação Psicológica, 5*(1), 21-31.

Siqueira, M. J. T., Mendes, D. Finkler, I., Guedes, T., & Gonçalves, M. D. S. (2002). Profissionais e usuárias (os) adolescentes de quatro programas públicos de atendimento pré-natal da região da grande Florianópolis: Onde está o pai?. *Estudos de Psicologia (Natal), 7*(1), 65-72.

Soares, J. F. (2007). Melhoria do desempenho cognitivo dos alunos do ensino fundamental. *Cadernos de Pesquisa, 37*, 135-160.

Souza, S. M. Z. L. (2003). Possíveis impactos das políticas de avaliação no currículo escolar. *Cadernos de Pesquisa, 119*, 175-190.

Sposito, M. P. (2002). As vicissitudes das políticas públicas de redução da violência escolar. In M. F. Westphal (Ed.), *Violência e criança* (pp. 249-266). São Paulo, Brazil: Edusp.

Teixeira, M. A. P., Oliveira, A.M., & Wottrich, S. H. (2006). Escalas de práticas parentais (EPP): Avaliando dimensões de práticas parentais. *Psicologia Reflexão e Crítica, 19*(3), 433-441.

Trindade, Z. A., & Menandro, M. C. S. (2002). Pais adolescentes: vivência e significação. *Estudos de Psicologia (Natal), 7*(1), 15-23.

Valente, A. L. (2003). O Programa Nacional de Bolsa Escola e as ações afirmativas no campo educacional. *Revista Brasileira de Educação, 24*, 166-182.

Viecili, J., & Medeiros, J. G. (2002). A coerção e suas implicações na relação professor-aluno. *PsicoUSF, 7*(2), 229-238.

Viégas, L. S., & Souza, M. P. R. (2006). A Progressão continuada no estado de São Paulo. *Psicologia Escolar e Educacional, 10*(2), 247-262.

Wagner, A., Carpenedo, C., Melo, L. P., & Silveira, P. G. (2005). Estratégias de comunicação familiar: a perspectiva dos filhos adolescentes. *Psicologia: Reflexão e Crítica, 18*(2), 277-282.

Wagner, A., Falcke, D., Silveira, L. M. B. O., & Mosmann, C. P. (2002). A comunicação em famílias com filhos adolescentes. *Psicologia em Estudo, 7*(1), 75-80.

Zenorine, R. da P. C. (2007). Estudos para a construção de uma escala de avaliação da motivação para aprendizagem—EMAPRE. Tese de Doutorado, Universidade São Francisco, Itatiba.

CHAPTER 15

CONCLUDING THOUGHTS

Tying it All Together With a Comparative Look at the Education of Young Adolescents

Vincent A. Anfara, Jr., Steven B. Mertens, and Kathleen Roney

INTRODUCTION

It has been noted that formal education (i.e., schooling) is the most commonly found institution and the most commonly shared experience in the contemporary world (Dale & Robertson, 2003). It is not surprising that in an increasingly international world, characterized by a "knowledge economy," that the relative success of national educational systems has become an explicit concern of policymakers. Specifically, policymakers are focused on their country's production of human capital which significantly contributes to the civic and economic development of the country and, ultimately, to that country's ability to be globally competitive.

Policymakers are becoming increasingly concerned with national standards as reported in the international comparisons of student achievement (e.g., Trends in Mathematics and Science Study [TIMSS] and Programme for International Student Assessment [PISA]). Rightly or wrongly, there is a widespread international assumption that those coun-

An International Look at Educating Young Adolescents
pp. 345–389

tries with the most "successful" education systems (i.e., defined as a high ranking on the international comparisons) will forge ahead in the global economy of this postmanufacturing age. In short, it is believed that the means must be found to encourage (require, force, or even cajole) students to learn more and to do so in more efficient and effective ways. As a consequence of this, there has been a tendency to want to borrow policies and practices that appear to be effective in producing high academic performance on tests like TIMSS and PISA.

In this final chapter, we offer a comparative analysis of the education of young adolescents in the 14 countries presented in this volume. We commence this chapter by highlighting three major themes in the education of young adolescents across nations: (a) the growing realization that schooling should respond to the needs of young adolescents, (b) the necessity of understanding the role that context (cultural, political, economic) plays in schooling, and (c) the role of educational discourse in relation to the goals or purposes of schooling. Taking these three themes a step further, we believe that in responding to young adolescents' developmental needs, the cultural contexts, and the goals as stated in educational discourse, that countries are creating organizational and structural arrangements, along with revisions to curriculum, instruction, and assessment that have contributed to an appearance of "sameness" in the essential components of schooling for young adolescents across the world.

This final chapter, then, will examine these three themes and this issue of sameness, the "homogenization" of the education of young adolescents. It needs to be recognized that the analysis presented in this concluding chapter is based solely on the information contained in each of the chapters. The editors of this book (also authors of this concluding chapter) were, therefore, limited to the information presented by each chapter author and relied on the accuracy and completeness of what was reported.

RESPONSIVENESS TO DEVELOPMENTAL NEEDS

The first theme that is evident is the remarkable realization that teacher-directed/dominated instruction and rote memorization are not producing the desired educational results. Addressing this issue in the context of an international education environment, Rudduck and Flutter (2000) suggested that "Teachers are very aware of the difficulties of engaging all pupils in learning and know that schools have changed less in their deep structures in the past 20 or 30 years than young people have changed" (p. 86). Indeed, from the various chapters presented in this volume of the *Handbook of Middle Level Education Research* series, it seems that students are less and less content to be passive recipients of learning. Like workers who are more productive when they are active participants and understand their role in the overall process, so students need to be actively engaged. As Goleman (1996, cited in Broadfoot, 2001) stated so well,

> After more than a century in which educational theory has tended to assume that it is an individual's cognitive ability—often called their intelligence—that determines their potential to learn, it is now finally being recognized that learning dispositions, that combine both cognitive and affective dimensions, are of crucial importance in this respect just as they are in the successful execution of workplace roles. (p. 264)

Confidence, motivation, perseverance, and self-esteem, among other qualities, are all beginning to be seriously considered in the international context as key components in successful learning. As Broadfoot (2001) noted, we must shift the "focus of research concern away from the factors that influence the ability to learn and towards those that impact the desire to learn" (p. 264).

This first theme speaks clearly to the need for schools to respond to the needs of young adolescent students across the world. Those of us who are familiar with *This We Believe: Successful Schools for Young Adolescents* (National Middle School Association, 2003) and *Turning Points* (Carnegie Council on Adolescent Development, 1989) are familiar with the importance of developmental responsiveness in creating learning environments for young adolescents. There is, likewise, a list of other publications (e.g., National Association of Secondary School Principals's *Breaking Ranks in the Middle*, 2006) which support this fundamental tenet of the middle school concept. We hold, though, that more research from an international and comparative perspective needs to be conducted which focuses on addressing the developmental needs of learners across the contexts of multiple nations. Numerous questions surface, including: Are the tenets of the middle school philosophy that are consistently agreed on by all of the major American players (e.g., National Middle School Association, National Association of Secondary School Principals, Association for Supervision and Curriculum Development, Carnegie Corporation, the National Forum to Accelerate Middle-Grades Reform) now taking on some degree of international importance? Do the tenets of the middle school philosophy withstand scrutiny and application in a global context?

If nothing else, the comparative analysis attempted in this concluding chapter, and the research we desire to see conducted, can provide "the kind of critical reflection that may move the field [of middle level education both nationally and internationally] forward in new directions" (Virtue, this volume, p. xx). There is no argument that the "knowledge base in middle level education is built on a foundation of research conducted in the United States and elsewhere in the English-speaking world. [But] the field ... needs to embrace diverse perspectives and alternative ways of knowing if it is transcend Anglophonic parochialism and achieve relevance abroad" (Virtue, p. xx).

CULTURAL CONTEXT

The second theme deals with cultural context. The way in which individual pupils, needs, interests, and abilities interrelate with, and are affected by, the various sociocultural settings students experience at home, at school, and in their peer group is still relatively poorly understood, though their significance is increasingly being recognized. Recent research in comparative education has emphasized the importance of these contextual components. Indeed, in any educational setting, there is a complex network of contextual factors at work. These include factors associated with the students' "learning biography," teachers' understandings and professional priorities, the ethos and structure of the particular classroom and larger institution in which schooling takes place, and the culture and policy priorities that characterize any given country. According to Broadfoot (2001),

> The importance of the relationship between national context, institutional ethos and particular classroom practices in mediating the development of a learner's identity is now increasingly being recognized by comparativists (e.g., Elliott et al., 1999) as a means of explaining the significant variations in national levels of achievement which have been revealed by the series of international comparative tests. The essence of this involves exposing or illuminating the "black box" of the classroom and school as well as more fully understanding the experiences and attitudes of the students themselves. (p. 261)

In an attempt to capture the rich network of cultural elements (see the first section of each chapter in this volume), we present Table 15.1 (contextual narrative) which focuses on the following four areas: (1) religious influence; (2) cultural context—social forces; (3) political and economic forces; and (4) education, writ large, from policy to issues of practice.

Chapter authors were asked to set the stage for their readers by providing information about their country and its significant cultural norms and issues, including issues like the role of women, compulsory education, infant mortality, illiteracy, population migration, religious issues, location/geography, individualist/competitive versus collectivist/cooperation beliefs, economic well-being, and other social issues deemed to be critical to understanding the education system. We noted some similarities and differences across the countries with regard to the cultural context.

Table 15.1. An Overview of Contextual Narrative

Country	Religious Influence	Cultural Context—Social Forces	Political and Economic Forces	Education
Australia	• Catholic/Christian (48%) • non-Christian (5%) • no religion (16%)	• Foreign-born population • 92% Caucasians; 2% aboriginal • Extensive social welfare system		• 85% literacy rate • State's responsibility • Compulsory to age 15 or 16, depending on the state • Recent move to nationalize core curriculum
Brazil	• Catholic majority; Protestantism, Spiritism, Islam, Judaism coexist	• Multiracial	• Largest economy in South America, 8th largest in world • 30% living in poverty • Gender equality is a fundamental right (since 1988), however, women are less likely to be employed	• Educational inequalities exist—e.g., illiteracy rate among White and Black population
China		• Family planning policy—2 children per family • Dramatic increase in aging and life expectancy—results in housing, health care, retirement income, care giving challenges	• State established—1949 • Single-party system (Communist) • Long-running dispute over political status of Taiwan • Industrialization leads to increased environmental challenges—water and air quality • A global manufacturing power • Large research and development • Most populous country in the world • Growing economy, but widening rural-urban economic gap	• Goal is to educate all the people of China • 17% illiteracy rate

(Table continues on next page)

Table 15.1. (Continued)

Country	Religious Influence	Cultural Context—Social Forces	Political and Economic Forces	Education
Germany	• Catholics and Protestants (60%) • No church affiliation (30%) • Islam—4%		• Liberal market system	• A state responsibility for the most part
India		• Familial preferences for males keeps girls illiterate • Caste system determines occupation, education, and interactions	• World's largest democracy • War-torn over boundary issues • On cutting edge of science and technology • Immense poverty • A regional superpower • Second most populous nation in the world	• Education is the bastion of the elite • Government is beginning to provide basic education for all its children • Free and universal primary education
Ireland	• Catholic	• Increase in immigrants to Ireland from outside EEC	• 1973 admission into the European Economic Union • Strong economic growth since 1990s • Increasing number of women in workforce	
Lebanon	• Muslim and Christian	• Arabic country • Highest % of females in work force in Arab world • Lack social progress • Mass emigrations • Male births are preferred • Gender inequality perpetuates	• Confessional distribution of power • Religious courts control personal status laws • Recovering from 15-year civil war (1975-1990) • Recent political violence and instability • 60% earn under $800 per month • Lack economic development	• Highest literacy rate • Compulsory and free Grades 1 - 8 • No gender differences in attendance or completion of primary school • Gender equality in access to basic education

New Zealand	• Christianity played role in shaping education, but less so today	• Bicultural becoming multicultural due to flow of immigrants	• Social democracy • Agricultural, tourism, and service industries dominates economy • First county to adopt universal suffrage for men and women • High percent of women in government leadership roles	• State school system predominates • Private state-integrated church-aligned schools co-exist • 99% literacy rate
Russia	• Christianity (Russian Orthodox)	• Recent decrease in immigration • Although better educated, women are minority in senior management positions	• Move from strict totalitarianism • Official documents claim equal rights for men and women	• Highly centralized • Obligatory and free ages 6-18
Rwanda	• Descended from Catholic and Protestant religions (93%) • Muslim (4%)	• Two ethnic groups/tribes • Extended family support system in family compounds • 60% below poverty line • Females face gender-based violence and consequence of HIV infection	• Independence: July 1, 1962 • Following 1994 genocide, caution and fear prevail • World's highest rate of female parliamentarians • Labor-intensive work for females	• Gender equality in primary school • Compulsory and free education at primary level • Inequitable literacy and drop-out rates between males and females • 74:1 pupil/qualified teacher ratio
South Africa			• Apartheid legislation	• Two (unofficial) systems: white and black middle class children; majority of South African working class poor children

(Table continues on next page)

Table 15.1. (Continued)

Country	Religious Influence	Cultural Context—Social Forces	Political and Economic Forces	Education
South Korea	• Confucianism	• Internet service and broadband items are household items • Lack of natural resources prompts dependence on human resources	• Remarkable economic growth reliant on scientific and technical manpower • Major products are information and technology • Goal: To be one of the strongest IT societies in the world	• Academic elitism • Emphasis on gifted children programs in science and math • Extensive use of private tutoring organizations
Turkey	• Secular country—99% Muslim • Christianity and Judaism free to practice	• Patriarchal family units • High context and indirect society • Gender equality before the law is not reflected in workforce practices nor participating in governmental processes	• Recent economic growth	• Mandated religious courses start at 4th grade; non-Muslims are exempt • High illiteracy rates differ by region and gender • Overall educational level is low • Compulsory education in primary school (Grades 1-8)
United Arab Emirates	• Muslim religion is requirement for citizenship • Traditional Muslim costume worn	• Tribal nation • Women in the workforce challenges division of labor in household • Extended family live in large homes, sometimes walled-in compounds • Unequal roles for boys and girls	• Young country—1971 • Tribal leaders • Provides low-cost excellent health care • Subsidizes dowry and child costs • Positioning for global presence in the marketplace • High standard of living for nationals	• Free education • Compulsory for boys and girls through Grade 9

In addressing religious issues we found that except for three, the authors contextualized the education of young adolescents within a faith-based tradition. Some commented that religion played an important role in the early days of education in their country and updated us on the movement today away from religious influence over schooling (Germany, New Zealand). Social factors of note include gender issues. For example, we read that families contribute to the process of fostering illiteracy among girls (India), gender inequality prevails (Lebanon, Turkey, United Arab Emirates), male births are preferred (India, Lebanon), and an increase of women in the workforce is happening (Ireland, Lebanon). Likewise, authors commented about immigration—while Russia is experiencing a recent decrease in immigration, New Zealand and Ireland are experiencing increases in immigrants to their countries.

Political and economic forces were found across countries. Thirty percent of the population is living in poverty in Brazil, India reports immense poverty, and 60% earn under $800 per month in Lebanon. On the other hand, economic growth is also noted. While China is positioning itself as a global manufacturing power, India, Ireland and South Korea view themselves as on the cutting edge in science and technology. Tourism and service industries dominate the economy in New Zealand. Sadly, recent wars and political unrest are reported by China, India, Lebanon, Rwanda, and South Africa.

Finally, in providing the contextual narrative authors offered general comments about education in their countries. Education is provided free by the government and is compulsory for students in Russia; in India, Rwanda, and Turkey it is compulsory for primary grades; in Lebanon for first to eighth grades, and in Australia and the United Arab Emirates through grade nine. Literacy rates are reported by Australia, China, Lebanon, New Zealand, Rwanda, and Turkey.

HISTORY AND ORGANIZATION OF
SCHOOLING FOR YOUNG ADOLESCENTS

Focusing on the history of educating young adolescents (ages 10-15) in their countries, authors were asked to describe what the schooling of young adolescents is like—what kinds of curricula, instructional practices, and assessment systems exist or are supposed to exist? How are schools organized to educate young adolescents? What organizational structures and teaching practices are found in schools dedicated to teaching young adolescents? Table 15.2 provides a snapshot of what is found within each chapter regarding the (a) historical background, (b) curriculum, (c) instruction, (d) assessment practices, and (e) organization and structure of schools for young adolescents.

Table 15.2. An Overview of the History and Organization of Schooling for Young Adolescents

Country	Historical Background	Curriculum	Instruction	Assessment Practices	Organization and Structure
Australia	• Churches and individuals establish first schools in early nineteenth century • Dual system of government funded church/denominational schools and national schools are created in mid-nineteenth century • Schooling becomes compulsory for ages 6-15 by mid-twentieth century • Recent emergence of nondenominational, low-fee paying private Christian schools	• 11 core subjects • Specify range of outcomes; provide framework to achieve outcomes; recognize and accommodate diversity	• Cater to developmental and social challenges of young adolescents: outcomes based, • Students move between classes taught by subject area specialist teachers	• School-based (teacher-made), state-based (at completion of Years 9 & 10), and national (at Years 3, 5, 7, & 9)	• Three to 4 years of compulsory junior secondary schooling (Years 7–10) • Dedicated middle schools exist with K-12 in private, increasing number in public sector • 40-80 minute blocks of instructions (periods)
Brazil	• Education benefited the ruling class • 19020s new educational ethos established • State's role in education—expansion of teaching and quality of public schools • Parallel educational system established for purpose of producing qualified work force • 1971 affirmed compulsory and free education ages 7-14	• National Curriculum Parameters—benchmarks for elementary and middle schools • Transversal Themes—address current issues	• Attends to bio-psycho-social characteristics of young adolescents	• Basic Education Assessment System samples fourth and eighth grade elementary grades and third grade of middle school • Exams in Portuguese and math with emphasis on reading and problem-solving • Standardized tests and socioeconomic questionnaires	• Ages 10-15 attend fourth to eight grade of elementary school and first grade of middle school

China	• Indigenous educations system ended in mid-nineteenth century; infiltration of foreign missionaries establishing missionary schools • Experimented with various approaches to education in early twentieth century • Creation of People's Republic of China and Chinese communists take power—Marxist views influence a standard body of intellectual knowledge in mid-twentieth century • Vacuum for criticism and creativity	• Centralized, encyclopedist tradition • Textbooks and teaching materials approved by State • 13 basic studies	• Long rows of desks bolted to the floor • Teacher-focused, prescribed and undisputed prepare students for examinations • Recent move to quality-oriented education, using such models as inquiry learning, cooperative learning		• Three-level, basic nine-year compulsory education system: primary (6 years), junior-senior middle schools (3 years) • Junior/lower middle schools (begin at 1-12 years of age) • Class size: 40–50 students • Two semesters totaling 9 months
Germany	• Eighth century schools served religious purposes • Middle ages education became compulsory • Nineteenth century a stratified school system was established, along with teacher training institutes • Twentieth century formation of Federal Republic to direct federal states to set educational policy and prevents strong central power	• Few choices regarding 12	• Varies according to track of schooling—lower track uses real-world examples, does not required theory; secondary modern resembles lower track, but with theory attached; highest level proofs and insight are important, less real-world examples are used • Teacher move from class to class for 45-minute classes	• Semester report cards distributed • Three to four written tests in core subjects each semester • No multiple choice tests	• Middle school students tracked according to learning ability: practical and less academic abilities, secondary modern, Gymnasium/highest track, and comprehensive school • 24:7 average middle school class size • Children with severe handicaps or learning disorders attend special needs schools • Ministry of Education creates framing guidelines for teacher training • August-July with 12 weeks of holiday throughout the year

(Table continues on next page)

Table 15.2. (Continued)

Country	Historical Background	Curriculum	Instruction	Assessment Practices	Organization and Structure
India	• Focus on collective vs. individual • Resistant to the category of young adolescence in human development • Late twentieth century campaign to improve education, including teacher training	• Set by board • Ten mandatory subjects, optional subjects include computer science, home economics, and business management, among others	• Language of instruction differs from school to school (English, Hindi) • Focused on student's ability to reproduce facts and information • Textbook driven	• Determined by board • Year-end high stakes testing/examinations—2 hour essays every subject—graded by teachers • Class 10 exam assesses 3 years of cumulated material over a 10-14-day period—graded by out-of-school subject area teachers	• States provide free and compulsory education under age 14 • Ages 10-15 fall into upper primary and secondary school systems (Classes 5 through 10) • Private schooling is available
Ireland	• Roots in British colonial history differentiated by gender • Hedge schools illegally educated Catholics • Religious patrons established secondary schools • Current system is collaborative—state controls curricula, assessment, management, staffing, organization and facilities; immediate management controlled by managing bodies • Strong religious influence being replaced by secular influence • Introduction of Transition Year Programme (TYP)	• Literary- and humanities-based • Compulsory (academic) and non-compulsory (art, languages), courses • Guidelines set by Department of Education and Science for TYP syllabi • Hidden curriculum focuses on development of individual potential	• JCSP necessitates flexibility in student-centered teaching methodologies • TYP offers extra-curricular options to Junior Cycle	• Junior Cycle of three years begins at age 11 or 12 • Junior Certificate Exam accredited by State Examinations Commission • TYP reports include variety of recommended instruments	• Two levels: primary (ages 4-11); secondary (ages 12-17) • Junior Certificate School Programme (JCSP) introduced as alternative to Junior Cycle and targets potential drop-outs • Trend toward mixed-gendered education

Lebanon	• Public education system resembles French system • Three types of schools: public schools operated by Lebanese government; subsidized private religious schools (Lebanese run); private school, not subsidized	• Centralized by Ministry of Education • Focus on seven core subjects and four optional subjects • Disparities exist among public schools	• French is official language for education	• Includes 12 years for 6-18-year-old students: elementary (6 years), 3-year middle/intermediate cycle (Grades 7–9) • Secondary education includes a three year cycle (ages 15-18) • Vocational track is available at middle level
New Zealand	• Unique pedagogy for middle schooling not historically recognized • Experiment of Nelson Central School for years 5-9 finished in 1911 • Junior highs developed in 1922 • Intermediate schools came about in 1932 through government legislation but ended in 1957 • Recent political struggle concerning type of school structure for young adolescents • Official documents reflect increasingly robust discourse concerning developmental needs of young adolescents	• Integrated designs	• Years 7-8 delivered by primary teachers; years 9-10 delivered by secondary teachers	• Compulsory from ages 6-16 • Two-tiered structure: primary years 1-8, ending with intermediate school, and secondary, 9-13 • 83% years 7-8 educated in full primary and intermediate schools

(Table continues on next page)

Table 15.2. (Continued)

Country	Historical Background	Curriculum	Instruction	Assessment Practices	Organization and Structure
Russia	• Five periods: • religious schools focused on reading and writing religious books and orthodox services • government schools served interest of tsar government • public education implement different pedagogical approaches • Soviet based on strict communist ideology • Post-Soviet compulsory education	• Focus on humanitarian and scientific knowledge			• Preprofessional specializations for middle and high school levels
Rwanda	• Roots in Belgian colonial period—paternalistic • Roots in Rwandan history after 1962 independence—government sponsored • Christian Mission primary schools (Grades 1-8) served affluent Rwandans • Private schools created by Rwandan families	• Similar to Belgian curriculum, i.e., all students follow same academic preparation • Content determined and created by government • Second phase at secondary level provides professional career/vocational curriculum	• Dependent on resources, e.g., books, electricity, technology • Homework assigned according to availability of resources • Teacher lecture with some Q/A • Teachers circulate for 60-minute class periods • School administrators evaluate teacher quality	• Teacher-made assessments • State exams determine move from level to next • State exams are evaluated holistically by two educators	• Two levels: primary (Grades 1-6), secondary (7-12) • Academic courses taught to young adolescents in first three years of secondary level • School day: 7:30 a.m.- 4:30 P.M., with break for lunch

South Africa	• 1948 Nationalist government introduced Bantu Education to prepare natives for life in designated tribal areas with limited infrastructure and work opportunities • Twentieth century apartheid is national policy; Nationalist government took over teacher education • Late-twentieth century uprising against collapses schooling	• Fundamental Pedagogics—a series of propositions that brooked no analysis or critique, dominated apartheid years	• Learner-centered classroom practices • English was adopted as language of instruction	• Primary, senior primary (ages 9-12) and junior secondary (ages 13-15)
South Korea	• Early beginnings in schooling cultivated morals based on Confucianism and Buddhism • Nineteenth century Christian missionaries introduced modern schools • Mid-twentieth century established systematic public education (6-3-3-4 pattern)	• National curriculum based on ideal: contributing to the overall benefit of mankind • Electives and extracurricular activities, in addition to ten required subjects with Korean language arts, English, math, science and social studies to be the most important	• Teacher-centered focus on rote learning and memorization • Teacher is authority figure • Students have little time to develop critical thinking ability, creativity, or aesthetic sensitivity • Teaching license required • End-of-semester tests based on product rather than process	• Seven-hour day, 34-week school year • Six to seven 45-minute class periods per day • System administered by Ministry of Education and Human Resources Development • 20:8 student-teacher ratio

(Table continues on next page)

Table 15.2. (Continued)

Country	Historical Background	Curriculum	Instruction	Assessment Practices	Organization and Structure
Turkey	• Ottoman Empire established Ministry of Public Instruction—religious school dominate • 1924: contemporary education system was established—all schools become coeducational, teacher training developed	• 13 required courses, two electives, and enrichment courses	• Teachers certified in subject area circulate to classrooms • Recent move away from behaviorist (direct instruction) to constructivist methods has been difficult to implement	• Common teacher made assessments include multiple choice, right/wrong solutions	• Two forms—formal and nonformal—free • Four levels in formal: pre-school, primary (elementary and middle), high school, postsecondary • Nonformal: alternate training on developing reading, writing, job skills for enhanced standard of living • Compulsory for 5 years of elementary school • Average class size: 36
United Arab Emirates	• Current system has evolved from 4 different types of schooling—religious schools; o families teaching household/occupational skills; schools opened by businessmen • Currently government funded for national students includes monies for books, equipment, uniform, boarding and transportation from K-university	• Responsibility of Federal Ministry of Education • Emirates schools may develop own curriculum • Technical, agricultural, or commercial for national students choosing technical secondary • English, Arabic, science, mathematics, social studies, Islamic studies • Revised curriculum concentrates on thinking skills	• Arabic used in Emirati schools • English in primary schools • English throughout science, math, and technology classes • Seven 45-minutes lessons per day as teachers circulate • No student work on walls in government schools; model schools are colorful, displaying student work • Site advisors evaluate and provide professional development for teachers	• Two semesters with monthly assessments (September-December, and February-May); final exams in December and May • Final grade is average of both semester final grades • Higher literacy rate for females	• Currently three levels: primary (Grades 1-6), preparatory (7-9), high school (10-12) • Single-gender schools • Limited guidance services • Untrained in young adolescent issues social deal with issues • Expert lecturers brought in to deal with psychological and biological changes happening in young adolescents • School year begins in August, ends in May

When reading the history of educating young adolescents (ages 10-15) we discovered that seven of the countries' educational systems share early beginnings in religious schools—Australia, China, Germany, Ireland, Rwanda, Russia, Turkey, and the United Arab Emirates. Similarly, early beginnings of schooling in South Korea cultivated morals based on Confucianism and Buddhism until nineteenth century missionaries introduced modern schools. Second, it is reported that schools served the upper class in Brazil, Ireland, Russia and Rwanda. Lastly all countries eventually established some form of compulsory, public education

When addressing how schools are organized to educate young adolescents, curriculum, instruction, and assessment frame the presentations. For many of the countries—Australia, China, Germany, India, Lebanon, South Korea, and Turkey—the curriculum is composed of certain subjects identified as core or basic. Instruction is described as attending to the developmental characteristics of young adolescents in Australia, Brazil, Ireland, and South Korea. For China, Germany, India, Rwanda, South Korea, Turkey, and the United Arab Emirates, chapter authors report teacher-centered, subject-driven instruction, but noted a shift toward more student-centered approaches. State-based and/or high stakes assessment practices are reported for Australia, Brazil, India, Ireland, Rwanda, South Korea, and the United Arab Emirates.

The organization and structure of schools for young adolescents varies. Schooling for young adolescents crosses school levels. For example, in South Africa, students, ages 9-12, attend senior primary schools then move to junior secondary schools for ages 13-15. Brazil, India, Lebanon, Rwanda, and the United Arab Emirates have similar cross-grade configurations. An interesting alternative to the Junior Cycle organization for educating students ages 12-17 in Ireland is the Junior Certificate School Programme. It is hoped that this alternative will stem the rise in drop-out rates during the Junior Cycle.

EDUCATIONAL DISCOURSE: OUTCOMES OF THE SCHOOLING OF YOUNG ADOLESCENTS

The third theme deals with the educational discourse that characterizes the education of young adolescents in countries across the globe. The effects of globalization can be seen in educational discourses where governments around the world discuss similar educational agendas and goals. These agendas include items like investing in schooling to develop human capital, preparing better skilled workers for the economic growth of the state as well as for global competition, and developing lifelong learners. Perhaps less obvious is the interplay between these espoused goals and the means adopted to achieve them. Such relationships may be quite surprising.

In addition to nations engaging in these "education" discussions focused on the purposes and goals of schooling, we find intergovernmental organizations such as the United Nations, the Organization for Economic Cooperation and Development (OECD), and the World Bank promoting global educational agendas. Nongovernmental organizations, like those concerned with human rights and environmentalism, are also trying to influence schooling throughout the world.

In relation to the countries represented in this volume of the *Handbook of Research in Middle Level Education* series, we find the typical and expected outcomes that deal with human capital, economic development, and multiculturalism (because of the fact that there is a mass migration of workers across the globe). Examples of the topics of these education discourses include (note: the list of countries at the end of each item includes examples and is meant to be exhaustive):

1. wanting to meet the international standards for education (United Arab Emirates, Ireland);

2. desiring to integrate all sectors of the society; produce social cohesion (India, South Africa); strengthening nationalism and national sovereignty (Turkey);

3. increasing student enrollment in schools through addressing accessibility, gender inequities, and social and economic class divisions (India, Ireland);

4. creating a workforce that will allow the country to compete globally (India, South Africa, South Korea);

5. promoting life-long learning (Australia, Ireland);

6. encouraging participation in the civic and economic life of the country (Australia, South Korea, Brazil, Ireland);

7. developing the necessary skills and knowledge for the workplace (Australia, Ireland);

8. fostering the values, knowledge, and competencies for a full and satisfying life (New Zealand, Turkey, South Korea, Brazil, Ireland);

9. preventing juvenile delinquency, violence, and political militancy among working class youth (South Africa, Brazil); and

10. struggling to regain the reputation as the "most literate country" (Russia).

According to Broadfoot (2003), this educational discourse has resulted in governments around the world anxious to learn about educational practices in other countries, even calling on other countries for their expertise in fixing what is perceived to be a "fault" in the current system of schooling. As an example of this phenomenon, we see the United Arab Emirates using eight outside providers from five countries (Great Britain, United States, New Zealand, Lebanon, and Canada) to provide the expertise for the reform of its educational system. Supporting the belief that we need to learn from each other, Dale (2005) wrote that with globalization the world can no longer unproblematically be apprehended as made up of autonomous states. Indeed, this assumption of a global community has been fundamental to much of the work in comparative education and the basis for the comparisons that have been undertaken.

THE ISSUE OF SAMENESS: CURRENT ISSUES, REFORM INITIATIVES, AND NATIONAL POLICIES

The three themes explicated above led us to examining what appears to be a remarkable sameness in what is happening in the education of young adolescents worldwide. When looking at the current issues and reform agendas that are confronting these countries, we easily divided the items discussed in each chapter into five categories: (1) curriculum, instruction, and assessment (CIA); (2) teacher-related issues; (3) accessibility of schooling; (4) accountability; and (5) an area labeled "other issues" (see Table 15.3). These categories are consistent with what Kubow and Fossum (2003) characterized as the recent shift in comparative and international education research toward an examination of education-related issues, such as equity and access, and concerns about teacher quality and preparation.

Curriculum, Instruction, and Assessment (CIA)

What we found most often in relation to CIA was that most of the countries were trying to create more student-centered curriculum and instruction. The authors of the chapters on the United Arab Emirates, India, China, Australia, and New Zealand all made reference to "curriculum becoming more student centered," to "creating more child-friendly curriculum, instruction, and assessment." In addition to this focus, there were numerous mentions across these countries about focusing on study skills (India), meeting the diverse needs of young adolescents (India, Australia, New Zealand, Ireland, Brazil), making curriculum more relevant

Table 15.3. An Overview of Current Issues, Reform Initiatives, and National Policies

Country	Curriculum, Instruction, and Assessment (CIA)	Teacher-Related Issues	Accessibility of Schooling	Accountability	Other Issues
Australia	• Students actively engaged in learning utilizing real-world contexts • Integration of curriculum, instruction, and assessment facilitating transdisciplinary studies • Innovative leadership involved with school-based reform • Instructional practices geared to developmental needs of students; active, self-directed learning; outcome based; and vocationally relevant • Vocational relevance of curriculum is questionable • Curriculum is narrow with a lack of focus on arts and humanities	• Middle school teaching as a specialization area for teacher training • Expanding teachers pedagogical skills • Enhancing the status of the teaching profession • Lack of quality professional development that is ongoing • Need teacher preparation programs		• Increasing public confidence in quality of schooling through standards of achievement	• Lack of effective leadership at local and state levels
Brazil	• Lacking sufficient educational materials	• Teachers not adequately prepared for new teaching requirements and assessment system • More professional development needed • Not enough qualified teachers • Low status of profession	• Training schools funded by industry to produce a qualified work force • Few students finish basic education with a satisfactory level of achievement • Special education students have a right to an education	• Attempting to maximize educational programs in relation to diversity	• Violence in schools and issues like bullying are being addressed • Need to focus on self-esteem of students

China	• Promote quality and relevance of curriculum • Reform curriculum and textbooks • Replace teacher-centered methodologies with student-centered practices • More authentic assessment • Community service components in curriculum • Promoting English as a second language • Need for education focused on sexuality, reproductive health, HIV/AIDS	• Require teachers to obtain a degree • Improve teacher training curriculum • National teacher training center established. • Teacher shortage	• Nine years of compulsory education • Assist girls from poor areas and ethnic minorities to attend schools • Increase middle school enrollment • Not enough middle schools • Rural students are disadvantaged in relation to urban students	• Pressure to achieve academically	• Focus on primary schooling and higher education causes a lack of focus on middle schools • Funding is low • Young adolescents not valued by society
Germany	• Focus is on recall and facts, not problem solving strategies • Efforts to redirect instructional practices • Integrated teaching is being initiated	• Focusing on teacher preparation programs	• Three kinds of schools based on economic background with unequal access to higher educational opportunities	• Reforms implemented in response to Sputnik in the 1960s • Poor performance of students in international comparisons	• Rising levels of bad student behavior and a cultural divide between schools and their students
India	• Creating more "child-friendly" curriculum, instruction, and assessment • Focus on study skills • Meet the diverse needs of young adolescents • Students exposed to three languages	• Concern for the quality of teacher training • Lack of teachers	• Trying to make middle schools more accessible and affordable to all students • Need to address marginalized populations like girls, rural students, and students in certain castes and tribes • Increase student enrollment	• Private versus public schools and differential educational quality • Two thirds of students are not in schools • High-stakes testing determines careers of students at middle school age	• Stress on students is high

(Table continues on next page)

Table 15.3. (Continued)

Country	Curriculum, Instruction, and Assessment (CIA)	Teacher-Related Issues	Accessibility of Schooling	Accountability	Other Issues
Ireland	• Move away from emphasis on rite learning to personal development of student • Teaches encouraged to engage in a wide variety of teaching methodologies and approaches	• Tension between teachers having to teach the content of the examinations and being encouraged to address the needs of the student beyond academics	• Catholic Church gives enrollment preference to students who are Catholic • Gender-based performance disparities with girls outperforming boys • Fee-paying schools serve middle and upper-middle class students • State pays a high proportion of teacher salaries in fee-based schools which affords these schools more resources • Lower class students in nonfee paying schools and these schools have fewer resources	• Performance of students on international comparison tests is important and closely monitored • Student profiles are created to track performance and to intervene in case of potential drop out or other problems • Transition Year Program includes extracurricular activities, work experiences, self-exploration, community work projects	• Catholic Church played (and continues to play) a major role in the development of the educational system • Funding allocated to schools on an "examination result" basis

Lebanon	• Extracurricular activities provided • Career guidance counselors and academic advisors added to services • Courses in technology, computer literacy, and a second foreign language added • Theme-based curriculum developed • Cooperative learning implemented • Arts added to curriculum (music, acting, drawing, etc.) • Curriculum still portrays girls in limited roles • Textbooks created by content experts not curriculum specialists—therefore not engaging or relevant to students		• Strong emphasis on academics at the exclusion of socioemotional issues
New Zealand	• Integrated approach to curriculum • Student-centered curriculum designs • Exploratory curriculum • Pastoral care (managing self, relating to others, participating and contributing) important along with academic achievement	• Emergence of middle schools • Need to develop middle-grades teacher preparation programs	• Achievement gap between sectors of society	• Transition from primary to middle schools is problematic • Low student motivation and engagement in schooling

(Table continues on next page)

Table 15.3. (Continued)

Country	Curriculum, Instruction, and Assessment (CIA)	Teacher-Related Issues	Accessibility of Schooling	Accountability	Other Issues
Russia	• Apply Western credit-hour system • Prevocational (professional) courses in the 8th and 9th grades • More courses in culture, environmental issues, and societal development	• Teachers experience a lot of job-related stress • Teachers lack knowledge of test taking strategies to teach students	• Various types of schools available based on social class/wealth. • "Additional schools" to help prepare for tests like TOEFL, GRE, GMAT	• Trying to parallel Russia's education system with the European System • More public involvement in education system • Nationwide system of evaluation of the quality of schooling • Students not adept at navigating national standardized testing with tables, diagrams, and text	• Transitioning from school to school results in decrease in academic performance • Stress is high for students due to academic overload • Country losing strength as an educational powerhouse
Rwanda	• Promote health education to reduce the incidence of HIV/AIDS • Move away from memorization of teacher lectures • National curriculum materials are used • Struggling about what to teach in relation to genocide	• Only 51% of teachers are qualified/certified	• Fee-free education at primary and secondary levels by 2020 • Education for girls • Attention to special education students • Schools run by Catholic and Protestant missionaries serve more affluent families • Students need to assist families with chores and income generation • Lack of money for school-related items • Gender equity as issue	• Examinations now required for entry into secondary schools • Students have a difficult time passing state examinations	

South Africa	• Attempt to use learner-centered instruction, but teachers do not understand the philosophy • Classrooms characterized by data recall, drill, and rote learning, not higher-order thinking skills • Students are passive learners • Trying to implement learner-centered curriculum that is based in real-world experiences of students	• Teachers have poor conceptual knowledge of the subjects they teach and little content knowledge • Teacher education preparation programs are inferior • Teachers lack motivation	• Two educational systems: elite and White and Black middle class; other system serves African working class and poor	• Achievement levels are quite low	• Need for curriculum leadership
South Korea	• Students as passive learners: rote learning and memorization are common • Curriculum not responsive to needs of young adolescents • Reform trying to create student-oriented curriculum	• Teachers considered to be of high quality • More qualified teachers than in other countries • Many teachers of English who do not feel competent to teach speaking and listening skills • More attention is being given to teacher preparation and professional development to help in student-centered reforms • New teacher evaluation system	• Tutoring outside of school hours • Use of technology has contributed to equal access to schooling (cyber home-schooling for students in rural and remote areas) • Policies developed for gifted and talented students	• Examinations used to decide access to further educational opportunities	• Student motivation to study is very low • Students suffer from stress due to emphasis on high-stakes testing

(Table continues on next page)

Table 15.3. (Continued)

Country	Curriculum, Instruction, and Assessment (CIA)	Teacher-Related Issues	Accessibility of Schooling	Accountability	Other Issues
Turkey	• Moving from teacher-centered to student-centered CIA • Drill and practice • More guidance and counseling implemented. • Social, emotional, and physical outcomes identified as educational outcomes • Emphasis on authentic assessment	• Few professional development opportunities to help implement more constructivist curriculum and instruction and to further educational reform started in 2004 • Insufficient pedagogical knowledge	• Differential access by region of country, SES status, and gender • Two main systems: formal and nonformal • Private tutoring for those who can afford it • Ethnic minorities have problems of access to education in their native languages	• Use of high-stakes examinations to decide access to additional educational opportunities as well as for international comparisons	• Infrastructure is severely lacking in quality and quantity • Bullying and conflict resolution are being researched
United Arab Emirates	• Becoming more student centered and outcome-based • Rewrite textbooks to parallel curriculum • Extend students ability to read, write, and talk in English • Use of computers as instructional tools	• New college established to train teachers • Use of retired military and police for teaching • Professional development for teachers • Pedagogical skills to facilitate teaching content in English	• Model middle schools established	• Standards and assessment of student performance applicable to private schools • High-stakes examinations twice a year in every grade level • Aiming for international standards in achievement • Underperformance of students on national testing	• Short school day and tear cited for underperformance of students

and integrated (Australia, New Zealand, Germany, Turkey, Brazil), providing more counseling and guidance opportunities for young adolescents (Lebanon), developing theme-based curriculum (Lebanon), implementing cooperative learning and other learner-centered instructional practices (Lebanon, South Africa), broadening the curriculum to include the arts (Australia, Lebanon), and promoting health education (Rwanda, China).

Teacher-Related Issues

In the realm of teaching, most of these countries are involved in establishing new colleges and programs for teacher preparation (United Arab Emirates, China, Australia, New Zealand, South Africa, Germany, and South Korea). Teacher shortages were noted in India, Brazil, China, and Rwanda. Other issues related to teachers involved the need for more quality professional development (United Arab Emirates, Australia, Turkey, and Brazil), more refined pedagogical skills to teach content/subject areas in English (United Arab Emirates), and reports of job-related stress (Russia) and lack of teacher motivation (South Africa).

Accessibility of Schooling

Many of the countries discussed in this book are trying to make middle school more accessible for students. In some instances, the infrastructure is simply not in place to allow for more students to attend school. In other situations, accessibility is tied to social class, caste, where one lives (rural versus urban areas of the country), or gender. India is an example where marginalized populations include girls, rural students, and students in certain castes or tribes. China is suffering from a lack of middle schools as it tries to increase enrollment for girls, especially those from rural areas. In some instances, accessibility is tied to affordability (India, Rwanda, and Germany) or to educational status. Two thirds of India's young adolescents are not in school. Rwanda is currently trying to focus on the needs of special education students. Accessibility is also linked to a differentiation by type of school. Germany, as a case in point, has three different types of schools which provide unequal access to higher educational opportunities. In Ireland, access to resources depends to a large degree on whether one attends fee-based or non-fee-based schools. Accessibility in countries like Rwanda, Turkey, India, and South Korea is based on high-stakes examinations, allowing those who excel on these examinations to continue to have access to educational opportunities.

Accountability

Accountability is a major theme running throughout all of the chapters in this volume. A prominent feature of the systems of accountability is high-stakes testing (United Arab Emirates, India, Rwanda, Russia, Germany). Accountability is very likely one of the "threads" that runs throughout all of these countries, but some authors did not mention this dimension.

Other Items

In this category we found school transitions to be an issue in New Zealand and Russia, the lack of effective leadership to be problematic in Australia, low student motivation and a lack of engagement in schooling in New Zealand, and stress to be a major factor in Russia and India.

The discussion of these five areas highlights for us the amazing similarities in issues as these countries attempt to provide for the education of their young adolescents. In many ways, these issues are quite similar to those we face in the United States.

RESEARCH AGENDAS AND FUTURE DIRECTIONS

Across the 14 countries in this volume of the *Handbook*, a number of research topics and agendas focusing on young adolescents were identified and discussed. In examining these we are able to group the topics into three areas: (a) current research, (b) research methodologies, and (c) important findings (see Table 15.4).

Current Research

Interestingly, the main themes and topics of the international research described herein are not dissimilar to current research on young adolescents in the United States. In some countries the establishment of a national research agenda has served to guide the direction of the research focusing on young adolescents; whereas in other countries efforts are underway to develop national research agendas or research topics specifically designed to address issues and concerns around young adolescents.

In terms of current research, there were a number of countries that identified similar topics that were currently the focus of national research agendas or individual researchers, including:

Table 15.4. An Overview of Research

Country	Current Research Topics	Methodologies	Important Findings

Australia	• No national coordination of young adolescent research
	• Regionally, priority research areas have been established (e.g., New South Wales)
	• Priority research areas:
	  ○ Assessment & accountability
	  ○ Cooperation between schools
	  ○ Curriculum issues
	  ○ Environmental sustainability
	  ○ Info & comm technologies
	  ○ Quality teaching
	  ○ Resourcing
	  ○ Respect & responsibility
	  ○ Socially just schooling
	  ○ Student engagement
	  ○ Workforce development
		• Numerous research studies published over past decade, however, few of these based on objective research
		• Growth in "official" reports; again with little empirical research
		• Many of these "studies" rely on single cases, anecdotal data, and self-reported data analyses
		• Most middle schools have not yet generated any convincing evidence of improved learning
		• Most existing research evidence on effectiveness of middle schools is related to student & teacher attitudes toward middle school
			• Higher achievers in literacy and numeracy in year 9 are more likely to stay in school, have higher college entrance performance, and are more likely to gain employment
			• Young adolescent achievement varies depending on SES and demographics
			• Males are more likely to take math & science courses than females
			• Issues of resources for schools in rural and remote areas
			• Indigenous students and non-English speaking students consistently perform lower than other Australian students

(Table continues on next page)

Table 15.4. (Continued)

Country	Current Research Topics	Methodologies	Important Findings

Brazil	• National research on young adolescents being conducted in field of psychology (educational, developmental, social, & health)
	• Main themes are nearly identical to those investigated nearly 20 years ago
	  ○ Greater concern with issues related to young adolescent health
	  ○ family relations, and
	  ○ development and validation of national measures of cognitive, motivational, socioemotional variables
	• increase in theoretical studies and literature reviews
		• larger scale (regional) quantitative studies with more representative samples predominate current research
		• large number of studies based on convenience samples
		• fewer number of qualitative & mixed methods studies
		• descriptive and correlational studies predominate
		• recent efforts toward construction of national assessment tools
		• efforts underway to create tools to assess family relationships
			• current studies on the following:
			• street children
			  ○ see institutions as being valuable to their lives
			  ○ need for support systems
			• violence and young adolescence
			  ○ vandalism, theft, & physical aggression
			  ○ drugs & alcohol are causal factors of violence
			  ○ violence also attributable to social inequity
			• young adolescence & family
			  ○ forms of communication and links to psychosocial problems predominate the research
			  ○ family support critical to success of young adolescents
			• drugs and young adolescence
			  ○ major problem for young adolescents (marijuana is main illegal drug)
			  ○ nonusers typically had stronger family ties
			• sexuality and young adolescence
			  ○ majority of focus on STDs and evaluation of programs aimed at healthy development

China	<ul><li>Noticeably absent from international studies/comparisons<ul><li>this limits ability for international cross-comparisons</li></ul></li><li>currently there are 2 significant areas of research:<ul><li>paradox of Chinese adolescent learner</li><li>young adolescent use of technology</li></ul></li></ul>	<ul><li>paradox of Chinese adolescent learner<ul><li>authoritarian instruction</li><li>memorization as a tool for concept development</li><li>strictness in classrooms seen as nurturing & motivational for students</li></ul></li><li>young adolescent use of technology<ul><li>less technology use in schools versus out of school</li></ul></li><li>many Chinese students being "addicted" to Internet usage</li></ul>
Germany	<ul><li>1990s saw strong development in research on student achievement<ul><li>Usually connected to international comparisons (TIMMS, PISA)</li><li>Led to sophisticated sampling techniques and data analyses</li><li>Extensive empirical research on classroom instruction (mainly math & science)</li></ul></li><li>In comparison, current state of research on teacher education is lacking<ul><li>Current focus on more research on teacher education and professional competencies</li><li>Research currently lacks a common theoretical basis</li></ul></li></ul>	<ul><li>Focus on differences in international student comparisons suggests that teacher education programs may vary</li><li>Germany included in six-country study, *Mathematics Teaching for the 21st Century* (MT21) and the larger IEA study, *Teacher Education and Development: Learning to Teach Mathematics* (TEDS-M)</li><li>Examination of "professional competencies"</li></ul>	<ul><li>MT21 found:</li><li>Significant differences were noted among the six countries in terms of math, math pedagogy, and general pedagogical knowledge of future teachers</li><li>Teacher education matters</li><li>Math teachers trained as part of elementary program were at a disadvantage</li></ul>

(Table continues on next page)

Table 15.4. (Continued)

Country	Current Research Topics	Methodologies	Important Findings

India	• Academic achievement dominates current young adolescent research agenda
	  ○ Research is multifaceted (physiological aspects, TV viewing patterns)
	• How subject content is absorbed by students
	• Computer science
	• Role of environment in daily lives
	• How minority students are coping with both being young adolescents and the school system
	  ○ Problems faced by tribal children, Muslims, non-native language speakers
	• Role of academics, career development, and vocational & technical training
		• Preference in Indian journals for quantitative research studies
		• Questionnaires, random sampling, and correlational analysis are popular methodologies
		• Although some studies have a qualitative dimension, the majority of research is quantitative
		• More recently, there is suggestion for more qualitative studies
			• Instruction is focused primarily on preparing students for comprehensive high-stakes examinations
			• Burgeoning area of research is focused on tools used to plan lessons
			• Nonformal education is less prestigious than the formal education system
			• Conflict faced by young adolescents in the use of leisure time; found that this was very stressful

Ireland	• Streaming/banding/mixed ability classes	• Use of mixed methods, with an emphasis on combining both quantitative and qualitative data	• Found that grouping of students based on abilities was detrimental to students that were placed in lower-ability classes • Ireland ranked in top one third on educational well-being ○ As examined across 6 dimensions (material, health & safety, education, family/peer relationships, behaviors & risks, and subjective well-being)

Lebanon	• Global Classrooms Model United Nations (GC-MUN) targets young adolescent students worldwide
	• In Lebanon, GC-MUN is administered by students at the Lebanese American University
	• "Teach for Lebanon" is a new program set to begin in fall 2008
	  ○ Students will be taught life skills including academic-linguistic proficiency, computer literacy, and conflict resolution strategies
			• Two main issues highlighted in 2006 report:
			• Diagnosis of critical educational issues and matters in order to raise awareness
			  ○ Highlighted specific problems that reform policies will address
			• Creation of a realistic and practical vision that gives priority to critical matters
			• Success of new reform plan requires a new educational administration that can move to next phase of formulating new educational strategies

	Foci of Research	Methodology	Outcomes/Findings
New Zealand	<ul><li>Reviews of middle school literature</li><li>Integrative curriculum at the middle level</li><li>Young adolescents' experiences of schooling</li><li>Māori learners</li><li>Transition to secondary school</li></ul>	<ul><li>Use of a variety of methodologies including quantitative, qualitative, and mixed methods</li></ul>	<ul><li>Proposal to implement integrative curriculum à la Beane, not multidisciplinary model as proposed by Jacobs</li><li>Improving Māori experiences in main stream classrooms and the interactions between these students and teachers can improve student achievement</li><li>Research on transitions to secondary schools found:<ul><li>Reduced engagement</li><li>No impact on achievement; found that students' prior achievement was greater influence than transition</li><li>Some students report academic and social difficulties with transition</li></ul></li></ul>
Russia	<ul><li>Nationwide studies on various research programs; found that research has focused primarily on two main areas:<ul><li>Axiological, theoretical, and legislative foundation of the content theory of secondary education</li><li>Development of secondary education as a factor of the competitive capacity of Russia on the world arena</li></ul></li><li>Additional research has focused on federal programs such as:<ul><li>Children of Russia</li><li>Prevention of drug misuse and illegal drug circulation</li><li>Electronic Russia</li></ul></li></ul>	<ul><li>Studies have been conducted at international, national, regional, and local levels</li><li>Most studies have used mixed methods</li><li>Focus on normative rather than exploratory approaches</li><li>Quantitative methods commonly used for exploring student achievement</li><li>Schools and research institutions lack modern statistical tools and knowledge as to appropriate applications of techniques</li><li>Therefore, descriptive analyses are more common than inferential</li></ul>	<ul><li>In national study, 20% of students were identified as being "at risk" due to deteriorating health conditions, especially female students</li><li>Irregular nutrition, lack of physical activity, smoking and alcohol use significant problems for young adolescents</li><li>Physical and emotional environments at most secondary schools do not support normal, healthy development</li></ul>
Rwanda	<ul><li>Gender and poverty issues</li><li>Special education</li><li>Science and technology</li><li>HIV/AIDS education</li><li>Most research topics designed to assist with the nation's application for international funds and grants.</li></ul>	<ul><li>Predominant methodology is quantitative design, with outcomes reported in statistical findings</li></ul>	<ul><li>Enrollment</li><li>Repeater and drop-out rates at all levels</li><li>Gender parity</li><li>Health</li><li>Literacy</li></ul>

(Table continues on next page)

Table 15.4. (Continued)

Country	Current Research Topics	Methodologies	Important Findings
South Africa	• South African National Research Foundation (NRF) established seven research focus areas, of which two are applicable to education: ○ Education and the challenges for change ○ Indigenous knowledge systems • These include investigation of issues of teaching and learning as it pertains to young adolescents • NRF has commissioned a new research project to conduct an audit and interpretive analysis of research undertaken over the past 10 years, followed by a meta-analysis of these data. From this, a research agenda will be developed.	• The past 3 decades has seen a preponderance of qualitative research in science education • Hopeful that NRF audit will shed new light on educational methodologies	• Research on language issues • Comparative and interpretive studies are helping to shape national policy • More focused studies on language and mathematics
South Korea	• Educational systems and policies are major research topics • General middle school topics include: ○ Comprehensive evaluation system ○ Gifted and talented education ○ Perceived school issues (students)	• Various methodologies including qualitative, quantitative, and mixed methods are employed • Quantitative is most favored method (more than 70% of studies conducted using quantitative) ○ Survey/questionnaire is major instrument to explore educational research questions • Qualitative methods practically nonexistent prior to 1990s due to lack of training	• One study suggests that students are not happy with life in general ○ Increased drop out, class avoidance, and interference with other students • Another study suggests that achievement gap between schools is different according to different subjects ○ Students in schools in more affluent areas achieve at higher level compared to students in schools in less affluent areas

| Turkey | • In recent years have seen improvement in quantity and scope of middle school education research
• Majority of research occurs in mathematics, science, and instructional technology
• Research focuses on cognitive and affective domains, curriculum and textbook analyses, instructional strategies, student outcomes, and teacher education.
• Current emphasis on effectiveness of reform curriculum, technology integration, measurement and assessment, learning environment, and rural versus urban education | • Predominance of convenience sampling; random sampling beginning to emerge
• National studies are primarily focused on results of high-stakes tests and international studies (e.g., PIRLS and PISA)
• Middle school education research is predominantly quantitative in nature
• Some use of qualitative methods; mixed methods approaches are rare | • Benefited greatly from international studies in terms of understanding international standing of Turkish students' achievement levels and the curricula and pedagogical strategies used in high-achieving countries
• PIRLS results showed that Turkey was one of two countries with large numbers of students that did not attend pre-K schooling and with the largest class sizes
• Results of these studies have helped inform current reform movement |
| United Arab Emirates | • Ministry of Education has a research department which is responsible for collecting educational research on an annual basis and generate a report
 o Includes a variety of topics related to teachers, students, parents, subjects, teaching strategies, behaviors, and education system
 o Additional topics include student achievement, behaviors, and professional development
• Presently, planning is underway to reform assessment and evaluation systems in middle grades education | | |

- student achievement, assessment, and accountability (Australia, Germany, India, South Korea, Turkey, and the United Arab Emirates);
- teacher education/preparation and professional development (Australia, Germany, India, South Africa, Turkey, and the United Arab Emirates);
- young adolescent health and wellness (Brazil, Russia, and Rwanda);
- young adolescent developmental and environmental factors (Australia, Brazil, China, India, Lebanon, and Russia);
- technology and integration of technology (Australia, China, India, Lebanon, Russia, Rwanda, and Turkey);
- curricular and pedagogical issues (New Zealand, South Korea, Turkey, and the United Arab Emirates); and
- issues of heterogeneous grouping and student diversity, including gender, race, ethnicity, and poverty (India, Ireland, New Zealand, Russia, and Rwanda).

In addition, there were a number of research topics specific to individual countries: family and community relationships (Brazil), gifted and talented education (South Korea), workforce development (Australia), transition to secondary school (New Zealand), special education (Rwanda), rural versus urban education (Turkey), and specific subject focus such as mathematics and science (Turkey).

Research Methodologies

A number of varying methodologies have been employed across the countries, ranging from philosophical approaches (qualitative, quantitative), data collection strategies, and data analyses and sampling techniques. As can be seen from the following list, several countries report multiple methodological approaches, whereas others, report the predominance of one methodological approach:

- qualitative studies (New Zealand, South Africa, and South Korea);
- quantitative studies (Brazil, India, New Zealand, Russia, Rwanda, South Korea, and Turkey);
- mixed methods (Ireland, New Zealand, Russia, and South Korea);
- predominance of descriptive and correlational studies (Brazil and India);

- survey research (India and South Korea); and
- convenience sampling (Brazil and Turkey).

Research on young adolescents in several countries was also described as problematic for a variety of reasons, including, lack of empirical research (Australia), the need for more qualitative research methods (India), lack of modern statistical tools/applications (Russia), and the need for more sophisticated sampling techniques (Brazil and Turkey).

Important Findings

As described above, current research across many of these countries focus on a number of similar topics including, student achievement or student outcomes, student health and well being, and student diversity:

- student achievement
  - o if students achieve well in middle school, they will continue to do so in secondary school and at the university (Australia);
  - o students in more affluent schools achieve at higher levels compared to students in schools in less affluent areas (South Korea); and
  - o benefits from participation in international achievement studies in terms of understanding link between pedagogical strategies and higher achievement (Turkey)
- student diversity, including gender, race, ethnicity, and poverty, and grouping practices
  - o student achievement varies depending on socioeconomic status and student demographics (Australia);
  - o indigenous Australians and non-English speakers consistently perform lower than traditional Australian students;
  - o grouping based on ability levels found detrimental to students (Ireland); and
  - o by mainstreaming Māori students we find more positive classroom experiences and higher student achievement (New Zealand)
- student health and well-being
  - o drugs, alcohol, and social inequity are casual factors of violence (Brazil);
  - o family support is critical to success of young adolescents; strong family ties strongly correlated with lower drug use (Brazil);

o twenty percent of Russian students identified as being "at risk" due to poor health conditions; lack of physical activity, increased smoking and alcohol consumption; and

o a study from South Korea indicating that students are not happy with their lives, possibly leading to increased drop outs.

A number of research findings are specific to individual countries or regions. In Germany, teacher education/preparation appears to matter to student outcomes; more specifically, math teachers trained as elementary teachers were at a disadvantage in teaching young adolescents in middle schools. In New Zealand, research on the transition to secondary schools found reduced student engagement in school, some reports of academic and social difficulties, and little impact of transitioning on student achievement. Research in Brazil has recently focused on the condition of "street children" that currently constitute a significant proportion of the young adolescent population in several large Brazilian urban centers. Research on young adolescents in a few countries has been driven by their country's participation in international comparative studies (Germany, Ireland, South Africa, and Turkey). Additionally, several countries are currently engaged in varying levels of dialogue and discourse to development national research programs (Australia, Lebanon, South Africa, and the United Arab Emirates).

Future Directions

The recognition that additional research was needed to address the concerns of young adolescents was a universal topic for future directions in all of these countries (see Table 15.5). In some countries there is a recent trend toward the development of new, or the refinement of existing, national research programs or agendas, focused explicitly on young adolescent education (Australia, China, India, Russia, Rwanda, South Africa, and the United Arab Emirates). Another area identified by several countries as a focus of future research was the developmentally appropriate curriculum and instruction in middle schools (Australia, China, Germany, Lebanon, New Zealand, Russia, South Korea, and the United Arab Emirates). Other countries identified additional areas in need of additional research, including:

• addressing the issues of equity, grouping practices, and student diversity, including gender, race, ethnicity, and poverty (New Zealand, Rwanda, and Turkey);

Table 15.5. An Overview of Future Directions

Country	Future Directions
Australia	• Expanding transition programs • Encouraging a focus on teacher/student relationships • Raising confidence & motivation of students • Improving literacy & numeracy skills • Targeting professional development • Recognition that policy and strategy at the government & bureaucratic levels need to become more coherent & coordinated • Development of framework for a national curriculum

Brazil	• Future research should address the following:
	  o Investigate topics relevant to educational praxis
	    ■ How do teachers react to and what are their expectations in relation to repeating students or those with learning difficulties in the classroom?
	    ■ How are educational professionals dealing with repeating students?
	  o Research on background and components of motivation of young adolescents
	• Existing research—which is primarily self-reported surveys—should be complemented with other methodologies including observations
	• Need for research on effects of professional development programs

China	• New, national educational policies are being created based on China's robust economy and modernization • Conflict with emerging policies and traditional cultural values • Attention to educational infrastructure is critical to future direction of education of young adolescents • More research on social, emotional, and academic needs of young adolescents • Extensive research needed on how to provide teachers with effective professional development to ease the transition from transmission-acceptance model of pedagogy to more student-centered approaches
Germany	• Need to connect research on student achievement, classroom instruction, and teacher education • Need to externally validate MT21 findings about professional competencies of middle school teachers (e.g., observe classroom instruction, assess achievement of students) • Use of longitudinal research designs would be beneficial • Lack of in-depth qualitative studies; most studies focusing on middle schools are based on large-scale assessments (TIMMS, PISA)

(Table continues on next page)

Table 15.5. (Continued)

Country	Future Directions
India	• National education plan includes a 67% increase from 2003 to 2008 for middle school growth • Challenge of educating 75% of student population that is not privately schooled; what to do with students that have historically been neglected by the school system • Currently there is a large population of "out of school" youth who have dropped out to seek employment in rural and urban areas • India is recognizing that government initiatives are critical to fill the gap of those marginalized in middle schools • Need to pay more attention to teacher outreach, recruitment, and retention

Ireland	• While there have been some recent changes in the administration of Ireland's Department of Education and Science, it is likely that existing policies will remain intact. These include a focus on:
	  o Individualism
	  o Technological innovation
	  o Inclusiveness
	• Trends toward coeducational and multidisciplinary schools will also likely continue

Lebanon	• Several initiatives underway to improve middle school education in private schools:
	  o Differentiated instruction in writing and reading
	  o Implementation of block scheduling; facilitates integration of subject matter
	  o Civics teachers collaborating with university personnel to pilot a project to integrate technology
	• Due to demand from higher education, it has become necessary to readjust middle school education to be less traditional and more inductive and "hands-on"

New Zealand	• For many years, education in New Zealand has been conceptualized and practiced as either elementary or secondary • Students in the middle schools have historically struggled and new—middle school—pedagogical approaches are being recommended; however, to date, there has not been any systematic implementation of recommended middle school concepts • Need more serious focus on education of minority groups, particularly young Māori men

Russia	• Ministry of Education and Science of the Russian Federation is planning on implementing a national project called, *Education*
	• Goals of the project are to…
	  o Provide access to high-quality education for all students
	  o Meet the demands of current and future educational needs by providing properly trained professionals
	  o Create conditions for lifelong learning
	  o Create conditions for involvement of children and youth in economic, social, political, and cultural life
	  o Develop scientific and technical potential
	  o Support innovative activities in education
	• More specifically, middle school students will …
	  o Benefit from installation of internet access within every school
	  o Free hot lunches
	  o School buses for rural areas
	  o Improved school learning conditions
	• Philosophically, Russian Federation agrees that young adolescents should have equal access to high-quality education, social support, benefits, health care, and healthy physical development and emotional development regardless of gender, age, social status, and place of residence

Rwanda	• Ministry of Education is in the process of reconfiguring educational structure and is proposing that primary education be extended three years to include young adolescents • Currently, addressing issue of unqualified teachers • Given international political view of Rwanda, government needs to continue working to improve image and attract outside funding sources for social programs • Research agenda needs to be developed to address issue of better understanding, on part of teachers and administrators, of the educational needs of young adolescents • Need to conduct long-term qualitative studies and case studies to further understanding about national issue of drop outs and gender inequity

South Africa	• Primary educational concern in South Africa, a country with 11 official languages and numerous other languages, would be the agreement of a common language of instruction
	• Presidential Education Initiative (PEI) recommendations include:
	  o Decrease of mother tongue instruction in the lower grades and consequent increase in use of English as medium of instruction
	  o Need to address the mismatch between languages spoken by teachers and their pupils

(Table continues on next page)

Table 15.5. (Continued)

Country	Future Directions
South Korea	• Officials in the Republic of South Korean acknowledges the need to propel all educational systems to prepare students for twenty-first century, the era of globalization and knowledge-based society • By implementing student-centered curriculum, government hopes to bring about educational success for all students • Emphasis on gifted programs in science, math, and foreign language (particularly English)
Turkey	• Turkey's desire to join the European Union is strongly influencing their reliance on international testing (e.g., TIMMS, PISA) • Infusion of EU monies into education has served to help address discrepancies between eastern and western Turkey, as well as new school construction in remote areas and hiring teachers for these schools • Need to continue problem of teacher shortage
United Arab Emirates	• Ministry of Education is implementing new plans to develop the level of education in all grade levels and to achieve international standards • Focus on teacher and administrator preparation • Shift from teacher-focused curriculum to more student-centered • In 2008, government introduced a set of by-laws to ensure that all children receive a quality, uniform education; accreditation process will be used to evaluate schools

- improving student achievement (Australia, Germany, and South Korea);
- evaluating the effects of teacher preparation and professional development (Australia, Brazil, China, Rwanda, and the United Arab Emirates);
- assessing the developmental needs of young adolescents (China and India); and
- developing and using alternative research methods such as qualitative, mixed methods, and longitudinal designs (Germany, Rwanda, and South Korea).

CONCLUSION

Education has been situated within national borders. It has been shaped by the demands within each nation-state to prepare labor for participation in its economy, to prepare citizens for participation in the polity, and, in some instances, for global economic competition. This approximate congruence between the nation-state and formalized education becomes problematic as globalization blurs national sovereignty. If our contemporary discussion of education, and in particular middle level education, is going to have meaning, it must move beyond assumptions about national boundaries and goals that are internal to national agendas. This discussion must look outward. As was already stated, comparative and international research in middle level education can serve as a catalyst for critical self-reflection and knowledge expansion within the field. Beane (2005) argued

> What is needed is a reexamination of the middle school concept to see where it has the strength to sustain itself, where it must face up to persistent contradictions, and how it might be pushed to a stronger, more complete, and more compelling vision of its possibilities. (p. xiv)

There is no better place to reexamine the middle school concept than in the school systems of countries across the world. There is no argument that the "knowledge base in middle level education is built upon a foundation of research conducted in the United States and elsewhere in the English-speaking world. The field ... needs to embrace diverse perspectives and alternative ways of knowing if it is transcend Anglophonic parochialism and achieve relevance abroad" (Virtue, this volume, p. xx).

It has been said that we know more about reforming middle schools than any other component of the American educational system. While this may be true, we have been rather unsuccessful in convincing policymakers and practitioners to adopt and implement the middle school concept in middle schools across the United States. The implementation we have seen has been reserved to a small percentage of the total number of middle schools. In many instances, implementation has been only partial and has not been able to withstand changes in school-level or district-level administration. As we have struggled with multiple indictments against middle schools (starting in the mid-1990s) and the poor performance of students on eighth grade national and international assessments, we hold firm that what we know is *best* for the creation of learning environments for young adolescents. We defend the philosophy from the perspective that it has not truly been implemented on a large-enough scale, that only a small percentage of teachers have been specifically prepared to teach this age group, and that the necessary resources have not been devoted to ensuring its success.

We noted in the start to this chapter that we saw a "sameness" developing in the education of young adolescents in countries across the world. This sameness seems to be embracing the need to look at more student-centered approaches to curriculum, instruction, and assessment. It will be interesting to see how the "middle school philosophy," as developed by the major advocates of middle grades education in the United States, plays out in an international arena. It will be important to see if this philosophy can withstand crossing national boundaries. One thing is for certain. We must begin an international dialogue which allows us to bring to the table what we know—what has worked and what has not worked in the schooling of young adolescents. We can only envision positive benefits from this international dialogue.

REFERENCES

Beane, J. A. (2005). Foreword. In E. R. Brown & K. J. Saltman (Eds.), *The critical middle school reader* (pp. xi-xv). New York: Rutledge.

Broadfoot, P. (2001). Editorial: Culture, learning and comparative education. *Comparative Education, 37*(3), 261-266.

Broadfoot, P. (2003). Editorial. Globalization in comparative perspective: Macro and micro. *Comparative Education, 39*(4), 411-413.

Carnegie Council on Adolescent Development. (1989). *Turning points: Preparing American youth for the 21st century.* New York: Carnegie Corporation of New York.

Dale, R. (2005). Globalisation, knowledge economy and comparative education. *Comparative Education, 41*(2), 117-149.

Dale, R., & Robertson, S. (2003). Editorial. Introduction. *Globalization, Societies, and Education, 1*(1), 3-11.

Elliott, J., Hufton, N., Hildreth, A., & Illushin, L. (1999). Factors influencing educational motivation: A study of attitudes, expectations and behaviour of children in Sunderland, Kentucky and St. Petersburg. *British Education Research Journal, 25*(1), 75-94.

Goleman, D. (1996). *Emotional intelligence: Why it can matter more than IQ.* London: Bloomsbury.

Kubow, P. K., & Fossum, P. R. (2003). *Comparative education: Exploring issues in international context.* Upper Saddle River, NJ: Merrill/Prentice Hall.

National Association of Secondary School Principals. (2006). *Breaking ranks in the middle: Strategies for leading middle level reform.* Reston, VA: Author.

National Middle School Association. (2003). *This we believe: Successful schools for young adolescents.* Westerville, OH: Author.

Rudduck, J., & Flutter, J. (2000). Pupil participation and pupil perspective: Carving a new order of experience. *Cambridge Journal of Education, 30*(1), 75-91.

ABOUT THE CONTRIBUTORS

ABOUT THE EDITORS

Steven B. Mertens is an assistant professor in the Department of Curriculum and Instruction at Illinois State University. Prior to his current position, Dr. Mertens served as a senior research scientist at the Center for Prevention Research and Development (CPRD) at the University of Illinois. During his tenure at CPRD, Steve served as the project director for the design, research, and evaluation of several large-scale evaluations and research studies of comprehensive middle-grades reform projects, including Michigan Middle Start, Mid South Middle Start, and Turning Points. He and his colleagues have published more than 30 research articles, book chapters, and reports addressing varying aspects of middle grades school reform and improvement; recent books include the *Encyclopedia of Middle Grades Education* (with Anfara & Andrews, 2005) and *A Practitioner's Guide to Understanding and Applying Middle Grades Research* (with Flowers & Mulhall, 2007). Currently Steve serves as a board member of the National Forum to Accelerate Middle-Grades Reform, Council Member for the American Educational Research Association's (AERA) Middle Level Education Research Special Interest Group, as well as several editorial board positions. He recently completed a 6-year term as a member of the National Middle School Association's Research Advisory Board.

Vincent A. Anfara, Jr. is an associate professor of educational administration and supervision at The University of Tennessee, Knoxville. He received the PhD in educational administration from the University of New Orleans in 1995. Before entering the professorate, he taught for 23 years in both middle and high schools in Louisiana and New Mexico. His research interests focus on middle school reform, school improvement planning, leadership in middle schools, issues related to student achievement, and qualitative research approaches. He is past chair of the National Middle School Association's Research Advisory Board and past-president of the American Educational Research Association's Middle Level Education Research Special Interest Group. He has authored over 60 articles published in journals including *Middle School Journal*, *Research in Middle Level Education Annual*, *Education and Urban Society*, *The Journal of School Leadership*, *NASSP Bulletin*, the *International Journal of Leadership in Education*, and *Educational Researcher*. Vincent is also the author/editor of nine books related to middle grades education. Recent works include *The Encyclopedia of Middle Grades Education* (with Andrews & Mertens, 2005) and *The Developmentally Responsive Middle Level Principal: A Leadership Model and Measurement Instrument* (with Roney, Smarkola, DuCette, & Gross, 2006).

Kathleen Roney is an associate professor in the Department of Elementary, Middle Level and Literacy Education at University of North Carolina Wilmington, where she also serves as program coordinator for the middle grades education undergraduate and graduate programs. She has more than 25 years in teaching and administration at the elementary, middle grades, secondary level, and higher education level. Among her professional affiliations is membership in the American Educational Research Association, Middle Level Education Research (past president) Special Interest Group of AERA, National Middle School Association, North Carolina Association of Professors of Middle Level Education, and North Carolina Middle School Association. She has published in a variety of research journals, and has coauthored two books: *The Developmentally Responsive Middle Level Principal: A Leadership Model and Measurement Instrument* (NMSA, 2006), and, *Creating Healthy and Effective Middle Schools: Research That Supports the Middle School Concept and Student Achievement* (NMSA, 2008). Additionally, she has presented at more than 35 international, national, and regional conferences.

ABOUT THE AUTHORS

Wafa Abdul-Rahman Al Hashimi is a citizen of the United Arab Emirates. She earned both her bachelor's and master's degrees from Zayed University. She currently teaches mathematics to preparatory students (young adolescents) at the Al Mawaheb School for Girls in Abu Dhabi. In 2008, she was presented with the Rashid Award for Scientific Excellence.

Her writing has been published in the Zayed University College of Education journal, *Teachers, Learners, and Curriculum*.

David Anderson is an associate professor of educational leadership at Eastern Michigan University. He has worked with numerous educational policy organizations, including the Bureau of Accreditation and School Improvement Studies, the National Science Foundation, and the National Board for Professional Teaching Standards. He teaches courses in comparative, international, and multicultural education, leadership theory, organizational theory, decision theory, policy analysis, and research methods. He has presented his research through the Comparative and International Education Society.

Huda Ayyash-Abdo is an associate professor of education and psychology in the Department of Social Science at the Lebanese American University. Her research interests are in school counseling and the development of culturally appropriate approaches in counseling for Lebanon and the Arab region. She is published in the fields of school counseling, developmental counseling psychology, and counselor training education.

Rima Bahous is an assistant professor of education and teaching English to speakers of other languages in the Department of Education at the Lebanese American University. Her research interests are in TESOL and education. Her current research includes student engagement in disadvantaged schools, social justice (injustice) in educating youth, multicultural discourse, and alternative forms of assessment.

Supriya Baily is an instructor at George Mason University in the Initiatives in Educational Transformation graduate program. She previously spent more than a decade working with nonprofit organizations, conducting research on international education programs, and writing proposals for funding for education projects. She received her doctorate in international education from George Mason University and is building a research agenda that addresses how communities evolve as the disenfranchised seek to become more empowered.

Penny Bishop is an associate professor of education at the University of Vermont. In 2008 she served as a Sir Ian Axford Public Policy Fellow in Wellington, New Zealand, studying the education of young adolescents. A former middle grades teacher, Penny is the coauthor of several middle schooling books and holds positions on both the National Middle School Association's Research Advisory Board and AERA's Middle Level Education Research Special Interest Group.

Sigrid Blömeke is a professor of teacher education and instructional research in the Department of Education at the Humboldt University of Berlin. Blömeke is the German National Research Coordinator of IEA's Teacher Education and Development Study: Learning to Teach Mathematics and the NRC of the six-country study Mathematics Teaching in the 21st Century (MT21). A recent major publication is her book *Professionelle Kompetenz angehender Lehrerinnen und Lehrer. Wissen, Überzeugungen und Lerngelegenheiten deutscher Mathematikstudierender und -referendare*.

Evely Boruchovitch earned her PhD in education at the University of Southern California and a psychology degree at the State University of Rio de Janeiro. She is an associate professor in the Educational Psychology Department of the School of Education, University of Campinas and a researcher with the Brazilian National Research Foundation. She has previously published a book, several papers, book chapters, and coedited three books. Her current research interests include issues related to motivation and self-regulation.

Sharon Lynne Bryant, as assistant professor in the College of Education at Zayed University, recently completed a residency at the Hong Kong Institute of Education where she served 4 years as the deputy head of the Curriculum and Instruction Department and 7 years as the director of the Hong Kong Assessment Network. Her research interests lie in the areas of curriculum studies, information technology, teaching and learning strategies, and evaluation and assessment.

José Aloyseo Bzuneck earned a PhD and master's degrees in psychology at the University of São Paulo and a bachelor's degree in philosophy at the Pontifícia Universidade Católica. He is an associate professor at the Education Department of the School of Education of Londrina State University and a member of the Brazilian Educational Psychology Association. He has coauthored two books and published several papers and books chapters. His current research interests are focus on motivation and self-regulation of adolescents and university students.

Robert M. Capraro is an associate professor of mathematics education in the Department of Teaching, Learning, and Culture at Texas A&M University and codirector of the North Texas STEM Center. His areas of research are mathematics teaching and learning, mathematical representation, teacher preparation, and research methods. He is the author or coauthor of more than 30 journal articles and book chapters on mathematics education, quantitative research methods, and teacher education.

Tony Dowden is an early career researcher and lecturer of education at the University of Tasmania, Australia. He has taught in several secondary schools in New Zealand. In 2007 NZARE honored Tony with its Sutton-Smith Doctoral Award for his thesis on curriculum integration with respect to the needs of young adolescents. He is especially interested in curriculum designs for middle schooling that are ethical and genuinely relevant, challenging, integrative and exploratory for young people.

Martin Dowson is a professor of educational Psychology at the Australian College of Ministries and adjunct professor of research at the University of Western Sydney. He is author of over 140 peer-refereed publications, including those appearing in the *Journal of Educational Psychology, Contemporary Educational Psychology*, and *Review of Educational Research*. Professor Dowson's primary research interests are in student motivation, cognition and achievement, and educational and psychological measurement. He is a senior consultant to both government and universities on issues concerning adolescent education.

Anja Felbrich is a research scientist in the Department of Education at the Humboldt University of Berlin. Anja is a member of Germany's research team of IEA's Teacher Education and Development Study: Learning to Teach Mathematics and of the six-country study Mathematics Teaching in the 21st Century. Her research is focused on opportunities to learn in teacher education and features of teacher educators.

Marília Saldanha da Fonseca earned a PhD in education at the State University of Campinas, a master's degree in education at Rio de Janeiro State University, and a bachelor's degree in education at the Sociedade Universitária Augusto Motta, Rio de Janeiro. She is a collaborating professor at Centro Universitário de Barra Mansa and a researcher of National Secretary of Public Policies for Drugs. Her current research interests are drug abuse prevention and continuing education.

Inna Gorlova is a doctoral fellow at Eastern Michigan University in the Educational Leadership program. She was a Ford Foundation Fellow with the Institute for International Education. She has 2 decades of experience in Russian higher education having taught at the universities and working for nonprofit organizations on educational projects with grants from Eurasia Foundation, Soros Foundation, the USAID, and IREX. Her research interests include international comparative and global education, multicultural education, and international exchanges.

Lisa Hervey is a research assistant at the Friday Institute for Educational Innovation at North Carolina State University pursuing a PhD in literacy and technology. She earned her BS in education from Central Michigan University and her MEd from NCSU in reading. She received her National Board for Professional Teaching Standards certification while teaching middle grades language arts. Her research focuses on adolescents and technology integration using the technological pedagogical content knowledge framework for teachers.

Johannes König is a research scientist in the Department of Education at the Humboldt University of Berlin. He is the project manager of IEA's *Teacher Education and Development Study: Learning to Teach Mathematics* in Germany. His research is focused on measuring general pedagogical knowledge.

Ali Riza Küpçü is a doctoral student at Ataturk Faculty of Education, Marmara University, Istanbul, Turkey. His research interests include proportional reasoning and mathematical problem solving. He teaches mathematics methods courses to education majors at Marmara University.

Kathleen F. Malu, an associate professor in the Department of Secondary and Middle School Education at William Paterson University of New Jersey, teaches anthropology in education at the undergraduate level and literacy courses in the Graduate Reading Program. She is secretary for the Middle Level Education Research SIG of AERA and has a chapter published in Volume 5 of *The Handbook of Research in Middle Level Education* series. Her research interests include middle level issues, multicultural education, multiple literacies, and teacher education.

Mona Nabhani is an assistant professor of education in the Department of Education and the Director of the Teacher Training Institute at the Lebanese American University. Her current research includes student engagement in disadvantaged schools, social justice (injustice) in educating youth, as well as differentiated instruction in the primary years.

Pat Nolan is referred to by the New Zealand Association for Intermediate and Middle Schooling as the "Godfather" of middle schooling in New Zealand. Following a notable university career characterized by many partnerships with classroom teachers, Pat is editor of the association's journal, *Middle Schooling Review*. His academic, research and school development work, along with his advocacy for young people for over 30 years, are currently helping to shape national policy on middle schooling in New Zealand.

Serkan Özel is a fifth-year doctoral student in educational psychology program with the specialization in educational technology. His BS and MS degrees are in mathematics education from Bogazici University, Turkey. His research interests include integrating technology in teaching, specifically the teaching and learning of mathematics, with consideration of attending to the needs of multicultural students and representational systems. Ozel's expertise is instructional design and technology. He has authored three journal articles and two book chapters.

Toni Sills-Briegel is an associate professor in the College of Education at Zayed University. Toni has edited and authored more than 50 articles and books in the field of education. Her most recent books, *Soul of Sand* and *Soul of Sea*, are collections of poetry about the United Arab Emirates that complement the photography of Gloria Kifayeh. She coedits the College of Education journal, *Teachers, Learners, and Curriculum*.

Hiller A. Spires, who received her PhD from the University of South Carolina, is a professor of literacy and technology in the College of Education and senior research fellow at the Friday Institute at North Carolina State University. She conducts game-based literacy research with middle grade students and teachers and directs the New Literacies Collaborative (newliteraciescollaborative.org) where she studies new literacies in America and China. She served on the 2008 American-Asian Summit on Educational Partnerships planning committee.

Aaron Thornburg is a PhD candidate in the Department of Cultural Anthropology at Duke University. He earned his BA in anthropology at the University of Florida and an MPhil in linguistics at Trinity College in Dublin, Ireland. His research focuses on information and communication technology/media and Irish Gaelic (Gaeilge) among transition-year students in the greater Dublin area. He recently completed a year as a fellow in the Spencer Foundation's Discipline-Based Scholarship in Education program.

David C. Virtue is an assistant professor of middle level education and founding affiliated faculty with the Office of International and Comparative Education at the University of South Carolina. His research interests include immigrant and refugee education, middle level teacher education, and teacher certification policy. He has done research in Denmark and has published his international work in *Kappa Delta Pi Record* and *Language of the Land: Histories of Language and Nationalism Within Educational Settings*.

Paul Webb is a professor of science education and director of the Research, Technology and Innovation Unit in the Faculty of Education at the Nelson Mandela Metropolitan University, South Africa. His research interests have been in the fields of the nature of science, classroom discussion, teaching science in disadvantaged schools and, currently, in developing new insights into the notion of scientific literacy.

Z. Ebrar Yetkiner is a doctoral student in the Department of Teaching, Learning and Culture at Texas A&M University. Her research interests include mathematics education and statistics. She has coauthored three journal articles and four book chapters on mathematics education and quantitative research methods.

Bogum Yoon is an assistant professor of literacy in the Department of Reading at Texas Woman's University. Her research interests include critical literacy, cultural and social identity, and teacher education on English language learners. Yoon's most recent articles are published in *American Educational Research Journal* and *The Reading Teacher.*

Junzhen Zhang received his MEd in educational technology from Hebei University in Baoding China in 1991. He has been a professor in educational technology at Shanxi Datong University since 1998 working with elementary and middle school teachers. He was a visiting scholar at the University of South Florida's College of Education in 2000-2001 and served as a visiting scholar at the Friday Institute for Educational Innovation at North Carolina State University in 2008.

Printed in the United States
212272BV00011B/3/P